ESSENTIALS OF EDUCATIONAL MEASUREMENT

fifth edition ════════════════════

ESSENTIALS OF EDUCATIONAL MEASUREMENT

ROBERT L. EBEL

DAVID A. FRISBIE

University of Iowa

 PRENTICE HALL, Englewood Cliffs, New Jersey 07632

Library of Congress Cataloging-in-Publication Data

Ebel, Robert L.
    Essentials of educational measurement / Robert L. Ebel, David A.
  Frisbie. —5th ed.
      p.   cm.
    Includes bibliographical references and index.
    ISBN 0-13-284613-6
    1. Educational tests and measurements. 2. Examinations-
  Evaluation. 3. Examinations—Design and construction.
  4. Examinations—Interpretation.   I. Frisbie, David A. II. Title.
LB3051.E22   1991
371.2'6—dc20

                                            90–39616
                                          CIP

Editorial/production supervision and
   interior design: **Susan E. Rowan**
Cover design: **20/20 Services, Inc.**
Manufacturing buyer: **Bob Anderson**

Essentials of Educational Measurement
is the fifth edition of the book
formerly titled *Measuring Educational Achievement.*

©1991, 1986, 1979, 1972, 1965 by Prentice-Hall, Inc.
A Division of Simon & Schuster
Englewood Cliffs, New Jersey 07632

Printed in the United States of America
10 9 8 7 6 5 4 3 2 1

ISBN 0-13-284613-6

Prentice-Hall International (UK) Limited, *London*
Prentice-Hall of Australia Pty. Limited, *Sydney*
Prentice-Hall Canada, Inc., *Toronto*
Prentice-Hall Hispanoamericana, S.A., *Mexico*
Prentice-Hall of India Private Limited, *New Delhi*
Prentice-Hall of Japan, Inc., *Tokyo*
Simon & Schuster Asia Pte. Ltd., *Singapore*
Editora Prentice-Hall do Brazil, Ltda., *Rio de Janerio*

Contents

8

True–False Test Items   133

9

Multiple-Choice Test Items   154

10

Other Objective-Item Formats   179

11

Essay-Test Items   188

16

The Nature of Standardized Tests   286

17

Using Standardized Achievement Tests   303

18

Standardized Intelligence and Aptitude Measures   330

Appendixes

Preface

This fifth edition of *Essentials of Educational Measurement*, like the previous editions, has been designed as a textbook for introductory measurement courses and as a reference for practitioners engaged in the development and use of educational measures. The evaluation needs of teachers have been weighed heavily in making decisions about content coverage and emphasis, but consideration also has been given to the needs of administrators, counselors, instructional designers, and researchers. The goal has been to foster understanding and application rather than simply to provide information. But the level is intended to be introductory; no previous study of educational measurement or statistics is expected.

The most significant organizational changes in this edition are the addition of a chapter on nontest evaluation methods and the deletion of the chapters on personality measures and recent developments. Chapter 14, Nontest and Informal Evaluation Methods, describes the development and use of observation schedules, checklists, rating forms, questionnaires, and a variety of oral questioning techniques. This chapter was added in recognition of the significance of these methods in everyday classroom assessment and in an attempt to draw greater attention to the need to obtain high-quality information when these procedures are used.

The chapter-end projects and problems sections have been moved to the Instructor's Manual, and the glossary has been dropped to provide space for expansion without increasing overall length. Questions for individual study or class discussion have taken over some of the space and a new set of appendixes accounts for the remainder. The first three appendixes are components of a classroom evaluation plan (Grade 6 Health) that are referenced throughout the text to illustrate the application of test-development concepts and procedures. The last three appendixes provide lists of topics that are appropriate to consider when planning in-service instruction about standardized test selection, administration, and score interpretation for teachers.

The first three chapters deal with fundamental educational measurement concepts and current testing issues. A major modification in Chapter 2, and throughout the text, is a change in usage of the term *criterion-referenced* to the more common usage found in the literature. Chapter 3 includes an expanded discussion of classification systems (taxonomies) for learning outcomes.

The treatment of reliability has been extended further to provide greater detail on criterion-referenced situations, especialy decision consistency. The validity chapter has been rewritten entirely to give proper emphasis to construct validation evidence and to clarify the role of intrinsic rational validity evidence. In addition, Chapter 7 gives greater attention to planning for criterion-referenced tests and to developing tables of specifications for all kinds of tests.

The chapters on item writing have undergone only minor revision: the multiple true–false section has been moved to the true–false chapter and the discussion of holistic and analytical scoring of essays has been expanded. The chapters on test administration, test evaluation, and grading have been modified only slightly in organization and content. The topic of standardized testing, particularly achievement testing, has been addressed by adopting "informed use" as the main theme. Chapter 17, for example, has been revised completely to describe and illustrate score-interpretation procedures. In addition, this chapter also presents a discussion of several key issues in school testing programs that most educational measurement texts do not address. The chapter on intelligence and aptitude testing also has been revised substantially to give primary focus to score interpretation and use.

I want to acknowledge the valuable and generous contributions to this work made by others. First, I am grateful to several colleagues who furnished constructive reactions to chapter drafts: Tim Ansley, Doug Becker, Bob Forsyth, H. D. Hoover, Mike Kane, Mike Kolen, Dave Lohman, Rick Stiggins, and Jon Twing. In addition, I thank Len Feldt for his support, Kim Volk for her able word-processing assistance, and Bob Jordan for his helpful library work. I also appreciate the efforts of Fred Finch and Bill Zwack of the Riverside Publishing Company in obtaining illustrations. Finally, thanks are due to my family for the patience and understanding they have shown and to Bob Ebel for the solid foundation he established with the first three editions of this book.

D. A. F.

ESSENTIALS OF EDUCATIONAL MEASUREMENT

1

The Status
of Educational
Measurement

THE PREVALENCE OF TESTING

As the last decade of this century unfolds, there is more educational testing occurring than we have ever witnessed before. Like many other educational phenomena, however, testing seems to fall in and out of favor in cyclic fashion over time. Usually the era of peak demand is followed by a period of increasing criticism of the inadequacies of testing and of the inability of tests to address our most pressing educational problems. By decade's end we likely will have come full circle from the 1970s when charges of racial/ethnic bias dominated our thoughts and contributed to a decrease in educational testing.

The most recent escalation in the use of tests gained impetus from such educational movements as "excellence," "effective schools," "public accountability," and "minimum competency." The pressure of these movements brought both more and different kinds of testing to the schools. Teachers continued as usual to give classroom tests to assess learning outcomes and to motivate their students to learn. And schools continued as usual to administer standardized testing programs to monitor the progress of each grade group and to assess curricular strengths and weaknesses. However, in many states this teacher and district testing was supplemented by a host of other testing programs mandated by the state or by the district itself. Thus, students and teachers alike continually found themselves in some phase of testing—preparing to take a test, administering or taking a test, or reviewing or explaining the results from some kind of a test.

Unfortunately, there has been too much testing—too little use of good tests and too little good use of well-developed tests. For example, achievement tests designed to identify strengths and weaknesses of individual pupils have sometimes been given for the purpose of differentiating schools of varying quality or for making achievement comparisons among a group of states. Increased pressures on educators to produce high test scores has led to the unhealthy state of test-driven curricula. That is, the curriculum taught by teachers is determined more by the content of the upcoming mandated test than by the goals, values, and perceived needs of the local community. As a result, in many places the *avoidance* of the potential negative consequences of testing has begun to shape educational practice and policy far more than it should.

The heightened demand of policymakers and the public for test information has contributed to hurried test preparation and to ill-advised uses of existing tests. Often good tests are used for purposes other than what their makers intended. Unfortunately, too, some of these tests are not of very high quality. Too many of them are produced under severe time constraints by individuals with little special training in test development and no special aptitude for the task.

All educators—teachers, administrators, counselors, curriculum coordinators, and instructional designers—need to know more about educational measurement than they have had an opportunity to learn. Most states have no teacher certification requirements that specify a test and measurement course, and most teacher preservice programs of study have no such requirement. Thus, such specialists as counselors, principals, and reading diagnosticians, for whom teacher certification may be a prerequisite to special certification, have no foundation in educational measurement as they prepare for and practice their specialty. For these and other reasons, the measurement practices of teachers and other educators are influenced primarily by lore—what they experienced as students, what they have seen or heard from colleagues, and what they have learned incidentally through related coursework or short-term professional development experiences.

The status of achievement testing in noneducational settings is not much different. Employment testing by personnel specialists in business and testing for licensure or certification decisions by professional examining boards are both on the upswing. Tests of achievement dominate decision making in these situations, and the quality of these tests varies drastically from one circumstance to the next. The decisions made on the basis of scores from such tests are no less critical than many of those made in our schools. These are "strong tests"; the consequences for test takers are great because the decisions will influence career paths, economic opportunities, and social acceptance by peers. They are high-stakes tests because there is much to lose or much to gain, depending on the decision that results from the scores.

The excessive pressures brought on by high-stakes decisions should serve to reduce the amount of testing that takes place as we near the century's end. And the realization that a test score provides limited information of less-than-perfect accuracy should help to curb the tide also. But tests will not go away permanently or even sink to low obscurity. Nor should they. If we want to motivate and reward efforts to learn, if we want effective and productive schools, if we want to deal fairly with individuals on the basis of their capabilities and accomplishments, we need more good testing, not simply less testing. Despite the current prevalence of educational testing, we are far from receiving the full bene-fits that could be obtained from the wise use of good tests.

SOME CHRONIC COMPLAINTS ABOUT TESTING

Even in periods of unprecedented amounts of testing, there are those who decry the use of tests and whose goals are to highlight the misuses of tests or the harm done to students by them. Of course, not all tests are skillfully prepared, not all test scores are used in prudent ways, and no test score is likely to be free of error. The wise use of test scores requires an understanding of the issues raised by critics and an ability to distinguish constructive criticism from emotional reac-tion or uninformed opinion. Because some of the most frequent charges have implications for test development and test-score interpretation and use, it is ap-propriate to consider their merits early on in the study of educational measure-ment.

1. *Standardized test makers control what students learn.* It is possible for the developers of a commercial achievement test to construct their instrument to include only those items that meet their own personal criteria of relevance, diffi-culty, and timeliness. But unless the content represents the essential topics of current textbooks, unless the items reflect the recommendations of national cur-riculum councils and committees, and unless the content is deemed relevant by district test selection committees, such tests will not be sold. A test that might be considered ahead of its time or behind recent developments will die a quick death because many school personnel will fear that such a test will yield a set of very low scores and, more importantly, useless information. The success of commercial test developers is measured in the marketplace. The most successful tests are those that respond to curricular changes and emphasis rather those that attempt to effect such changes.

To the extent that a school modifies its curriculum—what is taught, when it is taught, and how much effort is devoted to teaching it—so that test scores will improve, some may say the test is controlling the curriculum. However, the effects of such instructional modifications can be considered both positive and negative. Instruction that is measurement driven is *purposeful* instruction, whether or not the intentions are laudable. For example, when the domain of instruction is lim-ited only to the ideas that will be tested, understanding and retention both will be enhanced. But the scope of the curriculum is likely to be narrowed severely, perhaps to the total exclusion of subject areas not covered by the tests. Slow learners are likely to experience greater success and less frustration in such an environment, but the more talented students are likely to experience greater boredom, more frustration, and lower achievement levels. Trade-offs abound.

Teachers and administrators are faced with the decision about how much the test should influence instructional emphases. Unfortunately, parents, school board members, superintendents, and other school personnel are reluctant to explain low test scores in terms of test–curriculum content mismatches. Instead, current sentiments are to treat low scores as an indication of failure on the part of the school. Most often the appropriateness and quality of the test instrument remain unquestioned and are assumed to be ideal. We are not in the habit of considering competing explanations for a set of test scores, whether they be high or low, but we *are* in the habit of uncritically accepting the quality and appropriateness of the test instrument.

A school that focuses instruction on what the tests measure surely should teach other things as well. Even in the basic skills areas that the test does sample there should be ample class time and teacher time to venture into interesting and important areas not covered by the standardized tests. Standardized tests can dominate local curricula only to the extent that school administrators and teachers permit.

2.   *Test scores are inflated because of teaching to the test.* If the effectiveness of instruction is to be judged on the basis of students' performance on a test, the temptation may be strong for the teacher to prepare students to answer the specific questions that will be included on the test. This is often referred to as teaching to the test. When the negative consequences of low scores are significant for the teacher—loss of job, low salary increase, reassignment to a less favorable setting—there is great urgency to ensure students' scores will not be too low. The morality of the decisions often takes a back seat to practicality and survival.

The pressures of accountability encourage this type of teacher behavior, but, more importantly, unrealistic and inappropriate achievement goals with their associated rewards and punishments imposed on teachers may require it. For example, teachers with average-achieving classes who are faced with goals requiring above-average achievement gains must either give up or beat the system. Teaching the test questions and corresponding answers is one response. And as one state found out, erasing wrong student responses and marking correct ones in their places after the test administration is another. The higher the stakes are, the bolder the stakeholders will become, especially in circumstances of unreasonable expectations or requirements.

An important distinction should be made between teaching to the test (that is, attempting to fix in students' minds the answers to particular test questions) and teaching material to be covered by the test (that is, attempting to give students the capability to answer questions *like* those in the test on topics covered by the test). The first is thoroughly reprehensible. The second reflects purposeful teaching. Just as there is no justification for giving away the answers to particular questions, so there is no justification for testing performance on skills or general ideas that students were never taught. Teachers whose work is to be assessed are entitled to know what the students will be expected to do. Such an assessment must be thoroughly relevant to the instruction it is intended to assess. Since a test can never elicit more than a sample of performance, usually much more will be taught (and learned) than can be tested. However, the test should seldom go beyond what students have had an opportunity to learn.

3.   *Tests make students anxious and stressful.* Claims that testing is harmful to students have taken many forms: tests threaten and upset students; some students even break down and cry when faced with a test; if students get a low score on a test, they will become discouraged and quit trying; student's self-concepts will be damaged seriously; and testing is incompatible with educational procedures designed to be supportive of students.

There is undoubtedly anecdotal evidence to support some of these claims. Common sense suggests, however, that the majority of students are not harmed by testing. There are no substantial survey data that would contradict common sense on this matter. Teachers seem concerned much more often with students who don't care enough how well or how poorly they do on tests than with the relatively exceptional instances of students who seem to care too much.

It is normal and biologically helpful to be somewhat anxious when facing any real test of performance in life. But it is also a necessary part of growing up to learn to cope with the kind of tests that life inevitably brings. Of the many challenges to a child's peace of mind caused by such things as angry parents, playground bullies, bad dogs, shots from the doctor, and things that go bump in the night, tests surely must be among the least fearsome for most youngsters. Unwise parental pressure can in some cases elevate anxiety to harmful levels. But usually the child who breaks down in tears at the prospect of a test has problems of security, adjustment, and maturity that testing did not create and that cannot be solved by eliminating tests. Indeed, more frequent testing might help to solve the problem.

A student who consistently gets low test scores on material that the student has tried hard to learn is indeed likely to be discouraged. If this does happen, the school cannot claim to be offering a good educational program, and the teacher cannot claim to be doing a good job of teaching. Most low test scores, however, go to students who, for whatever reason, have not tried very hard to learn. In the opinion of the teachers of such students, it is the trying rather than the testing that is more in need of correction.

4. *Standardized tests are biased against some students.* Standardized tests of educational achievement have been attacked for their alleged bias against racial/ethnic minorities, against either males or females, or against students with poor reading skills. The reason for the attack, at least in part, is that such students tend to score lower on standardized tests than their age-mates. But surely lower scores alone do not signify bias. If they did, every spelling test would be biased against poor spellers, and every typing test against persons who never learned to type. A test is biased only if it yields measures that are consistently lower than they should be.

That students who do poorly on a particular test written in English might do better if the test were in Spanish, or if the questions were presented orally, does not mean that the original test is biased against them. It simply means that they have not learned enough of what the particular test measures. Its linguistic context is part of the test. The particularity of what the test does and should measure does not constitute bias.

The score of a student on an achievement test indicates how successfully the test questions were answered under the conditions of the test. The reasonable assumption usually is made that the student would be equally successful with other tasks requiring the same knowledge or ability. Consequently, if a test score is judged to be an inaccurate indication of the student's level of achievement in the domain covered by the test, bias is not the likely explanation. It is more likely that the conditions for testing were undesirable or that a reasonably good test was chosen for a purpose other than the one for which it was intended originally.

Suppose we present third graders with this math problem-solving item: "A football team scored two touchdowns, no extra points, and one field goal in the first quarter. How many points did the team score altogether in that quarter?" Surely this item is biased against students who cannot add, as it is intended to be. But it is also biased against those who do not know the scoring rules of football, as it probably should not be if it is intended to measure math problem-solving ability. The item probably favors American males over American females and probably disadvantages those who know football as a game some of us call "soccer," a game in which there are no touchdowns. For which other subgroups might this item be biased?

5.   *Paper and pencil objective tests measure only the most trivial learning.* It would indeed be foolish to claim that all relevant measurement of achievement could be accomplished with a carefully designed multiple-choice or true–false test. In many situations we need to examine a behavioral process or the characteristics of a product developed by the student: the surgery of a medical student, the therapy session of a counselor in training, the use of a microscope in a lab, the draft of a one-act play, a persuasive speech, or a swan dive. An indirect measurement of skill is no substitution for the real thing when the behavior in question can be observed directly and evaluated with reasonable realism, precision, and economy.

In situations where objective-test items are as appropriate as essays or performance measures, the ability to measure more than trivial learning is largely in the hands of the test maker. Items that measure rote learning and recall of unimportant detail are the easiest to write, especially for inexperienced item writers. Thus, all of us who have been tested with objective items by inexperienced test developers can attest to the frustration brought on by items made difficult by the obscurity of their content or by the ambiguity with which they were stated. Only a small collection of such experiences is required before we are tempted to draw the conclusion that paper and pencil objective tests do not (cannot) measure worthwhile instructional outcomes. Of course, an equal number of more positive experiences should elicit a nearly opposite conclusion. Only the skill of the test developer and the nature of the important content to be measured influence the quality and usefulness of a given test.

Finally, the increased interest in recent years in giving more curricular emphasis to higher-order thinking skills has raised questions about how to measure the achievement of these skills. The ability to analyze, predict, evaluate, deduce, or distinguish cannot be measured, some have said, with objective-test items. Undoubtedly, skill beyond the level of remembering often will need to be demonstrated through task performance or product development to be assessed adequately. But in many content domains, only the skill of the item writer precludes the development of items that measure important higher-order abilities. Skill, practice, and extra effort are the fundamental requirements of good item writing, as will be seen in later chapters.

6.   *Test scores need to tell what students can do rather than how students rank in a group.* The fact is, both kinds of scores are important, and we need tests that will provide each type. For example, I may not be satisfied to know that Jess is the best swimmer in her class. Rather, I want to know if she can swim far enough to save herself in the pool. If she can swim halfway across the pool, that still may not be far enough, even if it is "best" in the class. When it comes to such activities as swimming, writing one's name, driving a motorcycle, or dispensing medica-

tion, being the best in some group may be quite inadequate: ranking is not enough.

Scott can swim 100 yards and spell 310 words. Is he a better swimmer or speller? Knowing only what he can do is not sufficient for deciding about relative strengths and weaknesses. If it were important to decide which is better, I need to know how other five-year-olds swim and spell. Suppose I learn that no other five-year-olds in Scott's YMCA swim class can swim 100 yards and three girls in his kindergarten class can spell more than 310 words. Is Scott a better swimmer? This is an issue to be explored in greater depth later, but for now it will be sufficient to point out that, as long as the comparison groups are different from one another, the question must remain open. If we learn that everyone else in Scott's swimming class can spell at least 325 words, what conclusion can be drawn about Scott's strengths and weaknesses?

In sum, we need different kinds of information for different kinds of instructional decisions: what students can do and how they rank with others are both important. Beyond that, knowing the type of information most needed in a given situation and how best to obtain it are key issues faced by teachers at all instructional levels.

SOME CURRENT ISSUES AND DEVELOPMENTS

Mandated Assessment

The continuing press for accountability has led to more testing, more emphasis on test results in policymaking, and new developments or advances in test-related methodology. *Mandated assessment* is the term that describes the collective testing programs organized at the state (or local) level in response to legislation enacted by state (or local) governments. The mandate varies from state to state regarding the flexibility accorded local school districts to implement an assessment program and to use the results. In some states, for example, local districts have the option of conducting an assessment, but in others the legislation dictates the grade levels, subject areas, and specific purposes of testing for every district. Virtually every state has enacted some form of statewide assessment law, and new legislation is introduced annually in many states as assessment experiences uncover unanticipated gaps in implementation.

The emphasis placed on testing in response to state and local mandates can be seen by reviewing this contrived, but realistic, testing program for one school district:

1. *State assessment.* Tests in mathematics and reading must be administered to all students in grades 2, 4, 6, 8, and 10 of every district during a two-week period in May. Results are summarized by the state and reported to each district in September.
2. *Graduation competency test.* High school sophomores are given tests in reading, math, health, and consumer education to determine if they have the minimum knowledge required for high school graduation as determined by the local dis-

trict. Those who fail may be retested again as juniors and, if necessary, as seniors. Test content coverage and standard setting decisions are made locally.

3. *Middle school promotion test.* The school district requires pupils at the end of fifth grade to pass tests in reading, mathematics, and language skills for promotion to grade 6. Those who fail any test must attend summer school and pass a comparable test before they may enroll in middle school.

4. *Writing assessment.* Writing samples are collected near the end of grade 6 and are scored locally to determine the extent to which writing skills are being developed. This local assessment does not provide individual student scores, but it does provide information by classroom to describe the nature of group achievement. Curriculum adjustments in terms of focus and time allocation are made on a building by building basis after examining the results.

5. *End-of-course tests.* High school students completing these courses are required to pass a district-wide comprehensive test to receive graduation credit for the course: U.S. history, American government, algebra, geometry, biology, and chemistry. Students who fail to achieve minimum performance levels may opt for summer school study in the area of deficiency and retest with a comparable form of the test. These tests are intended to ensure equality in academic demands in the course within and between buildings and to enforce minimum standards of performance in each course.

Of course, other forms of assessment take place throughout the school year interspersed among the preparation, administration, and reporting activities associated with the mandated tests. In grades 1, 3, 5, 7, 9, and 11 the district administers a traditional achievement-test battery to help fulfill the need for administrative, instructional, and guidance information that mandated programs do not furnish. A test of cognitive abilities is administered in grades 2 and 5, an aptitude battery is given in grade 8, and many high school students take any number of college scholarship and admission tests.

The sheer volume of testing has led a number of measurement specialists to lobby for a consolidation of testing so that one test administration might effectively serve multiple purposes. Considerable experimentation is taking place to develop acceptable testing procedures and reporting methods that will accommodate the variety of needs with a reduced amount of testing. Two developments that warrant brief mention in this regard are customized testing and district report cards.

Customized testing, as the term implies, allows states or districts to have tests tailor-made to their own content specifications rather than to select one that was designed to represent the curriculum of the mythical "typical school in the nation." The district identifies its instructional objectives from a publisher catalog and specifies how many test items should be used to measure each one. The publisher selects items that match the chosen instructional objectives from its large bank of test items. Custom test booklets are printed, tests are administered and scored, and results are reported in terms of mastery of the various instructional objectives. This mastery testing program may be a useful supplement to the district's traditional standardized testing program.

Another form of customized testing that has been tried in an effort to reduce the amount of time devoted to testing has serious limitations. In this method a district (or state) chooses a sample of math and reading items from a standardized achievement battery for administration in its assessment program. These items, along with a few others chosen by the district, are administered and then, using complex statistical procedures, the scores on the full-length standardized math and reading tests are estimated. The whole purpose here is to obtain nationally normed test scores without giving the entire tests. There are at least two problems with these procedures that make the norms inapplicable: (1) the district chose only items on which its students could do well and (2) the test taken by the district was different (context of the items, length) from the one taken by the norming schools. The implication of both of these conditions is to overestimate the performance of district pupils relative to the national group. (See Way, Forsyth, and Ansley, 1989, for further details associated with context effects in customized testing.)

The state or district report card is the most popular method under development for reporting the results of statewide assessment, among other information, at the school-district level. Typically, the report provides school-building achievement-test score averages by grade level and compares those with the averages of other buildings in the district and in the state. To help the report reader develop an understanding of achievement in the school, student characteristics are described and compared with those in other buildings in the district and the state. For example, the distribution of racial/ethnic background, limited-English ability, and family income levels might be presented to help explain current student academic performance. Information about instructional resources, school finances, and student attendance and mobility might be presented for similar purposes. The report card method shows promise for improving the interpretability of test scores for a school district. The wide range of information presented helps focus attention on factors that seem to relate to school achievement. But there is much we do not know about how such factors as family income level, per pupil expenditure, educational levels of teachers, and racial/ethnic backgrounds of students influence the achievement of individual pupils.

Legislated statewide testing has evolved over the past 20 years to address public accountability concerns. It is likely to remain with us in some form for the indefinite future, and it is likely to provide further motivation for improving test development and reporting practices.

National Assessment of Educational Progress

The quest for school accountability that emerged in the post-Sputnik era made both educators and legislators realize that no useful mechanism existed to provide information about how much young people nationwide had learned in school. No dependable guides existed for steering public policy regarding priorities for educational spending or needed curriculum reform. Plans were laid in the mid-1960s for the National Assessment of Educational Progress (NAEP), a project that would survey the knowledge, skills, and attitudes of young Americans in several subject areas and report this information to educational decision makers, practitioners, and the public. Initial assessments in each of ten learning areas—science, writing, citizenship, reading, literature, music, social studies, mathematics, career and occupational development, and art—have been updated periodically to gauge progress. More limited assessments, called *probes*, have been conducted in such areas as basic life skills, health, and energy. The reports of each assessment include selected exercises (test items) and the proportion of the sample tested that chose each multiple-choice alternative.

Many of the factors that shaped the initial structure and goals of NAEP in the 1960s have changed. For example, there is less public confidence in the ability of the school to do its job, there are greater demands for some form of accountability, and the once modest role of the federal government in education has changed to a prominent one. Beginning in the late 1970s, charges were made that NAEP was failing to serve the audience that needed serving; its results needed to be more useful (Comptroller General, 1976; Wiley, 1981). Subsequently, the funding for NAEP to the Education Commission of the States was not renewed and the contract was awarded to Educational Testing Service, based on a redesign of the purposes and technical procedures proposed for future assessments (Messick, Beaton, and Lord, 1983). Included in those new plans for NAEP were assessment of functionally handicapped students, assessment of limited-English proficiency students, and computer-assisted assessment procedures.

The social/political climate of the 1980s left many congressional and educational leaders dissatisfied with the national assessment data available to them. A study committee appointed by the U.S. Department of Education reviewed NAEP and made its recommendations in the report, "The Nation's Report Card" (Alexander and James, 1987). Another significant redesign of NAEP ensued, with considerable effort directed toward a testing plan that would permit state by state comparisons of achievement by 1990. Such comparisons, viewed as dangerous and inappropriate by the original designers of NAEP, are considered essential by current policymakers to respond to accountability needs and to motivate states to improve education in their jurisdictions.

The 1990s expansion of NAEP requires that all states administer NAEP tests to representative samples of their students in selected grades. (Add this form of "imposed" testing to the illustration of mandated assessment in the previous section.) No doubt the extra testing required by NAEP will raise issues related to school time, personnel requirements, and need for dollars to support state-level participation.

There are many good reasons to believe that the state by state comparisons made possible by NAEP are a bad idea. First, despite the apparent demand for these data, there is no useful plan in place or no explicit purpose given for using state-level results. A state's ranking, either within the 50 states or relative to its border neighbors, is more likely to provide fuel for political fires than to improve the quality of education in the state. Second, it is unlikely that states can agree on the essential content to be measured at each grade level for which comparisons are to be made. As a result, the content is likely to be low-level, minimum essentials that a majority of students have mastered. (If such compromising were unnecessary, more of the current statewide assessment programs would use the same or similar tests to conduct their state programs.) Third, content compromising will hamper the development of tests that are difficult enough to help show actual differences in achievement from state to state. That is, if the state scores are all fairly high, the scores of the highest-scoring five states may not look much different from the scores of the lowest-scoring five states.

Fourth, the meaningfulness and value of the scores from tests representing a low-level, "plain-vanilla" content domain are very questionable. For example, there will be much in the science curriculum of Missouri schools that students will learn but NAEP will not test. Why should Missouri be interested in the scores from such a test? The lowest common denominator curriculum represented by test content will necessarily be far lower than what we see in widely used standardized achievement test batteries. Fifth, the costs of gathering the state-level NAEP scores probably cannot be justified in terms of the benefits states can accrue. The hidden and indirect costs to states and school districts may exceed the direct costs funded by the federal government or allocated by each state legislature. If all these resources could be divided and channeled to instructional programs and school facilities in each state, the impact on educational quality would certainly be greater. Bold leadership on the state level is needed to redirect the state by state comparison efforts.

The Impact of Computers

Advances in computing, especially with regard to the microcomputer, continue to provide new opportunities for more efficient, more realistic, and more accurate measurement of educational achievement. A textbook description of new developments seems futile since the technological changes are likely to be regarded in historical terms by the time the print reaches the audience. Even so, these changes reach the classroom implementation phase at a snail's pace, especially those related to testing.

A major but somewhat hidden impact of computers on testing has been in the area of theoretical measurement developments. The increased capacity and speed of computing have made it possible for researchers to perform simulations requiring complex and lengthy statistical analysis that previously were too cumbersome to carry out. The developments have been outlined and detailed by Bunderson and Inouye (1987) in terms of four generations of computing in educational measurement.

One of the most noteworthy theoretical advances made possible by technological improvements has been computerized adaptive testing. The computer creates a test for the examinee during the test administration process by "adapting" to the examinee's most recent response. If the last response was wrong, an easier item is selected; if is was correct, a harder item is selected. This continuous bouncing from easy to hard, or vice versa, allows the examinee's achievement level to be determined quickly with a relatively small number of items. Adaptive testing requires less than half the number of items and testing time relative to conventional methods. And though efficiency is the main advantage at this stage, this method is likely to prove to be more accurate, more versatile in terms of types of items that can be presented, and more economical than our traditional group test-administration procedures. When the capabilities of video disk and voice synthesis are added, it is easy to see that adaptive testing can revolutionize the entire testing process in the near future.

New and revised software packages for microcomputers are making the classroom testing process more efficient for teachers and more fitting for individualization of instruction. Item banking allows teachers to reduce test preparation time and to access test questions that have been designed to accompany their other instructional materials. In some cases the test can be administered by the computer and scored by the time the student has finished. Responses and scores from all students can be stored in the computer and summarized in a convenient report for the teacher at a later time. In other cases, a desk-top scoring machine attached to a microcomputer can score answer sheets and provide a summary analysis report for the teacher within minutes.

Another significant impact of the computer has been in the processing and reporting of the results of standardized testing. Computers can easily aggregate scores for buildings, districts, and states, and they can disaggregate scores of subgroups to monitor the achievement of pupils in special programs. Laser printers can display test scores attractively and in ways that are most convenient and meaningful for each of the several different users. Since the way test scores are organized and formatted on a report has such an influence on whether the reports are even used, the flexibility made possible by computer changes may be among the most prominent factors impacting testing policy during this last decade of the century.

Despite the many positive contributions of computer technology to testing, there are some potential negative side effects worth contemplating. The most troublesome may be the fact that computers can provide teachers with more information about test results than they understand and are able to use. More inservice work and careful design of software both can address this problem. Second, the availability of an item bank means that teachers need to write fewer items themselves and, thus, they obtain less of the much needed practice required to nourish good item-writing skills. Of course, this potential problem is greatly diminished when teachers build and maintain their own banks. Third, the quality of the items in a commercially prepared purchased item bank is not necessarily higher than the caliber of items the teacher might prepare. So increased reliance on item banks may yield poorer measures of achievement than what teachers could develop on their own. Finally, the use of computers to administer a test may impede the performance of some test takers, even though it may yield more valid results for others. (In what ways might some test takers be put at a disadvantage?) All these potential negative effects can be examined through empirical research, but a heightened awareness of their possible influence may be most effective in minimizing their impact.

Licensure and Certification Testing

The amount of testing done to license professionals or to certify individual competence for employment has surged as much as any other kind of testing. Our government tries to control the delivery of unsafe, fraudulent, or unnecessary services to John or Jane Q. Public by licensing only individuals who are capable of providing such services. Thus beauticians, auto mechanics, physicians, semitruck drivers, and realtors, among others, are required to demonstrate the possession of sufficient knowledge and skill about their work through licensure testing so that the public will be protected. In addition, many professional organizations provide testing programs to certify that certain of their members have specialized skills and knowledge beyond those required by a government agency.

Though licensure or certification requirements may include a certain college degree, so many hours of related work experience, or endorsement letters from licensed practitioners, test scores most often carry the most significant weight in the decision. Thus it is reasonable to question, as many have done, whether a paper–pencil objective test can measure the possession of many of the skills deemed essential for safe and trustworthy practice. Should a mechanic be required to demonstrate ability to diagnose an engine problem? Should a dentist demonstrate a tooth restoration on a live patient before being licensed? Is a multiple-choice test score sufficient information for certifying an emergency medical technician? Probably not.

A number of the important issues associated with licensure testing can be seen by considering some of the difficult questions related to testing for teacher licensure by state governments. If prospective teachers complete an accredited teacher preparation program and obtain a bachelor's degree, why is there a need to test them? If program quality actually varies so much from college to college, does that mean the accreditation process should be overhauled instead? If teachers are to be tested, what kinds of content should be covered? If writing skills are to be assessed, what standard should be used to define minimal acceptable performance? If ability to develop a sound lesson plan is deemed to be an essential professional skill, should an objective test be used to check knowledge of the process and the purpose of lesson planning? If teachers need to demonstrate effectiveness in the classroom as a prerequisite to renewing a license, should students' achievement-test scores be required as evidence? In view of the purpose for licensing teachers, is it logical to offer a lifetime license to a teacher after, say, ten years of satisfactory service? Who should provide the "final" answers to all these questions? Most states are working independently toward answers to these questions, and some are cooperating with educational researchers to develop prototype procedures for teacher evaluation. No doubt computer simulations, video chronologies, and work-product portfolios will be used to capture the many facets of "teacher" that will need to be evaluated. We need to be able to measure teacher competence in such a way that we are convinced we have measured the proper characteristics and we could obtain nearly the same results if someone else did the measuring on another occasion.

The Impact of the Courts

As might be anticipated, while the amount of testing has increased and the importance of test scores in decision making has swelled, more legal challenges of test-dominated decisions have developed. The grievances seldom have been directed at the instruments themselves, however. Most often plaintiffs have questioned the relevance of the test score as a criterion in the decision process or they have argued that the use of the scores leads to discrimination—disproportionate selection or rejection of members of certain racial/ethnic groups. Thus, it is the consequences of using test scores in certain ways, and not particular tests, that have been scrutinized most frequently by the courts. Consequently, court decisions provide some guidance for test developers, but mainly they provide direction for the just use of test scores.

Scores from intelligence and cognitive ability tests have been used to group students in buildings and classes for instructional purposes. The courts have said that such ability grouping practices have perpetuated racial segregation in some cases (*Stell* v. *Savannah*, 1964) and have created segregation in others (*Hobson* v. *Hansen*, 1967; *Diana* v. *State Board of Education*, 1973). In the case of *Larry P.* v. *Wilson Riles* (1979), it was ruled that the use of intelligence-test scores to place children in classes for the educably mentally handicapped was illegal because it had a disproportionate effect on black children in the California districts in question.

Discrimination or equal protection has been central to most court decisions involving educational testing. In *Bakke* v. *California* (1978), the plaintiff had been rejected by a medical school and then learned that a minority applicant with lower test scores had been admitted. The U.S. Supreme Court ruled that Bakke should be admitted, but it only implied that the use of different standards for applicants of different races was inappropriate. However, the court did indicate that it was proper for the race of an applicant to be considered in making admission decisions. In another case, when the state of Florida implemented its high school graduation test, a class action suit was brought against the state because a disproportionate number of minority students failed the test. Charges of bias were dismissed (*Debra P.* v. *Turlington*, 1983) and the court agreed that the use of tests of minimum competence for awarding a high school diploma was legal. However, it suspended the use of the test in Florida for four years. By that time all students who had received any part of their education in previously segregated schools would have had an opportunity to be graduated from high school. Thus, opportunity to learn the material covered by the graduation test was judged to be a significant criterion for establishing the appropriateness of its use. Perhaps the most significant outcomes of this case were the distinctions it helped to make between what *is* taught, what *should* be taught, and what is *intended* to be taught. To the extent these three domains differ, only the first is a legitimate standard for establishing the relevance of the content of a graduation competency test.

Discrimination has been an issue with respect to court cases involving employment testing as well. In *Griggs* v. *Duke Power Company* (1971) the court ruled that requirements for employment, such as a passing test score, must be shown to be relevant to some aspect of success on the job. Furthermore, the court decided that it is permissible for the use of test scores to result in disproportionate selection from different racial groups *if* the user can demonstrate that the test measures knowledge or skill required by the job. This same idea was the basis for the outcome of *U. S.* v. *South Carolina* (1977). The use of the National Teachers Examinations (NTE) by the state of South Carolina resulted in disproportionate failure rates for minority certification candidates. But because teacher educators provided evidence that the content of their teacher preparation programs included the content found on the tests, the court rejected racial discrimination as the basis for explaining the higher failure rate of minority examinees.

The notion of disproportionate impact was also at the heart of another dispute, commonly referred to as the Golden Rule case, which was settled out of court. The Golden Rule Insurance Company brought suit against the Illinois Department of Insurance, a credentialing agency, and Educational Testing Service (ETS), the state's testing consultant, because too many minority applicants for its insurance broker positions failed the state's test. The settlement requires ETS to follow certain rules in selecting test items for future versions of the Illinois test. For example, when selecting between an item that previously has been equally difficult for blacks and whites and an item that has been harder for blacks, the former must be chosen. (For further details about the controversial procedures required by the Golden Rule settlement, see several related articles in the second issue of Volume 6 of *Educational Measurement: Issues and Practices*, 1987.)

Finally, scholarship selection procedures were at issue in a suit brought by the American Civil Liberties Union (ACLU) against the New York Department of Education. The court said the purpose of the state scholarship program was to reward achievement in high school, not academic promise in college. Therefore, since the exclusive use of the Scholastic Aptitude Test (SAT) score for awarding scholarships resulted in a sizable disparity favoring males, the court said the *procedure* discriminated against females. (There is ample evidence that the high school grades of females are higher than those of males.) The judge concluded that the most appropriate resolution was to use a composite of high school grade-point average and SAT score as the selection criterion (Staff, 1989).

While all the cases cited above involved the use of tests, the crucial issue in most of them was a matter of social policy. And what was on trial was the fair and appropriate use of test scores in decision making rather than the tests themselves. Is desegregation in school important enough to justify some apparent sacrifice of optimum learning conditions (Stell, Hobson)? Is it proper for employers to specify employee qualifications that are not related directly to job requirements (Griggs)? Should a seemingly "good" test be disqualified as a selection device because of its adverse impact on minorities (Larry P., South Carolina, Debra P.)? In attempting to right old wrongs, should selection procedures discriminate to the advantage of minority test takers (Debra P., Bakke)?

The issue that underlies the testing controversies that have ended up in court has everything to do with what a test is perceived to measure as it relates to how the scores are to be used. And this is *the* fundamental issue that underlies the procedures we will address in subsequent chapters on item writing and test building. Most well-developed, technically sound tests were built with a particular purpose in mind and are less useful for other purposes for which we might consider them. Why might it be inappropriate, for example, to use the scores from a high school graduation competency test to select the recipients of three college scholarship awards?

Standards for Testing Practice

In view of the increases in the amount and the significance of testing, it seems reasonable to expect state and federal governments would regulate and control the development and use of tests. Shouldn't the public be protected from poorly made tests or inappropriate uses of them, just as they should be protected from inept insurance sellers, fraudulent lawyers, or low-grade beef? Aside from the truth-in-testing legislation from New York state in 1979, no other legislation—state or federal—has been directed at the control of the testing industry or at the protection of test takers' rights. Fortunately, the testing profession has been active in developing standards of practice, albeit unenforceable, for makers and users of tests.

The *Standards for Educational and Psychological Testing* (American Psychological Association, 1985), also referred to as the *Standards*, is the most recent form of a document that has been prepared and revised over a 30-year period by educational and psychological test specialists. Though they distinguish essential and important aspects of test development, the *Standards* are not intended primarily as prescriptions for commercial test publishers. Instead, they are intended to distinguish appropriate and inappropriate test use and to describe the types of evidence users should seek and developers should furnish to support a specific use of the scores from a test. There are no legal ramifications for violators, and no professional sanctions will be placed on those who fail to adhere to these standards. However, professionals can exert pressure on their colleagues to conform when the beliefs and values of the profession have been documented in writing and published widely as a consensus for reasonable practice. Thus, despite their lack of teeth, the *Standards* are essential to the profession and, not so indirectly, to consumers whose test-taking rights are seldom protected legally or formally.

A more recent effort of similar intent has been the preparation of the *Code of Fair Testing Practices in Education* (1988), a document more limited in both scope of content and intended audience that the *Standards*. The *Code* has separate lists of responsibilities for test developers and test users and is written to communicate with the general public rather than only testing professionals. Its sections on developing and selecting appropriate tests, interpreting scores, striving for fairness, and informing test takers are intended to highlight the proper use of tests rather than to broaden the existing *Standards* in any way. The publication and mass distribution of the *Code* by the five sponsoring professional organizations is a clear indication that many testing professionals see the need for self-regulation of sorts. It also demonstrates a keen desire for test takers to be treated fairly and for tests to be used properly.

There has been some interest in creating a type of consumer protection agency for testing that would function much like the Consumer's Union, the Underwriter's Laboratory, or any of the various accrediting bodies for schools and universities. In fact, the Center for the Study of Testing Evaluation and Educational Policy at Boston College has received grant funds to explore the feasibility of creating such an organization. One possible outcome of the study could be the formation of an organization that would certify (1) the quality of existing test instruments, (2) the procedures used by testing companies to develop their instruments and to perform their statistical analysis for scale and norms development, and (3) the proposed uses of existing tests for certain specific selection, placement, certification, or licensure decisions. There is still considerable debate about whether a testing "watchdog" is needed and whether the cost passed on to test takers to support this protection is worth the potential benefit to consumers. No doubt when the stakes are very high, all relevant parties—makers, users, and takers—will be persuaded about the value of independent review and subsequent certification of the process. Opinions are likely to diverge more widely, however, as the stakes decrease.

THE PRINCIPAL TASK OF THE SCHOOL

When one considers the reasons why schools were built, the reasons why both children and adults attend them, and the activities that go on inside them, it seems apparent that the main purpose of the school is to facilitate cognitive learning. However, this thesis has been challenged throughout the years by those who have argued that schools should be concerned *primarily* with, for example, development of moral character (Ligon, 1961), life adjustment (U.S. Office of Education, 1951), enhancing self-confidence (Kelly, 1962), or even the restructuring of society (Counts, 1932). Clearly, all these are worthy purposes. And since learning can contribute to the attainment of each, they are not actually alternatives to learning as much as they are reasons for learning. But should they be given primary emphasis in defining the task of the school? Should they form the foundation for the school curriculum? Don't they have more to do with ultimate, lifetime goals than with the means the school should use to help students achieve those goals?

Many educators disagree with those who espouse "higher" goals than cognitive learning for education. While most teachers would acknowledge the ultimate importance of character, adjustment, self-confidence, and the good society, there are several reasons they might give for why none of these should replace learning as the school's primary focus of attention. One reason is that the school is a special-purpose social institution. It was designed and developed to do a specific task: to facilitate learning. Other agencies are responsible for other aspects of the complex task of helping people to live good lives together. For example, there are families and churches, legislative assemblies and courts, factories and unions, publishers and libraries, and markets and moneylenders. To believe that the *major* responsibility for ethical character, life adjustment, social reconstruction, or personal happiness must rest on the schools is as presumptuous as it is foolish.

Even the private, parochial, and home schools that have emerged as alternatives to public school education have sought to make the transmission of knowledge their primary function, secondary to the other goals that may have led to their formation. The instructional methods they choose to use, the curricular supplements they choose to endorse, and the physical facilities and environment they choose for their setting do not overshadow the fostering of cognitive learning as their main function. The special responsibility of every school is to provide training, instruction, and education. The task of facilitating learning is challenging enough, and important enough, to occupy nearly all a school's time and to consume nearly all its energy and resources.

Another reason for believing that the schools should continue to emphasize learning is because of the basic, instrumental importance of learning to all human affairs. With their gift of language, human beings are specially equipped for verbal learning. Cognitive excellence is their unique excellence. The more they know and understand, the better, more effective, and happier they are likely to be. How better can schools help youngsters toward happiness than by increasing their knowledge and understanding of themselves and the world around them? How else can adjustment be facilitated, character developed, or ability to contribute to society increased? Cognitive learning is effective in reaching all these goals, but is not the only means.

The psychological process we call conditioning also can be used to achieve some of these same goals. It works by making use of rewards and punishments to establish specific, habitual responses to certain specific conditions. Much of our behavior was molded, especially during our first years of life, by the processes of conditioning, or behavior modification. Even as adults we are very much subject to its influences. If the schools were concerned only with training and if their sole mission was to establish certain specific, unvarying responses or behavior patterns, then they should depend heavily on conditioning, because conditioning could probably get the job done more quickly and effectively than the cognitive learning process could. But what conditioning cannot do is give a person flexibility and freedom in choosing future behavioral responses. Conditioning is better suited to the training of horses or dogs than to the development of human beings to live happy, useful lives as free men and women.

People who object to the emphasis on learning as the school's main function may do so because they think of learning as academic specialization, designed mainly to prepare a person for further learning, and remote from the practical concerns of living. There may be some justification for this view. But learning need not be, and ought not be, the learning of useless things. It can and should be the student's main road to effective living. And as long as cognitive learning is the focus of our schools, there is a need for ways to determine the extent and type of learning that has occurred. Tests can be, and should be, among the most useful instructional tools for planning new learning activities and for monitoring students' progress in attaining the learning goals presented to them.

The Role of Affective Outcomes

Teachers and test developers are sometimes accused of overemphasizing cognitive learning, with consequent neglect of the affective determiners of behavior. Some people believe most teachers are preoccupied with what their students know; students, they say, are most concerned with what they like or dislike and how they feel. Furthermore, they submit, the most profound challenges in our society are not cognitive. They are challenges to our social unity and our social righteousness, to our ethical standards and moral values, and to our courage and compassion. If our schools dwell too much on cognitive outcomes, they will fail to contribute as they should to meeting these other important challenges.

Such viewpoints are not without foundation. Feeling is as real and as important a part of human nature as is knowing. How we feel is almost always more important to us than what we know, and how we behave is a paramount concern for those with whom we share our lives. And since behavior is often determined more by how we feel about a situation than by what we know about it, clearly the affective dimension will play a most significant role in meeting the challenges of society.

Should schools give up some of their concerns for cognitive learning in favor of affective outcomes? Such a reemphasis should not occur for a variety of reasons. Many affective goals can be reached, at least in part, through cognitive means. Affect and cognition are not independent aspects of the personality: how we feel about a problem or an event depends in part on what we know about it. Wisdom does not guarantee happiness, but the lack of it often entails great unhappiness. The affective failures among student—the alienated, the dropouts, the pushouts—can nearly always be traced to some prior cognitive failure of theirs or ours. Psychologists who try to help people with problems of affect usually use cognitive means. The psychotherapy they practice is essentially a cognitive process of fostering self-knowledge in the patient. Training sessions and courses in human relations focus on the cognitive aspects of bias and prejudice and attempt to create a new awareness (cognizance) of interpersonal relationships by expanding the knowledge base of participants.

No teacher can afford to ignore the affective side effects of efforts to promote cognitive learning. In fact, the affective disposition to learn—the willingness to attend and respond—must be considered by teachers in assessing the entering behaviors of their students for each instructional unit. But teachers should not use their concern for affect as an excuse for paying less attention to cognitive outcomes.

THE POTENTIAL VALUE OF TESTING IN EDUCATION

There is currently much testing in education, but tests seldom contribute as much as they could to effective instruction. How much is learned in any particular course of instruction depends largely on how much the students want to learn and on how hard the teacher works to help them to learn it. These efforts by students and teachers depend, in turn, on the immediate and ultimate rewards or satisfaction that seem likely to result from their efforts. Tests can be used to provide recognitions and rewards for success in learning *and* teaching. They can be used to motivate and direct efforts to learn. In short, they can be used to contribute substantially to effective instruction.

Tests have sometimes been used very successfully to stimulate efforts to learn. For example, in the Iowa Academic Contest that began in 1929 (Lindquist, 1960), high school students were offered tests in each of the major subjects of study: English, history, geometry, physics, and so on. Those who received the highest scores on the local test were invited to a district contest where a similar but somewhat more difficult test was given. Those who scored highest on the district tests were invited to the state contest where they took a third level of tests. Those who scored highest on these tests were offered scholarships to the State University.

This academic contest was used by some high school principals to provide incentives for both students and teachers to work hard. In some schools the local contest winners were recognized at a school assembly and in news stories. In conferences with teachers whose students had done well on the tests, the principal offered congratulations and support for continued efforts to teach effectively. In conferences with teachers whose students had not done well, the principal tried to identify things that the principal or the teacher might do to make students more successful the next year. Thus the whole school was led to believe that learning was important and that successful efforts to learn would be rewarded. An environment conducive to learning was created in the school, and every student, not just the contest winners, benefited from it.

In many schools, unfortunately, tests are not used so effectively to stimulate and facilitate learning. Test scores do not matter very much, and unless they matter they cannot contribute much to effective instruction. There are several reasons, none of them very good, why some teachers and school administrators depreciate testing and do as little of it as possible. The tests are criticized as having little value or as being actually harmful. Doing a good job of testing demands skills that many educators know that they lack and requires work that their lives are more comfortable without. Testing involves comparison and competition. Even though these are facts of life, some teachers believe that schools should protect their students from competition as much as possible. Unless all students can win, none should be allowed to win. Thus some schools are content with a comfortable mediocrity as long as the public will tolerate it.

Heavily taxed citizens in many states are not willing to tolerate mediocrity in their schools. They are asking for evidence that their tax dollars are buying excellence in education. They are asking that the schools do something, or demanding that communities do something, to correct the conditions that educators blame for low achievement in learning. Since public school teachers and administrators are public employees, it is entirely proper for the public to hold their schools accountable for doing the best job possible under the circumstances.

There are two things, both involving the use of tests, that teachers and schools can do, and ought to do, to justify their stewardship to the community. Each teacher ought to present evidence periodically to the school administration that the students he or she has been teaching have made substantial progress in learning. Each school ought to present evidence periodically to the community that the students in the school are making substantial progress in learning. It is not sufficient for teachers and schools to describe their processes of instruction and to claim that they know how to do a good job of educating children. The public is more interested in the product than in the process, and it would like to see evidence to support the claims.

Of course, not all evidence of learning can be, or should be, furnished in the form of test scores, whether from teacher-prepared or standardized tests. Public performances and displays of student creative efforts, portfolios of student work products, and in-class observations by teachers and administrators can and should be used to support the positive efforts of students and teachers. It is possible to use tests effectively to promote and document learning also. However, effective test use requires that *both* teachers and administrators be knowledgeable about and skilled in the use of educational tests. The remaining chapters of this book are devoted to the presentation of concepts and principles that will contribute to the development of many of these essential skills.

SUMMARY PROPOSITIONS

1. The most recent surge in educational testing is part of an historical cycle pattern of test use.
2. Mandated testing and the accompanying potential negative consequences have unduly shaped the curriculum and teaching practices of many schools.
3. Educators have not had an opportunity to learn as much as they need to know about educational measurement.
4. The influence standardized tests have on the local school curriculum is probably more beneficial than harmful.
5. "Teaching to the test" is deplorable if it means giving students answers to the particular questions on a test; it is commendable if it means helping students learn what they must know to answer questions like those on the test.
6. Claims that testing harms students tend to be exaggerated and seldom are substantiated.
7. Test bias may exist to some extent on some tests, but it cannot account for substantial differences in test scores between different cultural groups.
8. Objective tests can provide highly valid, precise, and convenient measurements of most of the important outcomes of education.
9. Comprehensive instruction can benefit from two kinds of test information—scores that tell what students can do and scores that show how students rank among their peers.
10. State and district assessment programs required by law are intended to evaluate the general quality of the educational program or to identify specific competencies held by students "ready" for high school graduation.
11. A district's customized testing program is no adequate replacement for a nationally standardized testing program.
12. One significant contribution of the National Assessment of Educational Progress was to provide a model that states might adapt for designing and operating statewide assessment programs.
13. Test assembly and administration can be accomplished efficiently with the use of computers without sacrificing test quality.
14. The use of purchased item banks by teachers could have a negative impact on test quality, as well as on the development of teachers' item-writing skills.
15. Testing to certify competence or to license practitioners often requires a demonstration of processes or products that a paper and pencil testing approach cannot accommodate.
16. Court cases of the last several decades that involved testing were focused nearly exclusively on the social consequences of testing and fair test use rather than on the tests themselves.
17. The *Standards for Educational and Psychological Testing* represent an effort by the testing profession to monitor itself and to provide a form of consumer protection to test takers and users.
18. There are good reasons for believing that the primary task of the school is to facilitate cognitive learning.
19. Among the limited means that schools can use to help students become effective and happy adults, cultivating their cognitive abilities is the most appropriate and desirable.
20. Schools should seek to attain affective ends only through cognitive means.
21. Tests could be used to promote learning better if both teachers and administrators systematically provided test results to the community as evidence of the educational progress of students.

QUESTIONS FOR STUDY AND DISCUSSION

1. What useful purposes could be served by a mandated *national* testing program?
2. Why is there no federal school curriculum, a common core for all schools in the United States?
3. Under what kinds of circumstances might "teaching the test" be appropriate and desirable?

4. What kind of evidence should be furnished to support someone's claim that a particular test is biased against a given ethnic group?

5. How should the standards for a high school graduation competency test be established?

6. What are the pros and cons of making available state by state comparisons of achievement-test scores?

7. What functions might be served by a testing "watchdog" organization that would provide protection to test consumers?

8. Which individuals or agencies should be assigned major responsibility for developing inter-personal skills, societal values, and personal attitudes in young people?

2

Measurement and the Instructional Process

EVALUATION, MEASUREMENT, AND TESTING

The purpose of evaluation is to make a judgment about the quality or worth of something—an educational program, worker performance or proficiency, or student attainments. That is what we attempt to do when we evaluate students' achievements, employees' productivity, or prospective practitioners' competencies. In each case the goal is not simply to describe what the students, employees, or other personnel can do. Instead we seek answers to such questions as: How good is the level of achievement? How good is the performance? Have they learned enough? Is their work good enough? These are questions of value that require the exercise of judgment. To say simply that evaluation is the process of making value judgments understates the complexity and difficulty of the effort required. Once it has been determined that evaluation is needed, the evaluator must decide what kind of information is needed, how the information should be gathered, and how the information should be synthesized to support the outcome—the value judgment. Thus, evaluation is as concerned with information gathering as it is with making decisions. In addition, the term is used to refer to the product or outcome of the process. That is, we might, for example, submit our evaluation (the product) of Scott's school performance to his parents following our evaluation (the process) of his accomplishments. In this respect evaluation has a dual connotation.

Evaluation: Formative and Summative

The terms formative and summative were introduced by Scriven (1967) to describe the various roles of evaluation in curriculum development and instruction. *Formative evaluation* is conducted to monitor the instructional process, to determine whether learning is taking place as planned. *Summative evaluation* is conducted at the end of an instructional segment to determine if learning is sufficiently complete to warrant moving the learner to the next segment of instruction. The distinctions between these two types of evaluation have implications for test development and use in the classroom and in the evaluation of educational programs. As will be noted later, information gathered primarily for summative purposes may be used on occasion for formative purposes as well.

The major function of *formative evaluation* in the classroom is to provide feedback to the teacher and to the student about how things are going. Such feedback provides an opportunity for the teacher to modify instructional methods or materials to facilitate learning when feedback indicates things are not going well. Formative evaluation requires the gathering of fairly detailed information on frequent occasions. Information is obtained through teacher observation, classroom oral questioning, homework assignments, and quizzes or informal inventories. Much of what a teacher does in leading class discussions or answering student questions should be regarded as formative evaluation. The role of tests is likely to be quite small. Only in highly systematized programs of individualized instruction are tests used prominently for formative evaluation.

However, formal classroom tests, such as unit tests or final examinations, are the most frequently used tools of summative evaluation. The major function of summative evaluation in the classroom is to determine the status of achievement at the end of an instructional segment, to determine how well things went. Relative to formative evaluation, there is greater finality associated with summative evaluation. The information gathered is less detailed in nature but broader in the scope of content or skills assessed. Figure 2–1 compares some of the distinguishing characteristics of the two types.

Obviously, both types of evaluation are necessary components of classroom instruction. In some cases, information gathered for summative purposes may be useful in a formative sense. For example, the scores on a unit test may be used to evaluate achievement at the end of that unit. At the same time the scores reflect progress in the course and in the broader instructional program. In such circumstances the tests should be designed to yield useful information

Figure 2-1. Characteristics that Distinguish Classroom Formative and Summative Evaluation

	Formative	*Summative*
Purpose	Monitor progress	Check final status
Content Focus	Detailed, narrow scope	General, broad scope
Methods	Observations, daily assignments	Tests, projects
Frequency	Daily	Weekly, or every 2-3 weeks

for summative evaluation purposes, but the scores might be used incidentally as gross indicators of progress in the broader context.

Measurement: Assigning Numbers

Measurement is the process of assigning numbers to individuals or their characteristics according to specified rules. Measurement requires the use of numbers but does not require that value judgments be made about the numbers obtained from the process. We measure achievement with a test by counting the number of test items a student answers correctly, and we use exactly the same rule to assign a number to the achievement of each student in the class. Measurements are useful for describing the amount of certain abilities that individuals have. For that reason, they represent useful information for the evaluation process. But can we measure all the important outcomes of our instructional efforts?

Education is an extensive, diverse, and complex enterprise, not only in terms of the achievements it seeks to develop, but also in terms of the means by which it seeks to develop them. Our understanding of the nature and process of education is far from perfect. Hence it is easy to agree that we do not now know how to measure all important educational outcomes. But, in principle, all important outcomes of education are measurable. They may not be measurable with the tests currently available. They may not even be measurable in principle, using only paper and pencil tests. But if they are known to be important, they must be measurable.

To be important, an outcome of education must make an observable difference. That is, at some time, under some circumstance, a person who has more of it must behave differently from a person who has less of it. If different degrees or amounts of an educational achievement never make any observable difference, what evidence can be found to show that it is in fact important? But if such differences can be observed, then the achievement is measurable, for all that measurement requires is verifiable observation of a more–less relationship. Can integrity be measured? It can if verifiable differences in integrity can be observed among individuals. Can mother love be measured? If observers can agree that a hen shows more mother love than a female trout, or that Mrs. A shows more love for her children than Mrs. B, then mother love can be measured.

The argument, then, is this: *To be important an educational outcome must make a difference. If it makes a difference, the basis for measurement exists.* To say that Rita shows more "spunk" than Ned may not seem like much of a measurement. Where are the numbers? Yet out of a series of such more–less comparisons, a scale for measuring people's spunk can be constructed. The Ayres scale for measuring the quality of handwriting is a familiar example of this (Ayres, 1912). If a sequence of numbers is assigned to the sequence of steps or intervals that make up the scale, then the scale can yield quantitative measurements. If used carefully by a skilled judge, it yields measurements that are reasonably objective (that is, free from errors associated with specific judges) and reliable (that is, free from errors associated with the use of a particular set of test items or tasks).

Are some outcomes of education essentially qualitative rather than quantitative? If so, is it reasonable to expect that these qualitative outcomes can be measured? It is certainly true that some differences between persons are not usually thought of as more–less differences. This person is a man; that one is a woman. This person has blue eyes; that one has brown. This person speaks only French; that one speaks only German. But we can express these qualitative differences in quantitative terms, too. This person has more of the characteristics of a man; that one has less. This person has more eye-blueness; that one has less. This person has more ability to speak French; that one has less.

We may think of the weight of a man, his age, or the size of his bank account as quantities, while regarding his health, his friendliness, or his honesty as qualities. And if they serve to differentiate him from other men because he exhibits more or less of them than other men, they become quantitative qualities. It is difficult to think of any quality that interests us that cannot also be quantified. "Whatever exists at all exists in some amount," said E. L. Thorndike (1918, p. 16). And William A. McCall (1939) has added, "Anything that exists in amount can be measured" (p. 18).

Testing: A Form of Measurement

Tests represent one particular measurement technique. A *test* is a set of questions, each of which has a correct answer, that examinees usually answer orally or in writing. Test questions differ from those used in measures of attitudes, interest or preference, or certain other aspects of personality. Ideally, the questions in tests of achievement or many tests of intelligence have answers that content experts can agree are correct; correctness is not determined by the particular values, preferences, or dislikes of a group of judges.

All tests are a subset of the quantitative tools or techniques that are classified as measurements. And all measurement techniques are a subset of the quantitative and qualitative techniques used in evaluation. A major concern in this text, but certainly not the only one, will be with the development of tests that can contribute to summative evaluation of student learning. Other measurement and evaluation techniques are useful for other evaluation purposes, but tests that measure relevant school learning with precision are the most useful tools available to teachers for most classroom summative evaluation needs.

EVALUATION IN THE TEACHING PROCESS

The evaluation of learning takes place in an instructional context and, consequently, that learning environment shapes the reasons why we evaluate, influences the purposes for evaluating as well as how we evaluate, and determines how we should use the outcomes of our evaluating. Evaluation is an integral part of instruction, it is not a separate entity that somehow is loosely attached to the teaching process. The instructional process and the role of evaluation in it both must be understood as background to the study of educational measurement. To that end, the role of evaluation in instruction will be described using a model that explains how the teaching process works.

The Basic Teaching Model

There are many models that describe the variety of approaches to teaching found in our schools, but the Basic Teaching Model (BTM), introduced by Glaser (1962), accounts for the fundamental components of most other specific teaching models, such as the Socratic approach, the individualized instruction approach, or the computer-dominated instructional approach (Joyce and Weil, 1980). Few teachers probably follow the BTM steps explicitly to guide their instructional activities. And though we do not specifically endorse the use of the BTM or any other particular model, we do advocate instructional approaches, by whatever name, that account for the fundamental functions represented in the BTM as described next.

The main purposes of the BTM are to identify the major activities of the teacher and to describe the relationships between activities. Figure 2–2 is a diagram of the model. Our primary interest is the Performance Assessment component, but we cannot understand completely the role of evaluation without understanding how Performance Assessment affects, and is affected by, other teaching activities. *Instructional Objectives,* the first component of the BTM, represents the teacher's starting point in providing instruction. What should students learn? What skills and knowledge should be the focus of instruction? What is the curriculum and how is it defined? The second component, *Entering Behavior,* indicates that the teacher must try to assess the students' levels of achievement and readiness to learn prior to beginning instruction. What do the students know already and what are their cognitive skills like? How receptive to learning are they? Which ones seem self-motivated? This component indicates a need for evaluation information *before* instruction actually begins.

Once the teacher has decided what will be taught and to whom the teaching is to be directed, the "How?" must be determined. The *Instructional Procedures* component deals with the materials and methods of instruction the teacher selects or develops to facilitate student learning. Does the text need to be supplemented with illustrations? Should small group projects be developed? Is there computer software available to serve as a refresher for prerequisites? At this point instruction could begin, and often it does. But unless the teacher makes plans to evaluate students' performances, the students and teacher will never be

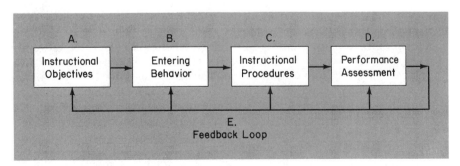

Figure 2-2.   The Basic Teaching Model (DeCecco and Crawford, 1974).

sure when learning is complete. The *Performance Assessment* component helps to answer the question, "Did we accomplish what we set out to do?" Tests, quizzes, teacher observations, projects, and demonstrations are evaluation tools that help to answer this question. Thus evaluation should be a significant aspect of the teaching process; teaching does not occur, according to the model, unless evaluation of learner performance occurs.

The model shows a fifth component, the *Feedback Loop*, that can be used by the teacher as both a management and a diagnostic procedure. If the results of evaluation indicate that sufficient learning has occurred, the loop takes the teacher back to the Instructional Objectives component, and each successive component, so that plans for beginning the next instructional unit can be developed. (New objectives are needed, entering behavior is different, and methods will need to be reconsidered.) But when evaluation results are not so positive, the Feedback Loop is a mechanism for identifying possible explanations. (Note the arrows that return to each component.) Were the objectives too vaguely specified? Did students lack essential prerequisite skills or knowledge? Was the film or text relatively ineffective? Was there insufficient practice opportunity? Such questions need to be asked and frequently are. However, questions need to be asked about the effectiveness of the performance assessment procedures also, perhaps more frequently than they are. Were the test questions appropriate? Were enough observations made? Were directions clear to students? The Feedback Loop returns to the Performance Assessment component to indicate that we must review and assess the quality of our evaluation procedures, after the fact, to determine the appropriateness of the procedures and the accuracy of the information. Unless the tools of evaluation are developed with care, inadequate learning may go undetected or complete learning may be misinterpreted as deficient.

In sum, good teaching requires planning for and using good evaluation tools. Furthermore, evaluation does not take place in a vacuum. The BTM shows that other components of the teaching process provide cues about what to evaluate, when to evaluate, and how to evaluate. Our purpose is to identify such cues and to take advantage of them in building tests and other assessment devices that measure achievement as precisely as possible.

Evaluation Planning

Most teachers spend considerable time planning their instruction to help ensure its effectiveness and to provide for such practicalities as scheduling facilities, equipment, and the time of other instructional personnel. Often the details of evaluation are overlooked, however, as teachers attend to the selection of reading excerpts, the preparation of handout materials, and the previewing of films, videotapes, or tutorial software. But if we are to get the most out of the limited time allocated to evaluation activities, planning is just as crucial for it as for other aspects of instruction.

Teachers usually make written plans for upcoming instruction, whether it is for the start of the year or semester, the beginning of a new unit, or the introduction of a daily lesson. Figure 2–3 describes how these three levels of instruction might be viewed separately to make evaluation plans for addressing each of three separate information needs. For example, during the first few weeks

Figure 2-3. Examples of Methods that Serve Varying Purposes in an Evaluation Planning Guide

Type of Information	LEVEL OF INSTRUCTION		
	Course	Unit	Daily Lesson
Entering Behavior	Cumulative folders, questionnaires, observation, oral questioning	Pretest, oral questioning, checklist, observation	Observation, oral questioning, homework results
Formative Evaluation	Unit tests, projects, papers, observation, participation patterns	Quizzes, oral questioning, results, participation records	Teacher questioning, student questioning, quizzes, activity observation, nonverbal observation
Summative Evaluation	Final examination, comprehensive project, research paper, performance ratings	Unit test, written project, work product, presentation, participation record, performance checklist	[Ordinarily not applicable]

of school, teachers spend considerable time "sizing up" their class, both the group and the individuals in it (Airasian, 1989). Teachers might review cumulative record folders or solicit specific background information from students, but most data gathering is unplanned observation and questioning directed more toward social and emotional behaviors than academic ones. Teachers should plan for their evaluation needs, no matter which level of instruction they happen to be considering. By deciding in advance what kind of information they need and how it might be obtained, evaluation will be done efficiently and will yield complete and helpful information.

Another reason for developing an evaluation planning guide for a unit, for example, is that the teacher will be forced to plan for assessing the achievement of some of the hard-to-measure outcomes of instruction. For example, the teacher may plan to evaluate the achievement of the 12 main objectives in a science unit by using an objective test, two essay items, and a laboratory observation checklist. Without the planning, however, last-minute attention to evaluation might result in the use of only an objective test. Test-planning activities that will be discussed in Chapter 7 will help to decide how "testable" objectives can be measured. But in the absence of an evaluation planning guide for the unit, nontestable outcomes may get lost in the shuffle. An assessment of science achievement should reflect learning of all relevant objectives, not just those that are most easily assessed.

Finally, it can be seen from an inspection of Figure 2–3 that evaluation activities vary depending on the level of instruction and the type of information needed. Note, for example, that standardized achievement-test scores, found in cumulative folders, are useful on the course level, but only for providing information on entering behavior. They are much less useful as summative evaluation information, and they are of little value at the unit and daily lesson levels. Note, too, that summative evaluation of daily lessons is not meaningful because such lessons are seldom ends in themselves. Which methods seem more helpful for formative than summative evaluation purposes? Why isn't homework included under the summative evaluation heading? In which other category do you find most of the components that are listed under formative evaluation at the course level?

Appendix A is a sample Evaluation Planning Guide prepared for a sixth-grade health unit on physical fitness. Activities corresponding to the middle column of Figure 2–3 are grouped according to the three different types of information needed. This guide forms the basis for subsequent illustrations of various aspects of test development and evaluation as we proceed through this text.

FUNCTIONS OF ACHIEVEMENT TESTS

To teach without evaluating the extent of learning would be foolish. Some educators who have become frustrated by the limitations of tests might suggest that schools do not need tests or that we might even do a better job of educating students if tests were banned. But none of these individuals is likely to argue that evaluation is not needed. They seem to recognize that learning cannot be promoted effectively by teachers and students who have no particular goals or who pay no attention to the results of their efforts. Certainly, if tests were abandoned, some other means of assessing achievement would have to be used in their place. Unfortunately, perhaps, no other means that is as efficient, as dependable, and as beneficial to the educational process has been discovered yet.

The major function of a classroom test is to measure student achievement and thus to contribute to the evaluation of educational progress and attainments. This is a matter of considerable importance. To say, as some educators have, that what students know and can do is more important than their scores on a test implies, quite incorrectly in most cases, that knowledge and the scores are independent or unrelated. Or to say that testing solely to measure achievement has no educational value implies, also quite incorrectly in most cases, that test scores are unrelated to educational efforts, that they do not reward and reinforce effective study, that they do not penalize unproductive efforts, or that they do not tend to discourage lack of effort.

Tests often do help teachers and instructors to assign meaningful and accurate grades. Because these grades are meant to be a comprehensive measurement of student achievement, because they are reported to students and their parents to indicate how effective their efforts have been, and because they are entered in the permanent school record and may influence opportunities for future education and employment, it is important that teachers and instructors take seriously their responsibilities for assigning grades. Students are urged, quite properly, not to study *merely* to earn high grades. But in terms of the students' present self-perceptions and future opportunities, there is nothing "mere" about the grades they receive.

A second major function of classroom tests is to motivate and direct student learning. The experience of almost all students and teachers supports the position that (1) students do tend to study harder when they expect an exam than when they do not and (2) they emphasize in their studying those things on which they expect to be tested. If students know in advance (as they should) that they will be tested, if they know what the test will require, and if the test does a good job of measuring the achievement of the essential course objectives, then its motivating and guiding influence will be most wholesome.

Anticipated tests should be regarded as extrinsic motivators of learning efforts, and internal desires or needs to achieve should be regarded as intrinsic motivators. Since both kinds contribute to learning, the withdrawal of either would probably lessen the learning of most students. For a fortunate few, intrinsic motivation may be strong enough to stimulate all the effort to learn that the student ought to exert. For most of us, however, the motivation provided by tests and other influential factors is indispensable. What we stand to gain or what we might lose in a given situation is motivating to all of us. We live with such trade-offs. Tests help us make many of our decisions about trying to learn—whether to try, how hard to try, and when to stop trying.

Classroom tests do serve other useful educational functions. The process of building them should cause instructors to think carefully about the objectives of instruction in a course. It should cause them to define their objectives operationally, that is in terms of the kinds of tasks a student must be able to handle to demonstrate achievement of those objectives. And from the students' perspective, the process of taking a classroom test and discussing the outcome afterward can be a richly rewarding learning experience. As Stroud (1946) put it long ago,

> It is probably not extravagant to say that the contribution made to a student's store of knowledge by taking of an examination is as great, minute for minute, as any other enterprise he engages in. (p. 476)

Hence, testing and teaching should not be regarded as mutually exclusive or as competitors for valuable instructional time. They are intimately related parts of the total teaching effort, as the BTM illustrates.

LIMITATIONS OF ACHIEVEMENT TESTS

It is easy to show that mental measurement falls far short of the standards of logical soundness that have been set for physical measurement. Ordinarily, the best it can do is provide an approximate rank order of individuals in terms of their ability to perform a more or less well defined set of tasks. Unlike the inch or pound, the units used in measuring this ability cannot be shown to be equal. The zero point on the ability scale is not clearly defined. Because of these limitations, some of the things we often do with test scores, such as finding means, standard deviations, and correlation coefficients, ought not to be done if strict mathematical logic holds sway. Nonetheless, we often find it practically useful to do them. When strict logic conflicts with practical utility, it is the utility that usually wins, as it probably should.

It is well for us to recognize the logical limitations of the units and scales used in educational measurement. But it is also important not to be so impressed by these limitations that we stop doing the useful things we can legitimately do. One of those useful things is to measure educational achievement.

Are some outcomes of education too intangible to be measured? No doubt there are some that we speak of often, like critical thinking or good citizen-ship, that are so difficult to define satisfactorily that many of us have given up trying. To this extent they are intangible, hard to measure, and hard to teach purposefully. We may feel intuitively that critical thinking and good citizenship, for example, are immensely important. But if we are unable to state objectively what they consist of, it is hard to show that the concepts they might stand for are, in fact, important.

The processes of education that a particular student experiences prob-ably have subtle and wholly unforeseen effects on that individual, and possibly on no one else. Some of these effects may not become apparent until long after the student has left school. These, too, could be regarded as intangible outcomes. It is unlikely that any current tests, or any that could conceivably be built, would measure these intangibles satisfactorily. In individual instances they might be cru-cially important. But since they may be largely accidental, subtle, and quite possi-bly long delayed in their influence, the practical need to measure them may be no greater than the practical possibility of measuring them.

Finally, it should be recognized that paper and pencil tests do have some limitations. They are well adapted to testing verbal knowledge and understand-ing and the ability to solve verbal and numerical problems. These are important educational outcomes, but they represent an incomplete list. Outcomes in the realms of physical development or social skills attainments cannot be assessed readily with paper–pencil tests. Performance tests of physical development or controlled observations of behavior in social situations would be expected to offer more promise than a paper and pencil test.

However, it is important to remember that the use of alternative mea-sures of achievement does not in any way lessen the need for objectivity, rele-vance, and accuracy. To achieve these qualities of excellence in measurement may well be even more difficult in performance testing and observational rating than it is in paper and pencil testing. But the usefulness of the measurements depends on these qualities.

Alternatives to Tests

Teachers obtain information about the educational progress and attain-ments of their students from many sources and with the use of many tools other than tests. Many of these were identified in Figure 2–3 as alternatives to tests, supplements to tests, or replacements where tests seemed inappropriate or illogi-cal. For example, teachers observe informally–and almost constantly–what stu-dents do and say. Some of these observations are recorded on charts or lists and some are simply stored in memory for later retrieval. Evaluations of student per-formances or products also can be defined and quantified in a comprehensive and systematic way with the help of rating scales.

In many cases, information obtained from nontest sources is essentially descriptive and provides no direct measurement of ability or achievement in learning. Of course, if the information does not result in numbers, it does not constitute a measurement. (As noted in an earlier section, measurement consists of assigning numbers to persons or things so that the larger numbers indicate greater amounts of some characteristic of those persons or things.) Assessments of students' abilities *can* be made on the basis of descriptive information. Because these assessments are bound to be qualitative, not quantitative, they provide only limited and very imperfect indicators of achievement. Such descriptions are dominated by terms like excellent, mediocre, worthwhile, well written, satisfactory, and quite good. Qualitative descriptions of direct or indirect behavior observations, however specific and objective, may have some value in assessing achievement, but they are no adequate replacement for a well-prepared classroom achievement test.

Ratings of performance or products, on the other hand, *do* involve assigning numbers to things and, hence, do constitute measurements. Thus, they are useful in differentiating individuals who possess different amounts of the traits measured by the ratings. These kinds of rating scales tend to measure certain aspects of achievement that tests are less well equipped to measure. Consequently, while they seldom can replace tests, they frequently provide useful supplements to the information provided by tests.

Many teachers use ratings of a student's discussion participation and of the student's written work as part of the basis for evaluating learning. It is important to note that the value of ratings, as well as of a test or any other measurement of achievement, depends on their reproducibility, accuracy, and appropriateness. Assessments of achievement ordinarily should not be limited to tests, but the alternatives and supplements that are available must be used with full realization of their limitations and pitfalls. Chapter 14 is devoted to a discussion of the development and use of nontest alternatives for gathering achievement information.

INTERPRETING MEASUREMENTS

The result of measuring is a number, but that number has no inherent meaning and, consequently, is not a useful contributor to decision making. To make the number useful, or meaningful, it is necessary to compare it with something. If Gail, a 23-year old female, weighs 62 gauchos, what does that mean? If it is 8 bukas between your town and mine, what does that number mean? If Tonya got 15 right on an algebra test, what does that 15 tell us? My score of 23 on the Attitude Toward Computers Scale means nothing by itself. I need to *reference* it, or compare it, with something that has meaning in order to interpret my score. What are these "somethings?"

When we step down from the scale after weighing ourselves, we lend meaning to the number we read by referencing it to any of several other numbers: our expectation for how much we think we should weigh; the result from our last weighing; the weights of other individuals of our own height, gender, or age; or a listing of numbers that define such terms as obese, overweight, about right, underweight, and emaciated. Similar kinds of comparisons can be made to interpret a test score. If my expectation for myself was a score of at least 85 on a midsemester exam, then actual scores of 67 or 92 each will have quite different meanings to me. If my score of 92 is 15 higher than my score on this same test a week ago, my score obtains meaning in terms of growth or change by referencing my first score. Knowing that three-fourths of my classmates obtained scores above 92 also supplies interpretative information. And, finally, if I know there were 115 total test points, my 92 means I know 80 percent of the content represented by the 115-point test. In sum, test scores or any other measurement results can be made meaningful by referencing them separately to some expected or desirable score level, to the scores of other individuals, or to scores that represent different performance levels. How *should* a test score be interpreted? Which kind of referencing is most appropriate? These simply stated questions have important but complex answers.

There are two main types of score interpretations—norm referenced and criterion referenced—but there are a number of specialized terms used to describe certain aspects of each of the two types. In addition, though these terms most precisely describe types of test-score interpretations, they are used frequently by educators to describe kinds of tests. That is, a norm-referenced test is one that permits the user to make norm-referenced interpretations from it. It is important to understand the differences between the various types of score interpretations because it is possible to apply more than one type to the scores obtained from a single test. Despite this possibility, it is seldom advantageous to interpret a given set of scores in more than one way; good tests tend to be built to optimize the user's ability to make only one type of interpretation. As a result, there are important variations in the procedures adopted for constructing tests that will yield one type of interpretation rather than the other. Likewise, there are important differences to consider in evaluating the characteristics of a test or its scores, depending on the type of score interpretation the evaluator has in mind. A close look at these score interpretation differences will help provide the background for test development and evaluation and for assessing appropriate and inappropriate score use.

Norm-referenced Interpretations

When we reference the scores of other individuals (or groups) to obtain meaning, we make a *norm-referenced* interpretation. The term "norm" relates to "normal," which connotes typical, usual, or average. Thus, norm-referenced interpretations involve comparing a person's score with the average score of some relevant group of people. Is it above or below the group average? Is it slightly above or well above average? In fact, we compare Bob's geometry score with the scores of *all* his classmates, not just with the average, to determine his relative standing or rank in the class.

Obviously, the meaning we obtain from a norm-referenced interpretation depends a good deal on the nature of the norm group with which comparisons are made. An individual belongs to several groups simultaneously and, therefore, his or her relative standing might vary from group to group. For example, Bob is in Mr. Schroeder's fifth-period geometry class, and Mr. Schroeder has three geometry classes with 30 students each. Bob may have the second highest score in his class but only the tenth highest in the three classes. If we say Bob had the highest score in some *other* group, which group might that possibly be?

The term *treatment referenced* has been used in certain research or program evaluation contexts to describe norm-referenced interpretations involving groups rather than individuals (Millman, 1974a). When two or more groups are each exposed to a different instructional treatment or strategy, the usual goal of summative evaluation is to compare the achievement scores of the groups. Treatment-referenced interpretations are made when the score (average) of one group is compared with the scores (averages) of other groups that have experienced the same, rival, or no instructional treatment. Tests designed to yield such interpretations contain items that are sensitive to instruction; that is, they are much easier for students who have been instructed than for those who have not been. Interpretations are made in reference to the varying methodological treatments or instructional levels. The mean score of a particular group takes on significance only when compared with the mean of some other group. For example, "The team-taught class scored higher than the control group" or "High-ability students who used calculators scored the same as low-ability students who did not use calculators." No direct reference is ordinarily made to test-item content or subject matter to derive meaning from the scores. Achievement scores obtained through most of the "methods" research in the education literature are interpreted in a treatment-referenced fashion. In addition, school norms, or norms for school averages, that are reported from the scoring of standardized achievement tests are best labeled treatment referenced.

Group referenced is the broad term we find convenient to use in referring to norm-referenced and treatment-referenced collectively. Both kinds of interpretation involve comparing a single score with a group of scores. In the first case, these are scores of individuals. In the second, these are scores of groups of individuals. The distinction is an important one because, when we want to interpret the performance of, say, a class of first graders, we should compare their average score with the averages of other first-grade classes, not with the scores of other individual first-grade pupils. The consequences of using the wrong norm group for making comparisons will be explained in greater detail in Chapter 16.

Criterion-referenced Interpretations

A criterion-referenced interpretation is made when we compare a person's score with scores that each represent distinct levels of performance in some specific content area or with respect to a behavioral task. Meaning is obtained by describing what the person can do, in terms of various gradations, in an absolute sense. Glaser (1963) first used the term to highlight the need for tests that can describe the position of a learner on a performance continuum, rather than the learner's rank within a group of learners. For example, we may want to know if Bob can solve geometry problems that require an understanding of the properties of the rhombus and trapezoid, but we do not care so much how well or poorly his performance compares with that of his classmates. Such interpretations are important when the goal is to determine whether students have the prerequisites to profit from a new instructional unit or if they have learned the essential ideas in a unit before moving on to a new unit.

After over 25 years of using the term criterion referenced, there is much confusion, even among measurement specialists, about what the term means. Part of the confusion stems from the fact that "criterion" is used in several other ways by testing specialists. Another part of the confusion relates to the wide variety of interpretations that can be classified correctly as criterion referenced (Nitko, 1980). Both Hively (1974) and Millman (1974b) recognized this ambiguity and offered the term *domain referenced* as a more exact description of a test designed primarily to optimize absolute or content-related interpretations: "(Criterion) carries surplus associations to mastery learning that are best avoided by using the more general term 'domain' instead" (Hively, 1974, p. 6). A domain can be broadly conceived as (1) a large number of closely related but separate skills or behaviors, (2) several loosely related but separate skills or behaviors, (3) several somewhat related clusters of homogeneous skills or behaviors, or (4) one single skill or behavior. This broad conceptualization is consistent with Millman's definition of a domain-referenced test (DRT) as "any test consisting of a random or stratified random sample of items selected from a well-defined set or class of tasks (a domain)" (1974b, p. 315). A single instructional objective or a cluster of instructional objectives that defines a unit of instruction both could be considered domains. In the latter case, each objective might be referred to as a subdomain.

The use of instructional objectives gives rise to a special type of domain-referenced interpretation called *objectives referenced*. When the items in a test represent all the instructional objectives of interest to the test users, scores can be interpreted in terms of mastery of each of those objectives. The interpretation is mastery or nonmastery when the domain is a single objective. If the domain is a cluster of instructional objectives, the interpretation may center on either the proportion of objectives mastered or mastery versus nonmastery of each objective in the domain. Daily quizzes and curriculum-embedded tests used for formative evaluation purposes are examples of measures used to obtain objectives-referenced interpretations.

The major difference between domain-referenced and objectives-referenced interpretations is in the amount of inference that must be made about what examinees know. Domain-referenced interpretations are made when test items represent only a (random) sample of the behaviors or skills of interest. Some behaviors included in the domain definition may not be included among or may be underrepresented by the items in the test. Inferences must be made on the basis of *both* sampled and unsampled behaviors. Course final examinations, course proficiency tests, "chapter" achievement tests, and commercially prepared achievement batteries are likely applications for domain-referenced interpretations. However, when all behaviors in the domain of interest are represented completely by the test items, inferences about other behaviors are unnecessary. Score interpretations can be made in reference to only the cluster of behaviors (objectives) or to each single behavior for which items are included in the test. Unit pretests and posttests are possible applications for objectives-referenced interpretations.

In many instructional settings the content domain of interest is not so easy to describe because its constituent elements are not easily identifiable. Domains in mathematics and foreign language may be much easier to define, for example, than those in literature or social studies. Of course, domain-referenced interpretations are meaningful only to the extent that the domain of interest can be communicated to those who are trying to understand the meaning of the score. It should be apparent, also, that even when the domain is defined and communicated clearly, misinterpretation will occur if the test content does not reflect the intended domain well. An example will illustrate several of these points.

Suppose we want to measure students' skills in using the dictionary. With that goal in mind we could begin to write test items, but the content domain of interest will be relatively ill defined. A well-defined domain, however, might be described by listing these particular uses of the dictionary: to check spelling, to determine word meaning, to determine pronunciation, and to identify parts of speech. (Note the definition specifically excludes determining plural forms and syllabification.) A test designed to yield domain-referenced interpretations should be expected to contain items requiring demonstration of each of the four skills listed. A score of 74 percent indicates extent of mastery of that collection of skills, but it yields no information about the separate subskills or subdomains. If such objectives-referenced interpretations are needed, separate domain definitions will be needed and separate subtests will need to be constructed to ensure that the subdomains are being measured thoroughly. Then four scores, one for each subdomain, would be obtained so that separate decisions about the mastery of each skill (objective) could be made.

Cutoff-score Interpretations

There is another score-interpretation situation that merits special consideration because it is so easy for the outcome to result in misinterpretation. Here are some examples first.

1. You need a score of 88 percent to earn a B grade.
2. You will be placed in German 202 if your score is in the range from 40 to 52.
3. A TOEFL score of at least 280 is needed for admission.
4. Those who score 16 or higher will be awarded five credit hours for Calculus I.
5. The passing score on the certification test is 120.

These are situations in which the score users are not particularly interested in domain scores or in norms. Instead, some minimal standard of performance is the most logical reference for obtaining score meaning. It appears, on the surface at least, that this is just another form of criterion-referenced interpretation because each cutoff score represents a performance standard. But does it? What is the basis for choosing 88 percent rather than 85 or 87 percent for the B cutoff score? What level of content proficiency does a calculus test score of 16 represent, or does a score of 16 simply "promote" the top 10 percent of the test takers out of Calculus I?

Whenever a cutoff score is used as a basis for score interpretation, we must know the rationale for selecting the cutoff score in order to determine whether norm-referenced or criterion-referenced interpretation is being used. For example, a test might be given to identify the talented eighth graders who could benefit from an enriched algebra course next year. Those in the top 20 percent (the top 16 students out of the class of 80) might be selected. Whatever score separates the top 20 percent is the relevant performance standard for this

Figure 2-4. Interpretive Statements Distinguishing Norm-Referenced and Criterion-Referenced Interpretations

A.   *Norm-Referenced Interpretations*

1. Rico got the highest score in the class.
2. No other 5th grade class in the district has a lower average vocabulary score.
3. Sara's score of 77 is well above the class average of 58.
4. Prince won the "Best of Show" award at the pet show.
5. Ben's percentile rank on the listening test is 35.
6. The average score of the "Writing to Read" students was higher than the average of the other students.
7. My GRE score is 450.

B.   *Criterion-Referenced Interpretations*

1. Erica can correctly name the capitals of 47 states.
2. Jody has achieved 3 of the 9 science goals.
3. Katie has a perfect score.
4. Billie missed 6 of the 8 items dealing with adding unlike fractions.
5. Andy correctly spelled 93% of the words from this quarter's list.
6. Bert can type 52 words/minute without errors.
7. I got half of the true-false capitalization items right.

group. This is obviously a norm-referenced interpretation because each student's outcome depended on his or her ranking in the group.

The cutoff also could have been established by determining a content-based performance standard. Instead of setting a quota for the algebra class size, the math department could identify those students who have command of certain basic mathematical skills and concepts that are deemed essential for the proposed course. The math teachers might examine the test item by item to determine how many items each thinks a student must answer correctly to meet the prerequisites. A cutoff score using the average judgment of the teachers might be set. This method of setting the cutoff score is based on a content performance standard and thus qualifies as criterion-referenced interpretation.

The statements in Figure 2–4 are intended to summarize the discussion of types of score interpretation by providing examples that distinguish the two types. See if you can verify that each statement is listed under the proper heading. At the same time, try to differentiate examples of norm-referenced from treatment-referenced interpretation. In the bottom section, which statements are examples of objectives-referenced interpretation?

SUMMARY PROPOSITIONS

1. Evaluation is an information-gathering process that results in judgments about the quality or worth of a performance, product, process, or activity.

2. The results of formative evaluation are used primarily to monitor learning and improve the instructional process.

3. The results of summative evaluation are used pri-

marily to make final judgments about the extent of learning or the quality of the instructional program.

4. Measures are tools of evaluation that require a quantification of information.

5. Any important outcome of education is necessarily measurable, but not necessarily by means of a paper and pencil test.

6. It is a mistake to believe that qualities cannot be measured.

7. All tests are measures, and all measures are included in the set of qualitative and quantitative techniques of evaluation.

8. The Basic Teaching Model is a conceptual description of the essential ingredients of the teaching process. Its components—instructional objectives, entering behavior, instructional procedures, performance assessment, and feedback loop—represent the general activities one would expect to find among the procedures of successful teachers, regardless of the specific teaching model they employ.

9. The relationship of evaluation activities to the other essential aspects of teaching can be described with the Basic Teaching Model.

10. An evaluation plan describes the methods to be used in an instructional segment to obtain information about entering behavior and information for formative and summative purposes.

11. The measurement of educational achievement is essential to effective formal education.

12. The primary function of a classroom test is to measure student achievement accurately.

13. Classroom tests can help motivate and direct student achievement and can contribute to learning directly.

14. The development of a good classroom test requires the teacher to define the course objectives in specific terms.

15. The fact that educational measurements fail to meet high standards of mathematical soundness does not destroy their educational value.

16. Educational outcomes that are said to be intangible because they are not clearly defined are as difficult to attain through purposeful teaching as they are to measure.

17. The imperfect tests we now use serve us far better than we would be served by the use of qualitative assessments alone.

18. Criterion referenced and norm referenced more precisely describe kinds of test-score interpretations than types of tests.

19. Domain referenced and objectives referenced, both types of criterion-referenced interpretations, are applied in situations where the test content is either a sample of interest or the entire universe of interest, respectively.

20. Norm-referenced interpretations involve comparing one person's score with the scores of other individuals, but treatment-referenced interpretations compare the score of one group with the scores of other groups.

21. Criterion-referenced interpretations involve comparing one person's score with a set of absolute performance standards.

22. When a cutoff score is used, the underlying interpretation may be either absolute or relative, depending on the method used to establish the cutoff score.

QUESTIONS FOR STUDY AND DISCUSSION

1. How is the process of evaluation different from the process of measuring?

2. In what ways do formative and summative evaluation often take place in employee performance appraisal in various work settings?

3. What are some important educational outcomes that seemingly cannot be measured by any available means? What is the basis for establishing the importance of these outcomes?

4. Thinking back to a course you have taken recently, how were the components of the BTM evidenced in the teacher's behaviors? Which components seemed to have been missing, if any?

5. In which component of the BTM does the evaluation planning process probably best fit?

6. For what reasons might the results of daily assignments be better categorized as formative rather than summative evaluation? What are the implications of the distinction?

7. If the use of paper and pencil tests were abolished at all educational levels, what might some of the important direct and indirect consequences be for students, teachers, and others?

8. What kinds of group-referenced interpretations do teachers and administrators make most frequently?

9. Under what circumstances might we be interested in knowing only whether a specific examinee scored above or below the average score of a certain group?

10. Why might it be difficult to make useful norm-referenced interpretations with scores from a test designed to provide criterion-referenced interpretations?

11. What are some practical examples of the use of cutoff scores that do *not* provide content-related interpretations, that is, indications of what examinees can do?

3

Measuring Important Achievements

THE COGNITIVE OUTCOMES OF EDUCATION

If we look at what actually goes on in our school and college classrooms, labs, libraries, and lecture halls, it is reasonable to conclude that the major goal of education is to develop in students a *command of substantive knowledge*. Achievement of this kind of cognitive mastery is certainly not the only concern of educators, parents, and students, but it is the central concern. What is this important knowledge and how does it relate to understanding, thinking, and performing? We need answers to these questions so that we can decide which achievements our educational tests should measure.

Knowledge Versus Information

Knowledge originates in information that can be received directly from observation or indirectly from reports of observations. Anything we hear, read, smell, or otherwise experience can become part of our knowledge. If it is remembered, it does become knowledge. But if it is only remembered, without being thought about, it remains mere information, the most elementary and least useful form of knowledge. If, on the other hand, information becomes the subject of our reflective thought, if we ask ourselves, "What does it mean?" "How do we know?" "Why is it so?", we may come to *understand* the information. It can be integrated into a system of relations among concepts and ideas, all of which constitute a structure of knowledge. This process of encoding is essential to enable later retrieval; observations that are not encoded in some way cannot be recalled.

Information that is stored in our memory by semantic encoding, that is, by associating its meaning with information already stored, is powerful, useful, and satisfying relative to information stored merely by episodic encoding (Anderson, 1983). In the latter case, information is stored by associating it with other information related to our personal experience. Telephone numbers, what we wore two days ago, and what we plan to do next weekend are examples of information that is episodic. We may not remember that we learned the meaning of "prognosticator" in seventh grade (episodic encoding), but we likely still remember what it means (semantic encoding). Information that has been assimilated into our existing structure of knowledge is likely to be a more permanent possession than information that is simply remembered (Boulding, 1967).

The source of our verbal knowledge exists in our minds in the form of tacit knowledge (Polanyi, 1964) and as such is a purely private possession. But when concepts can be abstracted from these images and expressed in words, and when the relations among the concepts can be expressed in sentences, then the information imagery is converted into verbal knowledge. This kind of knowledge can be communicated, it can be recorded and stored for future reference, and it can be manipulated in the process of reflective thinking. Thus verbal knowledge is a very powerful form of knowledge. The peculiar excellence of humans among all other earthly creatures is their ability to produce and use verbal knowledge.

If a structure of verbal knowledge consists entirely of a system of articulated relations among concepts and ideas, can it be described completely by listing the elements (propositions) that compose it? Might not a complex structure involve relations or dimensions that are not expressed by the constituent elements of the structure? Certainly, a listing of the elements of a structure may lack some that have not been perceived or expressed in words. But to cite an example of such an unperceived and unexpressed element, one would have to perceive and express it. It could then be added to the list. The conclusion that a structure of verbal knowledge can be described by listing the concepts and propositions that compose it appears to be logical. The whole in this case appears to be precisely equal to the sum of all the parts.

Propositions Represent Knowledge

If the primary goal of education is to help students build and use structures of verbal knowledge, it follows that tests designed to measure achievement should be composed of items that help to determine the extent to which students possess these structures of verbal knowledge. Two ideas from Cohen and Nagle (1934) about propositions seem particularly germane in this context: (1) knowledge is of propositions and (2) a proposition is a statement that can be said to be true or false. (Our use of the term here is not limited to the basic "if–then" statements used in logical analysis in the field of philosophy.) Propositions are expressed in sentences, but not all sentences are propositions. Those expressing questions or commands cannot be said to be true or false, nor can those that report purely subjective wishes or feelings. Propositions are always declarative statements about objects or events in the external world. For example:

The earth is a planet in the solar system.

A body immersed in a fluid is buoyed up by force equal to the weight of the fluid displaced.

As we consume or acquire additional units of any commodity, the satisfaction derived from each additional installment tends to diminish.

William J. Bryan failed in his bid for election to the presidency of the U.S. in the campaign of 1896.

The relation of propositions such as these to objective-test items of the true–false variety is direct and simple. Less obvious is the fact that such propositions are implicit in most other types of objective items—multiple choice, matching, short answer, or completion. What we test in each case, beyond students' ability to understand the language used in the test item, is their knowledge of the underlying proposition that makes one answer correct and others incorrect. All the propositions cited above probably deserve to be preserved and passed on to future generations. Contrast them with these propositions:

Rain fell in New York on December 1, 1991.

The cost of living in Canada increased by two-fifths of a point during October, 1985.

Work-limit tests are mentioned on page 136 of *Educational Measurement*, edited by E. F. Lindquist.

Objective test items ought not to be based on propositions such as these, but sometimes, unfortunately, they are.

Despite the fact that the major goal of education is to develop in students a command of substantive knowledge of propositions, it is not easy to identify or state propositions that are suitable as bases for objective test items. To be suitable, propositions need to meet at least four criteria:

1. They must be concise, worded as accurately and unambiguously as the precision of knowledge and language permit.
2. They must be true, as established by a preponderance of experts in the field.
3. They must be worthy of remembering, as judged by experts in the field.
4. They must represent knowledge unique to the field, that is, principles and concepts not generally known by those who have not studied the subject matter.

The difficulty of finding or creating propositions that meet these standards in some areas of study may raise questions about the value of study in that field. Furthermore, if relevant test items are too difficult to prepare, it may be because the structure of substantive knowledge is too ill defined or because the item writer understands too little of the structure.

Appendix B is a list of propositions taken from some of the instructional materials used in the sixth-grade health unit on physical fitness. Do these propositions meet the four criteria of a suitable proposition enumerated above? Note that these propositions state "what is so" rather than what should be done during instruction or what the learner should be able to do. Note also that these statements can only represent the verbal knowledge to which instruction is devoted. Physical skills or affective outcomes that we may want students to acquire cannot be represented by propositions.

Performance Requires Knowledge

Our concern here is with the measurement of the cognitive outcomes of education. The term *cognitive ability* is used narrowly and specifically to refer to whatever particular kind of task can be done using the mind. Intelligence, general mental ability, general numerical ability, verbal fluency, and ability to reason are examples of generalized abilities outside the realm of the meaning of cognitive ability as used here. Here are some examples of what we mean by cognitive ability:

Ability to trace the route of the Pilgrim voyage
Ability to calculate the square root of a number
Ability to outline the economic theories of J. M. Keynes
Ability to trace the circulation of blood
Ability to describe the origins of the Industrial Revolution
Ability to identify the parts of a flower by name
Ability to describe a method for removing tarnish from copper

These abilities indicate what a person can do. They require applications of knowledge to perform specific tasks or to answer particular questions. They can be taught specifically and are learned specifically.

Most written tests used to measure school achievement, professional capabilities, or qualifications for effective performance on the job should be tests of specific cognitive abilities like those listed above. To acquire any such cognitive ability, a person must learn how to do it. To perform a cognitive task, one must know how to do it. The basis of any cognitive ability is knowledge. Experience and practice may develop and perfect the ability, enabling the person to perform the tasks more efficiently and accurately. But the basic requirement is that the person know how the task is to be done. To suggest that a person might lack the ability to do something the person knows perfectly well how to do is hardly reasonable. Knowledge is the key.

It is sometimes said that individuals possess knowledge they do not know how to use. They may indeed. Based on this supposition, the inference is sometimes drawn that knowledge alone is not enough; something more is necessary. But such an inference is open to question. It may be that the individual lacks sufficient knowledge of the right kind. Or those who cannot apply knowledge they possess may simply lack the knowledge of how to apply it. The problem may not be the inadequacy of knowledge per se, but inadequacies in the specific knowledge possessed.

The contribution of knowledge to effective human behavior is sometimes questioned. Knowledge alone is not enough, says the businessman. It does not guarantee financial success. Knowledge alone is not enough, says the college president. It does not guarantee scholarly achievement. Knowledge alone is not enough, says the religious leader. It does not guarantee virtue. Knowledge alone is not enough, says the philosopher. It does not guarantee wisdom.

They are all right, of course. Knowledge alone is not enough. But in our complex world of chance and change, no one thing or combination of things will ever be enough to guarantee financial success or scholarly achievement or virtue or wisdom. Although this is true, few would deny that the command of substantive knowledge does contribute greatly to the attainment of these and other ultimate goals.

Some have argued that knowing *how* does not always require knowing *that* (Ryle, 1949). But are the two really so distinct and unrelated? For cognitive tasks, would not a sufficient amount of relevant knowing *that* enable a person to know *how*? If you know *that* to find the quotient of two common fractions you must invert the divisor and multiply, and all that those words mean, do you not know *how* to divide common fractions? In general, if we wish to teach someone *how* to do something, is there any better way than to teach them *that* this, this, and this must be done?

Surely, knowing is not the same as doing. If the doing involves physical manipulation, it may require psychomotor skills that knowing cannot supply. Even in the realm of pure mental tasks, practice may increase facility. But facility aside, can doing any mental task require more than knowing perfectly well how to do it? If so, what is that "something more?" The best way to prepare learners to complete a cognitive task is to help them acquire the knowledge of how to complete it. The basis of that knowledge is necessarily verbal knowledge. Given sufficient motivation to attempt to complete a task, sufficient verbal knowledge about how to complete it should enable learners to do so successfully.

Knowledge, Thinking, and Understanding

Thinking, understanding, and performing are among the significant goals of education, but none of these behaviors can be produced or nurtured without a substantive knowledge base. Thinking is a process and knowledge is a product, but the two are intimately related (Aaron, 1971). New knowledge cannot be produced internally or used without thinking, and thinking always involves knowledge. Thought processes are wholly dependent on the knowledge being processed. Knowing how to think can be distinguished from knowing what is so but cannot be separated from it. Acquiring knowledge and learning how to think thus would seem to be interdependent goals. To say that schools should teach students how to think instead of teaching them knowledge is to urge the impossible. In sum, the best way to teach people how to think is to help them acquire useful knowledge; the ability to think is necessarily dependent on having something to think about.

To assimilate new information, learners must incorporate it into their own structure of knowledge. They must relate it to what they already know. Relating is understanding. Thunder is understood better when it is related to lightning. Fermentation is understood better when it is related to bacteria. In general, the understanding of any separate thing involves seeing its relations to other known things. And knowledge that is understood is more useful than knowledge that is only information.

Teachers can give pupils information. But they cannot give them understanding, for a person's understanding is a private, personal possession created by the one who seeks it. We earn for ourselves the right to say "I understand." How much we know about a subject depends not only on how much information we have obtained from others or from our experiences. It depends also on how much we have thought about that information, related it to and tested it against other elements of information we have received. This is a primary purpose of study. We ask students to study because we expect such activities will cause them to think about relationships between what they know and what we want them to learn. New information that can be associated with present knowledge by elaborate means will be remembered and understood; information that enters the structure of knowledge with superficial associations likely will not be understood, but it may be remembered. Learning activities and homework that do not foster understanding are correctly perceived as "busy work."

To be understood, information must become part of a coherent structure of knowledge. When occasion for its use arises, we must be able to remember it and see its relevance. When all this is true, we can say we have command of the knowledge. Possession of knowledge is not enough. The bad name rote learning has in some educational circles stems from too much emphasis on possession and not enough emphasis on command.

Finally, what we know probably is known with widely varying degrees of understanding. At the low end of the scale are things that are simply known, like the middle name of an acquaintance, or like the formula Einstein proposed to express the relation of energy to matter. Understanding may be absent either because there is little to be understood, as in the case of the middle name, or because too little is known on the subject or too little time has been spent in thoughtful attempts to understand, as in the case of the Einstein formula. The possibility of finding new relations and thus gaining more understanding always exists. However, most of us settle for understanding less about most subjects than we actually could understand; the cost of learning more seems greater than the knowledge would be worth to us. No doubt the presence of such sentiments provides one of the greatest challenges to teachers as they attempt to facilitate student learning. How do we increase the worth to students of knowing something or decrease the "cost" of learning it?

Describing Cognitive Outcomes

Educational achievement in most courses consists of acquiring command of a store of usable knowledge and in developing the ability to perform certain tasks. For convenience, knowledge can be categorized as verbal facility and practical know-how. Abilities usually include anything from ability to explain or ability to apply knowledge to ability to take appropriate action in practical situations. In other courses the goals may be to develop the ability to calculate or the ability to predict.

The terms that some educators have used to identify or describe achievement are more impressionistic than demonstrative. Their categories of achievement are based on hypothetical mental functions like comprehension, recognition, analysis, scientific thinking, or synthesis—functions that are not directly observable or readily understood. Consequently, such categories are of little value for use in describing either what we wish to measure or what is being measured by a particular test item.

Nearly all important aspects of achievement—knowledge or abilities—

can be described by the type of behavior required to demonstrate attainment of the achievement. Nearly every test item on a good classroom achievement test can be classified using one of these seven categories:

1. Understanding of terminology (or vocabulary)
2. Understanding of fact or principle (or generalization)
3. Ability to explain or illustrate (understand relationships)
4. Ability to calculate (numerical problems)
5. Ability to predict (what is likely to happen under specified conditions)
6. Ability to recommend appropriate action (in some specific, practical problem situation)
7. Ability to make an evaluation judgment

The usefulness of these categories in the classification of items testing various aspects of achievement depends on the fact that they are defined mainly in terms of overt behavior requirements, rather than in terms of presumed mental processes that may be required for successful response. Items belonging to the first category always designate a term to be defined or otherwise identified. Items dealing with facts and principles are based on descriptive statements of the way things are. If the question asks, Who? What? When? or Where? it tests a person's factual information. Items testing explanations usually involve the words *why* or *because*, while items belonging to the fourth category require the student to use mathematical processes to get from given information to the required quantities. Items that belong in either of categories 5 or 6 are based on descriptions of specific situations. "Prediction" items specify *all* the conditions and ask for the future result; "action" items specify *some* of the conditions and ask what other conditions (or actions) will lead to a specified result. In "judgment" items, the response options are statements whose appropriateness or quality is to be judged on the basis of criteria specified in the item itself.

The fundamental concern of test developers is the process of translating the relevant structure of knowledge into tasks (test items) that require a demonstration of the knowledge and abilities of that specific structure. To do so requires that the elements of the structure be identified so that test items can be written based on them. These elements can be represented in a variety of ways—propositions, instructional objectives, or goal statements—and with varying levels of specificity. To the extent that we are able to dissect the knowledge structure and describe its components precisely, the measurements of achievement that result will be most useful and most meaningful in describing the cognitive outcomes of education.

USING INSTRUCTIONAL OBJECTIVES

The knowledge and understanding on which the instructional efforts in our schools are focused is the same knowledge and understanding that tests of achievement ought to measure. The specific knowledge we expect students to learn is represented in the Instructional Objectives component of the Basic

Teaching Model described in Chapter 2. The teacher's job is to define the structures of knowledge, the concepts and relationships that should form the basis of instruction. Statements of instructional objectives can be useful for instructional planning, for promoting intentional learning, and for developing tools for performance assessment. What are instructional objectives and where do they come from? How can they be used to enhance our evaluation efforts?

The Derivation of Instructional Objectives

Instructional objectives are statements that describe the abilities students should be able to display to demonstrate that important concepts and principles have been incorporated into their own structures of knowledge. These statements indicate what the learner should be able to do at the end of an instructional sequence. Because the development of cognitive abilities ought to be the primary concern of our schools, the delineation of these important abilities is no trivial matter. Particularly at the elementary and secondary school levels, the job of deciding what students should learn, what they should know, should not be left to the classroom teacher alone. Most purposeful formal learning is organized in the context of a curriculum defined in terms of grade levels and subject matters. For example, the instructional objectives of a seventh-grade mathematics class must fit into the entire organizational plan; they should not be decided solely by the personal preferences, interests, or capabilities of each different seventh-grade mathematics teacher in the school district.

The derivation of instructional objectives in an organized curriculum is outlined in Figure 3–1. The pyramid develops from a small set of *educational goals* that indicate the purpose of the instructional program. These goals are broad, general statements that are the foundation of the educational program. Parents, teachers, school board members, and administrators decide jointly what the educational goals of the schools should be. For example, "To develop the skills necessary to live as an independent adult" may be a goal specified for the middle school curriculum. To accomplish this goal, *level objectives* are prepared for each of the middle school grade levels. A level objective for grade 7 might be: "To use basic mathematical concepts and processes to solve problems encountered in daily living."

The level objective for the seventh grade, one of several, suggests the need for a mathematics course. The purpose of the course is to address all the level objectives related to mathematics content. Another tier of objectives is needed to define in more detail the mathematics curriculum for grade 7. One *course objective* might be to "compute with ratios and proportions to solve practical word problems." Once course objectives such as this have been specified, teachers must organize them logically and sequentially. Typically, such activities result in the formation of instructional units, defined by yet more detailed descriptions of the abilities students should attain—*instructional objectives*. An example from a unit on ratios and proportions might be: "To compute the price per ounce of several comparable grocery commodities to determine the least expensive." The final tier, *prerequisite knowledge*, suggests that new learning builds on prior learning and that students' entering behaviors must be considered in planning the instructional procedures for a particular unit.

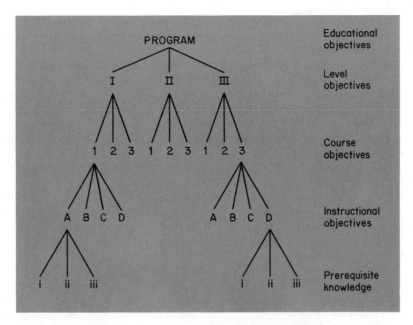

Figure 3-1. The Source of Instructional Objectives—The Pyramid Effect.

The pyramid illustrates that instructional objectives are derived from a few broad educational goals through successive stages in hierarchical fashion. Each stage yields more statements, collectively, than the prior stage, and the statements generated at any one stage are more precise than those in the prior stage in indicating the nature of the ability to be achieved. In fact, the writing of instructional objectives can become a seemingly endless task if the writer attempts to separate cognitive abilities into increasingly finer components.

Stating Instructional Objectives

In contrast to educational goals and level objectives, instructional objectives should be prepared primarily by those who will do the teaching. The statements should be written in a form and at a level of specificity that will make them most useful for their intended purposes. Objectives that have been prepared to guide instructional planning or to communicate intended learning outcomes to students can also be used for evaluation planning and test development. For example, the cognitive abilities indicated by instructional objectives are prescriptive of the type of evaluation tool to use (observation, objective test, research paper, essay, or project) to assess achievement. And when a test seems most appropriate, each objective suggests the most appropriate type of test item (essay, multiple choice, problem type). The nature of the objectives also may suggest how frequently evaluation should occur and, perhaps, how much formative evaluation is needed.

Though there is general agreement among educators about the value of and the role of instructional objectives, there remains little agreement about how such statements should be prepared. Most, however, will agree that *explicit statements* are more helpful than *implicit* statements, no matter how the objectives are intended to be used. Explicit statements contain a verb that indicates in operational, behavioral, or observable terms what the learner must do to demonstrate attainment of the objective. Examples of such verbs are listed in Figure 3-2. Contrast them with the verbs from implicit statements. It is not possible to tell when someone knows, thinks about, or comprehends, but we can observe them explaining, developing, and defining.

The approach to developing objectives recommended by Gronlund and Linn (1990) incorporates both implicit statements—what they call general learning outcomes—and explicit statements, what they call specific learning outcomes. Their method probably parallels the thought processes most of us would use to develop separate (explicit) instructional objectives. For example, "Knows where to use commas in writing" is a general outcome because it has an implicit verb in it. Some specific learning outcomes can be developed that indicate the kind of behaviors we are willing to accept as evidence for attainment of the general learning outcome. Here are some examples: separates names of city and state, sets off introductory clauses, separates quotation from rest of sentence, and ends complimentary close of a letter. Of course, it is the specific outcomes that are most useful for evaluation instrument development. For which purposes might general outcomes be particularly useful?

The most prescriptive advice for preparing instructional objectives was offered by Mager (1962) as part of the trend toward individualized programs of instruction in the post-Sputnik era. His three criteria for a good instructional objective are still useful to consider for work in performance domains or in individualized instruction, but only the one that calls for a statement written in behavioral (explicit) terms is widely applicable.

How do propositions relate to instructional objectives? Is it necessary or useful for teachers to have both? The anatomy of an instructional objective consists of a content portion, the underlying proposition, and an operational part, the verb. Consider this sample objective: "The learner should be able to explain how frequent exercise can contribute to body efficiency." The underlying proposition is that exercise *does* enhance efficiency with respect to the respiratory and circulatory systems. The learner should *explain* how this happens rather than merely recognize (1) that it happens, (2) that it affects lung capacity or heart

Figure 3-2.   Verbs that Distinguish Explicit and Implicit Statements of Instructional Objectives

Explicit, Behavioral, Observable	Implicit, Non-Behavioral, Inferential
identify, explain, describe, rearrange, summarize, select, develop, predict, differentiate, define, compare, write	know, consider, understand, enjoy, discuss, realize, remember, judge, perceive, think about, comprehend, imagine

strength, or (3) that aerobics are particularly useful for this purpose. Thus propositions are an essential ingredient in instructional objectives (an expression of the relevant content), but they are not one and the same. Propositions are of content knowledge; instructional objectives are of performance with respect to content. The sample instructional objectives shown in Appendix C are based on some of the propositions listed in Appendix B. Consider how some of the propositions could be translated differently into instructional objectives, depending on how the learner is expected to "operate" on that content.

How instructional objectives should be prepared for a specific situation may be dictated by the teaching model adopted. For example, individualized approaches to instruction (Bloom, 1968; Glaser, 1968; Keller, 1968) require explicit statements of objectives to define and organize the curriculum, to plan instructional activities, to monitor learner progress, and to advance the learner through the curriculum. Domain-referenced or objectives-referenced tests are essential measures of achievement in these teaching models. Regardless of the teaching model, instructional objectives can be useful to test constructors as guides to determining the nature of test content and the differential emphasis of topics within a test. Highly specific statements may even be useful in suggesting particular questions or types of questions to ask.

Taxonomies of Educational Achievements

A number of educators have devoted considerable effort to reducing the ambiguity associated with stating instructional objectives and translating these objectives into relevant test items. In doing so, some have divided learning outcomes into three nonoverlapping domains: cognitive, affective, and psychomotor. The first taxonomy of educational objectives stemming from this work, *The Cognitive Domain: Handbook I* (Bloom and others, 1956), commonly called "Bloom's Taxonomy," provides six categories for classifying cognitive behaviors: *knowledge, comprehension, application, analysis, synthesis,* and *evaluation.* The categories are intended to be hierarchical in terms of the intellectual demand required of the learner. That is, knowledge, the remembering of information, is less demanding than comprehension, the relating of concepts or the translation of ideas from one form to another. Evaluation, the most demanding, requires judgments using criteria remembered or formulated by the learner. Each major category is further subdivided, and test items are presented in the handbook to illustrate how achievement can be measured at each taxonomic level.

The taxonomy for the cognitive domain has received the most attention from test constructors because it has been available the longest and because it describes the kinds of abilities test constructors are most interested in measuring. A major contribution of this taxonomy has been the awareness it has created regarding the intellectual level at which instructional objectives and test items are written. That is, teachers who may have written most of their objectives to require simple remembering or recall of information have come to realize that they actually intended for students to understand and apply knowledge. By using the taxonomy to classify objectives, teachers can reflect more readily on whether their expectations are appropriate.

Though the cognitive taxonomy can be somewhat useful for classifying objectives in terms of the level of behavior required, it is much less useful for classifying test items. Unfortunately, some teachers and test constructors have failed to realize this shortcoming. The problem can be illustrated with the following test item. To which category of the taxonomy does this item relate most directly?

1. **Why is a fusible alloy better than its constituents for use in automatic fire sprinkling systems?**
    a. **The alloy generally has a lower melting point.**
    b. **The alloy generally can withstand greater water pressure.**
    c. **The alloy generally has a higher melting point.**
    d. **Each of the constituents is a better conductor of electricity than the alloy.**

On the surface this item appears to measure achievement beyond the recall level, perhaps comprehension or even application of principles. However, a full assessment cannot be made without knowing what events transpired during instruction. If the fire sprinkler illustration was used as an example in class or in a text, the item is a measure of recall of that information. Only if the item presents a novel situation can it be categorized as an application item in terms of Bloom's cognitive taxonomy. It is very difficult to pinpoint the mental processes involved in answering a particular test question, even when we know what took place during instruction.

It was precisely this difficulty that led Ebel (1965) to create a different categorization system, one to be used with items rather than objectives and one that depends on observable operations rather than inferred mental processes. *Ebel's Relevance Guide*, as it has come to be called, was described earlier in this chapter in terms of these seven categories: terminology, factual information, explanation, calculation, prediction, recommended action, and evaluation.

Classification systems for the affective and psychomotor domains have been developed to deal with outcomes that require more than cognition. *Handbook II: The Affective Domain* (Krathwohl, Bloom, and Masia, 1964) is similar in purpose to *Handbook I*, but relates to interests, values, and attitudes. The five categories are arranged hierarchically in terms of increasing level of involvement by the learner: receiving, responding, valuing, organization, and characterization by a value. Taxonomies for the psychomotor domain have been proposed by several educational psychologists (Harrow, 1972; Kibler and others, 1981). The categories of each system vary but generally relate to gross bodily movements, finely coordinated bodily movements, nonverbal communications, and speech behaviors.

Finally, a classification scheme attributed to Gagné (Gagné and Driscoll, 1988) incorporates all three domains in differentiating learning outcomes. The major categories are shown in Figure 3–3 to contrast them with the systems of both Bloom and Ebel. The table masks the fact that Gagné's intellectual skills category has four subcategories—discriminations, concepts, principles, and problem solving—that each may match up better with one of the other rows of the other two systems. It should be apparent that these three systems should not be expected to have a close association throughout because each was created to serve a different purpose. For that reason, too, some categories are not interchangeable across systems. Is it conceivable that a fourth system, yet to be developed, might

Figure 3-3. Comparison of Classification Systems of Bloom, Ebel, and Gagné

Bloom's Taxonomy	Ebel's Relevance Guide	Gagné's Learning Outcomes
A. Knowledge	Terminology Factual Information	Verbal Information
B. Comprehension	Explanation	Intellectual Skills Cognitive Strategies
C. Application	Calculation Prediction	
D. Analysis		
E. Synthesis		
F. Evaluation	Recommended Action Evaluation	
G.		Attitudes
H.		Motor Skills

use some categories from each of these systems to achieve some special purpose? (Choose one of the classification systems and use it to classify the sample objectives provided in Appendix C. Compare your results with those of another member of your class to see how well you agreed.)

Interest in promoting critical or higher-order thinking skills (HOTS) has lead several educators to try to develop a taxonomy of thinking skills. But there has been little agreement about what categories should be included or even whether such a classification system would be helpful. The kind of mental activity that most of us would consider higher thinking can be described by rows B through F of Figure 3-3. These are "beyond the knowledge or recall level," which itself is a useful way to describe HOTS. As we have noted earlier, thinking can occur only when there is something to think about—new information or an existing knowledge structure. Even learning how to think requires "how to" knowledge. Consequently, an independent thinking curriculum seems to be illogical and unnecessary as long as "the use of verbal knowledge" is a prominent strand in each aspect of the school curriculum.

SUMMARY PROPOSITIONS

1. A major goal of education is to develop in the students a command of substantive knowledge.
2. Knowledge is information that has been integrated into a structure of relations between ideas.
3. A structure of verbal knowledge can be described by listing the concepts and relationships of which it is composed.
4. All verbal knowledge can be expressed in propositions.
5. Propositions provide the basis for most good objective achievement-test items.
6. Thinking necessarily produces knowledge, but knowledge must be present for a person to have something to think about.

7. The prerequisites for performing a cognitive task are the desire to do it and the knowledge of how to do it.
8. Understanding is a strictly internal process that involves the meaningful attachment of new ideas to an already existent structure of knowledge.
9. Nearly all questions that ask *Who? What? When?* or *Where?* are properly classified as factual information questions.
10. Items intended to test various aspects of achievement ordinarily can be classified more reliably on the basis of overt item characteristics than on the basis of the mental processes they presumably measure.
11. The major source of the instructional objectives that describe student outcomes is a series of statements of objectives derived from a set of educational goals.
12. Explicit statements of learning outcomes are more useful for most purposes than implicit statements.
13. The taxonomies of educational objectives are more useful to teachers for instructional planning than for evaluation planning or test development.
14. The categories of Ebel's Relevance Guide describe the various observable behaviors a test taker must demonstrate to respond successfully to achievement-test items.
15. The categories of Bloom's Taxonomy (cognitive domain) are intended to describe the nature of the intellectual demand required by each of several instructional objectives.

QUESTIONS FOR STUDY AND DISCUSSION

1. What does it mean to have command of knowledge?
2. What advantages does a person have who can understand rather than simply know something?
3. Why are true propositions of greater interest than false propositions to those who teach and measure?
4. Why is it not possible to represent important educational outcomes from the affective or psychomotor domains in the form of propositions?
5. What are some of the criteria high school learners probably use to decide that their understanding of a particular idea (for example, use of metaphor) is as deep as they care for it to be?
6. What do we mean when we say students should "comprehend what they read"?
7. What features distinguish educational goals from instructional objectives?
8. What advantages does Bloom's Taxonomy have over a two-category system with the labels Lower-order Skills and Higher-order Skills?
9. What factors often cause separate judges to disagree so frequently and so substantially in their classifications of instructional objectives using Bloom's Taxonomy?
10. If your task was to develop a new taxonomy for categorizing cognitive learning outcomes so that your system would generate high agreement among judges, what features would you build into your system to accomplish this task?

4

Describing and Summarizing Measurement Results

There is a variety of statistical concepts and techniques that enable test users to interpret scores and that assist test developers in assessing the quality of their instruments. In particular, many of the methods of making norm-referenced score interpretations depend on the mean and standard deviation of the scores of the norm group. And when a test has been given, statistical procedures help to summarize and describe the performance of the class. These same statistical methods provide information about the effectiveness of the test instrument in providing norm-referenced or criterion-referenced interpretations—whichever the test developer had in mind. The purpose of this chapter is not to duplicate the content of a good statistics text, but to describe statistical ideas that form a foundation for the measurement concepts to be considered in subsequent chapters.

FREQUENCY DISTRIBUTIONS

A *frequency distribution* is a two-column list that describes a set of scores in a concise and systematic manner. One column lists all possible scores in the set from highest to lowest, and the other column, the frequency column, shows the number of examinees that obtained each score. Table 4–1 shows the scores of a class of 30 students on a spelling test of 25 words. A frequency distribution for these scores is shown in Table 4–2. This distribution of scores is a useful visual aid for identifying the relative position in the group of any one student and for obtaining a picture of overall group performance at a glance.

Table 4-1. Scores of 30 Students on a 25-Item Spelling Test

Aaron	16	Franco	20	Kim	20
Barbara	19	Gary	17	Lori	17
Barry	20	Gaea	18	Marcia	23
Ben	17	Helen	21	Marcy	23
Brent	21	Jack	14	Nathen	19
Camille	24	Jeff	19	Patrice	22
Donald	15	Jerry	22	Richard	21
Doreen	18	Joanne	18	Scott	19
Earl	20	Kelly	21	Travis	21
Faith	16	Ken	20	Wendy	15

Frequency Polygons and Histograms

The information summarized by a frequency distribution also can be represented pictorially by a frequency polygon or a histogram. The frequency polygon is also known as a line graph. Figure 4–1 is an example of a frequency polygon using the scores of the 30 examinees obtained on the 25-item spelling test. The score scale is depicted along the horizontal line and the frequency scale is shown on the vertical line. An alternative representation is the histogram or bar graph, shown in Figure 4–2.

Frequency polygons and histograms are equally useful for describing a set of test scores efficiently. Detailed procedures for constructing both types of graphs can be found in most introductory statistics textbooks.

Characteristics of Frequency Polygons

Frequency polygons come in all shapes and sizes, as evidenced by the variety shown in Figure 4–3. These curves are frequency polygons like the one in Figure 4–1, except these have been smoothed. That is, the jagged lines have

Table 4-2. Frequency Distribution of 30 Spelling Scores

Score	Frequency
25	0
24	1
23	2
22	2
21	5
20	5
19	4
18	3
17	3
16	2
15	2
14	1
13	0

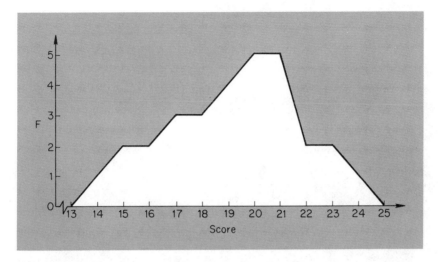

Figure 4-1. Sample Frequency Polygon

been replaced by a smooth curved line, and the vertical line used to determine frequencies has been omitted. Such modifications usually indicate that the polygon does not represent any one set of data precisely, but it depicts a general distribution having certain prominent characteristics.

Often there is considerable economy associated with describing or sketching the frequency polygon for a set of test scores rather than enumerating each score or even preparing a frequency distribution. But to communicate such a general picture, the characteristics that help distinguish frequency polygons from

Figure 4-2. Sample Histogram

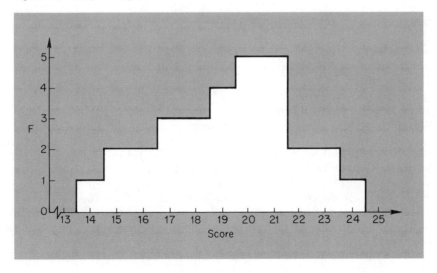

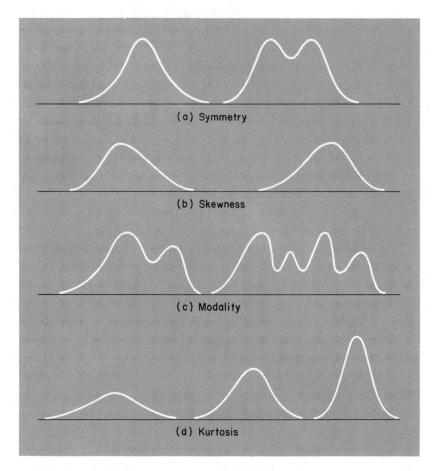

Figure 4-3. Frequency Polygons Illustrating Varying Characteristics

one another must be known and understood. Four of these important characteristics are illustrated in Figure 4–3, and others will be noted in subsequent sections of this chapter.

A *symmetric* curve is one that has two halves, each a mirror image of the other. It is possible to draw a straight vertical line through each of the top two polygons in Figure 4–3 so that, if we were to fold either figure on that line, the two halves would appear as one. Nonsymmetric or asymmetric curves are those that do not have this property. Such curves are said to be *skewed*. In part (b) of Figure 4–3, each skewed curve has a large "hump" and a long tail extending in one direction. The curve on the right is negatively skewed and the one on the left is positively skewed. Note that the direction in which the tail extends on the score scale indicates whether the curve is skewed positively (to the right where positive numbers are found) or negatively (to the left where negative numbers might be found). Can you draw a line of symmetry for the figures in part (b)?

Since polygons can differ in the number of humps or peaks they contain, modality is another distinguishing characteristic. The *mode* of a score distribution is the most frequently occurring score.[1] A curve is *uni*modal if it has *one* mode, *bi*modal if it has *two* modes, and *multi*modal if it has *many* modes. When a frequency polygon has more than one peak, we must look to the tallest to describe its modality. Part (c) of Figure 4–3 shows a unimodal curve and a bimodal curve. Note that the curve with four peaks has two that are taller than the others and those two are equally tall. How should the modality of the polygon in Figure 4–1 be described?

The last row of Figure 4–3 illustrates the *kurtosis* property of frequency polygons. Kurtosis relates to the relative flatness or peakedness of the curve. The names describing these curves (platykurtic, mesokurtic, and leptokurtic) can be remembered by associating the prefix of the term (platy, meso, lepto) with a visual image of the shape of the curve.

To test your understanding of the properties of frequency polygons and their interrelationships, try to draw a figure to verify that each of the following statements is true:

1. Not all skewed distributions are unimodal.
2. Some leptokurtic distributions are not symmetric.
3. A rectangular distribution is multimodal.
4. Not all bimodal distributions are symmetric.
5. A single distribution can be symmetric, unimodal, and mesokurtic.
6. Some platykurtic distributions are skewed.

DESCRIBING SCORE DISTRIBUTIONS

Two particularly important characteristics of a distribution of scores are (1) the typical or average score and (2) the amount of dispersion or variability of the scores. The statistics used to report the typical score—measures of central tendency—are the mode, median, and mean. To report dispersion, we are likely to use the range or the standard deviation as a measure of variability.[2]

Central Tendency

The *mode* was defined previously in considering modality as a property of a frequency polygon. It is the most frequently occurring score, and it may have more than one value (as in Figure 4–1). The *median* is the score above which and below which exactly half of the scores are found: the middlemost score. For the scores 5, 4, 3, 2, 1, the median is 3; for the scores 8, 7, 5, 2, the median is 6, halfway between 7 and 5. In simple cases like these, if the distribution contains an even number of scores, the median is the average of the two middle scores.

[1]Some statistics textbooks refer to all identifiable peaks of a curve as modes, and some distinguish major and minor modes based on differences in height. For simplicity, we will retain the meaning "most frequently occurring score" throughout this book.

[2]Another measure of dispersion, the semi-interquartile range, is used so infrequently to describe test scores that we have chosen not to discuss it here. Most introductory statistics textbooks describe its computation and use.

Thus the mode must be a score actually obtained by an examinee, but the median need not be. When the score distribution is large and there are several people with tied scores in the vicinity of the median, the computational procedures are slightly more complicated. Table 4–3 shows four examples of computing the median. Can you infer from these examples what the general procedure is? Because the median also is the 50th percentile, the procedures described later in this chapter for computing percentiles should be used for finding the median.

The *mean* is the average score, obtained by summing all the scores and dividing that sum by the total number of scores. For the scores 5, 4, 3, 2, 1, the sum is 15 and the mean is 3. These operations are represented by the formula

$$\overline{X} = \frac{\Sigma X}{n} = \frac{15}{5} = 3 \tag{4.1}$$

where $\overline{X}$ is the mean, ΣX is the sum of the scores, and n is the number of test scores.

Ordinarily, the median is easier to calculate than the mean, especially when the number of scores is small. If the score distribution is skewed, the median usually gives a more reasonable indication of the typical score than does the mean. Consider, for example, the set of scores 9, 9, 10, 11, 22. What are the values of the median and mean? Notice that the median (10) is more indicative of the "typical" score and that the magnitude of the mean (12) is influenced in the direction of the extreme score. Note also that four of the five scores are below the mean, but only two are below the median. If the 22 was changed to a score of 42, how would the median and mean each be affected?

For a variety of reasons, the mean generally is regarded by statisticians as a more precise and useful measure of central tendency than the median. However, we will find the median very useful for certain test-evaluation and test-score interpretation purposes.

So why are there three different ways to indicate central tendency? Why not just use the mean and forget the rest? The mode is easy to determine but not always unique. There may be two or more modes in a score distribution. The median generally is easier to determine than the mean, and in a very skewed distribution, the median is more like the typical score. Different situations suggest a need for one measure rather than the other, but in many cases it matters little which is used. For what kind of score distribution are the mean and median the same value? Is there any circumstance in which all three measures are equal?

Variability

The *range* of a distribution is a number that indicates how many score points the distribution covers. For the scores 8, 7, 3, 2, 1, the range is 8. Note that

Table 4-3. Examples of Computing the Median

A. 1,2,8,8,9,10	C. 1,2,6,6,6,10
$Md = 7.5 + \frac{1}{2} = 8.0$	$Md = 5.5 + \frac{1}{3} = 5.8$
B. 1,4,6,9,9,10	D. 1,2,2,2,3,10
$Md = 7.5 + 0 = 7.5$	$Md = 1.5 + \frac{2}{3} = 2.2$

this is *one more than the difference between the highest and lowest scores.* The range is a relatively gross indicator of the amount of dispersion in a set of scores because its value depends only on two scores, the most extreme scores in the entire distribution of scores. The set of scores 10, 9, 9, 9, 3 has a range of 8 also, but notice how different these two sets are in variability.

The most common and useful measure of variability is the *standard deviation.* A conceptual understanding of the standard deviation can be gained by learning how this statistic is computed. Calculating the standard deviation involves four steps.

1. Compute each person's *deviation score* by subtracting the mean from each person's test score.
2. Square each deviation score (multiply each deviation score by itself) and sum all of the squared deviation scores.
3. Divide this sum by the number of test scores.[3] This yields a quantity called the *variance.*
4. Find the square root of the variance. This value is the standard deviation. (Remember to verify that your answer makes sense, that it is not larger or smaller than it should be, logically.)

These steps can be represented by this formula for finding the standard deviation:

$$s = \sqrt{\frac{\Sigma(X - \overline{X})^2}{n}} \tag{4.2}$$

where s is the standard deviation, Σ is the symbol meaning "the sum of," and X is an individual's test score.

The calculation of the standard deviation is illustrated in Table 4–4 using the scores 5, 4, 3, 2, and 1. The scores are listed in column 1 and their sum is used to determine the mean. The deviation scores are calculated and listed in

Table 4-4. Calculating Standard Deviation

	(1) X	(2) $X - \overline{X}$	(3) $(X - \overline{X})^2$
	5	2	4
	4	1	1
	3	0	0
	2	−1	1
	1	−2	4
Sum	15	0	10

$$s = \sqrt{\frac{10}{5}} = \sqrt{2} = 1.41$$

[3]Statistically, this division yields a "biased" estimate of the variance. An unbiased estimate would be obtained by dividing by $(n - 1)$, one less than the total number of scores. Since most electronic calculators that are programmed to yield the variance or standard deviation use $n - 1$ as the divisor, the value they yield should be slightly larger than that obtained with equation 4.2. Check a statistics book to learn more about this distinction.

column 2. The squared deviation scores are shown in column 3 along with their sum. The sum, 10, divided by the number of scores, 5, yields the variance. The standard deviation, 1.41, is the square root of the variance. Is 1.41 a reasonable value for the standard deviation of these 5 scores? What does it mean?

Conceptually, the standard deviation is a number that indicates, on the average, how far the scores in a distribution are from their mean. If the scores are all very close together near the mean, the standard deviation should be a relatively small number. However, if the scores are spread out over a large range, the standard deviation should be a relatively large number. In Table 4–4, some scores differ from the mean by two points and some by one point, and one does not differ at all from the mean. Our answer, 1.41, seems reasonable as an average amount by which these scores differ from their mean.

The conceptual definition given above is not the *statistical* definition exactly. Why it is necessary to go through all the squaring and "unsquaring" business? The answer to this question requires more statistics than we should concern ourselves with here. But notice that to calculate the *average deviation score* (using the values in column 2), we would obtain zero, no matter what set of scores is used. The sum of the deviations from the mean is *always* zero. (This is how the mean is defined statistically.) The squaring and square root operations overcome this difficulty to yield a unique value for the standard deviation.[4]

Standard deviations are used in defining test standard scores, such as TOEFL, SAT, or ACT scores, in determining comparable or equivalent scores on two tests, in expressing the accuracy of a test score, and in controlling the weights of quizzes, project scores, and test scores in determining course grades. Variances, which so far have been used only to calculate standard deviations, will help in understanding some aspects of test reliability. Knowing a little about variances and standard deviations is a prerequisite to understanding important concepts about test scores, test characteristics, and other kinds of measures.

Normality

A frequency polygon that is symmetric, unimodal, and mesokurtic is, in plain talk, bell shaped. It is also called a *normal distribution*. The normal curve is a sort of standard that is used frequently as a reference point for describing a set of test scores. For example, we might make statements like: "It's nearly normal." or "It's a bit flatter than the normal curve." or "It's like a normal curve with fat tails." Some of the essential characteristics of the normal distribution are illustrated in Figure 4–4. In addition to it being unimodal, symmetric, and mesokurtic, all three of its measures of central tendency have the same value. The horizontal scale along the base is marked in standard deviation units with pluses and minuses corresponding to points above and below the mean, respectively.

The percentages shown in each area under the normal curve indicate how much of the total area under the curve lies within that area. In terms of the test scores in the distribution, the percentages indicate what portion of all the

---

[4]A formula that is equivalent to equation 4.2 and that is simpler computationally is

$$s = \sqrt{\frac{n \, \Sigma \, X^2 - (\Sigma \, X)^2}{n^2}}$$

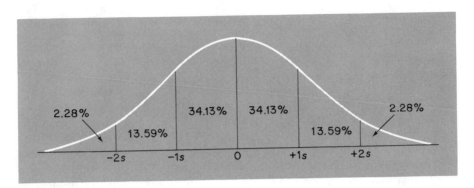

Figure 4–4. The Normal Distribution

scores are between the values shown on the base line. For example, about 34 percent of all scores are between the mean score and the score that is one standard deviation above the mean. It is useful to remember that (1) about 68 percent of the scores are between −1s and +1s, (2) about 95 percent of the scores are between −2s and +2s, and (3) about 2.5 percent of the scores are in each tail beyond ±2s. These rounded percentage values are accurate enough for our purposes; more exact decimal values can be found in tables in an introductory statistics book.

The normal distribution is a theoretical curve that is assumed to include an unlimited (infinite) number of scores or observations. Therefore, it extends without limit on either side of the mean well beyond ±3s. In practice and for convenience, it is often considered to extend from about three standard deviations below to three standard deviations above the mean. (Actually, 99.72 percent of all scores comprising the distribution are within those limits.) But the distribution of scores from a class of, say, 30 students typically will not show a range of scores encompassing six standard deviation units. The figures shown below indicate the ratio of score range to standard deviation that can be expected for groups of the size shown here (Hoel, 1947).

Sample Size	Typical Range in Standard Deviation Units
10	3.0
50	4.5
100	5.0
1000	6.5

The typical values shown are averages. For example, we should expect a set of 10 scores that form a shape like a normal distribution to range from about −1.5s to about +1.5s. There are too few scores in the distribution to *expect* that any one of them would be as far as 3 standard deviations above the mean, for example. It might be a useful computational check to realize that in a distribution of 25 test scores the highest score is more apt to be 2 than 3 standard deviations above the mean.

SCORE SCALES DESCRIBE PERFORMANCE

Since the scores on different tests, when taken by the same group, can have widely different means, standard deviations, and distributions, it is necessary to have some kind of standard scale to which all scores can be referred for comparison purposes. Percentile ranks and standard scores are both examples of such scales. We will discuss both kinds in some detail because they are so useful for interpreting scores from both teacher-made and standardized achievement tests.

Percentiles and Percentile Ranks

The percentile rank of a particular test score can be defined in three similar but significantly different ways. It is the percentage of scores in a distribution of scores that:

1. is below the given score, or
2. is the same as or below the given score, or
3. is below the midpoint of the score interval of the given score.

Table 4–5 shows the effects of using each of these different definitions to compute the percentile ranks of 5 hypothetical scores. The highest score gets a percentile rank of only 80 under definition 1. The lowest score gets a percentile rank of 20 under definition 2. The median score gets a percentile rank of 40 under definition 1 and of 60 under definition 2. But under definition 3 the median score gets a percentile rank of 50, as it should in a symmetric distribution of scores. In addition, the highest and lowest scores are both the same distance from the extremes of the percentile rank scale, as they also should be. For these reasons, definition 3 is preferred and we will use it here.

There are seven steps in the process of computing the percentile rank of a given score in a particular distribution using definition 3.

Table 4–5. Effect of Different Definitions of Percentile Ranks

Score	PERCENTILE RANK UNDER DEFINITION		
	1	2	3
5	80	100	90
4	60	80	70
3	40	60	50
2	20	40	30
1	0	20	10

1. Prepare a frequency distribution.
2. Beginning with the lowest score, add successive frequency values to obtain a column of cumulative frequencies.
3. For the given score, identify the cumulative frequency up to, but not including, the score.
4. For the same given score, divide its frequency by 2.
5. Add the values from steps 3 and 4.
6. Divide the sum from step 5 by the total number of scores.
7. Multiply the result by 100 to obtain a percentile rank (rounded to the nearest whole number).

Table 4–6 illustrates the computation of percentile ranks for the spelling scores from Table 4–1. Notice that the score scale extends from one score below the lowest score obtained to the highest score obtained. And the scale always includes all possible scores between the extremes, even when no student may have actually obtained some of those scores. The number of students who received each of the scores is shown in the second column of the table.

The third column gives a cumulative frequency for each score. It is calculated by counting the number of scores lower than the given score and adding the frequency at that score point. Consider the score 19, for example. There are 11 scores lower than 19 and four scores of 19. So we get a cumulative frequency of 15.

To obtain the percentile rank for a score of 19, the value in the fourth column, we proceed as follows. Take the cumulative frequency of scores *below* 19 (which is 11) and add to it half of the frequencies at a score of 19 (one-half of 4 is 2). The sum, 13, is divided by 30 (the number of scores) to yield 0.433. That quotient is multiplied by 100 (43.3) and then rounded to obtain 43. In summary, we take half the scores *at* the given score value plus all the scores *below*, we divide that sum by the total number of scores, and we change the result to a rounded percentage value. Can you verify that Andy's score of 21 has a percentile rank of 75?

Table 4-6. Computation of Percentile Ranks

Score	Frequency	Cumulative Frequency	Percentile Rank
24	1	30	98
23	2	29	93
22	2	27	87
21	5	25	75
20	5	20	58
19	4	15	43
18	3	11	32
17	3	8	22
16	2	5	13
15	2	3	7
14	1	1	2
13	0	0	—

Although *percentile* and *percentile rank* are used interchangeably by some, they really mean quite different things. We say that the percentile rank of 22 is 87, but the 87th percentile is 22. A percentile rank must be a number between 0 and 100, but a percentile is a score value in the distribution of scores, in this case between 14 and 24.

Suppose we want to find the 20th percentile, that is, the raw score below which 20 percent of the 30 scores are located. Follow these steps:

1. Determine how many scores should be below the percentile score in question: 20 percent × 30 = 6.

2. Find the *score interval* in which the sixth score from the bottom is located. (For this purpose, think of 17 as the midpoint of the score interval, 16.5 to 17.5.) The sixth score is in the interval 16.5 to 17.5.

3. Decide how many of the scores in that interval are needed. Since there are 5 scores *below* the interval and we need 6 altogether, we need 1 of the 3 scores from the interval.

4. The 20th percentile is found by adding the value of the lower limit of the score interval (16.5) to the fraction that represents the proportion of scores needed from the interval (one-third). Thus, 20 percent of all scores are below a raw score of 16.8.

Verify that the median, the 50th percentile, is 19.5. The median will have 15 of the 30 scores below it and above it. The fifteenth score from the bottom is in the interval 18.5 to 19.5. Since we need all 4 of the scores in that interval, the 50th percentile is 18.5 + 4/4 or 19.5. Is the 80th percentile 21.3?

Test scores expressed as percentile ranks are sometimes confused with test scores expressed as percent correct. They are, of course, quite different. A *percent correct score* is determined by an examinee's performance relative to the content of the test. It expresses the relation between the number of points awarded to a specific examinee's paper and the maximum possible number of points for any paper. Usually, the expectation is that few examinees in a group will receive percent correct scores less than some value near 70 percent, which is often set arbitrarily as the passing score. If the group as a whole does well on an examination, the percent correct scores will run higher than if the group as a whole does poorly.

A percentile rank, on the other hand, is determined solely by the relation between a specific examinee's score and the scores of other examinees in the group tested. Percentile ranks must necessarily range from near 0 to near 100, regardless of whether the group as a whole does well or poorly on the examination.

Percentile ranks differ from the original or raw test scores, and many other types of scores derived from them, in another respect. They are rectangularly distributed. Raw-score distributions, and those of many other types of scores, generally approximate a normal distribution in which the scores are concentrated near the middle, with decreasing score frequencies as one moves out to the high and low extremes. In a rectangular distribution the score frequencies are uniform all along the scale. The relation between a normal distribution and a rectangular distribution is illustrated in Figure 4–5.

Normal
Distribution

Rectangular
Distribution

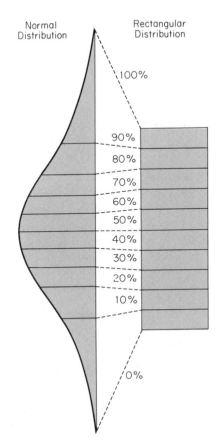

Figure 4-5. Relation Between Normal and Rectangular Distributions

It is clear from this figure that percentile ranks magnify raw-score differences near the middle of the distribution but reduce raw-score differences toward the extremes. Stated in other words, a difference of 10 percentile rank units near the extremes corresponds to a much larger raw-score difference than does the same difference in percentile ranks near the mean. For example, for a set of 100 scores that form a normal distribution, the number of scores between the 50th percentile and the 55th percentile is *the same as* the number of scores between the 90th and 95th percentiles. But the raw-score difference between the 50th and 55th percentiles is smaller than the raw-score difference between the 90th and 95th percentiles. The score differences in standard deviation units are 0.13 and 0.37, respectively. (This can be verified using a normal distribution table, found in most statistics books.) In view of this property, does it make sense that percentile ranks should not be averaged?

Standard Scores

Like percentile ranks, standard scores provide a standard scale, a common yardstick, by which scores on different tests by different groups may be compared reasonably. And like percentile ranks, standard scores inherently yield norm-referenced score interpretations. Standard scores typically are used to interpret the results from standardized tests. They are considered in this chapter because they can be related well to both the normal curve and to percentile ranks and because they are useful in the procedures for determining grades.

Linear standard scores. Raw scores are transformed into standard scores using the raw-score mean and standard deviation. The effect of this transformation is to create a new score scale that has a predetermined mean and standard deviation. One basic type of standard score, the *z-score,* is found using this formula:

$$z = \frac{X - \overline{X}}{s} \tag{4.3}$$

where X is the student's raw score, $\overline{X}$ is the mean of the raw scores, and s is the standard deviation of the raw scores. Notice that the numerator in this formula is the student's deviation score. The z-score indicates how many standard deviations from the mean (plus or minus) the student has scored. A student who scores at the mean has a z-score of 0. If the student has a raw score that is exactly one standard deviation *above* the mean, the z-score is $+1.0$. A z-score of -1.5 indicates the student scored one and one-half standard deviations *below* the mean. The z-score is seldom used itself to make score interpretations, but it is needed in further computation to yield some commonly used standard scores.

The *T*-score, for example, is computed using this formula:

$$T = 10(z) + 50 \tag{4.4}$$

And standard scores on the College Board's achievement tests or Scholastic Aptitude Test (SAT) were established with this formula:

$$\text{CEEB score} = 100(z) + 500 \tag{4.5}$$

The original standard scores used to report the results from the Iowa Tests of Educational Development (ITED) come from this formula:

$$\text{ITED score} = 5(z) + 15 \tag{4.6}$$

Finally, stanines are computed with the formula

$$\text{Stanine} = 2(z) + 5 \tag{4.7}$$

Stanine values are rounded to the nearest whole number.

Table 4–7 shows the characteristics of these linear standard scores and the relationships between them and percentile ranks in a normal distribution. To say that the transformation from raw scores to standard scores is *linear* means that if the corresponding pairs of scores, raw score and standard score, are plotted on a graph they would form a single straight line. This also means that the shape of the frequency polygon of the standard scores is the same as the shape

Table 4–7. Characteristics of Standard Scores in a Normal Distribution

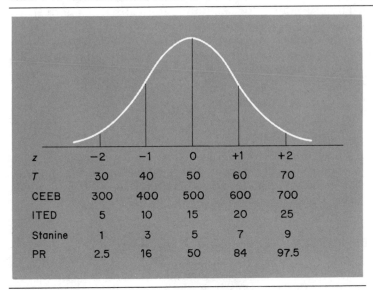

z	−2	−1	0	+1	+2
T	30	40	50	60	70
CEEB	300	400	500	600	700
ITED	5	10	15	20	25
Stanine	1	3	5	7	9
PR	2.5	16	50	84	97.5

of the raw-score frequency polygon from which the standard scores were derived. For example, the T-score distribution will be negatively skewed if the raw-score distribution was, the z-score distribution will be leptokurtic if the raw-score distribution was, and a bimodal, symmetric raw-score distribution will yield a standard-score distribution with those same properties.

Notice that the mean and standard deviation of each standard-score scale as shown in Table 4–7 is readily apparent in the corresponding formula for computing each. To create a new standard-score scale, we simply multiply the z-score by the standard deviation desired for the new scale and then add the value of the mean desired for the new scale. For example, if we wanted a J-score scale that would have a mean of 40 and a standard deviation of 12, the formula needed would be

$$J = 12(z) + 40 \qquad (4.8)$$

If a teacher adds 3 points to every student's raw score, have the raw scores been changed to a linear *standard score*? If so, how would you describe the new set of scores?

Normal curve equivalents (NCEs). If we wish to assume that the trait being measured by a test is normally distributed, it is possible to transform the obtained raw scores in a nonlinear fashion so that the new distribution will be normal. Obviously, it is not desirable to perform such a transformation on a distribution of scores that does not resemble the shape of a normal distribution. The main reason for normalizing a set of scores is to permit norm-referenced interpretations that take advantage of the properties of the normal curve. Stanines and other standard scores reported by publishers of standardized tests typically are normalized. The procedures for computing normalized standard scores are described in most introductory statistics textbooks.

The *normal curve equivalent* (NCE), a type of normalized standard score, has been made popular primarily because of its use in reporting evaluation results from Title I programs of the Elementary and Secondary Education Act (ESEA), also known as "Chapter I." NCEs are computed with this equation:

$$NCE = 21.06(z) + 50 \tag{4.9}$$

where the z is a normalized z. The computed NCE value is rounded to the nearest whole number and only values from 1 to 99 are used. As can be seen from Table 4–7, NCEs resemble T-scores in that both have means of 50, but the possible range of NCEs is the same as that for percentile ranks. What advantages might NCEs have over percentile ranks?

CORRELATION COEFFICIENTS

Correlation coefficients are statistics that show the extent to which scores from one measure are related to scores from the same individuals on a second measure. For example, there is a need for an index of the relation between sets of test scores when estimating some kinds of test reliability. If a single test is given to the same group on different occasions, or if two equivalent test forms are given to the same group, we use a correlation coefficient to estimate the degree of agreement between the pairs of scores on the two measures for each person. We also use correlation coefficients to help make predictions about future performance. How do the employment test scores of park rangers relate to the quality of job performance after a year of work? How do the TOEFL (Test of English as a Foreign Language) scores of Indonesian students relate to their success in graduate school at the University of Iowa?

Scatterplots Describe Relationships

A *scatterplot* or scatter diagram is a visual representation of the relationship between the scores from two measures for a single group of individuals. It is based on the same graphing methods used in algebra and geometry to plot straight lines, circles, and other figures. Each dot or point that is plotted is a pair of scores (X, Y) for a person on test X and test Y.

A correlation coefficient is a number that may range from $+1.00$, through zero, to -1.00 and that indicates two things. The sign (plus or minus) shows the direction of the relationship, and the magnitude of the number indicates the extent of the relationship. Perfect correlations, $+1.00$ or -1.00, rarely exist in practice, but both represent the *highest* possible correlation between two variables. A correlation of 0.00 means there is no relationship between the two variables.

A graphical representation of the pairs of scores from which a correlation coefficient can be computed is useful for two reasons. First, we can tell from a graph if the points tend to cluster about a single straight line. If they do *not,* a more complex method of computation is required. Second, we can estimate both the direction and magnitude of the relationship from visual inspection of the graph. The graph provides a means of checking the accuracy of calculations when the correlation coefficient has been computed.

Four scatterplots are shown in Figure 4–6 to illustrate the correlation of two sets of scores graphically. Each point in a graph represents a pair of scores, *X* and *Y,* for each person. In diagram *a,* the lower scores on test *X* are associated with low, moderate, and high scores on test *Y.* And the higher scores on test *X* also are associated with low, moderate, and high scores on test *Y.* Therefore, we can conclude there is little or no relationship between the two sets of scores. A similar analysis can be made of each of the other three diagrams to verify the value of the correlation coefficient estimates given. Another approach to inter-

Figure 4–6.   Sample Scatterplots Showing Varying Relationships Between Two Sets of Scores

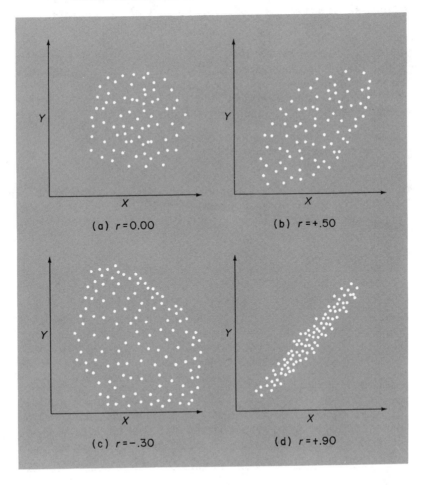

(a) $r = 0.00$

(b) $r = +.50$

(c) $r = -.30$

(d) $r = +.90$

preting the scatterplot is to ask how accurately we could predict someone's test Y score when we know their score on test X. The data in diagram d permit the most accurate prediction of test Y scores, while the data in diagram a suggest that our prediction would be a mere guess. Finally, we might observe the rank orders of individuals' scores on X and compare with those on Y. If the rankings are similar on both, the correlation is high and positive, but if the rankings are more nearly opposite on the two, the correlation is high and negative.

Computing Correlation Coefficients

There is a wide variety of correlation coefficients, each appropriate for certain conditions and each computed in a somewhat different manner. The most common type, the Pearson product-moment correlation, will be illustrated here. Suppose we have used an elaborate and time-consuming interview process to assess the communicative competence in Spanish of ten foreign service job applicants. Furthermore, we have given the applicants a 60-item multiple-choice test to measure the same type of competence. Is the relationship between the interview ratings and test scores high enough that we might be willing to drop the more expensive method and use only the more efficient one for future selection decisions? In other words, are these methods interchangeable in terms of how they rank order individuals? The results of the two measurements are shown in Table 4–8. Try to envision what the scatterplot would look like for these pairs of scores and then sketch it. What is your estimate of the correlation coefficient? The correlation is computed using the formula

$$r_{XY} = \frac{n \, \Sigma \, XY - (\Sigma \, X)(\Sigma \, Y)}{\sqrt{[n \, \Sigma \, X^2 - (\Sigma \, X)^2][n \, \Sigma \, Y^2 - (\Sigma \, Y)^2]}} \tag{4.10}$$

where n is the number of pairs of scores (or persons), Σ is the symbol meaning "the sum of," X is the score of a person on one measure, and Y is the score of the same person on a second measure. The various sums required to compute

Table 4–8. Measurements Used to Compute Correlation

Examinee	Interview Score (X)	Test Score (Y)	X²	Y²	XY
Daniel	10	57	100	3249	570
Liz	6	50	36	2500	300
Ben	3	33	9	1089	99
Carmen	5	44	25	1936	220
Ellen	8	53	64	2809	424
Rosa	2	25	4	625	50
Michael	4	33	16	1089	132
Robert	5	48	25	2304	240
Rhonda	10	59	100	3481	590
Albert	3	35	9	1225	105
Sum	56	437	388	20,307	2730

the correlation coefficient are shown at the bottom of each column in Table 4–8. We can substitute these values in equation 4.10 to complete the computation.

$$r_{XY} = \frac{10(2730) - (56)(437)}{\sqrt{[10(388) - (56)^2][10(20,307) - (437)^2]}}$$

$$r_{XY} = \frac{2828}{\sqrt{(744)(12,101)}} = \frac{2828}{3001} = 0.94$$

How does your estimate using the scatterplot compare with the computed result? What does the 0.94 mean?

The example used here is fairly simple, intended only to show what a correlation coefficient is and how it is calculated. Most situations in which a correlation coefficient is desired involve at least 30 pairs of scores and larger numbers or decimal values. Electronic calculators and computers both can provide greater efficiency and accuracy than the hand-computation process illustrated above. Finally, the raw-score formula (equation 4.10) can be modified to produce equivalent results when either deviation scores or z-scores are readily available.

$$r_{XY} = \frac{\Sigma(X - \overline{X})(Y - \overline{Y})}{n s_X s_Y} \qquad (4.11)$$

$$r_{XY} = \frac{\Sigma z_X z_Y}{n} \qquad (4.12)$$

Note that subscripts are used with s and z to distinguish between scores from the two measures (X and Y) for which the correlation is to be estimated.

Interpreting Correlation Coefficients

There are no absolute interpretations attached to correlations except for values that are very close to $+1.00$, 0.00, or -1.00. For example, the $+0.94$ correlation obtained above between interview ratings and test scores is probably close enough to $+1.00$ to warrant labeling this as a "near perfect" relationship or "extremely high." In most interpretive situations, however, it is helpful to relate the coefficient to those obtained in other more or less similar situations. Scores on equivalent forms of well-constructed achievement tests, for example, tend to yield correlations of about 0.70 to 0.85. Values of 0.90 to 0.95 would be considered particularly high for that situation, and values less than 0.65 might be considered somewhat low. On the other hand, ACT scores correlate about 0.50 with grade-point average at the end of the freshman year at most universities. Values of 0.60 would be considered somewhat high and values of 0.35 would be regarded as fairly low.

Coefficients of correlation are widely used to study test scores, build theories, and make predictions. If calculated accurately, they provide precise estimates of the degree of relationship among the data on which they are based. Two cautions are in order, however. First, the relationship expressed by a correlation coefficient is seldom a causal one. Other factors, each related to X and Y, probably explain why X and Y are related so highly. For example, if the grades of biology students correlate -0.60 with the number of hours of television watched in a typical week, this does not mean that frequent television watching directly causes low grades. But both variables may relate to number of hours spent on homework in the typical week, a variable that may explain why the correlation is moderately high and negative. (Grades would not necessarily go up if all television sets were turned off on week nights.) Second, when a coefficient obtained from one sample of individuals is used to estimate the correlation for either another sample from the same population or the entire population, the size of the sample should be noted. In general, small samples yield widely varying estimates of the correlation that would be obtained from other samples or from the entire population.

There is much more to know about the interpretation of correlation coefficients that we will not consider here. There is also much more to know about the computation of correlation coefficients—other methods of computing for varying circumstances and assumptions that must be made so that the results will be interpretable. Most introductory statistics books provide greater breadth and depth than we have tried to describe here.

SUMMARY PROPOSITIONS

1. To do an adequate job of interpreting a set of test scores, it is necessary to understand and use a variety of statistical tools: frequency distributions, percentile ranks, standard scores, and measures of central tendency, variability, and correlation.

2. A frequency distribution of scores is an ordered listing of score values that shows how many individuals obtained each of the scores in the list.

3. A frequency polygon or histogram provides a graphic means of representing the same information displayed by a frequency distribution.

4. Knowledge of the physical characteristics of a frequency polygon—symmetry, skewness, modality, and kurtosis—is helpful in supplying a general verbal description of a set of scores.

5. The median is either the middle score (when the number of scores is odd) or a point midway between the two middle scores (when the number of scores is even).

6. The mean of a set of scores is found by adding all the scores and dividing the sum by the total number of scores.

7. A few extremely high or extremely low scores tend to pull the value of the mean away from the median and in the direction of the extreme scores.

8. The variance of a set of scores is the average of the squared deviations of the scores (from the mean).

9. The standard deviation is the square root of the variance.

10. Conceptually, the standard deviation is a number that shows the average amount by which the scores in a distribution deviate from the mean.

11. The normal curve is a theoretical, symmetric, bell-shaped frequency polygon that has become a relative standard for describing certain types of test data.

12. The larger the number of scores in a group, the greater the expected range of scores in standard deviation units.

13. The use of percentile ranks permits comparison of performance from tests that may differ in the means, variability, or distribution of scores they yield.

14. The percentile rank of a given score is most appropriately defined as the percent of scores in a group that fall below the midpoint of the score interval in which that score is located.

15. A complete set of percentile ranks yields a frequency polygon that is rectangular in shape.

16. Percentile ranks are percent values between 0

and 100; percentiles are raw scores that may have any value on a given raw-score scale.

17. Conversion of normally distributed scores to percentile ranks increases apparent score differences near the center of the distribution and decreases them near either extreme of the raw-score distribution.

18. A z-score indicates the number of standard deviation units an individual has scored above (+) or below (−) the mean.

19. A standard score can be computed by using the values of the mean and standard deviation of the new scale to modify the z-score.

20. Normalized standard scores are provided by many test publishers so that the useful properties of the normal curve can be incorporated in the interpretation of the scores.

21. The correlation coefficient is a measure of the degree of relationship between two variables, based on paired values of the variables obtained from each of a number of persons or things.

22. Possible values of the correlation coefficient range from 1.00, expressing perfect positive (direct) relationship, through 0, expressing absence of relationship, to −1.00, expressing perfect negative (indirect) relationship.

23. A scatterplot is a graph that can be used to estimate the correlation—magnitude and direction—between the variables used in plotting it.

24. A relatively high correlation between two variables is not sufficient evidence for concluding that one variable can predict the other in a causal relationship.

25. Correlation coefficients obtained from small samples are subject to large sampling errors.

QUESTIONS FOR STUDY AND DISCUSSION

1. Why should score values be included in a frequency distribution even when no individuals obtained those scores?

2. What unique purposes might be served by frequency polygons? histograms?

3. Why might the median be more useful than the mean for describing typical performance on a sixth-grade promotion test?

4. How are the average deviation score and the standard deviation different, conceptually and computationally?

5. From what kinds of measures might we expect to obtain scores as high as 4 or 5 standard deviations above the mean?

6. What is the essential difference between a percentile rank and a percent-correct score?

7. Under what circumstances might it be useful to know that the correlation between two measures is about zero?

8. If a scatterplot for two variables forms a straight, horizontal line, how should the relationship between the two variables be described?

5

The Reliability
of Test Scores

THE MEANING OF RELIABILITY

Reliability is the term used to describe one of the most significant properties of a set of test scores–how consistent or error free the measurements are.[1] Scores that are highly reliable are accurate, reproducible, and generalizable to other testing occasions and other similar test instruments. For norm-referenced tests, this means that the use of a comparable test, under similar testing conditions on another occasion, will yield a distribution of scores that will place examinees in essentially the same rank ordering. The scatterplot of the scores from the two measures will be a set of points that cluster about a slanted straight line.

For criterion-referenced testing situations, reliability still refers to consistency, but placing examinees in the same order on two occasions is a less relevant goal. When the purpose is to estimate how much of a domain each student knows, testing with equivalent instruments on different occasions should yield the same percent-correct score for each student, not *just* the same ordering of test takers. When the purpose is objectives referenced, leading to mastery interpretations, the concern is not so much with reproducing the same score as with replicating the original decision—mastery versus nonmastery. Thus, the notion of consistency is the basis for the meaning of reliability, but how we conceptualize consistency for a certain measurement situation depends very much on the kind of score interpretation to be made. Could a given set of scores be considered

---

[1]Portions of this discussion of reliability were taken from an instructional module prepared for a series sponsored by the National Council on Measurement in Education (Frisbie, 1988).

quite reliable for criterion-referenced purposes, but not so reliable for norm-referenced purposes?

In view of the differences in interpretation of reliability for norm-referenced and criterion-referenced situations, separate discussions of the two will be presented. Similarities will be described in the last section of this chapter when criterion-referenced circumstances are addressed.

Definitions of Score Reliability

The classical definition of score reliability makes use of the idea of correlation and equivalent tests:

> *The reliability coefficient for a set of scores from a group of examinees is the coefficient of correlation between that set of scores and another set of scores on an equivalent test obtained independently from members of the same group.*

Three aspects of this definition deserve comment. First, it states that reliability is a property of a set of test scores, *not* a property of the test itself. A nutrition test could yield fairly accurate scores on a certain day when given to a particular class, but could yield fairly inconsistent scores when given to a different class or when given to the same class on another occasion. The more appropriate a test is to the level of abilities in the group, the higher the reliability of scores it will probably yield. The wider the range of achievement in a group, the higher the reliability of the scores obtained with a test of that achievement. Even though we may hear some individuals refer to a test as "very reliable," what they really mean (and what they actually should say) is that the scores obtained from a certain group on a certain day and under certain testing conditions could be reproduced readily with an equivalent test. That is, the scores are highly consistent.

Second, the definition specifies the use of a correlation coefficient as a measure of reliability. One of the characteristics of the correlation coefficient is that it provides a *relative* rather than an *absolute* measure of agreement between pairs of scores for the same persons. That is, the scores do not need to be the exact same numbers on the two occasions. If the differences between scores for the same person are small relative to the differences between scores for different persons, then the test will tend to show highly reliable scores. Conversely, if the differences between scores for the same person are large relative to the differences between persons, then the scores will show much lower reliability.

Third, the definition calls for two or more independent measures, obtained from equivalent tests of the same trait, for each member of the group. This is the heart of the definition. From this it follows that the various means of obtaining independent measurements of the same achievement will provide the basis for several distinct methods for estimating score reliability.

A Theoretical Representation

For theoretical purposes we assume that a test score can be partitioned into two components: a true score and an error score. The hypothetical true score of an individual is the average of the scores the person would obtain if tested on many occasions with the same test. The relationship between these scores is simply

$$X = T + E \qquad (5.1)$$

As an example, if we could separate test scores into their true and error components, we might have these values for two pairs of students:

	X	T	E		X	T	E
Scott	31	28	+3	Missy	35	40	−5
Mike	25	27	−2	Jenny	35	32	+3

Note that the boys have nearly identical true scores, but their observed scores make it appear as though their achievements are somewhat different. The girls, on the other hand, appear to have the same level of achievement, but measurement error masks the fact that Missy's real achievement level is higher. Mike and Scott are likely to be assigned different test grades, while Missy and Jenny probably would be assigned the same grade. Since we are unable to determine the size of an examinee's error score (E), we would like to be able to estimate how large the E score is, on the average, for the group tested. Then the interpretation of observed scores can be tempered by showing how much error might be contained in the score. To obtain the needed estimate, we take this theoretical development one step further.

The variance of the observed (raw) scores can be represented as

$$s_X^2 = s_T^2 + s_E^2 \qquad (5.2)$$

The variance is the square of the standard deviation of the scores, s_X^2, an indication of the amount of dispersion present in the score distribution. Equation 5.2 depends on these classical test theory assumptions: the errors are random (the correlation between error scores and true scores is 0.00) and the average error score in a distribution is zero (the positive and negative errors add to zero). The equation says that the observed test scores of a group vary for two reasons: (1) individuals in the group have different true scores and (2) error scores vary among examinees. The reliability of a set of scores can be expressed as the ratio of the variance of true scores to the variance of observed scores:

$$r_{XX} = \frac{s_T^2}{s_X^2} \qquad (5.3)$$

The reliability coefficient is a number that indicates how much of the variability in observed scores can be explained by the fact that examinees differ from one another in the trait being measured. When the ratio is large (near +1.00), it means that the raw scores are an accurate representation of the true differences that exist within the group tested. A relatively small ratio (approaching zero) means that random errors, not true differences, mainly explain why examinees obtained different scores.

Sources of Score Variability

A major goal of test makers is to maximize the true variance and minimize the error variance in the scores on their tests. What are the factors that influence each type of variance? What are the many reasons that explain why individuals in a group achieve different scores when they take a test that is appropriate for the ability level of the group?

As an example, Carlos and Marta might obtain different scores on the same geography test because Carlos knows more about the content covered by the test than Marta. We want our test scores to reflect this kind of difference, so no error is involved if this is the sole explanation for the score difference. However, all other possible explanations are potential sources of measurement error. Here are some examples:

1. Although Marta is an above-average reader, for some inexplicable reason she had to reread nearly everything on the test. She seemed unable to concentrate well enough to comprehend on the first reading. Carlos's attention did not seem to fluctuate in any unusual way during the test.

2. The teacher recognized both Carlos's and Marta's handwriting when scoring the essay responses. He seemed particularly lenient with one of Carlos's incomplete responses and probably should have awarded Marta a few more points for one of her responses.

3. Carlos was fortunate in that the two essay questions related closely to what he had most recently studied, but Marta had concentrated her study in several other areas instead. She might have been more successful had a different pair of essay questions been asked.

4. Marta did not read the instructions carefully and forgot to answer the five items on the back side of the last page. These items were marked as incorrect.

5. Carlos guessed correctly on four of five multiple-choice items, but Marta was correct on only two of the six guesses she made.

In these illustrations the errors that occurred affected Marta and Carlos differently and probably affected all others in the group in other various ways. These are called *random errors* because, if we were to give these students an equivalent test or give them the same test again, we would expect these kinds of errors to have a somewhat different effect on each examinee the second time. Each type of error might be present or absent in a specific testing situation for a given test taker. Sometimes the effect of an error will be fairly large, sometimes it will be fairly small, and sometimes it will be absent altogether.

Unlike random errors, *systematic errors* affect all examinees in the same way and cause all scores to be higher (or lower) than they ought to be. These kinds of errors do not contribute to score differences among test takers, but they do affect the absolute magnitude of each examinee's score. For example, there was a short-answer definition item that everyone got wrong (even though they all knew the definition) because they did not write a complete sentence. Or everyone got a certain true–false item wrong because the teacher mistakenly keyed the item "true" when it was actually "false." These situations contribute to each person's score in the same way, but each causes the scores to be in error, two points lower than they ought to be. How do systematic errors impact norm-referenced and criterion-referenced scores differently?

Thorndike (1951) has classified the possible sources of variance in scores

Figure 5–1.   Possible Sources of Variance in Score on a Particular Test (Thorndike, 1951).

I. *Lasting and general characteristics of the individual*
   A. Level of ability on one or more general traits, which operate in a number of tests
   B. General skills and techniques of taking tests
   C. General ability to comprehend instructions

II. *Lasting but specific characteristics of the individual*
   A. Specific to the test as a whole (and to parallel forms of it)
      1. Individual level of ability on traits required in this test but not in others
      2. Knowledge and skills specific to a particular form of test items
   B. Specific to particular test items
      1. The "chance" element determining whether the individual does or does not know a particular fact (sampling variance in a finite number of items, not the probability of guessing the answer)

III. *Temporary but general characteristics of the individual* (Factors affecting performance on many or all tests at a particular time)
   A. Health
   B. Fatigue
   C. Motivation
   D. Emotional strain
   E. General testwiseness
   F. Understanding of mechanics of testing
   G. External conditions of heat, light, ventilation, etc.

IV. *Temporary and specific characteristics of the individual*
   A. Specific to the test as a whole
      1. Comprehension of the specific test task
      2. Specific tricks or techniques of dealing with the particular test materials
      3. Level of practice on the specific skills involved (especially in psychomotor tests)
      4. Momentary "set" for a particular test
   B. Specific to particular test items
      1. Fluctuations and idiosyncrasies of human memory
      2. Unpredictable fluctuations in attention or accuracy, superimposed upon the general level of performance characteristic of the individual

V. *Systematic or chance factors affecting the administration of the test or the appraisal of test performance*
   A. Conditions of testing—adherence to time limits, freedom from distractions, clarity of instructions, etc.
   B. Unreliability or bias in subjective rating of traits or performances

VI. *Variance not otherwise accounted for (chance)*
   A. "Luck" in selection of answers by "guessing"

in an attempt to identify those that contribute to error and true score variance. His categorization scheme is reproduced in Figure 5–1. Some factors explain why an individual might obtain different scores on the same test on two occasions, and some explain why examinees tested on the same occasion might obtain scores that differ from one another. A detailed discussion of each category can be found in Stanley (1971). For our purposes, several generalizations can be drawn from the listing in Figure 5–1:

1. All the sources of variance do not necessarily operate in every testing situation.
2. Some factors contribute to error scores in some testing situations but contribute to true scores in other situations.
3. Reliability is not simply an intrinsic trait of a test; its value depends on the nature of the group tested, the test content, and the conditions of testing.

METHODS OF ESTIMATING SCORE RELIABILITY

There is a need to estimate test score reliability so that we can judge the extent to which measurement errors might interfere with the interpretability of the scores. Because reliability can be influenced by so many factors—the group tested, the test content, and testing conditions—it is not possible to settle on a single method for estimating reliability for all testing situations. At least five methods are used in practice to obtain the independent measurements necessary for estimating reliability. These methods yield coefficients of stability, equivalence, and internal analysis.

Stability Estimates

The test–retest method is essentially a measure of examinee reliability, an indication of how consistently examinees perform on the same set of tasks. The simplest and most obvious method of obtaining repeated measures of the same ability for the same individuals is to give the same test twice. This would provide two scores for each individual tested. The correlation between the set of scores obtained on the first administration of the test and that obtained on the second yields a test–retest reliability coefficient. Note that such temporary characterstics listed in Figure 5–1 as health, fatigue, memory fluctuations, and comprehension of the specific test task are likely to contribute to the error score when this method is used. The test–retest method is particularly useful in situations where the trait being measured is expected to be stable over time. Then, if the scores on the two occasions yield different rank orderings of the examinees, measurement error is the single most likely explanation for such differences.

A number of objections to the test–retest method have been raised, especially for use with achievement tests. One is that exactly the same test items are used both times. Since this set of items represents only one sample from what is ordinarily a very large population of possible test items, the scores on the retest provide no evidence on how much the scores might change if a different sample of questions were used (category II.B.1 from Figure 5–1). Another objection is that students' answers to the second test are not independent of their answers to the first. That is, their responses on the retest undoubtedly are influenced to some degree by recall, and possibly also by student discussion and individual or joint effort to learn the material in the interval between testings. A third objection is that, if the interval between the test and the retest is long, errors of measurement may get confused with real changes in student ability as a result of learning. Finally, readministration of the same test simply to determine how reliable its scores are does not appeal to most students and teachers as a very efficient use of instructional time. Lack of interest on the students' parts sometimes may make the second test a much poorer measure than the first, even though the actual test is the same in both cases. The test–retest method is not recommended for estimating the reliability of scores from classroom achievement tests.

Equivalent Forms Estimates

If two (or more) forms of a test have been produced in such a way that it seems likely that the scores on these alternate forms will be equivalent and if each student in a group is given two forms of the test, then the correlation between scores on the two forms provides an estimate of score reliability. A high-reliability estimate is evidence that the two test forms can be used interchangeably as measures of the same trait. But a relatively low estimate is an indication that the two sets of test items probably are not sampling the content domain of interest equally well. This kind of content sampling error (II.B.1 in Figure 5–1) is perhaps the most prevalent category of error affecting achievement-test scores. Consequently, estimation methods that are able to detect content sampling errors are most appropriate for achievement-test scores.

The major drawback to this approach is that teachers ordinarily do not prepare alternate forms of their achievement tests. Some have enough trouble building one good test for each testing occasion. However, all widely used standardized achievement tests *do* provide alternate test forms at each of several levels. When equivalent forms are used to measure progress or growth within a school year or to assess the effects of experimental treatments, evidence of high equivalent forms reliability is essential so that true educational gains are not masked or artificially elevated by measurement errors.

Internal Analysis Methods

The difficulties associated with the determination of test–retest and equivalent forms reliability coefficients encouraged the search for more practical methods. The methods described in this section are based on the administration of a single test and on the use of component subtests, information internal to the test, to estimate test-score reliability.

Split halves.   A common approach is to split a test into two reasonably equivalent halves. These independent subtests are then used as a source of the two independent scores needed for reliability estimation. One common method of splitting a test has been to score the odd-numbered items and the even-numbered items separately. Then the correlation between scores on the odd- and even-numbered items is calculated. Of course, splitting a test in this way means that the scores on which the reliability is based are from half-length tests. To obtain an estimate of the reliability based on the full-length test it is necessary to correct, or step up, the half-test correlation to the full-length correlation. (As you will see shortly, the length of a test has a very direct effect on the reliability of the scores we can get from it.) This is done with the help of the Spearman–Brown formula. When we need to predict the score reliability from a test twice as long as a given test, as in the split-halves method, the formula is

$$r_2 = \frac{2(r)}{r + 1} \tag{5.4}$$

where r is the reliability of the original scores. For example, if the odd-even correlation between two 25-item half-tests is 0.82, the reliability of the total-test scores (50 items) is 1.64 divided by 1.82, which is approximately 0.90.

The general Spearman–Brown formula is used to predict the new reliability expected from increasing the length of a test of known reliability by adding items similar to the original ones. The general formula is

$$r_n = \frac{n(r)}{(n - 1)(r) + 1} \tag{5.5}$$

where r_n is the reliability of the scores from the new, lengthened test, n is the number of times the original test is lengthened, and r is the reliability of the original test scores.

Suppose a given set of scores has a reliability of 0.50 and we wish to increase the original length of the test by nine times, adding new items equivalent in content and difficulty to the original items. The reliability of the scores from the new test is predicted to be

$$r_n = \frac{9(0.50)}{(9 - 1)(0.50) + 1} = \frac{4.50}{5.00} = 0.90$$

If the original test contained 20 items, the new test would need 180 equivalent items to yield a reliability of 0.90. Of course, for this prediction to hold, students should be expected to respond to 180 items without getting more bored or fatigued than they would get by responding to the original 20. And the added items should be similar to the original ones in terms of content, difficulty, and overall quality.

Kuder–Richardson. Two of the most widely accepted methods for estimating reliability were developed by Kuder and Richardson (1937). Their formula 20, abbreviated K–R20, is

$$r = \frac{k}{k - 1} \left[1 - \frac{\Sigma \, pq}{s^2} \right] \tag{5.6}$$

where

k = number of test items

p = proportion of correct responses to a particular item

q = proportion of incorrect responses to that item (so that p plus q always equals 1)

s^2 = variance of the scores on the test

This formula is applicable only to tests scored dichotomously (0 or 1), one point for each correct answer and no points for an incorrect answer. If the scores from a test are corrected for guessing or if some other form of weighted scoring is used, more complex variations of the formula must be used.

The Kuder–Richardson estimate for reliability will not necessarily yield the same result as the split-halves method.[2] Conceptually, K–R20 is the average correlation achieved by computing all possible split-half correlations for a test. That is, there are many ways to split a test into two halves, and some splits will yield two fairly equivalent halves, while others will yield somewhat nonequivalent halves. Since the K–R20 can be thought of as the average of all possible splits, its value will be larger relative to nonequivalent splits and smaller relative to fairly equivalent splits. The idea that similar methods can yield different results may be particularly important to consider when evaluating standardized tests for possible selection for a school testing program. The technical manual for one test may report split-halves reliability estimates, while the manual for another may report Kuder–Richardson estimates.

The computation of K–R20 requires information about the difficulty (proportion of correct responses) of each item in the test. If the test items do not vary widely in difficulty, a reasonably good approximation of the quantity pq can be obtained from information about the test mean and the number of items. This formula, K–R21, estimates the value of K–R20:

$$r = \frac{k}{k-1}\left[1 - \frac{\overline{X}(k - \overline{X})}{ks^2}\right] \tag{5.7}$$

Can you verify that K–R21 is 0.32 for a six-item test that has $\overline{X} = 3.3$ and $s^2 = 2.01$? For this same test, K–R20 was computed to be 0.40. One limitation of the K–R21 is that it always gives an *underestimate* of the K–R20 reliability coefficient when the items vary in difficulty, as they almost always do. If a test includes many items on which the average score is either near perfect (1.0) or near zero, this underestimate could be quite large. But if most of the items have average scores between 30 and 70 percent, the underestimate should be much smaller. A formula for correcting some of this underestimation was developed by Wilson, Downing, and Ebel (1977).

Coefficient alpha. Coefficient alpha can provide a reliability estimate for a measure composed of items scored with values other than 0 and 1 (Cronbach, 1951). Such is the case with essay tests having items of varying point values or attitude scales that provide responses such as "strongly agree" and "strongly disagree"

[2]An illustration of the computations of K–R20 can be found in Ebel (1979).

with intermediate response options. The formula resembles the one for K–R20 because K–R20 is actually a special case of the alpha procedure. The formula is

$$\alpha = \frac{k}{k-1}\left[1 - \frac{\Sigma s_i^2}{s^2}\right] \qquad (5.8)$$

where s_i^2 is the variance of a single test item. When alpha is used to estimate the reliability of scores from a test that is scored dichotomously, the result will be *exactly* the same as that calculated using K–R20.

Reliability of ratings. A method for estimating the reliability of essay-test scores uses the basic coefficient alpha formula given in equation 5.8. The formula is

$$r = \frac{k}{k-1}\left[1 - \frac{\Sigma s_i^2}{s_t^2}\right] \qquad (5.9)$$

where

$\quad k \quad$ = number of separately scored essay test questions
$\quad s_i^2 \quad$ = variance of students' scores on a particular item
$\quad \Sigma s_i^2$ = sum of the item variances for all test items
$\quad s_t^2 \quad$ = variance of the total essay scores

This method of estimating reliability of scores employs concepts from the statistical procedure called *analysis of variance.* A high reliability coefficient results when the total essay scores for examinees are quite variable *and* the item scores for individuals across the items are quite similar. In such circumstances the separate essay items are consistent in identifying individual differences in the achievement measured by the essay test as a whole.[3]

USING RELIABILITY INFORMATION

The reliability coefficient is an index of the amount of error associated with a set of scores and, thus, is an important piece of information needed for evaluating the meaningfulness and usefulness of those scores. In addition, the information about error can be used to make estimates of the true scores of examinees and to assess the practical significance of the difference between scores of two or more test takers. How all this can be accomplished is our next set of concerns.

Interpreting Reliability Coefficients

There are no absolute standards to serve as criteria for determining whether a given reliability coefficient is high enough. However, some relative standards have evolved over time for evaluating reliability under each of several

---

[3]An application of this method to a simple case is illustrated in Ebel (1979).

circumstances. For example, teacher-prepared tests tend to produce scores with reliability coefficients around 0.50. Most educators regard this value as acceptable for these circumstances. However, most published standardized tests have been shown to yield scores having reliabilities in the 0.85 to 0.95 range, values regarded as highly acceptable.

The standards for minimally acceptable values for test-score reliability need to be established in the context of score use. That is, how reliable the scores must be depends mostly on how the scores will be used—what kinds of decisions will be made and how much weight the test score will have in the decision. Experts in educational measurement have agreed informally that the reliability coefficient should be at least 0.85 if the scores will be used to make decisions about individuals *and* if the scores are the only available useful information. (This ought to be a very rare circumstance.) However, if the decision is about the scores of a *group* of individuals, like a class, the generally accepted minimum standard is 0.65.

Usually, we can tolerate reliabilities around 0.50 for scores from teacher-made tests if each score will be combined with other information—test scores, quiz scores, observations—to assign a grade for quarter or semester work. It is the reliability of the total score that results from combining the collection of measurements that should concern us the most; it is this total score, not the score from any one test, on which grading decisions will be made. When an important decision is made using a single score, we need to be concerned about the reliability of that single set of scores. For example, if a teacher uses a placement test to determine the most appropriate starting point in instruction for each student, those decisions will be important and little additional corroborating information will be at hand. Consequently, our standard for acceptable reliability for such placement-test scores should be noticeably higher than that for achievement-test scores that will provide information for grading.

Standard Error of Measurement

The reliability coefficient is a useful indicator of the extent to which a set of test scores is error free or error laden, but it furnishes no direct assistance in estimating the true scores of examinees. In almost all practical measurement situations, the only information available is the set of observed scores of the persons measured. Their true scores and error scores are both unknown. However, given the standard deviation of the distribution of observed scores and the reliability coefficient of those scores, the standard deviation of the hypothetical error scores can be estimated. This quantity is called the *standard error of measurement.* The formula, derived from equations 5.2 and 5.3, is

$$s_E = s_X \sqrt{1 - r} \tag{5.10}$$

The relationship of the standard error of measurement to true scores, error scores, and observed scores can be seen using the hypothetical test scores in Table 5–1. Note that for each of the five students the observed score equals the true score plus the error of measurement. The mean of the true scores is 15, and the mean of the errors of measurement is 0, which makes the observed score

Table 5-1. Reliability and Errors of Measurement

Students	True Scores	Errors of Measurement	Obtained Scores
Alissa	18	−2	16
Dan	9	+1	10
Jody	15	+2	17
John	21	+1	22
Sean	12	−2	10
Mean	15	0	15
Variance	18	2.8	20.8

Reliability $= \dfrac{18}{20.8} = 0.865$

$s_E = \sqrt{2.8} = 1.67$ (direct calculation)

$s_E = \sqrt{20.8\,(1 - 0.865)}$

$= 4.56 \times 0.367$

$= 1.67$ (from formula)

mean 15, also. The variances of each of the three types of scores are given in the next line of the table. The ratio of the true score variance to the observed score variance is 0.865, which is the reliability of this set of observed scores. The standard deviation of the errors of measurement is $\sqrt{2.8}$, or 1.67. When the values of s_X and r are substituted in equation 5.10, the value $s_E = 1.67$ is obtained. This shows that an estimate of the standard deviation of the errors of measurement can be obtained with the standard deviation of the observed scores and the reliability coefficient, without any information about the individual errors of measurement.

The standard error of measurement provides an indication of the absolute accuracy of the test scores using the observed score scale. For example, if the standard error of measurement for a set of scores is 3, then for slightly more than two-thirds of the observed scores (about 68 percent of them) the errors of measurement will be 3 or less score points. For the remainder of the scores, of course, the errors of measurement will be greater. For individual score interpretation purposes, the standard error of measurement is used to create a range of scores within which the person's true score is expected to be. Using the values from Table 5-1, we could be about 68 percent sure that Dan's true score is in the interval 10 ± 1.67 or 8.33 to 11.67. To be 95 percent sure, we would say Dan's true score is within the interval 10 ± (2)1.67 or 6.66 to 13.34. Note that the percentages 68 and 95 correspond to the percentages under the normal curve within one and two standard deviations, respectively, of the mean.

The standard error of measurement is the most common indicator of the amount of error contained in an observed test score. But its limitations have caused a number of researchers to consider additional ways of accounting for error when interpreting a test score. One shortcoming of the standard error of measurement is that it provides the same error estimate for everyone in the group, even though it is reasonable to expect individuals to have varying error scores. Methods that permit the computation of standard errors of measurement for each of several score ranges are described by Feldt and Brennan (1989). In addition, they describe procedures for obtaining error-score estimates for each individual in the tested group.

The Problem of Low Reliability

Suppose the K–R20 from the scores on a history unit test turns out to be 0.33 and the teacher decides this value is unsatisfactory. What should be done? After all, the scores seem to have *some* worth, though less than had been hoped originally. Perhaps the first action, when practical, should be to improve the conditions that contributed to the low reliability and then retest. But, ordinarily, test development and administration time constraints will preclude the "do over" alternative. A second alternative would be to retain the scores but discount them, that is, assign less weight to them in the decision process than had been planned originally. For example, if the scores were to count as 25 percent of the final grade, their weight might be dropped to 20 percent, or a bit less.

When discounting is employed, as described above, decision making can be affected in important (and usually negative) ways. For example, if the discounted scores related to significant prerequisites for later learning opportunities, the wisdom of the decision to discount the scores would be questionable. If the discounted scores were supposed to measure higher-order thinking skills in the content area or problem solving or application of content, subsequent decisions might be grossly misleading. In sum, the user must be aware of the trade-offs involved when using discounted or undiscounted scores, when either has relatively low reliability.

Low reliability is symptomatic of an unhealthy testing situation, just as high fever indicates unhealthy body tissue. We cannot tell in either case what the problem is, but the symptom suggests where to look. Was it the test, some characteristic of the examinees, or some aspect of the testing conditions? Was it a combination of these? The user should determine plausible explanations so that a decision can be made about whether to use the scores for their intended purpose.

FACTORS INFLUENCING SCORE RELIABILITY

When we understand the various factors that can impact the reliability of a set of scores, we can interpret and use the scores prudently, and we can attempt to manipulate those factors through test preparation and administration activities.

Test-related Factors

The reliability of achievement-test scores is affected by the number of items in the test, the extent to which test content is homogeneous, and the characteristics of the individual items—their difficulty and discrimination capability.

1. *Test length.* The Spearman–Brown formula (equation 5.5) indicates the theoretical relationship between score reliability and test length. The effect of successive doublings of the length of an original five-item test, which yielded a reliability of 0.20, is shown in Table 5–2. The same data are shown graphically in Figure 5–2. As the table and figure indicate, the higher the score reliability, the smaller the increase in reliability with added test length. Adding 60 items to a 20-item test could increase reliability from 0.50 to 0.80. But adding 80 more items to the 80-item test would raise reliability from 0.80 to only 0.89. To achieve perfect reliability, an infinite number of items would have to be used, which of course means that perfect reliability cannot be attained by lengthening any test.

Two assumptions, one statistical, the other psychological, are involved in the use of the Spearman–Brown formula. The statistical assumption is that the items added to the original test to increase its length have the same statistical properties as the original items. That is, the added items should have the same average difficulty as the original items, and their addition to the test should not change the average intercorrelation among the test items. The psychological assumption involved is that lengthening the test should not change the way examinees respond to it. If practice on items like those in the test facilitates correct response, if fatigue or boredom inhibits it, or if any other factors make the examinees respond quite differently to the lengthened test, reliability predictions based on the Spearman–Brown formula could be erroneous.

2. *Test content.* Homogeneity of test content also tends to enhance score reliability (Guilford, 1936). A 100-item test about the Vietnam War era is likely to provide more reliable scores than a 100-item test covering American history after the Civil War. Also the subject matter in some courses, such as mathematics and foreign languages, is more tightly organized, with greater interdependence of facts, principles, abilities, and achievements, than is the subject matter of literature or history. This is another aspect of test-content homogeneity that makes high reliability easier to achieve with tests of mathematics and foreign languages than with some other achievement tests.

3. *Item characteristics.* The items in homogeneous tests also tend to discriminate between high and low achievers better than items in tests covering more diverse content and abilities. But the ability of an item to discriminate is also heavily dependent on the technical quality of the item—on the soundness

Table 5–2. Relation of Test Length to Score Reliability

Items	Reliability
5	0.20
10	0.33
20	0.50
40	0.67
80	0.80
160	0.89
320	0.94
640	0.97
∞	1.00

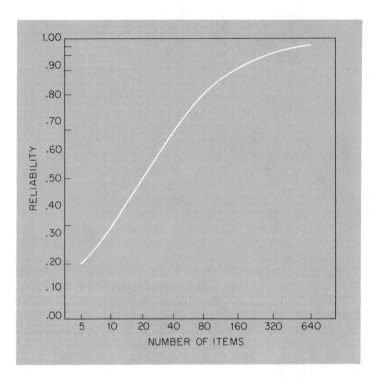

Figure 5-2. Relation of Test Length to Score Reliability

of the idea underlying the item, the clarity of its expression, and, for each multiple-choice item, the adequacy of the correct response and the attractiveness of the wrong answers to examinees of lower ability. The nature and determination of indices of discrimination and their relation to reliability will be discussed in greater detail in Chapter 13. For the present, it will be sufficient to say that the relation is close and important. Working to improve the discrimination of the individual items in most classroom tests is probably the most effective means of improving score reliability and, hence, test quality.

The difficulty of a test item affects its contribution to score reliability. An item that all examinees answer correctly, or all miss, contributes nothing to reliability. An item that just about half of the examinees answer correctly is potentially capable of contributing more to test-score reliability than an item that is either extremely easy or extremely difficult. Of course, such an item could also be totally nondiscriminating. Items of intermediate difficulty, that is, from about 40 to 80 percent correct responses, are all capable of contributing much to reliability. Items that more than 90 percent or fewer than 30 percent of the examinees answer correctly cannot possibly contribute as much. Contrary to popular belief, a good norm-referenced achievement test seldom should include items that vary widely in difficulty.

4. *Score variability.* Classroom tests are sometimes constructed and scored so that the range of scores obtained is much less than it could be, theoretically. For example, an essay test with a 100-point maximum score may be graded

with a view to making 75 a reasonable passing score. This usually limits the effective range of scores to about 30 points. A true–false test, scored only for the number of items answered correctly, has a useful score range of only about half the number of items. A multiple-choice test, on the other hand, may have a useful score range of three-fourths or more of the number of items in the test. Hence the scores from a 100-item multiple-choice test are usually more reliable than those from a 100-item true–false test. But students generally can respond to three true–false items in the time required to respond to a pair of content-parallel multiple-choice items (Frisbie 1973, 1974). With testing time held constant, a 150-item true–false test and a 100-item multiple-choice test produce equally useful score ranges and are likely to produce scores of equal reliability.

The dependence of reliability on score variability is illustrated by the hypothetical data in Table 5–3. The essay test was assumed to consist of ten questions, each worth a maximum of 10 points, with a score of 75 on the entire test set in advance as the minimum passing score. The other two tests were scored by giving one point for each correct answer; no "correction for guessing" was used. Each multiple-choice item is assumed to offer four alternative choices, so the expected chance score on that test is 25. The expected chance score on the true–false test is 75, half of the 150 items.

Notice that the expected variability of the true–false and multiple-choice tests, as reflected by the effective score range, is the same, and the reliabilities are nearly the same. However, the relatively small amount of variability expected in the essay scores would produce a reliability coefficient of only about 0.57. But this phenomenon is not simply a function of the difference between essay and objective tests. If we were to equate test lengths rather than testing time, a 100-item true–false test would yield an effective score range of 50 (100 − 50) and a corresponding reliability estimate of 0.76. While these are hypothetical data, based on deductions from certain assumptions, they are reasonably representative of the results we could expect teachers to achieve when using tests of these types.

Examinee-related Factors

Score reliability can be influenced by the amount of variability in achievement within the group tested, the testwiseness of the individuals, and student motivation. Teachers ordinarily do not try to manipulate achievement vari

Table 5-3. Hypothetical Test Statistics for Three Tests

Statistic	TEST TYPE		
	Essay	True–False	Multiple Choice
Number of items	100	150	100
Expected mean	87.5	112.5	62.5
Expected standard deviation	5	15	15
Effective score range	25	75	75
	(75–100)	(75–150)	(25–100)
Estimated reliability	0.57	0.88	0.91

ability, but they can and should try to improve both testwiseness and motivation in ways that will improve reliability.

1. *Group heterogeneity.* The reliability coefficient for a set of test scores depends also on the range of talent in the group tested. If an achievement test suitable for use in the middle grades of an elementary school is given to pupils in the fourth, fifth, and sixth grades, the reliability of the complete set of scores will almost certainly be higher than the reliability of any subset of scores from a single grade.

The reliability coefficient, as we have said, reflects the ratio of true score variance to observed score variance. The wider the range of talent in a group is, the greater the true score variance will be. If the variance of the errors of measurement is relatively unaffected by the range of talent, as should be expected, then the observed score variance will not increase as fast (that is, in the same proportion) as the true score variance. Thus, for several groups of increasingly heterogeneous achievement levels, (1) their true score variances will be increasingly higher, (2) their error variances will all be about the same, and (3) the reliabilities of their scores will be increasingly higher.

There are circumstances in which the students in a class are very similar to one another in their achievement of the objectives in an instructional unit. The standard deviation on the unit test is very small and the reliability coefficient is quite low, also. This may be a situation in which a high-quality test, when given properly, cannot yield scores of very high reliability. Dependable differences in achievement cannot be detected by most tests if those differences are negligible—too small to be of practical consequence. Though group homogeneity may be a plausible explanation for low reliability at times, we should not be too quick to ignore the signs of faulty test items before settling on group homogeneity as the most likely reason.

2. *Student testwiseness.* When the amount of test-taking experience and levels of testwiseness vary considerably within a group, such backgrounds and skills may cause scores to be less reliable than they otherwise would be. When all examinees in the group are sophisticated test takers, or when all are relatively naive about test taking, such homogeneity probably will not lead to much random measurement error. The rank order of scores is likely to be influenced only when there is obvious variability in testwiseness within the group. Students who answer an item correctly only because of their testwiseness, rather than their achievement of content, cause the item to discriminate improperly. As we noted earlier, poor item discrimination contributes to lowered reliability estimates.

3. *Student motivation.* If students are not motivated to do their best on a test, their scores are not apt to represent their actual achievement levels very well. But when the consequences of scoring high or low are important to examinees, the scores are likely to be more accurate. Indifference, lack of motivation, or underenthusiasm, for whatever reasons, can depress test scores in the same way that anxiety or overenthusiasm may. When motivation influences individuals in the group differently and inconsistently across testing occasions, random errors are likely to influence the scores.

Administration-related Factors

As with test-related effects and most examinee-related effects, test users usually can control the administration-related factors that might influence test scores. Two such factors, time limits and cheating, are considered here.

1. *Time limits.* Scores from a test given under highly speeded conditions will ordinarily show a higher internal consistency reliability coefficient than would be obtained for scores from the same test given to the same group under more generous time limits. But most of the increased reliability of speeded test scores is spurious—an artifact of the method of estimating reliability. If, instead of estimating reliability from a single administration of the speeded test, we were to administer separately timed equivalent forms of the test under equally speeded conditions, the correlation between scores on these equivalent forms would be less than the correlation estimated from a single administration. Hence the apparent increase in reliability that results from speeding up a test is usually regarded as a spurious increase.

Here is what causes the trouble. Scores on a speeded test depend not only on how many items examinees can answer, but also on how fast they can work to answer them. Thus, to estimate the reliability of scores on a speeded test, one must have estimates for both ability and speed. By splitting a test into halves or into individual items, one can get two independent estimates of ability. But there is no way of getting independent estimates of speed, short of timing separately the responses to individual items or parts of the test. When this is not done, the estimates of speed are not only dependent, they are forced to appear almost identical. The reliability of the "apparent" measurements of speed is very high. When this is combined with a valid estimate of the reliability of the measurements of ability, the composite estimate is overinflated. The implication of all this is that dependable estimates of test-score reliability can be obtained from a single administration of a test only if the speed at which examinees work is *not* an important factor in determining their scores. For achievement-testing purposes, it is widely held that a test is speeded if fewer than 90 percent of the examinees are able to attempt all items.

2. *Cheating opportunities.* Occurrences of cheating by students during a test contribute random errors to the test scores. Some students are able to provide correct answers for questions to which they actually do not know the answers. Copying of answers, use of cribs or cheat sheets, and the passing of information all give unfair advantage to some and cause their scores to be higher than they would be on retesting. The passing of information from class to class when the same test will be given to different classes at different times also reduces overall score reliability. The effect is to reduce artificially the true differences between students and, consequently, to make real differences more difficult to detect accurately. Of course, similar outcomes would be observed if some students gained access to copies of the test prior to its use. Since the effect of cheating is to raise the cheaters' observed scores above their true scores, extensive cheating contributes to inaccurate and less meaningful scores.

CRITERION-REFERENCED SCORE RELIABILITY

The whole idea of consistency of measurement, or reliability, relates as much to criterion-referenced scores as it does to norm-referenced ones. Some educators hold the mistaken notion that scores on criterion-referenced tests exhibit little or no variability. From this, they erroneously conclude that the methods of reliability estimation for norm-referenced scores, methods that depend on score variability, are inappropriate for criterion-referenced use. This last section will be devoted to discussing the variety of methods for determining consistency of measurement for several criterion-referenced testing situations, including the applicability of the "norm-referenced" methods.

Scores or Decisions

The reliability of scores from criterion-referenced tests can be understood better if we first examine the types of interpretations we might want to make with such scores. For convenience, these can be labeled as absolute performance, domain estimate, and mastery.

Absolute performance interpretations make use of a number scale that shows increasing levels of accomplishment or achievement for each successive numbered scale position. Examples are a 7-point scale used to evaluate themes, a 10-point rating form for judging the quality of a woodworking project, a 10-point scale for judging the quality of a figure-skating performance, or a 15-point scale used by a French teacher to judge the quality of short dialogues written and presented by pairs of students. In each of these cases, the score obtains meaning from the behavior descriptions attached to each scale point. A 13 describes what a student has achieved, and no reference to the performances of other students is required to bring meaning to the score. What must be done to demonstrate that the scores obtained from such a scale are reliable enough? Note that we cannot be satisfied with a "retest" that would yield a high correlation with the original scores. Correlation coefficients reflect the extent to which pairs of measurements are in the same *relative* position. Our concern is with maintenance of the same *absolute* position on retesting.

There are no generally accepted indices of reliability for scores based on absolute performance interpretations. However, appropriate evidence for consistency would include a demonstration that the average discrepancy between test and retest scores was small for the group in question. "Small" would need to be defined by the user, based mainly on the fineness of the behavior scale gradations. In addition, high agreement among independent raters of the same themes or projects or other performances is further evidence of the consistency of the scores. Again, absolute differences rather than relative differences must be examined.

Domain estimate interpretations are made when the scores indicate the percentage of some clearly defined content or performance domain attained by the student. Some of the common domains of interest are found in the basic skills curriculum of our elementary schools: names of the 26 letters of the alphabet, products from the multiplication of pairs of single-digit numbers, all words on the third-grade spelling scale, and name–location associations for the 50 states.

In each case, a test score obtains meaning from an understanding of what the "whole," the domain, constitutes. "Tommy knows 83 percent of his letters," is not very informative because we are likely to be most interested in which four letters Tommy has trouble identifying. To know that Rose-anna can spell 90 percent of the words on the third-grade list probably is insufficient by itself, even if we are told there are 780 words in all. Setting aside these shortcomings, how can the reliability of scores from a domain-referenced spelling test be determined? Since we are again interested in absolute interpretations, correlational methods will not be useful.

As with absolute performance interpretations, the most reasonable evidence of the reliability of domain estimate scores is a small average discrepancy score based on retesting. Again, no generally accepted methods have been developed for this purpose. The apparent lack of interest in reliability methods for domain-estimate interpretations may be a reflection of a general lack of interest in domain scores. Such scores are descriptive, but they offer no prescriptions for further instruction and, unless a cutoff score is introduced, they do not help the interpreter decide if performance is "good enough."

Mastery interpretations are actually absolute performance or domain estimate scores interpreted in terms of an absolute criterion. Here are some sample performance standards (often called *decision rules*) used in mastery interpretations:

1. A posttest score of at least 85 percent is needed to proceed to the next unit.
2. A score of at least 22 out of 25 is needed to pass the driver's test.
3. Anyone with a score below 40 will be placed in the special reading program.
4. Scores higher than 3 on the 7-point scale will be regarded as "acceptable performance."

When the interpretive goal is to make a decision about performance, the notion of consistency should be tied to the *decision* rather than the *score*. For example, if theme scores of 4, 5, 6, and 7 are all "acceptable" and Stephen had a 5 on his first theme, our concern should be whether we can replicate the decision on retesting. It should matter little if Stephen earns a 7 or a 4 on the retest, as long as the decision about his performance is the same. Thus, for mastery interpretations, score reliability takes a back seat to decision consistency with regard to measurement error. Whenever criterion-referenced scores are used to make dichotomous decisions such as pass–fail, mastery–nonmastery, proceed–remediate, any of several methods may be useful for estimating decision consistency.

Estimating Agreement

When dichotomous decisions such as mastery–nonmastery are the object of criterion-referenced interpretation, the consistency of classification is of interest. That is, if an equivalent test were administered or if the same test were readministered, how closely would classifications of individuals be repeated? Several complex, unwieldy computational procedures have been proposed to estimate agreement under these conditions. We will consider two of these as means to generating a deeper understanding of the decision consistency concept.

Suppose Mr. Zimmer has given a capitalization test to his fifth-grade class and wishes to make mastery decisions. He decides that the decision rule for mastery will be 26/30 items. The outcomes, summarized in the two columns of Table 5-4, show that 17 students were classified as masters and 8 were classified as nonmasters. The next day Mr. Zimmer gave the same test and obtained the classification results shown in the rows of Table 5-4, 18 masters and 7 nonmasters. The classification agreement can be determined by using this formula for percent of agreement:

$$P_A = \frac{a + d}{N} \tag{5.11}$$

where a is the number of examinees classified as masters on both occasions, d is the number classified as nonmasters from the two administrations, and N is the number of examinees. The index tells us that 80 percent of the decisions about these 25 students were consistent from one time to the next. Only 5 students (20 percent) were classified differently on the two occasions. The highest P_A can be is 1.00, but its lowest value is not likely to be 0.00. If we were to assign students to classifications randomly, by coin tossing, we should expect *some* agreement.

Kappa, a second coefficient of agreement, was developed to estimate how much the classifications that are based on testing will improve decision consistency relative to random classification. For example, if P_A turns out to be 0.60 for a certain situation, might that level of consistency be achieved by more efficient and economical means than testing? Kappa is computed using this formula:

$$K = \frac{P_A - P_C}{1 - P_C} \tag{5.12}$$

where P_C, the percent of agreement that could be expected by chance, is calculated from this equation:

$$P_C = \frac{(a + b)(a + c) + (c + d)(b + d)}{N^2} \tag{5.13}$$

Table 5-4.   Example of Decision Consistency Estimation

		Form A Administration 1		
Form A Administration 2		Master	Nonmaster	
	Master	a = 15	b = 3	18
	Nonmaster	c = 2	d = 5	7
		17	8	25

$P_A = (a + d)/N$
$P_A = (15 + 5)/25 = 0.80$

The values of $a, b, c,$ and d are represented in Table 5-4. Can you verify that P_C = 0.579 for the data in Table 5-4? What does this value mean? It means that about 58 percent of the pairs of classifications would be consistent, by chance, if the outcome from the second test administration were independent of those from the first. For our illustration, $K = (0.80 - 0.579)/(1 - 0.579) = 0.525$. If the value of kappa were close to zero, it would mean that our classifications were not any better than we could have done by chance, without testing. Thus $K = 0.525$ should be interpreted to mean that something other than random factors is accounting for the level of decision consistency obtained through the two test administrations. In other words, true scores rather than error scores are the primary reason that decisions were so consistent from one time to the next.

The illustration of obtaining an agreement coefficient is parallel to the test–retest method used with norm-referenced measures. However, when equivalent forms are available or when content sampling is a major concern, estimation procedures that parallel the norm-referenced equivalent forms methods should be used. Berk (1984) and Subkoviak (1984) have dealt with these and other related methods in some detail. In addition, Subkoviak (1988) has provided tables to ease the computational burden for calculating P_A and kappa.

Factors Affecting Decision Consistency

Many of the factors that affect the magnitude of reliability coefficients also affect agreement coefficients because errors associated with examinees, the test itself, and the testing conditions can occur in any measurement situation. And, of course, these factors often operate simultaneously rather than in isolation.

1. *The cutoff score location.* When the cutoff score is nearer the highest score or the lowest score, decision consistency will be greater. A cutoff score at about the median is likely to produce the most inconsistent decisions. This idea conforms with the notion that extreme levels of performance are easy to pick out, but shades of differences among typical performers are difficult to detect.

2. *The homogeneity of the scores.* If the test scores are homogeneous and the cutoff score is somewhere among them, the number of inconsistent decisions could be quite high. Much greater decision consistency should be expected when scores are highly variable and the cutoff score is located somewhere within the distribution. For example, even if the cutoff score is at the median, more consistency is likely to be achieved with scores from a rectangular distribution than from one that is negatively skewed.

3. *Test length.* Intuitively, it seems logical that the more opportunities we give examinees to perform, the more confident we can be in deciding what their ranking is, how much they know, or whether they can perform a specific task well enough. If a mastery decision rule requires 75 percent for passing, greater decision consistency should result from twelve trials than from eight or from eight items than from four.

The theory and technical advances associated with the reliability of scores from criterion-referenced measures have been developed and implemented slowly. For more advanced treatment of these topics and for additional computational illustrations, see Crocker and Algina (1986) and Kane and Brennan (1980).

SUMMARY PROPOSITIONS

1. Educational tests always yield less than perfectly consistent results because of content sampling errors, examinee performance errors, scoring errors, or administration errors.
2. The meaning of score consistency varies depending on the type of score interpretation: norm, criterion, or objectives referenced.
3. Test-score reliability can be defined as the correlation between scores on two equivalent forms of a test for a specified group of examinees.
4. Reliability can be defined theoretically as the proportion of observed-score variance due to true-score variance.
5. The reliability of scores for a given test may be affected by random error sources but not by sources of systematic errors.
6. Neither test–retest nor equivalent forms methods are practically useful for estimating the reliability of scores from a classroom test.
7. The Spearman–Brown prophecy formula is useful for estimating the reliability of scores from a lengthened or shortened test.
8. The Kuder–Richardson formulas yield estimates of score reliability from data on the variability of the test scores, variability of the item scores, and the number of test items.
9. Coefficient alpha may be used in place of the Kuder–Richardson formulas for estimating the reliability of scores from tests not scored dichotomously.
10. The more widely the items in a test vary in difficulty, the more seriously the Kuder–Richardson formula 21 may underestimate reliability.
11. The minimum acceptable level of score reliability is mainly a function of the intended use of the scores.
12. The standard error of measurement is an estimate of the general magnitude of errors, expressed in test-score units.
13. The standard error of measurement can be estimated by multiplying the standard deviation of the scores by the square root of a difference, which is 1 minus the reliability coefficient.
14. Longer tests composed of more discriminating items are likely to yield more reliable scores than shorter tests composed of less discriminating items.
15. Tests composed of homogeneous content are likely to produce more reliable scores than those containing heterogeneous content.
16. The more variable the scores obtained from a test, the higher their reliability is likely to be.
17. Scores obtained from groups heterogeneous in achievement are likely to be more reliable than those obtained from homogeneous groups.
18. Groups that are heterogeneous in testwiseness are likely to produce less reliable scores than homogeneous groups.
19. Internal consistency reliability coefficients are likely to be overestimates when the test is speeded.
20. The reliability of scores from criterion-referenced measures can be estimated appropriately with the methods used for norm-referenced measures.
21. It may be more important to estimate decision consistency than score reliability for tests used to make mastery decisions.
22. Percent of agreement and kappa are both methods of estimating decision consistency.
23. Decision consistency is affected by such factors as cutoff score location, homogeneity of score distribution, and test length.

QUESTIONS FOR STUDY AND DISCUSSION

1. Why might a set of scores be considered quite reliable for criterion-referenced purposes but low in reliability for norm-referenced purposes?

2. What misunderstandings are demonstrated by a person who states, "This test is not reliable"?

3. Why are systematic errors considered part of true-score variance rather than part of error-score variance?

4. How do systematic errors affect norm-referenced and criterion-referenced scores differently?

5. Why are stability estimates of reliability generally inappropriate for use with achievement tests?

6. What assumptions must be made when using the Spearman–Brown formula to estimate the reliability of scores from a shortened test?

7. What is the formula for computing the standard error of measurement for a set of T-scores?

8. How can the standard error of measurement be used to describe the error associated with a perfect score (100 percent) on a test?

9. Under what circumstances might the doubling in length of a 30-item test produce a decrease in score reliability?

10. How does the difficulty level of items affect the reliability of scores from a multiple-choice test?

11. Why are correlation-based reliability estimates less useful with scores from domain-referenced than norm-referenced tests?

12. What happens to the values of P_A and kappa when all examinees pass on both testing occasions?

6

Validity:
Interpretation and Use

There are good reasons why validity is such a misunderstood concept among both test users and test experts. As you will see, the meaning of this idea has evolved and continues to change slightly with each passing decade. Consequently, measurement specialists have been inconsistent in their use of the term, and many ideas have been proposed for bringing order to the confusion. Then, too, those who have a relatively incomplete understanding of *reliability* find it easy to confuse the two terms. Despite the potential for confusion, there is a need to understand the concept of validity because such understanding is itself the foundation for fair and proper use of tests and measurements of all kinds. All the precautions and special cares taken in the test development process, in the administration of tests, and in the reporting and interpretation of scores are intended to enhance validity. The main goal of this chapter is to describe the several facets of validity and the related principles that can be applied to ensure appropriate use of test scores.

THE MEANING OF VALIDITY

The term *validity*, when applied to a set of test scores, refers to the consistency (accuracy) with which the scores measure a particular cognitive ability of interest. Thus, there are two aspects to validity: what is measured and how consistently it is measured. The cognitive abilities referred to are abilities to perform observable tasks, abilities that require a command of substantive knowledge. The consistency of measurement refers to the reliability of the scores. Reliability is a necessary ingredient of validity, but it is not sufficient to ensure validity. Unless the test scores measure what the test user intends to measure, no matter how reliably, the scores will not be very valid. Thus, from this perspective, validity refers to the meaning of the scores obtained from a test administered to a certain group. Does a high score mean that the individual is particularly competent with respect to the knowledge the test is supposed to be measuring? Does a low score mean the examinee has little ability? What else might a high or low score mean?

Validity has traditionally been regarded as a test characteristic, but the most current thinking of measurement experts has changed that. The most recent *Standards for Educational and Psychological Testing* (American Psychological Association, 1985) associates the term with a set of test scores rather than with the test used to produce them. In particular, validity has to do with the meaning of the scores and the ways we use the scores to make decisions. We ask such questions as "How well do these scores reflect physics achievement?" or "How appropriate is it to use these math test scores to decide who should take algebra next year and who should not?" or "How appropriate is it to infer that high scorers on this certification test will be excellent teachers?" Here are some situations that illustrate a variety of validity concerns.

1. **The test is intended to measure higher-order thinking skills in earth science, but most items require only recall of facts, terms, and scientific principles.** It would be inappropriate to infer that high scorers can apply, solve problems, or interpret earth science information; the nature of the test items did not require the demonstration of such skills. The meaning of the scores is somewhat different from what the test developer intended. For what other purpose might these scores be more valid?

2. **The test is supposed to measure achievement of concepts and relationships associated with the democratic form of governance, but the questions require a very high level of reading skills and a highly developed vocabulary.** The meaning of the scores from this test is compromised by the "extra" verbal skills that are required. Low scorers may be poor readers rather than low social studies achievers. These scores are not a very good representation of the kinds of achievement the teacher expected to measure.

3. **The scores on the persuasive essay that was given as a final exam in ninth-grade English are used by the curriculum committee to assess the effectiveness of the curriculum in addressing writing mechanics—spelling, grammar, punctuation, and capitalization.** Unless "writing mechanics" was a scoring criterion for the essays, the scores will be influenced mainly by the amount and quality of evidence the writer offered to support the position taken. Even if writing mechanics was one of the scoring criteria, the scores will be "contaminated" by the other factors that were used to judge the quality of the essays. It is probably inappropriate to make curricular judgments about mechanics on the basis of these scores.

4. **Students noticed that the multiple-choice items of the reading test contained qualifiers (most, some, usually) in the keyed responses and absolutes (all, never, every) in most distracters.** This test was made easier than it was intended to be due to the idiosyncratic item-writing methods of the teacher. The scores may well measure testwiseness better than reading comprehension. Since

the scores may not have the meaning intended by the teacher, it would be inappropriate to decide how well pupils are progressing in reading on the basis of those scores.

   5.   **The test is a measure of word analysis skills—beginning sounds, ending sounds, and rhyming—but the teacher's enunciation and voice inflection help lead students to the correct answers.** The scores on this test may still be a measure of word–sound association skills, but their interpretation is complicated by the teacher's improper test-administration procedures. The value of the scores for their intended use—grouping for reading instruction—has been jeopardized because the meaning of the scores has been distorted.

   6.   **The directions on the math test indicated that "+" and "0" should be used to respond true or false; answers using "T" and "F" were scored as wrong, regardless of their correctness.** Obviously, the scores of those who failed to heed the directions will not be a measure of their mathematics achievement. Since it is unclear what the scores mean, it also is unclear how they should be used.

   These situations illustrate what validity is all about—the meaning of the scores we obtain from the administration of a particular test. There are many factors that can destroy or alter the meaning we had hoped to attach to a set of scores. Once the meaning of the scores has been distorted, the scores become less appropriate for their intended use. That scores are *more* or *less* distorted and *less* appropriate means that validity is a matter of degree. Scores are not absolutely valid or invalid for a particular use; such perfection is ordinarily not possible to achieve with the educational measures available to us. The burden is chiefly on the users of test scores to justify (1) their interpretations of a set of scores and (2) the appropriateness of their use of the scores. In either case, some form of tangible evidence is required to support the justifications.

EVIDENCE USED TO SUPPORT VALIDITY

The appropriateness of using test scores for making particular interpretations or decisions should be judged from evidence gathered and presented by the test user. There is a variety of evidence that might be presented to demonstrate the valid use of a set of scores, and most could be grouped into one of these categories: content related, criterion related, and construct related. *These are not types of validity, but types of validity evidence.* The content type is concerned with how well the test content represents the domain of abilities the user is trying to measure. The criterion type is concerned with relationships, usually represented by correlation coefficients, between the test scores and the scores on some criterion measure of relevant abilities. Finally, the construct type is concerned with the overall meaning of the scores, what the collection of responses to the individual items (total score) means as a psychological construct.

   It is convenient to discuss the three types of evidence separately, but doing so conveys the false impression that these are independent notions and that any one of them might be used, by itself, to support validity judgments. In fact, construct-related evidence incorporates the other two: both content- and criterion-related evidence are needed to support the meaning that should be attached to a particular set of scores.

The process of gathering evidence is called *validation*. The goals of validation are to provide evidence *for* a particular interpretation and *against* each of several other competing interpretations. That is, validation should show that the scores reflect the achievement of certain relevant skills and that they are not unduly influenced by certain irrelevant or extraneous skills or traits of the test takers. Furthermore, if the scores are to be used to make decisions (selection, placement, promotion, and so on) about examinees, validation should include the collection of evidence to support the appropriateness of each planned use. Note that the term "test validation" is just as imprecise as "test validity." Validation is of test scores and their use, *not* of instruments.

It is important to realize that the validation of scores can change over time as evidence changes or as the method of using scores changes. Suppose, for example, that Acme Industries hires secretaries partly on the basis of typing test scores obtained from all applicants. (The personnel department at Acme had determined several years ago that there was a correlation of 0.60 between typing scores and supervisor ratings of on-the-job typing speed and accuracy.) Today all Acme secretaries use microcomputers for word processing, and the keyboards and error-correction methods used are much different from those associated with the typewriter. In fact, if Acme continues to use its typing test, it will likely pass up some potentially excellent word-processing operators. Note that the meaning of the typing score has not changed, but the appropriateness of using it for selection has. Similar problems are encountered in using scores contained in school cumulative record folders or grades placed on college transcripts. As these data age, their meaningfulness for the present time changes and their value for making inferences about future performance may also change.

Content-related Validation Evidence

All test-score interpretations require that an inference be made. Tests usually contain only a sample of all possible items that could be used to measure the attainment of knowledge in the content area of interest. The score interpretations—whether norm referenced or criterion referenced—are based on the hypothetical universe of items, not just the sample used in the test. We *infer* that a student who answers correctly 75 percent of the items on a test would likely answer 75 percent of the items in the universe. For tests of school achievement, are such inferences appropriate? If we mean that 75 percent is a more accurate estimate than 80 or 70, for example, the inference is based on score reliability. On another different but similar set of items from that population, we would expect the student to answer about 75 percent of the items correctly.

However, another type of inference must be made that relates to another type of validation evidence. For example, with a written driver's license test, we want to infer that those who score higher on the test will be safer and more responsible drivers than those who score lower. To justify such inferences, the test content must be based on an explicit definition of "safe driving ability"—a delineation of the knowledge, skills, and understandings required for safe driving. A sample of some of the statements that might be offered to develop a safe driver definition are:

1. Distinguish the meanings of road signs of different colors.
2. Describe the function of a carburetor.
3. Describe the procedure for gaining control of a car that begins to skid on ice or snow.
4. Find the shortest distance between two cities using a highway map.
5. Identify the meaning associated with signs of varying geometric shapes.
6. Describe the procedures for changing a flat tire.

Some statements could be excluded from the definition because they represent useful skills, but skills not essential for safe driving. The even-numbered statements probably fit in this category. On the other hand, the definition likely would be considered incomplete without including statements such as "Differentiate between the meanings of solid and broken lines that define driving lanes." Once the definition has been made explicit, it is possible to compare test-item content with the definition to assess the relevance of the items. If the items have been written to match the domain definition precisely, the inferences we wish to make about safe and responsible driving can be highly valid. From this point of view, a major portion of the answer to the validity question is inherent in the test-development process. That is, content-related evidence is furnished simultaneously with test-development activities. The domain definition (boundaries of content to be included), judgments about the relevance of test items, and steps taken to achieve representativeness of content serve the dual purpose of guiding test development and documenting validation evidence.

Written documentation of the domain specifications, the nature of the test tasks, and the reasons for using those tasks provide intrinsic rational validity evidence (Ebel, 1983). The evidence is intrinsic because it is built into the test. It is rational "because it is derived from rational inferences about the kind of tasks that will measure the intended ability" (p. 7). When the test maker is also the test user, evidence for appropriate score use is built into the product; that is, both the specifications for test construction and the items themselves are necessary evidence for the validation process.

Most test makers, including teachers, aim to produce tests that demonstrate intrinsic rational validity evidence, but they seldom acknowledge this goal explicitly. They seldom regard the process of test construction as a process of validation; they seldom document in writing the reasons for particular decisions in test development. Useful written documentation to support intrinsic rational validity provides answers to these questions:

1. *About what set of abilities are inferences to be made?* As part of this description, it is sometimes useful to note certain extraneous abilities that should be excluded intentionally from the main ability of interest. For example, in tests of chemistry problem solving, reading ability should be minimized.

2. *What domain of knowledge, skills, or tasks provides a basis for such inferences?* A content outline that describes the tasks of interest is needed. The outline

should cover the entire universe of content to be measured, not just the content reflected by the specific test items that might be developed. Sometimes chapter headings in a text are a good starting point for defining the domain.

3. *What is the relative importance of the subdomains that comprise the domain definition?* Are there sets of related tasks that are more important than others? If so, the test development plan should reflect the differences so that more test items will be included for the more important subdomains. One subdomain might receive a weight of 10 percent, for example, while a more important one is assigned 25 percent.

4. *What kinds of test items have properties that will permit the testing of achievement of the domain elements?* For example, in view of the tasks outlined in step 2, are either essay or short-answer items more appropriate than multiple-choice items? Why?

5. *Do the test items adequately reflect the domain knowledge, skills, and tasks?* This question relates to the match between test-item content and the content specified in the domain outline. How well did the item writer translate the task descriptions into test items?

6. *Do the subsets of test items adequately represent the domain in terms of the relative importance of the subdomains?* Is the content weighting in the test consistent with the decisions made in step 3?

7. *What domain or subdomain, outside the domain of interest, is present in the test?* Are there extraneous factors that could interfere with the score interpretations the user wishes to make? Is reading ability, vocabulary level, or computational skill, beyond that intended, required to answer items correctly?

It may seem that intrinsic rational validity evidence is sufficient for the validation of achievement tests, but it is not. Such evidence focuses on the test—its domain, the relevance of its items, and the representativeness of its content. But as long as factors other than the test can influence the magnitude of the scores, evidence beyond test content is needed to support valid score interpretations. Content-related evidence alone is not sufficient because it fails to take into account response consistency (reliability) or other aspects of the testing environment that might impact score interpretation. For example, norm-referenced test items that fail to discriminate between high and low achievers may be content relevant and technically adequate. But such items will not help to produce a rank order of scores that will permit useful norm-referenced interpretations for selection or classification purposes. Because the test scores obtained will be somewhat low in reliability, they also will be deficient in terms of validity.

Content-related evidence for achievement tests also must be supplemented by information about the administration conditions, scoring criteria, and nature of examinees. Previous examples have shown how the test administrator can provide clues about correct and incorrect responses and how scoring rules can distort the meaning of scores. But, in addition to these factors, examinee characteristics other than achievement can cause scores to be higher or lower than they ought to be. For example, Messick (1989) lists these alternative explanations for low achievement-test scores: lack of sufficient knowledge, high anxiety, visual impairment, low level of motivation, limited English skills, and low level of concentration. Though low achievement may be the most plausible explanation for low scores, the burden is on the user to show that these other factors are not influencing the scores unduly. Such evidence is not to be found in the test; intrinsic rational validity evidence must be supplemented by information found in examinee responses, in the testing conditions, and in the scoring process.

We have long known that validity depends on the purposes for which test scores are used, the group with which the test is used, and the circumstances under which the test is used. Validity depends on more than the quality of the test. The responsibility of the test developer is to be as clear as possible about what is being measured and to produce a test that measures as accurately as possible. The responsibility of the test user is to make valid decisions using the test scores and all other available, relevant information, including documentation furnished by the test developer.

Criterion-related Validation Evidence

A criterion measure is an accepted standard against which some test is compared to validate the use of the test as a predictor. For example, scores on a dictation test are a generally accepted measure of spelling achievement. If we were to build and give a true–false spelling test, we might compare the true–false scores with scores obtained on a comparable dictation test to demonstrate that the true–false test is an acceptable measure of spelling achievement. The dictation test is the standard used for comparison in trying to establish the legitimacy of the new spelling test.

Criterion-related evidence takes either of two forms: one relates to determining present standing on a criterion measure and the other relates to predicting future performance on a criterion measure. The type of evidence needed for a given situation depends on how the scores from the test in question are intended to be used. For example, the true–false spelling test referred to above was intended to be used instead of the dictation test because of the increased efficiency in scoring afforded by the true–false test. *Concurrent* evidence would be useful to show that students appear in the same relative rank order on the two measures. A correlation coefficient of 0.80, for example, might be regarded as acceptable concurrent evidence.

When test scores are used to select individuals for admission, employment, extraordinary education opportunity, and the like, *predictive* evidence is needed. There is a need to show that a positive relationship exists between scores on the test (the predictor) and scores on some acceptable measure of future performance (the criterion). For example, a developmental screening-test score might be used to predict which five-year-olds are likely to succeed in kindergarten. If the criterion measure for "success" is "teacher's rating of social, emotional, and academic development at the end of kindergarten," the essential validity evidence might include the correlation between screening-test scores and teacher's ratings. If a correlation of, say, 0.60 is obtained, we might conclude that the test is a useful predictor of future performance; that is, there is support for using the scores to predict success in kindergarten.

The correlation between test and criterion scores has been regarded by many as the best kind of evidence to support valid achievement-test use. The correlation seems to provide an independent, objective validation of the subjective judgments and decisions that must be made during test development. But the validity of the scores from widely used tests of academic achievement has seldom been supported with impressive criterion-related evidence. This could mean that the tests are simply poor tests. But a more plausible explanation is that how well a test measures what it is intended to measure cannot be conveyed by the correlation between test scores and scores on the criterion measure. Why might this be so?

In some cases appropriate criterion measures are simply unavailable. What should be used as a criterion measure for a test of ability in fifth-grade arithmetic or a test of ability to understand contemporary affairs? The tests themselves are usually intended to be the best measures of these abilities that can be devised. If better measures were available to serve the role of criterion, they also should be more valid than the test under validation. That many test developers have failed to present convincing empirical evidence of the validity of the scores from their tests is not for want of concern, effort, or skill. It is because correlational evidence for the validity of scores from most achievement tests is essentially unproducible. The same can be said of scores obtained from most professional licensure examinations (Kane, 1982).

In many cases, appropriate criteria turn out to be difficult or nearly impossible to measure accurately. On-the-job performance ought to be an appropriate criterion for an employee selection test. But for any except the simplest jobs, what constitutes satisfactory performance is hard to define, expensive to assess, and difficult to measure impartially. The relevance of performance ratings as criteria for the validity of a written test is open to question, also. A written test cannot possibly measure many of the characteristics that contribute to high ratings for job performance. Such a test, however, can measure desirable characteristics that are unlikely to show up clearly on a performance rating. In situations like these, there is little justification for presenting evidence on correlation with a criterion as the *primary* evidence of validity.

A major problem with empirical test validation is the imperfect or uncertain validity of the criterion scores. Criterion scores themselves should be highly valid measures of the ability being tested. This also means the criterion scores should be quite reliable, and their reliability coefficient should be included as validity evidence. After all, a standard used for judging the validity of test scores certainly ought to be *at least* as valid as the scores being judged against that standard. The validity of the scores from the criterion measure needs to be addressed as rigorously and as thoroughly as the validity of the test scores in question.

Correlation procedures hold little promise for providing the main evidence of validity, but they may be useful in providing secondary, confirming evidence. If ability A is related in some degree to abilities B, C, and D, then scores from a test of A should correlate to some degree with scores from B, C, and D. If they do, the confidence that test A measures ability A is increased.

It is important to note that such secondary evidence of validity cannot take the place of content-related validity evidence. What test A measures is determined mostly by the tasks included in it. One cannot discover what test A measures only by studying the correlation of scores from test A with scores from tests B, C, and D. How do we know what these other tests measure? We would need to examine the tasks included in them, the conditions under which they were administered, the nature of the examinees, and the procedures for scoring. If these are the bases for the meaning of scores from tests B, C, and D, should they not be the bases for the meaning of scores from test A as well?

Concurrent and predictive evidence both require correlational data and, consequently, both situations are plagued by the problem of obtaining an appropriate criterion measure. The prediction of college freshman grade-point average using ACT scores illustrates the dilemma. Both measures reflect the ability to do college-level work, but certainly the criterion measure, grade-point average, is influenced by many other important factors—nature of the coursework, student effort and motivation, grading policies in the courses, and ability to establish supportive social relationships among peers. And the criterion measure will represent achievement in English, mathematics, and science only to the extent that coursework in those areas was taken by each student in the validation sample. Correlations between ACT composite scores and freshman end of year grade-point averages tend to be about 0.50. There is much these two measures do not have in common. Can a more satisfactory criterion be identified, one that is practical to implement and fair to students regardless of the pattern of courses taken in their first year? The criterion problem demonstrates the need for additional validity evidence to supplement the information supplied by correlational evidence, which itself is based on criteria of questionable validity. A variety of evidence, all pointing to the same conclusion about score validity, is the most convincing justification for test score use.

Construct-related Validation Evidence

The term *construct* refers to a psychological construct, a theoretical conceptualization about an aspect of human behavior that cannot be measured or observed directly. Examples of constructs are intelligence, achievement motivation, anxiety, achievement, attitude, dominance, and reading comprehension. Construct validation is the process of gathering evidence to support the contention that a given test indeed measures the psychological construct the makers intend for it to measure. The goal is to determine the meaning of the scores from the test, to assure that the scores mean what we expect them to mean.

If our purpose is to measure mathematics problem-solving achievement, for example, the goal of construct validation is to garner evidence that will show that the tasks in the test require math problem-solving ability. The definition of the construct that was used for test development defines the construct. In this case, if the definition indicates that all four arithmetic operations may be included and that all problems should require at least two steps for solution, then each test item will need to be reviewed for compliance. Since *neither* reading comprehension nor math computation is to be measured (they are separate constructs), our validation should include evidence that these constructs have no appreciable impact on the magnitude of the scores. Judgments by reviewers and correlations between problem-solving scores and (1) reading scores and (2) computation scores would be useful evidence. Score reliability evidence would be needed to show that random errors due to examinee characteristics or to administration conditions were not too influential in the scores. In addition, the scoring criteria should be reviewed to determine their appropriateness, and the scoring key should be reviewed to check its accuracy. It should be clear from this illustration that construct-related evidence incorporates a variety of content-related and criterion-related evidence because the meaning of a set of scores is related to both.

The main threats to construct validity have been referred to by Messick (1989) as construct underrepresentation and irrelevant test variance. The idea of underrepresentation means that some of the skills, or certain aspects of the ability (the construct), are not being measured thoroughly by the test. If our problem-solving test *should* have some problems that require *both* addition and multiplication, but there are none, the test "underrepresents" the problem-solving domain we defined. The idea of irrelevant test variance means that extraneous factors, other than the construct, are causing scores to be different from what they ought to be. Many of the variables that contribute to low reliability fall in this category. Some of these factors make the test easier than it should be—testwiseness, guessing, clues in the items, implausible wrong answers—and some factors make the test more difficult than it should be—need for well-developed reading or writing skills, fine visual acuity, garbled speech by the test administrator, anxiety due to unreasonable expectations. In the problem-solving example, irrelevant test variance could be introduced by the difficulty of computations required, the use of novel problem settings that require unique prior knowledge, severe time limits, or ambiguous item wording.

Concern for construct validity is at the heart of such questions as "Why did this student score so high on this test?" or "Why were all of the scores so low?" These questions raise doubts about whether the scores are measures of the construct the test maker had in mind or whether extraneous factors have overstated or underrepresented true achievement. Questions of construct validation have not always been raised with scores from achievement tests. But clearly they should be. The *meaning* of the scores from any test should be established before the scores are used to make decisions about examinees. Then questions of valid *use* are appropriate to raise, and evidence for the proposed uses should be gathered.

As originally conceived, construct validity was concerned with the validity of a hypothetical construct purportedly measured by a particular test (Cronbach and Meehl, 1955). The idea was applied primarily to psychological variables or personality inventories rather than to achievement tests. The methods employed were, and still are, intended to show that the construct under investigation is related in predictable ways to other constructs, as explained by some theory. Some of these methods and their uses are explained and illustrated by Messick (1989) in his comprehensive treatment of validity.

Questions about construct validity have always been posed when there appeared to be a discrepancy between what a test was supposed to measure and what it seemed to measure. Is this a test of understanding of scientific principles, as the title suggests, or is it really an intelligence test? Is that a test of intelligence or is it really a measure of verbal facility? Some test makers name their tests and describe what their tests are measuring, not in terms of the tasks they include, but in terms of the traits they presumably measure. That is why we have tests of rigidity, intelligence, persistence, creativity, tolerance, spatial relations, and many other traits. For tests like these, the question of whether the test really measures what it claims to measure does arise, as it should. Does the task of completing a figure analogy measure intelligence? Does ability to list unconventional uses for a brick measure creativity?

APPLYING VALIDITY PRINCIPLES

Two illustrations of the validation process will be presented to show how various instruments and various uses may require different kinds of validity evidence. In each case it is assumed that the instruments were developed in accord with generally accepted measurement principles, but the quality or success of that work needs to be examined through validation.

Kindergarten Readiness Test

Standardized achievement tests are available for use with kindergarten pupils to determine how well they have attained the academic skills taught in their kindergarten program. Some schools use the scores from a spring administration to determine which pupils should be promoted, which should be retained, and which should be placed in a transitional kindergarten program the next year. Is it appropriate to use such scores to make these kinds of placement decisions? How valid are the scores for this purpose? What do these scores mean?

Frisbie and Andrews (1990) set out to gather evidence related to the latter question by observing the administration of the *Iowa Tests of Basic Skills* in nearly 50 classrooms. The purpose was to observe teacher and pupil behavior during test administration to determine whether irrelevant sources of test variance might compromise the meaning of the scores. That is, if pupils called out answers, if pupils copied from one another, if some pupils burst into tears or became ill, if teachers provided hints, or if teachers read items improperly, then the scores would not be very meaningful indicators of achievement. If high scores or low scores could be explained mostly by factors other than skill attainment, the scores would not be useful for *any* purpose. Conclusions from this study were that (1) teachers and pupils had little difficulty using the test materials, (2) teachers were able to provide an atmosphere conducive to good test taking, (3) pupils who were properly supervised could provide useful responses, and (4) teachers nearly always followed published directions. In sum, it was determined that the readiness scores of groups of pupils can be very meaningful, but the scores of selected individuals might be questionable.

In view of these findings, if convincing content-related evidence for the readiness test scores were also available (that is, evidence in support of intrinsic rational validity), then the meaning of the scores from the readiness test would likely be viewed as acceptable. However, the second question, the one regarding use, has not yet been addressed. What can be done to show that it is or is not appropriate to make first-grade placement decisions with the readiness scores? Since placement into first grade is the typical direct path from kindergarten, the test user must demonstrate that low scorers would benefit more from retention (in a particular program) than from normal promotion. If this evidence were to be gathered empirically, some low-scoring kindergarten pupils would need to be retained (before evidence in favor of retention is in hand) so that the outcomes could be observed. Unfortunately, this has been the scenario in some school districts. That is, some pupils have been retained without ample evidence that benefits will be derived for the child. In many instances, the second question has been addressed on theoretical and practical grounds. Most often the conclusion has been that deficiencies in skills covered by a readiness test can be overcome, even in the short run, through intensive instructional engagement. It should not take a year to remediate pupils with low scores unless physical, emotional, or intellectual disabilities are implicated.

This validation example illustrates the need to separate the questions of "meaning" and "use" to gather evidence. It further demonstrates that validation is more than gathering judgments and numbers; it usually requires a logical analysis of the relationship between several constructs.

Driver's License Written Test

Usually, the scores from a written examination, a performance test, and a vision-screening exam are used in combination to decide who is eligible to obtain an automobile driver's license. The primary purpose of licensing drivers is to protect the public from those who might endanger the life and property of others through unsafe use of a motor vehicle. For the written test, the validity question is: "How appropriate is it to infer that high scorers will be safer, more responsible drivers than low scorers?" What do the scores mean? What kind of evidence would support the intended use of the scores for classification purposes? (Another relevant question that we will not deal with at this time is the basis for choosing a particular passing score.)

The validation process might begin by examining (1) the definition of "safe driving ability" established by the test builders and (2) the elements of the domain of relevant knowledge the definition encompasses. Then the relevance of the test items can be assessed by matching item content with domain definition. Items that require examinees to explain how to control a skidding car or to tell the meaning of road signs of various shapes or colors would probably be judged relevant. Items that require examinees to describe how a carburetor works or to find distances on a map are likely to be judged irrelevant. If no items deal with the differing meanings of solid and broken lines that define road lanes, the construct domain might be considered underrepresented. If most items deal with facts about laws to the exclusion of making judgments in certain driving situations, the representativeness of the content might be questioned.

Next the technical adequacy of the test items might be reviewed to determine how well the items help achieve the purpose of distinguishing safe and unsafe drivers. Readability should be assessed to determine if the vocabulary is too advanced or if the syntax is too complex. (Safe drivers need not be able to read English prose.) The keyed response should be checked for correctness and (for multiple-choice items) the plausibility of wrong answers should be considered. Test instructions, instructions to examinees about coding or making responses, and information provided to examinees about scoring (including whether to guess) should be checked for clarity and completeness.

The test administration and scoring conditions should be reviewed to determine if threats to the valid meaning of the scores have been controlled. Is supervision sufficient to prevent cheating by the examinees? If a computer terminal is used to present items, is ample instruction provided and is there provision for returning to an item to reconsider or change a response? If clerical hand scoring is done, are there procedures in place to check the accuracy of scoring? Estimates of score reliability provide some evidence about the influence of random errors from administration and scoring. (Is it clear that decision-consistency information is important here, too?)

What kind of criterion-related evidence should be gathered to support the use of the written test for licensing drivers? Is the performance test a useful concurrent criterion measure? It probably is not, because the driving test requires more than knowledge of the law and rules of the road. Performance behind the wheel also requires psychomotor abilities, abilities to see and to judge speed and distance, and mental alertness and concentration. There probably is no existing standard against which the quality of a written driver's test can be judged. Predictive evidence might be gathered if a suitable criterion for safe driving in the future could be determined. For example, if the scores on the test correlate 0.10 with number of traffic citations during the first 5 years after receiving a license, how germane is such evidence? Would number of accidents be a suitable criterion? How about number of accident-free hours of driving? The problem of deciding on a suitable criterion suggests that criterion-related evidence is not likely to have major weight in deciding how appropriate the written test scores are for making licensure decisions.

This validation illustration shows how important intrinsic rational validity evidence is for achievement tests and how documentation of that evidence during test development should expedite validation. It also demonstrates that content-related evidence alone is insufficient for making judgments about validity.

SUMMARY PROPOSITIONS

1. Validity is a property of a set of test scores rather than a property of a test instrument.
2. Valid test use requires good tests, those that conform to a clear specification of test content and yield highly reliable scores.
3. What a test of abilities measures is defined more clearly by the tasks it requires than by the name of the trait it is supposed to measure.
4. Evidence of valid use of tests of cognitive abilities is inherent in the test construction process, in the definition of the abilities, and in the rationales for including each of the test tasks.
5. Intrinsic rational validity evidence is needed, but is not sufficient by itself to establish the validity of achievement scores.
6. The value of criterion-related evidence for validity is highly dependent on the quality (validity) of the criterion measure.
7. The value of correlational evidence to support the valid use of a set of achievement scores is secondary to the value of direct judgmental evidence.
8. No adequate criterion measure exists with which to compare achievement tests for the purpose of providing evidence of valid score use.
9. Construct-related evidence focuses on how well the items represent all dimensions of the relevant domain and how well irrelevant factors are excluded from the measurements.
10. Construct-related evidence necessarily includes, but is not limited to, content-related and criterion-related evidence.

QUESTIONS FOR STUDY AND DISCUSSION

1. What misunderstandings are demonstrated by a person who states, "This is a valid test."?

2. Under what circumstances might a set of scores be considered quite reliable but not very valid?

3. What kinds of things could happen during the administration or scoring of an objective test that would probably reduce the validity of the resulting scores?

4. Why is intrinsic rational validity not enough to support the usefulness of scores from a classroom test to be used for grading?

5. How is the idea of construct underrepresentation accounted for by the process of documenting intrinsic rational validity evidence?

6. What specific student characteristics does high school grade-point average probably measure?

7. Why might a supervisor's ratings *not* be a useful criterion for measuring employee performance quality?

7

Achievement Test Planning

ESTABLISHING THE PURPOSE FOR TESTING

The stages of the test-development process begin with describing the purpose for testing. Why are we testing? What do we intend to measure? How will the test scores be used, or what kinds of score interpretations do we want to make? These are important questions to answer, but too often they are not answered prior to the item-writing phase. This is unfortunate because the answers lay the foundation for subsequent decision making as test-development or test-selection activities proceed.

A good test rarely serves multiple purposes equally well. Tests designed mainly to measure achievement precisely probably also are motivating to students and may be instructional as well. However, tests designed primarily to motivate students to study or to serve as learning devices are not likely to be good summative assessments of student learning. Most teacher-made tests are intended to provide precise measures of achievement that can be used to provide feedback to students and to report progress to their parents. And this should be their primary function.

A significant aspect of establishing the purpose for testing is deciding how the scores should be interpreted. What referent will be used to obtain meaning from the scores? Content? Scores of a norm group? Statements of objectives? For classroom testing purposes, the answer should be tied closely to the grading (reporting) system—to the referent used to give meaning to the quarterly or semester grades. For statewide competency testing, the scores are likely to be referenced to the content domain from which the test was developed. For personnel selection that is based on hiring the most qualified of those who are at least minimally qualified, norm-referenced interpretations probably are needed. And, finally, testing for professional certification or licensure probably requires criterion-referenced interpretations.

The implications of the decision about the type of score interpretation needed will become more apparent as we consider the separate aspects of test construction. The goal at each stage of construction is to do the things that will help to yield a distribution of the most valid scores, a distribution that has the characteristics that make possible the type of interpretations we had planned to make.

ALTERNATIVE TYPES OF TEST TASKS

The most commonly used types of tests are the essay, the objective (including short answer), and the mathematical problem type. Performance tests and oral examinations both are less common perhaps, but where they are used, the circumstances often favor their use over the other types. This section is devoted to a brief comparison of the characteristics of these various test types and to a description of the relative merits of each in situations where a choice is feasible.

Essay, Objective, and Numerical Problem

First, some common misconceptions need to be addressed. It is not true that luck is a large element in scores on one type and nearly or totally absent in another. On the contrary, all types can be written to require much the same kind and level of ability and, if handled carefully, can yield results of satisfactory reliability and validity (Coffman, 1966; Dressel, 1978). A good essay test or a good objective test can be constructed so that it will rank a group of students in nearly the same order as that resulting from a good problem test. But this is not to say that the various types can be used interchangeably with equal ease and effectiveness. (See Birenbaum and Tatsuoka, 1987, for an example in the area of diagnosing learner difficulties.)

Both essay and problem tests are less time consuming to prepare than objective tests. But the objective test generally can be scored more rapidly and more reliably than either of the other types, particularly the essay test. Where very large groups of students must be tested, the use of objective tests permits greater efficiency with no appreciable sacrifice in validity. But where classes are small, the efficiency is in the opposite direction, and essay or problem tests often are preferred.

The numerical problem type has the apparent advantage of greater intrinsic relevance—of greater identity with on-the-job requirements—than either of the other types. It is sometimes claimed that ability to choose an answer is different from, and less significant than, ability to produce an answer. But most of the evidence indicates that these abilities are highly related (Ward, 1982; Sax and Collet, 1968).

Because of the length and complexity of the answers they require, and because the answers must be written by hand, neither essay nor problem type tests can sample the content domain as comprehensively as an objective test. Writing is a much slower process than reading.

With objective tests and problem tests there is usually a good deal more objectivity, particularly in scoring, than with essay tests. The student usually has a more definitive task, and the reasons for giving or withholding credit are more obvious to all concerned. It is important to realize, however, that even the objective test is based on many subjective decisions as to what to test and how to test it. For the problem test there is the additional element of subjectivity in scoring that is not present in the objective test. How much credit to give for an imperfect answer and which elements to consider in judging degree of perfection are often spur of the moment, subjective decisions. In considering the relative merits of essay, problem, and objective tests, it is important to remember that *the only useful component of any test score is the objectively verifiable component of it*. To the degree that a test score reflects the private, subjective, unverifiable impressions and values of one particular scorer, the score is deficient in meaning, and hence in usefulness, to the student who received it or to anyone else who is interested in using it.

Whichever type examiners decide to use, they should strive to make their measurements as objective as possible. A measurement is objective to the extent that it can be verified independently by other competent measurers. It is conceivable that measurements obtained from a good essay test could be more objective in this sense than measurements obtained from a poor multiple-choice test. But it is fair to say that those who use essay tests tend to worry less about the objectivity of their measurements than those who use multiple-choice tests.

Most teachers probably choose the types of test items that seem most useful to them or that they feel most competent to use effectively. However, it is possible that force of habit or misconceptions prevent some teachers from trying other types that could prove more advantageous to them. The classroom testing practices of many school and college faculties probably could be improved by a periodic review of the types of tests being used.

Performance: Process and Product

For some instructional objectives, the most relevant tools of performance assessment require students to demonstrate their achievement through means other than paper and pencil. These situations frequently involve skill learning that contains one or more psychomotor components. Performance tests can be used to determine if students can apply the knowledge and skills they have practiced and learned. Methods of performance testing can be categorized broadly as identification tasks, work products, and simulations.

Identification tests may require students to name objects, differentiate between objects given their names, or identify objects according to their function or their relationship to other objects. Which of these rocks is limestone? or granite? or agate? Given a skeleton, what is the name of this bone? Where do the pectoral muscles connect? For what purposes is this saw (point to a coping saw) more useful than this one (point to a hack saw)? Which of these needles is most appropriate for administering a subcutaneous injection to a three-year-old?

Work-product tests can be used to evaluate procedures involved in accomplishing a task or to determine the quality of a product. Teachers can evaluate drawings and collages in art, button holes and souffles in home economics, tuned-up engines and table lamps in technical education, and penmanship or paragraph cohesiveness in language arts. In each case the goal is summative evaluation, even if observations of process are made as the student progresses toward completion of the project.

Simulations, the most common form of performance testing, are contrived situations established for the purpose of observing student behavior, assessing speed, accuracy, and quality of work, or determining if an appropriate outcome is achieved. Dance instructors watch their students do the swing or polka, music teachers listen for proper notes and cadence, and psychologists watch and listen to their counseling students in role-playing situations. Those who have been certified in CPR are aware that timing, position, and know-how are important, but the outcome is of paramount importance.

Performance tests can serve unique evaluation purposes, but they also present some unique measurement problems. Unless each student performs the same identification tasks and simulations or prepares the same work product, the tasks may not be comparable. Hence, the scores derived from them may not be comparable. Great care must be exercised by the test developer to ensure equivalent testing for all students in the class if scores are to be comparable. The scoring of performance tests tends to be quite subjective, even when an explicit grading guide is prepared. Identification tests and simulations are time consuming to prepare and administer, especially to large groups. On the whole, performance tests tend to be less efficient than objective tests. In many situations the validity of simulations is highly questionable; the most realistic simulations tend to be the most costly to develop and administer. Even when simulation scores yield high reliability, their cost is likely to be greater than their benefit. Despite these shortcomings, there are many circumstances under which performance testing is the only reasonable means of measurement. Guidelines for developing performance assessment tools to yield highly valid results have been detailed by Stiggins (1987). In addition, Chapter 14 describes methods of using checklists and rating scales, both of which are used prominently in performance assessment.

TEST SPECIFICATIONS

Once the purpose for testing has been established, the next step to ensuring that highly valid scores will be obtained is to develop a test plan. The procedures enumerated for addressing intrinsic rational validity should be followed here: describe the abilities of interest and the domain of knowledge and skills to be tapped, decide on the relative importance of the various subdomains, and decide which types of items will best require the demonstration of relevant knowledge. The firmest basis for the construction of such a test is a set of explicit specifications that indicate the following:

1. Types of test items to be used
2. Number of items of each type needed
3. Kinds of tasks the items will present

4. Number of tasks of each kind needed
5. Descriptions of content areas to be sampled
6. Number of items from each area needed
7. Level and distribution of the difficulty of the items

Test specifications of this kind are useful for several reasons: (1) they guide the work of the test constructor, (2) they can inform examinees about expectations and how they might prepare themselves, (3) they provide information to others who may want to select the test for their own particular use, and (4) they provide documentation as evidence for judging the validity of the scores obtained. (But since test specifications furnish a *plan* for test development, the surest basis for judging the usefulness of a test, or the validity of its scores, is an examination of the test items themselves.)

Defining Content Domains

How specifically must the content to be measured by a test be described? The answer to this important question relates most directly and depends most heavily on the type of score interpretation the user wishes to make. Obviously, we need to list the explicit instructional objectives of interest if our goal is to make objectives-referenced interpretations. When our goal is norm-referenced interpretation, the content domain can be defined more generally, but still the boundaries need to be identified. In many cases, the content of certain book chapters, articles, novels, study guides, or other instructional materials set the limits for eligible item content. When our need is to estimate how much of the content domain has been learned, the separate elements that comprise that domain need to be described. This is the case when domain-referenced interpretations are desired.

Figure 7–1 shows the type of domain specifications that might be provided for each of these kinds of score interpretations. If our primary purpose was to obtain norm-referenced scores, for example, the boundaries of permissible content could be described somewhat loosely. If two individuals, both familiar with the instructional program, were to build tests independently based on the description provided, two quite different tests could emerge. Furthermore, if written instructional materials were not available, a content outline developed by the teacher would be needed to establish the content limits (breadth and depth) of the test items.

Content specifications for domain-referenced testing must be explicit because the goal is to estimate how many of the identifiable pieces of the domain are held by, known by, or controlled by each examinee. In most cases the domain will be large enough that only a sample of the elements can be tested at one time. If a genuine, representative sample is to be obtained, the individual elements must be listed or described in such a way that their selection is possible. The illustration in Figure 7–1 has been abbreviated to conserve space, but the entire domain could be described by the 27 propositions listed in Appendix B.

Finally, the specifications for objectives-referenced tests are simply a listing of the instructional objectives of interest. Each objective is considered a content domain by itself, several items will be written to measure achievement of

A. Norm-Referenced

The content domain of interest is physical fitness as described by Chapter 11 of the health text. The main areas are:

1. Exercise and its benefits
2. Designing an exercise program
3. The role of sleep in good health

B. Domain-Referenced

The content domain of interest is physical fitness as defined by a separate list of 27 propositions related to exercise, exercise programs, and the contribution of sleep. Here are three sample propositions, one from each subdomain, from the full domain listing (Appendix B):

1. Exercise can improve blood vessel capacity and increase heart strength and lung capacity.
2. The benefits of aerobic exercise require a minimum of three 20-minute sessions weekly.
3. The sleep cycle can be affected negatively by poor body position, too much light, or too much noise.

C. Objectives-Referenced

The content domains of interest are these instructional objectives about physical fitness (Appendix C):

1. Distinguish the purposes and features of aerobic and anaerobic exercising.
2. Describe how nutrition and exercise jointly affect body weight.
3. Estimate the relative amounts of sleep required by individuals who vary in age, activity level, and general health condition.

Figure 7-1. Sample Content Domain Definitions for Three Types of Score Interpretations

each separate objective, and a score will be reported for each instructional objective. The three objectives in part C of Figure 7–1 are taken from Appendix C to illustrate the contrasting requirements for the domain definition. Note that when objectives-referenced interpretations are needed, as opposed to domain-referenced, no sampling of elements occurs and no inferences about content need to be made in score interpretation. With objectives-referenced situations, all the skills or knowledge of interest are tested, and consequently no estimates are made about untested knowledge or skill the examinees may possess.

Tables of Specifications

One of the devices often used to outline the content coverage of a test, as part of the test specifications, is a two-way grid, sometimes called a *test blueprint* or a *table of specifications*. The several major areas of content to be covered by the test are assigned to the several columns of the grid. The several major kinds of abilities to be developed are assigned to the rows. Each item may then be classified in one of the cells of the grid. Various numbers of items are assigned to each of the rows and columns. Knowing the proportion of items specified for a particular row and for a particular column, one can determine the proportion of items appropriate for the cell formed by that row and that column.

The sample table of specifications in Table 7–1 is for a 40-item norm-

Table 7-1. Table of Specifications for a 40-Item Test on Score Reliability

ABILITIES	CONTENT AREAS					
	Definition	Error Types	Methods	Factors	Interpret	TOTAL
Terms	4	2	4	0	2	12
Factual information	2	1	2	1	0	6
Explanations	2	3	1	2	0	8
Predictions	0	1	1	3	1	6
Recommended action	0	0	1	3	4	8
TOTAL	8	7	9	9	7	40

referenced test covering five aspects of reliability: definition, types of errors, methods for estimating, factors influencing, and interpretation of coefficients. The types of abilities examinees are expected to demonstrate are described using categories of Ebel's Relevance Guide. The table tells us, among other things, that (1) three items should require explanation regarding types of error, (2) the five content areas are similar in relative importance, and (3) 22 of the 40 items should require ability more complex than simply identifying or describing terms.

The two-way grid is a good first step toward providing balance in a test, but certain circumstances may warrant modifications. For some tests, for example, a one-dimensional classification scheme may be entirely adequate. When instructional objectives form the content base, the content dimension and the ability dimension are both present in each statement. The table of specifications in Table 7–2 depicts such a situation for a domain-referenced test. The objectives noted here are those found in Appendix C. Though each of the three content areas contains five instructional objectives, the projected composition of the test is approximately $\frac{1}{4}$, $\frac{1}{4}$, and $\frac{1}{2}$. Because some instructional objectives are compound statements, the number of separate objectives is 7, 7, and 12 for a total of 26. (For example, objective 13 actually consists of six separate objectives.) The percentages shown in the table are based on 26 separate statements, each considered to be equally important. How to apply differential weighting to these categories will be described shortly.

Categories of Ebel's Relevance Guide were used to describe the abilities dimension in Table 7–1 because Ebel's terms give an operational indication of the type of ability required. The various levels of Bloom's taxonomy are less useful because the meanings of Bloom's categories are more susceptible to misclassification or to classification disagreement among judges than are Ebel's. Alter-

Table 7-2. Table of Specifications for a Domain-referenced Test

Instructional Objectives	Content Areas	Percentage of Items
$O_1 - O_5$	Exercise	27
$O_6 - O_{10}$	Exercise programs	27
$O_{11} - O_{15}$	Rest and sleep	46

nately, in situations where affective or psychomotor objectives are to be evaluated, categories of those taxonomies are appropriate to use to describe the abilities dimension. Regardless of the classification system employed, all categories of the chosen system will not necessarily be used for a particular test. Also, there is no basis for presuming that each cell appearing in a table of specifications must be used. Which categories of Ebel's Relevance Guide have been omitted from the plan in Table 7–1? How many items related to definition will require recommended action? (Does this make sense?)

The table of specifications provides a snapshot of the range of content to be tested and it indicates the relative emphasis to be allocated to subtopics. What factors should the test planner consider in determining the percentage of test content (total points or total items) to be represented by each content area? In the absence of instructional objectives, the relative emphasis of the content areas can be gauged by considering these factors:

1. *Amount of content contained.* An area formed by eight propositions probably should have twice the weight of an area comprised of only four propositions.

2. *Amount of instructional time devoted.* A topic to which six class sessions were devoted probably should have three times the weight of a topic that required only two class sessions.

3. *Role as a future prerequisite.* If an area is regarded as essential background for a subsequent instructional unit, it may be deemed more important, and deserving more weight, than an area that is not a prerequisite.

4. *Other opportunities to evaluate.* When a content area might be evaluated again, as on a comprehensive final exam, it might be weighted less than an equally important area that will not be tested again. This might occur, for example, when a topic is tested by essay on a midterm exam but the final exam must be entirely objective items, for practical reasons.

5. *Need for subtest scores.* When scores are needed for subtopics, content within subtopics must be weighted to ensure content representativeness of the subtests. In essence, this means designing a mini table of specifications for each content area for which a score will be reported.

The percentages in a table of specifications should be thought of as the percent of test points to be allocated rather than test items to be used. This is especially important when more than one type of item is to be used and the maximum point value can vary among items. For example, a short-answer item requiring a definition may be worth 1 point, but another short-answer item that requires a list of three pieces of information might have a maximum score of 3 points. They represent 25 and 75 percent, respectively, of a two-item test in terms of the score points each makes available.

To guide test construction effectively and to inform prospective examinees adequately, the test specifications need to be fairly detailed. To answer the question "How detailed?" we might pose another question: If they were followed exactly by a competent item writer, would they be likely to produce an acceptable test? Obviously, specifications should be detailed enough to indicate what kinds of items should be written on what general areas of learning, but they should not be so detailed as to give away the actual questions that will appear on the test.

ITEM FORMAT SELECTION

With content specifications in hand, the test developer's next decision relates to the types of items to be used. When instructional objectives form the content base, the verb used in each statement supplies a strict standard for the type of item to consider or reject. Words like describe, design, graph, develop, and explain require some form of production on the part of the examinee, activity that cannot be demonstrated by multiple choice, true–false, or other objective-item types. Often the ideal measurement procedure must be compromised because of practical considerations, as when an objective, machine-scorable test is used instead of a writing sample to measure writing abilities. The trade-offs associated with essay, objective, and problem-type tests will be examined further to reveal the relative merits of each.

Comparison of Essay and Objective Formats

The following statements summarize some of the similarities and differences of essay and objective tests.

1. Either an essay or an objective test can be used to measure almost any important educational achievement that any paper and pencil test can measure.
2. Either an essay or an objective test can be used to encourage students to study for understanding of principles, organization and integration of ideas, and application of knowledge to the solution of problems.
3. The use of either type necessarily involves the exercise of subjective judgment.
4. The value of scores from either type of test is dependent on their objectivity and reliability.
5. An essay-test question requires students to plan their own answers and to express them in their own words. An objective-test item requires examinees to choose among several designated alternatives.
6. An essay test consists of relatively few, more general questions that call for rather extended answers. An objective test ordinarily consists of many rather specific questions requiring only brief answers.
7. Students spend most of their time in thinking and writing when taking an essay test. They spend most of their time reading and thinking when taking an objective test.
8. The quality of an objective test is determined largely by the skill of the test constructor. The quality of an essay test is determined largely by the skill of the test scorer.
9. An essay examination is relatively easy to prepare but rather tedious and difficult to score accurately. A good objective examination is relatively tedious and difficult to prepare but comparatively easy to score.
10. An essay examination affords students much freedom to express their individuality in the answers they give and much freedom for the examiner to be guided by his or her individual preferences in scoring the answer. An objective examination affords much freedom for the test constructor to express personal knowledge and values but allows students only the freedom to show, by the proportion of correct answers they give, how much or how little they know or can do.

11. In objective-test items the student's task and the basis on which the examiner will judge the degree to which it has been accomplished are stated more clearly than they are in essay tests.

12. An objective test permits, and occasionally encourages, guessing. An essay test permits, and occasionally encourages, bluffing.

13. The distribution of numerical scores obtained from an essay test can be controlled to a considerable degree by the grader; that from an objective test is determined almost entirely by the examination itself.

In view of these similarities and differences, when might it be most appropriate and beneficial to use essay items? Essay tests are favored for measuring educational achievement when:

1. The group to be tested is small, and the test will not be reused.

2. The instructor wishes to provide for the development of student skill in written expression.

3. The instructor is more interested in exploring student attitudes than in measuring achievements. (Whether instructors *should* be more interested in attitudes than achievement and whether they should expect an honest expression of attitudes in a test situation seem open to question.)

4. The instructor is more confident of his or her proficiency as a critical essay reader than as an imaginative writer of good objective-test items.

5. Time available for test preparation is shorter than time available for test scoring.

Essay tests have important uses in educational measurement, but they also have some serious limitations. Teachers should be wary of unsubstantiated claims that essay tests can measure "higher-order thinking skills" if such skills have not been defined. They also should question the validity of using essay tests to determine how well students can analyze, organize, synthesize, and develop original ideas *if the efforts of instruction were not directed toward such goals.* Unfortunately, there is a tendency in some classrooms for instruction to be geared toward establishing a knowledge base and for evaluation to be directed toward application of that knowledge—"What can they do with it?" One of the purposes of planning is to prevent the occurrence of such inconsistencies.

Comparison of Objective Formats

The most commonly used kinds of objective items are multiple choice, true–false, matching, classification, and short answer. Many other varieties have been described in other treatments of objective-test item writing (Wesman, 1971). However, most of these special varieties have limited merit and applicability. Their unique features often do more to change the appearance of the item or to increase the difficulty of using it than to improve the item as a measuring tool.

Multiple-choice and true–false test items are widely applicable to a great variety of tasks. Because of this and because of the importance of developing skill in using each one effectively, separate chapters are devoted to true–false and multiple-choice item formats later in this text.

The *multiple-choice* form of test item is relatively high in ability to discriminate between high- and low-achieving students. It is somewhat more difficult to write than some other item types, but its advantages seem so apparent that it has become the type most widely used in tests constructed by specialists. Theoretically, and this has been verified in practice, a given multiple-choice test can be expected to show as much score reliability as a typical true–false test with nearly twice that number of items. Here is an example of the multiple-choice type.

Directions: Write the number of the best answer to the question on the line at the right of the question.

Example: Which is the most appropriate designation for a government in which control is in the hands of a few people?

1. Autonomy	3. Feudalism	<u>4</u>
2. Bureaucracy	4. Oligarchy	

The *true–false* item is simpler to prepare and is also quite widely adaptable. It tends to be somewhat less discriminating, item for item, than the multiple-choice type, and somewhat more subject to ambiguity and misinterpretation. Although theoretically a high proportion of true–false items could be answered correctly by blind guessing, in practice the error introduced into true–false test scores by blind guessing tends to be small (Ebel, 1968). This is true because well-motivated examinees taking a reasonable test do very little blind guessing. They almost always find it possible and more advantageous to give a rational answer than to guess blindly. The problem of guessing on true–false test questions will be discussed in greater detail in Chapter 8. Here is an example of the true–false format.

Directions: If the sentence is essentially true, encircle the letter "T" at the right of the sentence. If it is essentially false, encircle the letter "F."

Example: A substance that serves as a catalyst in a chemical reaction may be recovered unaltered at the end of the reaction.   Ⓣ F

Those critics who urge test makers to abandon the "traditional" multiple-choice and true–false formats and to invent new formats to measure a more varied and more significant array of educational achievement are misinformed about two important points:

1. *Any* aspect of cognitive educational achievement can be tested by either the multiple-choice or the true–false format.
2. What a multiple-choice or true–false item measures is determined much more by its content than by its format.

The *matching* type is efficient in that an entire set of responses can be used with a cluster of related stimulus words. But this is also a limitation since it is sometimes difficult to formulate clusters of questions or stimulus words that are sufficiently similar to make use of the same set of responses. Furthermore, questions whose answers can be no more than a word or a phrase tend to be somewhat superficial and to place a premium on purely verbalistic learning. An example of the matching type is given here.

Literary Works	Authors
__b__ 1. *Paradise Lost*	a. **Matthew Arnold**
	b. **John Milton**
__e__ 2. *The Innocents Abroad*	c. **William Shakespeare**
	d. **Robert Louis Stevenson**
__d__ 3. *Treasure Island*	e. **Mark Twain**

The *classification* type is less familiar than the matching type, but possibly more useful in certain situations. Like the matching type, it uses a single set of responses but applies these to a large number of stimulus situations. An example of the classification type is the following.

Directions: **In the following items you are to express the effects of exercise on various body processes and substances. Assume that the organism undergoes no change except those due to exercise. For each item circle the appropriate number.**

1. **If the effect of exercise is to *increase* the quantity described in the item**
2. **If the effect of exercise is to *decrease* the quantity described in the item**
3. **If exercise should have no *appreciable effect* or *an unpredictable effect* on the quantity described in the item**

27.	**Rate of heart beat**	27.	①	2	3
28.	**Blood pressure**	28.	①	2	3
29.	**Amount of glucose in the blood**	29.	1	②	3
30.	**Amount of residual air in the lungs**	30.	1	②	3

The *short-answer* item, in which students must supply a word, phrase, number, or other symbol, is inordinately popular and tends to be used excessively in classroom tests. It is easy to prepare. In the elementary grades, where emphasis is on the development of vocabulary and the formation of concepts, it can serve a useful function. It has the *seeming* advantage of requiring the examinee to think of the answer, but this advantage may be more apparent than real. Some studies have shown a very high correlation between scores on tests composed of parallel short-answer and multiple-choice items, when both members of each pair of parallel items are intended to test the same knowledge or ability (Eurich, 1931; Cook, 1955).

This means that students who are best at *producing* correct answers tend also to be best at *identifying* them among several alternatives. Accurate measures of how well students can identify correct answers tend to be somewhat easier to get than accurate measures of their ability to produce them. There may be special situations, of course, where the correlation would be much lower.

The disadvantages of the short-answer form are that it is limited to questions that can be answered by a word, phrase, symbol, or number and that its scoring tends to be subjective and tedious. Item writers often find it difficult to phrase good questions about principles, explanations, applications, or predictions that can be answered by one specific word or phrase. Here are some examples of short-answer items.

Directions: On the blank following each of the following questions, partial statements, or words, write the word or number that seems most appropriate.

Examples:
What is the valence of oxygen? <u>−2</u>
The middle section of the body of an insect is called the <u>thorax</u>.
What major river flows through or near each of these major cities?

Cairo	<u>Nile</u>
Calcutta	<u>Ganges</u>
New Orleans	<u>Mississippi</u>
Paris	<u>Seine</u>
Quebec	<u>St. Lawrence</u>

Some test specialists suggest that a variety of item types be used in each examination in order to diversify the tasks presented to the examinee. They imply that this will improve the validity of the scores or make the test more interesting. Others suggest that test constructors should choose the particular item type that is best suited to the material they wish to examine. There is more merit in the second of these suggestions than in the first, but even suitability of item form should not be accepted as an absolute imperative. Several item forms are quite widely adaptable. A test constructor can safely decide to use primarily a single item type, such as a multiple choice, and to turn to one of the other forms only when it becomes clearly more efficient to do so. The quality of a classroom test depends much more on giving proper weight to various aspects of achievement and on writing good items of whatever type than on the choice of this or that type of item.

Item Complexity

There continues to be an interest by some test developers toward the use of items that present complex tasks, often based on lengthy or detailed descriptions of real or contrived situations. Some require the interpretation of complex data, diagrams, or background information. Figure 7–2 shows some examples of complex items presented by Bloom and his colleagues (1956). In some fields it is common to use items of this nature on licensure and certification written examinations, particularly if the examinee pool is not very large.

There are several reasons why complex items appear to be attractive. Since these tasks obviously call for the *use* of knowledge, they provide an answer to critics who assert that objective questions test only recognition of isolated factual details. Furthermore, since the situations and background materials used in the tasks are complex, the items presumably require the examinee to use higher mental processes. Finally, the items are attractive to those who believe that education should be concerned with developing a student's ability to think rather than mere command of knowledge (as if knowledge and thinking were independent attainments!).

However, these complex tasks have some undesirable features as test

(1) The item begins with a description of a dispute among baseball players, team owners, and Social Security officials over off-season unemployment compensation for the players. Examinees are asked whether the players are justified in their demands, not justified, or whether they need more information before deciding. Then, they are asked whether each one of a series of statements about the case supports their judgment, opposes it, or leaves them unable to say.

(Taxonomy, pp. 196–97)

(2) An unusual chemical reaction is described. Examinees are asked to consider which of a series of possible hypotheses about the reaction is tenable and how the tenable hypotheses might be tested.

(Taxonomy, pp. 183–84)

(3) Examinees are given a chart on which the expenditures of a state for various purposes over a period of years have been graphed. Then, given a series of statements about the chart, they are asked to judge how much truth there is in each.

(Taxonomy, pp. 118–19)

Figure 7-2. Descriptions of Complex Items

items. Because they tend to be bulky and time consuming, they limit the number of responses examinees can make per hour of testing time; that is, they limit the size of the sample of observable behaviors. Hence, because of the associated reduction in reliability, tests composed of complex tasks tend to be less efficient than is desirable in terms of accuracy of measurement per hour of testing.

Furthermore, the more complex the situation and the higher the level of mental process required to make some judgment about the situation, the more difficult it becomes to defend any one answer as the best answer. For this reason, complex test items tend to discriminate poorly between high and low achievers. They also tend to be unnecessarily difficult, unless the examiner manages to ask a very easy question about a complex problem situation. Even the strongest advocates of complex situational or interpretative test items do not claim that good items of this type are easy to write.

The inefficiency of these items, the uncertainty of the best answer, and the difficulty of writing good ones could all be tolerated if the complex items actually did measure more important aspects of achievement than can be measured by simpler types. However, *there is no good evidence that this is the case.* A simple question like, "Will you marry me?" can have the most profound consequences. It can provide a lifetime's crucial test of the wisdom of the person who asks it and of the one who answers.

Some item writers are drawn to complex items because they are *perceived* as requiring the *application* of knowledge. But any good item tests application of knowledge; good multiple-choice items, for example, require more than recall. And some items test for knowledge indirectly by giving examinees a task that requires knowledge. Numerical problems, discussed earlier, test for application of knowledge, as do error recognition spelling tests, tests that require the examinee to add or correct punctuation and capitalization, tests requiring editing of text, or those that require the dissection and labeling of sentence parts. When examinees are asked to interpret the meaning of a table, graph, musical score, cartoon, poem, or passage of test material, they are asked to apply their knowledge.

Items that require interpretation of materials often are referred to as context-dependent items. (They have no meaning outside the context of the material about which they are written.) They are widely used in tests of general educational development, tests whose purposes are to measure the abilities of students with widely different educational backgrounds. (Most succeed quite well in doing so.) However, they are less appropriate, convenient, and efficient in testing for achievement in learning specific subject matter. Test users should be skeptical of claims that context-dependent items measure *abilities* rather than knowledge, because the abilities they measure are almost wholly the results of knowledge.

Many of the indirect tests of knowledge, through special applications of the knowledge or the use of complex situations, can be presented in true–false, multiple-choice, short-answer, or matching form. Some are more conveniently presented in open-ended fashion, such as requiring the examinee to produce a diagram, sketch, or set of editorial corrections. The main point to be made here is that, while achievement can be tested most conveniently with one of the common item formats, there are occasions when other means may be more convenient, satisfactory, or palatable to those who are charged with providing evidence for valid score use.

NUMBER OF ITEMS

The number of questions to include in a test is determined largely by the amount of time available for it. Many tests are limited to 50 minutes, more or less, because that is the scheduled length of the class period. Special examination schedules may provide periods of 2 hours or longer. In general, the longer the period and the examination, the more reliable the scores obtained from it. However, it is seldom practical or desirable to prepare a classroom test that will require more than 3 hours.

A reasonable goal is to make tests that include few enough questions so that most students have time to attempt all of them when working at their own normal rates. One reason for this is that speed of response is not a primary objective of instruction in most K–12 and college courses and hence is not a valid indication of achievement. In many areas of proficiency, speed and accuracy are not highly correlated. Consider the data in Table 7–3. The sum of the scores for the first ten students who finished the test was 965. The highest score in that group was 105. The lowest was 71. Thus, the range of scores in that group was 35 score units. Note that, though the range of scores varies somewhat from group to group, there is no clear tendency for students to do better or worse depending on the amount of time spent. One can conclude from these data that on this test there was almost no relation between time spent in taking the test and the number of correct answers given.

A second reason for giving students ample time to work on a test is that examination anxiety, severe enough even in untimed tests, is accentuated when pressure to work rapidly as well as accurately is applied. A third is that efficient use of an instructor's painstakingly produced test requires that most students

Table 7-3. Relation Between Rate of Work and Test Scores[a]

Order of Finish	Sum of Scores	Range of Scores
1–10	965	35
11–20	956	32
21–30	940	31
31–40	964	32
41–50	948	52
51–60	955	25
61–70	965	27
71–80	1010	30
81–90	942	24
91–100	968	40

[a]Based on a test in educational measurement composed of 125 true-false test items taken by 100 students. The mean score on the test was 96.1. The tenth student finished the test after working on it for 50 minutes. The 100th student used 120 minutes.

respond to all of it. In some situations, speeded tests may be appropriate and valuable, but these situations seem to be the exception, not the rule. Though there are no absolute standards for judging speededness, measurement specialists have come to adopt this one: A test is speeded if fewer than 90 percent of the test takers are able to attempt all items.

The number of questions that an examinee can answer per minute depends on the kind of questions used, the complexity of the thought processes required to answer them, and the examinee's work habits. The fastest student in a class may finish a test in half the time required by the slowest. For these reasons, it is difficult to specify precisely how many items to include in a given test. Rules such as "use one multiple-choice item per minute" or "Allow 30 seconds per true–false item" are misleading and unsubstantiated generalizations. Only experience with similar tests in similar classes can provide useful test-length information.

Finally, the number of items needed depends also on how thoroughly the domain must be sampled. And that, of course, depends on the type of score interpretation desired. For example, a test covering 10 instructional objectives may require a minimum of 30 items when objectives-referenced interpretations are wanted, but 20 items might suffice for norm-referenced purposes.

Content Sampling Errors

If the amount of time available for testing does not determine the length of a test, the accuracy desired in the scores should determine it. In general, the larger the number of items included in a test, the more reliable the scores will be. In statistical terminology, the items that make up a test constitute a *sample* from a much larger collection, or *population*, of items that might have been used in that test. A 100-word spelling test might be constructed by selecting every fifth word from a list of the 500 words studied during the term. The 500 words constitute the population from which the 100-word sample was selected.

Consider now a student who, asked to spell all 500 words, spells 325 (65 percent) of them correctly. Of the 100 words in the sample, he spells 69 (69 percent) correctly. The difference between the 65 percent for the population and the 69 percent for the sample is known as a *sampling error*.

In the case of the spelling test, the population of possible questions is real and definite. But for most tests it is not. That is, there is almost no limit to the number of problems that could be invented for use in an algebra test or to the number of questions that could be formulated for a history test. Constructors of tests in these subjects, as in most other subjects, have no predetermined limited list from which to draw representative samples of questions. But their tests are samples, nevertheless, because they include only a fraction of the questions that could be asked in each case. A major problem of test constructors is thus to make their samples fairly represent a theoretical population of questions on the topic.

The larger the population of potential questions, the more likely it is that the content domain is heterogeneous; that is, it includes diverse and semi-independent areas of knowledge or ability. To achieve equally accurate results, a somewhat larger sample is required in a heterogeneous than in a homogeneous domain. And as we have already noted, generally a larger sample will yield a sample statistic closer to the population parameter than a more limited sample.

Since any test is a sample of tasks, every test score is subject to sampling errors. The larger the sample, the smaller the sampling errors are likely to be. Posey (1932) has shown that examinees' luck, or lack of it, in being asked what they happen to know is a much greater factor in the grade they receive from a 10-question test than from one of 100 questions. Sampling errors are present in practically all educational test scores. However, it is important to realize that such errors are not caused by mistakes in sampling. A perfectly chosen random sample will still be subject to sampling errors simply because it is a sample.

LEVEL AND DISTRIBUTION OF DIFFICULTY

There are two ways in which the problem of test difficulty can be approached. One is to include in the test only those items that any student who has studied successfully should be able to answer. If this is done, most of the students can be expected to answer the majority of the items correctly. Put somewhat differently, so many correct answers are likely to be given that many of the items will not be effective in discriminating among various levels of achievement—best, good, average, weak, and poor. The score distribution in this circumstance will be very homogeneous, as reflected by a small standard deviation. But when our goal is to make norm-referenced score interpretations, clearly such a test would yield scores of disappointingly low reliability.

The other approach, for norm-referenced testing, is to choose items of appropriate content on the basis of their ability to reveal different levels of achievement among the students tested. This requires preference for moderately difficult questions. The ideal difficulty of these items should be at a point on the difficulty scale (percent correct) midway between perfect (100 percent correct response) and the chance level difficulty (50 percent correct for true–false items, 25 percent correct for four-alternative multiple-choice items). This means the proportion of correct responses, the item p-value, should be about 75 percent correct for an ideal true–false item and about 62.5 percent correct for an ideal multiple-choice item. (The term *p-value* is used to refer to the difficulty of an item.) This second approach generally will yield more reliable scores than the first for a constant amount of testing time.

As we will see in the upcoming chapters on item writing, there are several methods item writers can use to manipulate the difficulty level of a test item prepared for a specific group. And for norm-referenced testing, such manipulations *must* be employed to create items of the desired difficulty level. Though it is possible to use the same methods to control the difficulty of items written for a criterion-referenced test, such manipulations would be inappropriate. For criterion-referenced measurement, the difficulty is built into the tasks or the knowledge descriptions that specify the content domain. When item writers manipulate item content to adjust perceived difficulty, they are in effect creating a mismatch between item content and the domain definition. These mismatches impact content relevance by underrepresenting legitimate content and by introducing irrelevant (or less relevant) content. In sum, part of the reason for not specifying the norm-referenced content domain too precisely is that it gives license to the item writer to create items of the most appropriate difficulty.

Some instructors believe that a good test should include some difficult items to "test" the better students and some easy items to give poorer students a chance. But neither of these kinds of items tends to affect the rank ordering of student scores appreciably. The higher-scoring students generally would answer the harder items and, therefore, earn higher scores yet. Nearly everyone would answer the easy items. The effect of easy items is to add a constant amount to each examinee's score, to raise all scores, but without affecting the rank order of students' scores. For good norm-referenced achievement measures, items of moderate difficulty—not too hard and not too easy—contribute most to discriminating between students who have learned varying amounts of the content of instruction.

Tests designed to yield criterion-referenced score interpretations likely will be easier in difficulty level than their norm-referenced counterparts. When testing for minimum competency or for mastery, the expectation is that most students have reached the minimum level or have achieved mastery. The items in these tests should be easy for most students but should be difficult for those who have not mastered the content the items represent. It should be clear that a test item in isolation is not easy or difficult. The difficulty of an item relates to the nature of the group and depends on the extent to which those in the group possess the ability presented by the task.

SUMMARY PROPOSITIONS

1. The most important function of classroom tests is to obtain precise measures of students' achievements.

2. The form of a test—essay, objective, problem— gives no certain indication of the ability being measured.

3. Whatever form of test is used, examiners should attempt to make their measurements as objective as possible.

4. When a performance test and an objective test can be used to achieve essentially the same purpose, the objective test likely will be more effi-

cient, be more relevant, and yield more reliable measurements.

5. The precision with which the content specifications for a test should be described relates to the type of score interpretation desired.

6. A table of specifications is a planning guide for ensuring adequate representation of content and abilities in a test.

7. The relative importance of a content subdomain in a test depends on such factors as the amount of content it contains and the amount of instructional time devoted to it.

8. The examiner can control the distribution of test scores more easily with essay than with objective tests.

9. It is unlikely that students study more effectively in preparation for an essay test than for an objective test.

10. Essay tests can be efficient when the group to be tested is small.

11. Multiple-choice and true–false items can be used to measure any aspect of cognitive educational achievement.

12. Situational or interpretive test items tend to be inefficient, difficult to write, difficult to "key" objectively, and unconvincing as measures of higher mental processes.

13. Most classroom achievement tests should be short enough, in relation to the time available, so that virtually all students have time to attempt all items.

14. The number of items to be included in a test should be influenced by the amount of time available, the accuracy desired in the scores, and the homogeneity of content to be sampled.

15. In most achievement tests, the items that contribute the greatest amount of useful information are those on which the proportion of correct response is halfway between 100 percent and the expected chance score.

QUESTIONS FOR STUDY AND DISCUSSION

1. How might a test whose purpose is mainly to provide instruction differ in important ways from one intended mainly to measure achievement?

2. What reasonable step might a science or math teacher take to obtain scores on a numerical-problem test that are just as objective as those that could be obtained from a multiple-choice or true–false test?

3. Why are performance tests often less efficient than objective tests when both are designed to serve the same purpose?

4. How can the content-domain definition for a norm-referenced test and a criterion-referenced test be distinguished?

5. Under what circumstances might a table of specifications appropriately exclude items in the factual information or terminology categories?

6. Why might scores from a numerical-problem test and a multiple-choice test be equally useful for norm-referenced purposes but not for criterion-referenced purposes?

7. What factors influence which students finish an exam first and which finish last?

8. Why is the rule "Use one true–false item for each 30 seconds of testing time" not likely to be an adequate generalization?

9. How do content sampling errors cause score reliability to be lowered?

10. Under what circumstances might it be appropriate to use items that are highly difficult for the group being tested?

11. What is probably meant by the statement, "Criterion-referenced tests aren't intentionally easy, they just are"?

8

True–False Test Items

From one point of view, true–false tests seem like a breeze—easier than they ought to be. From another, as many students would testify, they seem unnecessarily difficult, irrelevant, and frustrating. Some would say there are better ways of measuring achievement than by using true–false items. Yet this lack of endorsement is not universally shared among educators. A few, including the authors of this book, regard true–false items much more favorably (Ebel, 1975; Frisbie, 1973).

MERITS OF THE TRUE-FALSE FORMAT

The basic reason for using true–false test items is that they provide a simple and direct means of measuring the essential outcomes of formal education. The argument for the value of true–false items as measures of educational achievement can be summarized in four statements:

1. The essence of educational achievement is the command of useful verbal knowledge.
2. All verbal knowledge can be expressed in propositions.
3. A proposition is any sentence that can be said to be true or false.
4. The extent of students' command of a particular area of knowledge is indicated by their success in judging the truth or falsity of propositions related to it.

133

The rationale supporting the first statement was provided in Chapter 3. The second is almost self-evident. Is it possible to imagine an element of verbal knowledge that could not be expressed as a proposition? The third is a generally accepted definition. The fourth seems to be a logical consequence of the first three. It may, of course, be challenged on the basis of technical weaknesses in true–false items, but it is not likely to be rejected in principle.

To test a person's command of an idea or element of knowledge is to test his or her understanding of it. A student who can recognize an idea only when it is expressed in some particular set of words does not have command of it. Neither does the student who knows the idea only as an isolated fact, without seeing how it is related to other ideas. Knowledge one has command of is not a miscellaneous collection of separate elements, but an integrated structure that can be used to make decisions, draw logical inferences, or solve problems. It is usable knowledge.

Consider how one might test a student's command of Archimedes' principle. Clearly, to offer the student the usual expression of the principle as a true statement, or some slight alteration of it as a false statement, as has been done in items 1 and 2, is to misunderstand the true nature of knowledge.

(1) **A body immersed in a fluid is buoyed up by a force equal to the weight of the fluid displaced. (T)**

(2) **A body immersed in a fluid is buoyed up by a force equal to half the weight of the fluid displaced. (F)**

Instead the student might be asked to recognize the principle in some alternative statement of it, as in items 3 and 4 below.

(3) **If an object having a certain volume is surrounded by a liquid or gas, the upward force on it equals the weight of that volume of the liquid or gas. (T)**

(4) **The upward force on an object surrounded by a liquid or gas is equal to the surface area of the object multiplied by the pressure of the liquid or gas surrounding it. (F)**

Or the student might be required to apply the principle in specific situations such as those described in items 5 and 6 below.

(5) **The buoyant force on a one-centimeter cube of aluminum is exactly the same as that on a one-centimeter cube of iron when both are immersed in water. (T)**

(6) **If an insoluble object is immersed successively in several fluids of different density, the buoyant force upon it in each case will vary inversely with the density of the fluids. (F)**

Sometimes the use of an unconventional example can serve to test understanding of a concept.

(7) **Distilled water is soft water. (T)**

It is a popular misconception that true–false test items are limited to testing for simple factual recall. On the contrary, complex and difficult problems can be presented quite effectively in this form.

(8)   **The next term in the series 3, 4, 7, 11, 18 is 29.   (T)**

(9)   **If the sides of a trapezoid are consecutive whole numbers, and if the shortest side is one of the two parallel sides, then the area of the trapezoid is 18 square units.   (T)**

The reason why true–false tests are often held in low esteem is not that there is anything inherently wrong with the item form. It is rather that the format is often used ineptly by unskilled item writers. It has also been alleged that true–false tests are especially susceptible to guessing and that they have harmful effects on student learning, beliefs that have not been checked against experimental data. These alleged weaknesses of true–false items will be dealt with more fully later in the chapter.

Efficiency of True–False Items

In addition to providing relevant measures of the essence of educational achievement, true–false items have the advantage of being quite efficient. The number of independently scorable responses per thousand words of test or per hour of testing time tends to be considerably higher than that for multiple-choice items. Research evidence has shown that students can attempt three true–false items in the time required to attempt a pair of multiple-choice items (Frisbie, 1973, 1974). Offsetting this advantage in efficiency is a disadvantage in item discriminating power. Item for item, true–false tends to discriminate less well between high- and low-achieving students than multiple-choice (Ebel, 1980). In sum, a good one-hour true–false test is likely to be as effective as a good one-hour multiple-choice test.

Compared with other item formats, true–false test items are relatively easy to write. They are simple declarative sentences of the kind that make up most oral and written communications. It is true that the ideas they affirm or deny must be chosen judiciously. It is also true that the ideas chosen must be worded carefully, with a view to maximum precision and clarity, since they stand and must be judged in isolation. For this reason they must be self-contained in meaning, depending wholly on internal content, not on external context. But the basic skill involved in true–false item writing is no different from that required in any written communication situation. Those who have difficulty in writing good true–false test items probably have trouble expressing themselves clearly and accurately in other forms of writing.

Comparisons with Multiple-choice Items

An obvious difference between true–false and multiple-choice items is in the number of alternatives generally offered to the examinee. Another difference is in the definiteness or specificity of the task presented. It may be more difficult to judge whether a statement should be called true or false than to judge which of several alternatives is the best answer to a particular question. For example, students who mark a statement true may not be able to think of a counterexample—a situation or occurrence that would make the proposition false. Their search for a counterexample may be bounded by time limits or by the length to which they can stretch their mind or the depth of their retrieval system to which they can penetrate. The multiple-choice item, however, limits the universe of comparisons that the individual must make. Aside from all these differences, there are substantial similarities between the two item types.

Implicit in most multiple-choice items are one true statement and several false statements. Like true–false items, multiple-choice items also test knowledge and are based on propositions. When expertly written multiple-choice items are converted to true–false items, and both forms are administered to the same large group of examinees, the scores obtained correlate about as closely as their reliabilities allow (Frisbie, 1973). In another study, the oral administration of content-parallel multiple-choice and true–false tests to middle school special education students resulted in no differences in difficulty or reliability (Irvin, Halpern, and Landman, 1980). Part A of Figure 8–1 displays items testing essentially the same propositions in multiple-choice and true–false formats.

While most multiple-choice items are based on propositions, a few, like the example that follows, are not.

Which of the following sentences is stated most emphatically?
  a. If my understanding of the question is correct, this principle is one we cannot afford to accept.
  b. One principle we cannot afford to accept is this one, if my understanding of the question is correct.
  c. This principle, if my understanding of the question is correct, is one we cannot afford to accept.
  d. This principle is one we cannot afford to accept, if my understanding of the question is correct.

Items like this and the one in part C of Figure 8–1 involve some degree of personal judgment and are not derived from propositions. Consequently, they cannot be converted easily to true–false format and are better posed initially as multiple-choice items. Note that the content basis of item 4 is more apparent than it is for either 4a or 4b.

There are also questions that are much easier to present as true–false than as multiple-choice items because only two answers are plausible. For example, when we wish to ask whether two variables are related, or about the effect of increasing one variable on the size of the other, it is almost impossible to find more than two reasonable alternatives. Here are some examples.

(1)   Changing the temperature of a mass of air will change its relative humidity.   (T)
(2)   More amendments were added to the U.S. Constitution during the first ten years after ratification than during the next one hundred years.   (T)
(3)   An eclipse of the sun can occur only when the moon is full.   (F)
(4)   Increasing the length of a test is likely to decrease its standard error of measurement.   (F)

Commitment to the multiple-choice format has led some item writers to present what is essentially a collection of true–false statements as a multiple-choice item. Part B of Figure 8–1 provides an example. Though research findings on this question are mixed (Ebel, 1978; Hsu, 1979), logic suggests that more reliable measures of achievement can be obtained from independently scored true–

MULTIPLE-CHOICE VERSION	TRUE–FALSE VERSION
A. Equally Useful Formats	
(1) The equation $X^2 + Y^2 = 4$ is represented graphically by *a. a circle. b. an ellipse. c. a parabola.	(1a) The graph of $X^2 + Y^2 = 4$ is a circle. (T) (1b) The graph of $X^2 + Y^2 = 9$ is an ellipse. (F)
(2) What is the main function of a corrective lens? *a. Change the image that falls on the retina b. Change the amount of light reaching the retina c. Remove the blind spot on the retina	(2a) The main function of a corrective lens is to change the image that falls on the retina. (T) (2b) The main function of a corrective lens is to change the amount of light reaching the retina. (F)
B. Items Better Suited to True–False Format	
(3) Which of these is *not* characteristic of a virus? a. It can live only in plant and animal cells. *b. It is composed of very large living cells. c. It can reproduce itself.	(3a) A virus can live only in plant and animal cells. (T) (3b) A virus is composed of very large living cells. (F)
C. Items Better Suited to Multiple-Choice Format	
(4) Which of these best describes a good citizen? a. Someone who pays taxes b. Someone who has a job *c. Someone who obeys the laws	(4a) A good citizen can be described better as a law abider than as a taxpayer. (T) (4b) Having a job is more characteristic of good citizenship than is obeying laws. (F)

Figure 8-1. Multiple-Choice and Corresponding True–False Items

false items than from multiple-choice items formed by grouping one true statement with three that are false or by grouping one that is false with three that are true.

COMMON MISCONCEPTIONS ABOUT TRUE-FALSE ITEMS

There seems to be an *uncritical unacceptance* of the true–false format among educational researchers, writers, and testing personnel. The unfavorable attitudes about true–false items seem to be perpetuated by disappointing experience of test takers, frustrating results of test makers, and hearsay evidence. There have been few careful empirical studies of the charges most often brought against them. An analysis of some of the most frequently heard indictments follows.

The Impact of Guessing

A charge against true–false tests that many take quite seriously is that they are subject to gross error introduced by guessing. Several things can be said in response to this charge.

The first is that a distinction needs to be made between blind guessing and informed guessing. Blind guessing adds nothing but error to the test scores. Informed guesses, on the other hand, provide valid indications of achievement. The more a student knows, the more likely that informed guesses will be correct.

The second is that well-motivated students, taking a test of appropriate difficulty with a generous time limit, are likely to do very little blind guessing on true–false tests. They know that thinking is a surer basis than guessing for determining the correct answer. In one study, college students reported an average of only one response in twenty that was equivalent, in their opinion, to a blind guess (Ebel, 1968). Hills and Gladney (1968) have shown that scores in the chance range are not significantly different from above-chance scores as predictors of college grades. This suggests that scores in the chance range were not in fact the results of pure chance (blind guessing).

The third is that the influence of blind guessing on the scores of a test diminishes as the test increases in length. On a one-item true–false test a student has a 50 percent chance (1 in 2) of getting a perfect score by blind guessing, but on a two-item test it drops to 25 percent, on a five-item test to 3 percent, and on a ten-item test to 0.1 percent. On a 100-item test it becomes less than one chance in a million trillion trillion! The chance of getting even a moderately good score, say 70, on a 100-item true–false test by blind guessing alone is less than 1 in 1000.

The fourth and most significant response that can be made to this charge is that reliable scores could not be obtained from true–false tests if they were seriously affected by blind guessing. But, in fact, true–false classroom tests of 100 items have shown reliability coefficients of 0.85 to 0.95. These values are about as high as can be expected for any classroom test, regardless of the form of test item used. They support the conclusion that good true–false tests need not be vitiated by guessing.

Some testing specialists believe that the problem of guessing can best be dealt with by "correcting the scores for guessing." This is a misconception. The announcement that test scores will be corrected for guessing may deter *some* students from guessing, but it only magnifies the differences between the scores of lucky and unlucky guessers. In fact, its effect on the validity of the test scores is negligible. If guessing on a true–false test were to be extensive enough to affect the test scores seriously, there is almost nothing that a guessing correction could do to improve the accuracy of the scores.

The Ambiguity Charge

A second major criticism of true–false items is that they are frequently ambiguous. Although some items do indeed succumb to this charge, ambiguity is not an inherent weakness of the true–false item—especially if the ideas for the items are carefully chosen and if the items themselves are carefully worded. Furthermore, we must make a distinction between *intrinsic ambiguity* and *apparent ambiguity.* Students who say, "If I interpret the statement this way, I'd say it is true. But if I interpret it that way, I'd have to say it is false," are complaining about apparent ambiguity. If experts in the field have the same difficulty in interpreting a particular statement, the trouble may be intrinsic ambiguity.

Apparent ambiguity may sometimes be due to inadequacies in the students' knowledge. They have trouble interpreting a statement because the words mean something a little different to them than to the expert, or because the statement fails to evoke the necessary associations that would yield the intended interpretation.

Hence apparent ambiguity is not only unavoidable, it may even be useful. By making the task of responding harder for the poorly prepared than for the well-prepared student, it can help to discriminate between the two. Thus a student's comment that a test question is unclear is not necessarily an indictment of the question. It may be, rather, an unintentional confession of his or her own shortcomings.

Intrinsic ambiguity, on the other hand, the kind of ambiguity that troubles the expert as much as or more than it troubles the novice, is a real concern. It probably can never be totally eliminated, since language is inherently somewhat abstract, general, and imprecise. But in the statements used in true–false test items it should be minimized.

Of course, there is sometimes truth in the charge that true–false test items are ambiguous and lack significance: one reason is that teachers sometimes try to excerpt textbook sentences for use as test items. Even in a well-written text, few of the sentences would actually make good true–false test items. Many statements serve only to keep readers informed of what the author is trying to do or to remind them of the structure and organization of the discussion. Some are so dependent for their meaning on sentences that precede or follow them that they are almost meaningless out of context. Others are intended only to suggest an idea, not to state it positively and precisely. Still others comprise a whole logical argument, involving two or three propositions, in a single sentence. Another category of statements is intended not to describe what is true, but to prescribe what ought to be true. Finally, some are expressed so loosely and so tentatively that there is hardly any possible basis for doubting them. In all the writing we do to preserve the knowledge we have gained and to communicate it to others, there seem to be very few naturally occurring nuggets of established knowledge.

For this reason it is seldom possible to find in a text or reference work a sentence that can be copied directly for use as a true statement or transformed by a simple negation for use as a false statement. The writing of good true–false items is more a task of creative writing than of copying. This may be a fortunate circumstance, for it helps test constructors avoid the hazard of writing items that would encourage and reward rote learning.

A special source of ambiguity in true–false test items needs to be guarded against. It is uncertainty on the part of the examinee as to the examiner's standards of truth. If the statement is not perfectly true, if it has the slightest flaw, should it be considered false? Probably not; the item writer's task will be easier, and the test will be better, if the examinee is directed to consider as true any statement that has more truth than error in it, or any statement that is more true than its contradiction would be. The test builder's task then is to avoid writing statements that fall in the twilight zone between truth and falsehood.

Of course, even the most competent and careful item writer may unintentionally include a few intrinsically ambiguous items. Such items are usually quite easy to identify after the test has been given. The better students who miss these items will call attention to their ambiguity. If the test is analyzed, the ambiguous items are likely to show low discrimination or high difficulty. Post mortems such as this do nothing to correct past failures, but they can help examiners identify items that need to be revised or discarded and make them more sensitive to avoidable sources of ambiguity.

Reward for Memorization

Another of the common criticisms of true–false test items is that they are limited to testing for specific, often trivial, factual details. As a result, the critics say, students are encouraged and rewarded for rote learning of bits of factual information rather than for critical thinking and understanding. In support of this criticism, items like these are cited as typical of true–false tests:

The author of Don Quixote was Cervantes.   (T)
The chemical formula for water is H_2O.   (T)
The Battle of Hastings was fought in 1066.   (T)
Christopher Columbus was born in Spain.   (F)
There are six planets in the solar system.   (F)

If these were indeed the only kinds of questions that could be asked in true–false form, it would surely be of limited value. However, it is possible to ask questions that not only test students' comprehension of broader principles but also their ability to apply them. For example, one can test understanding of an event or of a process:

King John of England considered the Magna Carta one of his great achievements.   (F)
In the laboratory preparation of carbon dioxide one of the essential ingredients is limewater.   (F)

One can test knowledge of a functional relationship:

The more widely the items in a test vary in difficulty, the narrower the range of test scores.   (T)
If heat is supplied at a constant rate to melt and vaporize a substance, the temperature of the substance will increase at a constant rate also.   (F)

One can test the ability to apply principles:

It is easier for a poor student to get a good score (80 percent correct) on a true–false test if the test includes only 50 items than if it includes 100 items.   (T)
If an electric refrigerator is operated in a sealed, insulated room with its door open, the temperature of the room will decrease.   (F)

The time from moonrise to moonset is usually longer than the time from sunrise to sunset. (T)

Effects on Learning Outcomes

Critics of true–false tests sometimes charge that their use has harmful effects on learning: that they (1) encourage students to concentrate on remembering isolated factual details and to rely heavily on rote learning; (2) encourage students to accept grossly oversimplified conceptions of truth; and (3) expose students undesirably to error. How defensible are these charges?

True–false items need not emphasize memory for isolated factual details. Good ones present novel problems to be solved and thus emphasize understanding and application. Even those that might require recall of factual details do not necessarily reward rote learning, for facts are hard to remember in isolation. They are retained and can be recalled better if they are part of a structure of knowledge.

There is reason to believe that rote learning is something of an educational bogeyman, often warned against and cited as the cause of educational failure, but seldom practiced or observed. Rote learning is not much fun, and it promises few lasting rewards. Most students and teachers properly shun it. Perhaps its supposed prevalence results from an error in inference. It is surely true that rote learning always results in incomplete learning (that is, lack of understanding), but it does not follow that all incomplete learning is the result of too much rote learning. It may simply be the result of too little learning of any sort.

What of the second charge, that the categorical way in which answers are both offered and scored is likely to give students a false notion about the simplicity of truth? Evidence in support of this argument is seldom presented, and the argument itself is seldom advanced by those who have used true–false tests extensively. Test writers know students will challenge answers that disagree with their own. Often they will point to the complexity of the entire subject and will insist that a case can be made for the alternative answer. Usually the author concedes that the statement in question is neither perfectly true nor totally false. The discussion that normally follows tends to emphasize, rather than to conceal, the complexity, the impurity, and the relativity of truth. On occasion it leads to the conclusion that the item in question was simply a bad item, poorly conceived or carelessly stated.

Now consider the third charge: that true–false test items are educationally harmful because they expose the student to error. The argument is that the presentation of false statements as if they were true may have a negative suggestion effect, causing students to believe and remember untruths. However, Ruch (1929) tentatively concluded that the negative suggestion effect in true–false tests is probably much smaller than is sometimes assumed and is fully offset by the net positive teaching effects. Other experimental studies confirm this conclusion, and as Ross (1947) pointed out:

> Whether or not a false statement is dangerous depends largely upon the setting in which it appears. A false statement in the textbook, toward which the characteristic pupil attitude is likely to be one of passive, uncritical acceptance, might

easily be serious. But the situation is different with the items in a true–false test. Here the habitual attitude of the modern pupil is one of active, critical challenge. (p. 349)

In light of these findings, we conclude that well-conceived and well-developed true–false test items can contribute substantially to the measurement of educational achievement. The harm some fear they might do is trivial in comparison.

WRITING EFFECTIVE TRUE–FALSE ITEMS

The instructor who wishes to write a true–false item for a classroom test should begin by focusing attention on some segment of the knowledge that has been taught. It is assumed that the item writer is in firm command of that segment of knowledge and that it is something any capable student of the subject ought also to understand. This segment of knowledge is, or easily could be, described in a single paragraph such as those found in any good textbook adopted for the class. Accordingly, item writers usually find it easier and more effective to use instructional materials as the source of ideas for test items than to derive those ideas directly from educational objectives.

Suppose now that an item writer singles out a specific paragraph of text intended to help the student develop some segment of knowledge. Take, for example, this paragraph:

> Avoid giving examinees a choice among optional questions on an essay test unless special circumstances make such options necessary. If different examinees answer different questions, the basis for comparing their scores, their levels of performance, is eroded. Students who have answered different sets of questions actually have taken different tests. These different tests are not likely to be measures of the same achievements. And certainly when students choose the questions on which they can perform best, the set of scores for that group will mask the differences in achievement among examinees. That is, a narrow range of fairly high scores will probably result. Dependable norm-referenced score interpretations will be difficult to make because the small score differences would more likely be due to measurement error than to differences in achievement levels.
>
> Optional questions are sometimes justified on the ground that giving students a choice among the questions they are to answer makes the test "fairer." But if all the questions involve essential aspects of achievement in a course (as they ordinarily might), it is not unfair to any student to require answers to all of them. Furthermore, an opportunity to choose among optional questions may help the poorer student considerably, but may actually distract the well-prepared student.

The first question the item writer must pose is, "What are the most important ideas presented in this paragraph?" Here are three of several propositions that can be identified:

1. The use of optional essay items interferes with interindividual score comparisons.

2. The use of optional essay items usually contributes to reduced test-score variability.

3. The use of optional items usually results in reduced test-score reliability.

The next question is how these ideas can be expressed as true–false test items. At this point, a very important suggestion can be offered: *Always think of possible true–false test items in pairs, one true, the other false.* Of course, only one member of the pair is actually used in the test. However, unless a parallel but opposite statement can be made, the proposition is not likely to make a good true–false test item. Here are some item pairs derived from the ideas presented above.

1a. The use of optional rather than required essay items reduces the ability to make norm-referenced interpretations. **(T)**

1b. The use of optional rather than required essay items enhances the ability to make criterion-referenced interpretations. **(F)**

2a. The scores resulting from the use of optional rather than required essay items will exhibit reduced variability. **(T)**

2b. The scores resulting from the use of optional rather than required essay items will exhibit increased variability. **(F)**

3a. The reliability of scores from optional essay items is likely to be smaller than for scores based on required essay items. **(T)**

3b. The reliability of scores from optional essay items is likely to be larger than for scores based on required essay items. **(F)**

4a. The reliability advantage of using required versus optional essay items is due to differences in score variability. **(T)**

4b. The reliability advantage of using required versus optional essay items is due to differences in test lengths. **(F)**

Note that many variations can be developed from the propositions listed and that none of the items, or the propositions, is a reproduction of one of the original sentences. All items are designed to test for understanding, not simply for recall of sentences read or heard.

Guidelines for Item Development

There are five general requirements for a good true–false test item.

1. It should test the examinee's knowledge of an important proposition, one that is likely to be significant and useful in coping with a variety of situations and problems. It should say something worth saying.

2. It should require understanding as well as memory. Simple recall of meaningless words, empty phrases, or sentences learned by rote should not be enough to permit a correct answer.

3. The intended correct answer (true or false) should be easy for the item writer to defend to the satisfaction of competent critics. The true statements should be true enough and the false statements false enough so that an expert would have no difficulty distinguishing between them. Any explanation or qualification needed to justify an unconditional answer should be included in the item.

4. On the other hand, the intended correct answer should be obvious only to those who have good command of the knowledge being tested. It should not be a matter of common knowledge. It should not be given away by an unintended clue. The wrong answer should be made attractive to those who lack the desired command.

5. The item should be expressed as simply, as concisely, and above all as clearly as is consistent with the preceding four requirements. It should be based on a single proposition. Common words should be given preference over technical terms. Sentences should be short and simple in structure. Essentially true statements should not be made false by simply inserting the word *not*.

Here are some pairs of true–false test items that illustrate these requirements. *The first of each pair is an acceptable item, while the second is poor.*

1. The item tests an important idea.

(1) **President Kennedy attempted to solve the missile crisis by threatening a blockade of Cuba. (T)**

(2) **President Kennedy was 12 years older than his wife. (T)**

The difference in the ages between President Kennedy and his wife might be a subject for comment in a casual conversation, but it has little to do with the important events of the time. The Cuban missile crisis, on the other hand, brought the United States and Russia to the brink of war. How this crisis was handled is a far more important element in world history than a difference in ages between a president and his wife.

(3) **Words like *some, usually, all,* or *never* should be avoided in writing true–false test items. (F)**

(4) **Two pitfalls should be avoided in writing true–false test items. (F)**

Item 4 is the type of textbook sentence that sets the stage for an important pronouncement—but fails to make it. Item 3, on the other hand, tests the examinee's understanding of several important principles. Specific determiners like *some* and *usually* provide irrelevant clues when used only in true statements. If used in false statements, they tend to attract wrong answers from the ill-prepared student. Conversely, specific determiners like *all* or *never* are useful in attracting wrong answers from the uninformed when used in true statements.

(5) **More salt can be dissolved in a pint of warm water than in a pint of cold water. (T)**

(6) **Some things dissolve in other things. (T)**

A statement like that in item 6 is too general to say anything useful. Item 5, on the other hand, provides a test of the understanding of an important relationship.

2. The item tests understanding. It does not reward recall of a stereotyped phraseology.

(7) When a hand pushes a door with a certain force, the door pushes back on the hand with the same force. **(T)**

(8) For every action there is an equal and opposite reaction. **(T)**

(9) If the hypotenuse of an isosceles right triangle is seven inches long, each of the two equal legs must be more than five inches long. **(F)**

(10) The square of the hypotenuse of a right triangle equals the sum of the squares of the other two sides. **(T)**

Both items 8 and 10 are word-for-word statements of important principles that could be learned by rote. To test a student's understanding, it is desirable to present specific applications that avoid the stereotyped phrases, as has been done in items 7 and 9.

3. The correct answer to an item is defensible.

(11) Moist air is less dense than dry air. **(T)**

(12) Rain clouds are light in weight. **(T)**

Since a rain cloud seems to float in the air, it might reasonably be called light in weight. On the other hand, a single rain cloud may weigh more than 100,000 tons. One cubic foot of the cloud probably weighs about the same as a cubic foot of air. Since the cloud contains droplets of water, it could conceivably weigh more per cubic foot than cloudless dry air. On the other hand, moist air alone (item 11) weighs less per cubic foot than does dry air. Should the item also specify "other things being equal," for example, pressure and temperature? It might, but in the absence of mention, a reasonable person is justified in assuming that temperature and pressure should not be taken to be variable factors in this situation.

(13) The proposal that salary schedules for teachers ought to include skill in teaching as one of the determining variables is supported more strongly by teachers' organizations than it is by taxpayers. **(F)**

(14) Merit is an important factor affecting a teacher's salary. **(F)**

The first version is much more specific and much more clearly false than the second. Experts could agree on the answer to the first, but would be troubled by the intrinsic ambiguity of the second. Across the country it is no doubt true that the salaries of good teachers are higher than those of poor teachers. However, it is also true that the salary schedules of many school systems do not include merit as one of the determining factors.

(15) The twinkling of starlight is due to motion in the earth's atmosphere. **(T)**

(16) Stars send out light that twinkles. **(T)**

The answer to the second, unacceptable version of this item could be challenged by a reasonable, well-informed person on the following grounds. It is not the light sent out by the star that twinkles—that light is relatively steady. But because of disturbances in our atmosphere, the light that reaches our eyes from the star often appears to twinkle. That the second version is unacceptable is due either to the limited knowledge or to the carelessness in expression of the person who wrote it.

4. The answer to a good test item is not obvious to anyone. It tests special knowledge.

(17)   **Frozen foods are usually cheaper than canned foods.   (F)**

(18)   **Frozen foods of the highest quality may be ruined in the kitchen.   (T)**

(19)   **Most local insurance agencies are owned and controlled by one of the major national insurance companies.   (F)**

(20)   **Insurance agencies may be either general or specialized.   (T)**

Who could doubt the possibility of cooking any kind of food badly? How plausible is the belief that only general or only specialized insurance agencies could be found? The unacceptable versions, items 18 and 20, are too obviously true to discriminate high achievement from low. Both read like introductory sentences lifted from a textbook, sentences that set the stage for an important idea but do not themselves express important ideas.

5. To one who lacks the knowledge being tested, a wrong answer should appear more plausible than the correct one.

(21)   **By adding more solute, a saturated solution can be made supersaturated.   (F)**

(22)   **A supersaturated solution contains more solute per unit than a saturated solution.   (T)**

It appears reasonable to believe that adding more solute would turn a saturated solution into a supersaturated solution (item 21). But those who understand solutions know that it doesn't work that way. The added solute won't dissolve in a saturated solution. Only by evaporating some of the solvent or cooling it, can a saturated solution be made supersaturated. The student who tries to use common sense as a substitute for special knowledge is likely to give a wrong answer (which is all his knowledge entitles him to) to the first item. But the same common sense leads the student of low achievement to answer item 22 correctly. Thus the second version fails to function properly as a test of the student's command of knowledge.

6. The item is expressed clearly based on a single idea.

(23)   **The salt dissolved in water can be recovered by evaporation of the solvent.   (T)**

(24)   **Salt can be dissolved in water and can be recovered by evaporation of the solvent.   (T)[1]**

(25)   **At conception the sex ratio is approximately 3 boys to 2 girls.   (T)**

(26)   **Scientists have found that male-producing sperm are stronger and live longer than female-**

---

[1]Another unacceptable version that inappropriately combines two ideas might be: Salt dissolves in hot water; sugar dissolves in cold water.   (T)

producing sperm, which accounts for the sex ratio at conception of approximately 3 boys to 2 girls.   (T)

An item based on a single idea is usually easier to understand than one based on two or more ideas. It is also more efficient. One can obtain a more accurate measurement of a student's achievement by testing separate ideas separately than by lumping them together and scoring one composite answer right or wrong.

(27)   **Individuals who deliberate before making choices seldom find themselves forced to sacrifice one good thing in order to attain another.   (F)**

(28)   **Life is a continuous process of choice making, sacrificing one human value for another, which goes through the following steps: spontaneous mental selections regarding everything we want, conflicting preferences hold each other in check, hesitation becomes deliberation as we weigh and compare values, finally choice or preference emerges.   (T)**

The strong inclination of some teachers to use their tests as opportunities for teaching, or their misguided attempts to use textbook sentences as test items, may account for the appearance of such items as number 28. But if one looks for the central idea in item 28, and asks what misapprehension it might serve to correct, an item like number 27 may emerge. Item 27 is simpler, clearer, and better in almost every way than item 28.

7. The item is worded concisely.

(29)   **The federal government pays practically the entire cost of constructing and maintaining highways that are part of the interstate highway system.   (F)**

(30)   **When you see a highway with a marker that reads "Interstate 80," you know that the construction and upkeep of that road are built and maintained by the state and federal governments.   (T)**

The wording of item 30 is careless and redundant. It is the *highway* that is built and maintained, not its construction and upkeep. The personal touch ("when you see") may give the appearance of practicality, but does not affect what the item really measures at all. Finally, making item 30 true by including state as well as federal governments as supporters of the interstate highway system probably makes the item easier for the uninformed. Item 29 hits the intended mark more clearly because it is more straightforward and concise.

8. The item does not include an artificial, tricky negative.

(31)   **Columbus made only four voyages of exploration to the Western Hemisphere.   (T)**

(32)   **Columbus did not make four voyages of exploration to the Western Hemisphere.   (F)**

Some item writers try to turn textbook propositions into false statements for test items simply by inserting the word *not* in the original statement. The result is seldom good. The item usually carries the clear birthmark of its unnatural origin: It reads awkwardly and invites suspicion, which, if the item is indeed false, may give away the answer. Furthermore, these items tend to be tricky. An unobtrusive "not" in an otherwise wholly true statement may be overlooked by even a well-prepared examinee. Such items put students at an unnecessary disadvantage. Negatively worded statements have been shown to be more difficult and to create more confusion and hostility in examinees than positively worded true–false statements (Barker and Ebel, 1981).

Reducing Ambiguity

Why are multiple-choice items seldom criticized for being ambiguous, but true–false items seem to be faulted with regularity? The answer, we think, is in the item formats themselves. With multiple-choice items, the response that appears to be most correct, relative to the other alternatives, can be defended. There is relative comparison inherent in the item. With true–false items, however, the statement usually is absolute and examinees search their knowledge structures for alternatives. A true–false item that declares, "Mt. Palomar is a tall mountain," leads the examinee to a search for high peaks so that the tallness of Mt. Palomar can be judged relative to the heights of other mountains. A corresponding multiple-choice item may ask which is tallest and provide these choices: Mt. Whitney, Mt. St. Helen's, Mt. Palomar, and Grand Teton. Though Mt. Palomar is the lowest of the four peaks, by itself it certainly would fit most conceptions of tall. This simple illustration of the format differences suggests a solution to the ambiguity problem in some true–false items.

Most true–false items can be made essentially ambiguity free by introducing a comparison within the item. Here are some sample pairs of poor and improved items:

1a. **Open-book tests tend to be inefficient. (?)**
1b. **Open-book tests tend to be less efficient than closed-book tests. (T)**
2a. **Take-home exams usually are high in quality. (?)**
2b. **Take-home exams usually are higher in quality than in-class exams. (F)**
3a. **The use of closed-book, in-class tests contributes to high retention by students. (?)**
3b. **The use of closed-book, in-class tests contributes more to high retention by students than does the use of take-home tests. (T)**
3c. **The use of closed-book, in-class tests contributes more to high retention by students than to reduction of test anxiety. (T)**

In each item an internal comparison is introduced so that "inefficient," "high in quality," and "high retention" can be judged by a common standard.

In other cases, statements may be ambiguous because of the imprecise wording chosen by the item writer. Instead of saying "a long test," for example, say "a 100-item test." Instead of referring to "an easy item," describe it as "an item that at least 85 percent of examinees answer correctly." There is no choice between brevity and precision when writing true–false items. Though we seek both, brevity and imprecision lead to worse measurement consequences than does verbosity with clarity.

Enhancing Item Discrimination

The job of a test item is to discriminate between those who have and those who lack command of some element of knowledge, regardless of the type of interpretation to be made of the scores. Those who have achieved command should be able to answer the question correctly without difficulty. Those who lack it should find a wrong answer attractive. To produce items that will discriminate in this way is one of the arts of item writing. Here are some of the ways in which true–false items can be produced to promote discrimination.

1. Use more false than true statements.

When in doubt, students seem more inclined to accept than to challenge propositions presented in a true–false test. False statements tend to discriminate more sharply between students of high and low achievement than do true statements (Barker and Ebel, 1981). This may be due to what is called an "acquiescent response set." In the absence of firm knowledge, students seem more likely to accept than to reject a declarative statement whose truth or falsity they must judge.

Instructions for preparing true–false tests sometimes suggest including about the same number of false and true statements. But if the false statements tend to be higher in discrimination, it would seem advantageous to include a higher proportion of them, perhaps as many as 67 percent. Even if students come to expect a greater number of false items, the technique still seems to work. In one of the author's classes, students took a test on which two-thirds of the statements were false. After answering the questions and counting how many they had marked true, they were told the correct number of true statements and were given a chance to change any answers they wished. Most of them changed a number of answers, but they improved their scores very little, on the average. They changed about as many of their answers from right to wrong as from wrong to right.

2. Word the item so that superficial logic suggests a wrong answer.

(1)   A rubber ball weighing 100 grams is floating on the surface of a pool of water exactly half submerged. An additional downward force of 50 grams would be required to submerge it completely.   (F)

The ball is half submerged and weighs 100 grams, which gives one-half of 100 considerable plausibility on a superficial basis. The true case is, of course, that if its weight of 100 grams submerges only half of it, another 100 grams would be required to submerge all of it. Superficial logic also would make the incorrect answers to questions 2, 3, and 4 seem plausible.

(2)   Since students show a wide range of individual differences, the ideal measurement situation would be achieved if each student could take a different test specially designed to test him or her.   (F)

(3)   The output voltage of a transformer is determined in part by the number of turns on the input coil.   **(T)**

(4)   A transformer that will increase the voltage of an alternating current can also be used to increase the voltage of a direct current.   **(F)**

3. Make the wrong answer consistent with a popular misconception or a popular belief irrelevant to the question.

(5)   The effectiveness of tests as tools for measuring achievement is lowered by the appre-hension students feel for them.   **(F)**

Many students do experience test anxiety, but for most of them it facil-itates rather than impedes maximum performance.

(6)   An achievement test should include enough items to keep every student busy during the entire test period.   **(F)**

Keeping students busy at worthy educational tasks is usually commend-able, but in this case it would make rate of work count too heavily as a determi-nant of the test score.

4. Use specific determiners in reverse to confound testwiseness.

In true–false test items extreme words like *always* or *never* tend to be used mainly in false statements by unwary item writers, whereas such modifiers as *some, often,* or *generally* tend to be used mainly in true statements. When they are so used they qualify as "specific determiners" that help testwise but uninformed examinees to answer true–false questions correctly. But some *always* or *never* state-ments are true and some *often* or *generally* statements are false. Thus these specific determiners can be used to attract the testwise student to a wrong answer.

(7)   A 50-item test generally will be more reliable than a 75-item test.   **(F)**

(8)   In a positively skewed distribution the mean is always larger than the mode.   **(T)**

(9)   True statements usually are more discriminating than false statements.   **(F)**

(10)   A correlation of +0.28 is never considered to be higher than a correlation of −0.49.   **(T)**

5. Use phrases in false statements that give them the "ring of truth."

(11)   The use of better achievement tests will, in itself, contribute little or nothing to better achievement.   **(F)**

The phrases "in itself" and "little or nothing" impart a tone of sincerity and rightness to the statement that conceals its falseness from the uninformed.

(12)   To ensure comprehensive measurement of each aspect of achievement, different kinds of items must be specifically written, in due proportions, to test each distinct mental process the course is intended to develop.   **(F)**

As in questions 2, 3, and 4, superficial logic is predominant. But this item also displays the elaborate statement and careful qualifications that testwise individuals associate mainly with true statements.

Are teachers playing fair when they set out deliberately to make it easy for some students to give wrong answers to test items? We contend that if they want valid measures of achievement—that is, measures that correctly distinguish between those who have and those who lack command of a particular element of knowledge—it is the only way they can play fair. The only reason a test constructor sets out to make wrong answers attractive to those who lack command of the knowledge is so that correct answers will truly indicate the achievement they purport to measure.

MULTIPLE TRUE–FALSE ITEMS

Multiple true–false items resemble multiple-choice items in their physical appearance. However, rather than selecting one best answer from several alternatives, examinees respond to each of the several alternatives as a separate true–false statement. These separate statements have a common stem, like a multiple-choice item, but any number of the associated alternatives may be true. The number of alternatives per item or cluster need not remain constant throughout a given test. Here is a sample item:

**An ecologist losing weight by jogging and exercising is
  1. **increasing maintenance metabolism.   (T)**
  2. **decreasing net productivity.   (T)**
  3. **increasing biomass.   (F)**
  4. **decreasing energy lost to decomposition.   (F)**
  5. **increasing gross productivity.   (F)**

Notice that the alternatives are numbered consecutively throughout the test and each new stem is introduced by two asterisks or some symbol that makes the stem easily identifiable. The next item, for example, might contain choices 6 to 10, the next, choices 11 to 14, and so on.

The multiple true–false form has several appealing features relative to the multiple-choice format (Frisbie and Sweeney, 1982). Examinees can make at least three multiple true–false item responses, on the average, in the time required to answer a single multiple-choice item, a decided advantage in an hour of testing time. The longer test permits testing of a greater range or depth of content. In addition, it has been shown that a multiple true–false test prepared by converting items from multiple-choice form yields higher reliability estimates than the original multiple-choice test (Frisbie and Druva, 1986; Kreiter and Frisbie, 1989). Finally, two less critical outcomes can be noted. Students that were examined by both item types expressed an overwhelming preference for multiple true–false items and perceived them to be easier than the multiple choice.

Multiple true–false items can be developed using any of several strategies. Existing multiple-choice items can be converted easily to multiple true–false "clusters," sometimes without significant rewording of the stem. The response choices in some items would need to be modified so that each cluster would not contain a single true statement. The number of items per cluster may vary, and the number of true statements per cluster should vary throughout a given test from "all" to "none." In other words, the test constructor should avoid establishing a pattern for the number of true statements per cluster, just as the position of the keyed response should vary throughout a multiple-choice test.

The shortcomings of "multiple multiple-choice" items, like the one shown below, can be overcome by converting them to multiple true–false form. Consider this example from an elementary-level mathematics test:

For which of the quantities below is it more reasonable to estimate the quantity by measuring a sample rather than the whole population?
  I.   **The average life of a new brand of TV tubes**
  II. **The percent of American voters who favor the president's foreign policy**
  III. **The number of teachers in Jefferson School who usually ride the bus to school**
*A. **Both I and II**
 B. **Both II and III**
 C. **I only**
 D. **II only**
 E. **III only**

In multiple true–false form, the item might look like this:

**It would be more reasonable to measure a sample than the whole population to estimate the
  1. **average life of a new brand of TV tubes.   (T)**
  2. **percent of American voters who favor the president's foreign policy.   (T)**
  3. **number of teachers in Jefferson School who usually ride the bus to school.   (F)**

Note that it is possible to add more statements to the multiple true–false cluster quite readily, but to do so to the multiple multiple-choice item would increase its complexity for the item writer and the examinee. Both types of items require the same cognitive tasks, but the second item does the job more efficiently.

Finally, those who prepare multiple true–false items other than by a conversion method can begin the process using the recommendations provided next for preparing multiple-choice items. The task is simplified somewhat, however, because the item writer is not limited to only one correct answer in the set of responses developed. Any concepts, principles, or applications measured by multiple-choice items can be measured at least as well by multiple true–false items.

SUMMARY PROPOSITIONS

1. True–false items provide a simple and direct means of measuring the essential outcomes of formal education.
2. The low esteem in which true–false tests are sometimes held is due to inept use, not to inherent limitations.
3. True–false items provide information on essential achievement more efficiently than most other item forms.
4. Most important aspects of achievement can be tested equally well with either true–false or multiple-choice items.
5. It is less efficient to group true–false statements to produce a multiple-choice item than to require

separate responses to each of the true–false statements.

6. Informed guesses, as opposed to blind guesses, provide useful indications of achievement.

7. Students do very little blind guessing on good true–false tests.

8. The probability of an examinee achieving a high score on a true–false test by guessing blindly is extremely low.

9. True–false items that appear ambiguous only to poorly prepared students are likely to be powerful discriminators.

10. Few textbook sentences are significant enough, and meaningful enough out of context, to be used as true statements in a true–false test.

11. Statements that are essentially (but not perfectly) true or essentially (but not totally) false can make good true–false items.

12. True–false items can test students' comprehension of important ideas and their ability to use them in solving problems.

13. There are no firm empirical data to support the notions that true–false tests encourage rote learning, oversimplified conceptions of the truth, or the learning of false or incorrect ideas.

14. Generally, it is easier to develop test items from instructional materials than from statements of instructional objectives.

15. A useful strategy for developing true–false items is to create pairs of statements, one true and one false, based on a single idea.

16. Good true–false items express single, not multiple, ideas.

17. Generally, a good false statement cannot be created by inserting a negative ("not") in a true statement.

18. Ambiguity in items can be minimized by writing statements that contain an internal comparison of alternatives.

19. False statements tend to be more highly discriminating than true statements.

20. Specific determiners can be used in ways that will hinder rather than help the poorly prepared, testwise examinee.

21. False statements can be made to seem plausible by using familiar terms and phrases in seemingly straightforward factual statements.

22. Relative to multiple-choice items, multiple true–false items are more efficient, are easier to prepare, and yield more reliable scores.

QUESTIONS FOR STUDY AND DISCUSSION

1. How could a good true–false item and the proposition on which it is based be distinguished?

2. What are some logical explanations for the general advantage of multiple choice over true–false in terms of item discrimination?

3. Why might the task of responding to a true–false item be more difficult inherently than responding to a content-equivalent multiple-choice item?

4. What steps can a test constructor take to diminish the potential negative effects of guessing on true–false tests? multiple-choice tests?

5. How does the use of verbatim textbook sentences as true–false items contribute separately to ambiguity and to measurement of triviality?

6. What are the arguments that support and refute the idea that true–false items implant "untruths" or misinformation in the minds of test takers?

7. How does the addition of an internal comparison in a true–false item make it more like a multiple-choice item?

8. Under what circumstances might the advice "Use more false than true" have more negative than positive consequences for obtaining valid measures?

9. Why might it be bad advice to recommend that specific determiners *not* be used in true–false items?

9

Multiple-Choice Test Items

THE POPULARITY OF THE MULTIPLE-CHOICE FORMAT

Multiple-choice items have long been the most highly regarded and widely used form of objective-test item. They are adaptable to the measurement of most important educational outcomes: of knowledge, understanding, and judgment; of ability to solve problems, to recommend appropriate action, to make predictions. Almost any understanding or ability that can be tested by means of any other item form—short answer, completion, true–false, matching, or essay—can also be tested by means of multiple-choice test items.

The form of the multiple-choice item, with the stem asking or implying a direct question, provides a realistic, naturally appropriate setting for testing student achievement. There tends to be less indirectness and artifice in multiple choice than in some other item forms. Students often find multiple-choice questions less ambiguous than completion or true–false items. Instructors also find it easier to defend correct answers.

Finally, multiple-choice items seem to both instructors and students to be less susceptible to chance errors resulting from guessing than true–false items. It is easy to exaggerate the harm done by guessing and to place too much emphasis on the need to limit the amount of guessing students do. Yet no matter how little harm is done by guessing, instructors and students still perceive that it is less detrimental in multiple-choice than in true–false tests.

Multiple-choice items have withstood the test of time well. They have overcome barrages of criticism and they remain resilient to allegations that—like other objective items—they are superficial, ambiguous, and unduly susceptible to guessing. Usually, the critics have said or implied that the only good way to test is their way—essay testing or some form of performance testing. Their way presents more authentic tasks, they say, and permits the assessment of higher-order cognitive skills. The implications are that we must use one method or the other, not both, and that multiple-choice items measure only artificial behaviors attained through some form of rote learning.

Few objective tests or item formats are so perfect as to be above reproach from persistent, perceptive critics. But there are several weaknesses in the indictments that have been issued against all multiple-choice tests and items. First, the criticisms are rarely supported by unbiased empirical data, despite the fact that such data would be relatively easy to obtain. The shortcomings mentioned by critics should lower the discriminating power of the items and the reliability of the scores. Yet trained teachers and expert test makers have demonstrated repeatedly and continually that scores from multiple-choice tests can be highly reliable. The evidence against multiple-choice testing tends to be based on generalizations stemming from intuition or from isolated instances of poor tests or items.

In the second place, most critics seldom make a serious attempt to make a good case for a better way of measuring educational achievement. Others promote assessment of performance, particularly methods that would not require the use of paper and pencil. But such proposals seldom account for the limitations inherent in the performance tasks, the fallibility of the scores assigned by judges, or the costs in time and personnel required to carry out the process. There are strengths and weaknesses associated with all forms of assessment and users of each need to be aware of these pros and cons. Most importantly, educators should realize that no single approach to educational measurement is most appropriate for *all* instructional situations.

Even the most ardent advocates of objective testing do not claim perfection. They acknowledge, as we do, that multiple-choice test items can be subject to serious flaws and that, in general, they are not as clearly meaningful and sharply discriminating as they should be. Most users of objective tests would agree wholly with the observation that the scores they obtain are not as reliable as they might be, or ought to be, for maximum value. But they are not likely to abandon multiple-choice testing until a substitute with less serious shortcomings can be found. The implied alternatives, essay or performance testing, are clearly less convenient and efficient to use in many situations.

Production versus Selection

It is sometimes suggested that objective tests are inevitably more superficial and less realistic tests of a student's knowledge than are essay tests. The reasoning is that in suggesting possible answers to the student the examiner has done the important part of the task. But most good objective-test items require the examinee to develop, by creative, original thought, the *basis* for choice among the alternatives. Good objective-test items do not permit correct response on the basis of simple recognition, sheer rote memory, or meaningless verbal association. Consider the nature of the thought processes involved in selecting an answer to this question:

> **A child buys jelly beans which the grocer picks up, without regard for color, from a tray containing a mixture of jelly beans of three different colors. What is the smallest number of jelly beans the child can buy and still be certain of getting at least four jelly beans of the same color?**

The answers provided are 4, 7, 10, and 12.

Assume that examinees are seeing this particular problem for the first time, so that they cannot answer it successfully by simply repeating an answer someone else has given them. Assume, too, that problems of this kind are not of sufficient practical importance to have been made the subject of a special unit of study. These assumptions call attention to an important general principle of educational measurement. What a test item measures, that is, what a successful response to it indicates, cannot be determined on the basis of the item alone. Consideration must also be given to the examinee's previous experiences. These may differ significantly for different examinees. But in the case of the foregoing problem, the assumptions mentioned above may be quite reasonable.

How much different would the thought processes be, and how much more difficult would the problem be, if no answers were suggested and the task required production of the answer rather than selection? Producing an answer is not necessarily a more complex or difficult task, or one more indicative of achievement, than choosing the best of the available alternatives (Quellmalz, Capell, and Chou, 1980).

Hogan's (1981) thorough review of the research involving comparisons between free-response and objective tests led him to these conclusions: "In most instances, free-response and choice-type measures are found to be equivalent or nearly equivalent, as defined by their intercorrelation, within the limits of their respective reliabilities. Further, the choice-type measure is nearly always more reliable than the free-response measure and is considerably easier to score." Patterson (1926) reached the same conclusion nearly 55 years earlier. But despite the overwhelming empirical support for Hogan's conclusions, many practitioners continue to ignore the research or persist in believing that in their own situation the two must yield measures of quite different abilities.

The Process of Elimination

Students may sometimes arrive at the correct answer to a multiple-choice test item through a process of elimination. Rejecting responses that seem unsatisfactory, they are finally left with one termed the "right answer," not because they have any basis for choosing it directly, but simply because none of the others will do.

The availability of this process of elimination is sometimes regarded as a weakness of the multiple-choice item form. It is charged that students get credit for knowing something they really don't know. Most specialists in test construction, however, do not disapprove of the process of answering by elimination and do not regard it as a sign of weakness in multiple-choice items in general, or in an item where the process is particularly useful. (It might be noted in passing that an item that uses the response "none of the above" as a correct answer *requires* the student to answer by a process of elimination.) There are two reasons why this process is not generally deplored by test specialists.

In the first place, the function of achievement-test items is primarily to contribute to a measure of general achievement in an area of study. They are not intended primarily to provide an inventory of which particular bits of knowledge or skills a student has. The achievement of a student who answers items 1, 3, and 5 correctly but misses 2 and 4 is regarded as equal to the achievement of another student who answers items 2, 3, and 4 correctly but misses 1 and 5. Identifying exactly which things a student has achieved or failed to achieve is a matter of secondary importance except when objectives-referenced interpretations are needed for mastery or diagnostic decisions.

In the second place, the knowledge and ability required to properly eliminate incorrect alternatives can be, and usually is, closely related to the knowledge or ability that would be required to select the correct alternative. If education does not consist in the accumulation of unrelated bits of information, if the development of a meaningful network of related facts and concepts is essential, then the fact that a student responds in a reflective, problem-solving manner, choosing the best answer by rational processes (including the process of elimination), should be applauded rather than deplored. Of course, this reasoning depends on the use of multiple-choice items in which the distracters are plausible choices for uninformed or misinformed examinees. The ability to eliminate absurd or logically inappropriate choices is no proxy for a measure of useful verbal knowledge.

In practice, few multiple-choice test items are likely to be answered correctly merely by eliminating incorrect choices. Far more often the process of choice will involve comparative judgments of this alternative against that. It is unlikely that an examinee who is totally ignorant of the correct answer would have knowledge enough to eliminate with certainty the incorrect alternatives. This is especially likely to be true if the item is well enough constructed so that all the available alternatives, correct and incorrect, have some obvious basic similarity. For these reasons, it seems safe to conclude that the problem of answer choice by a process of distracter elimination need not be regarded as a serious one.

THE CONTENT BASIS FOR CREATING MULTIPLE-CHOICE ITEMS

Like true–false items, multiple-choice items are developed most conveniently and most appropriately on the basis of ideas expressed or implied in instructional materials. In Chapter 8 two paragraphs of test material were reproduced and these three propositions were extracted from them:

1. The use of optional essay items interferes with interindividual score comparisons.
2. The use of optional essay items usually contributes to reduced test-score variability.
3. The use of optional essay items usually results in reduced test-score reliability.

To develop multiple-choice test items on the basis of propositions like these, it is necessary to:

1. Formulate a question or an incomplete statement that clearly implies a question (the item stem).
2. Provide an acceptable answer to the question, stated in a few well-chosen words.
3. Produce several plausible (but incorrect) answers to the question (the distracters).

This sequence of steps was followed to develop a multiple-choice item corresponding to each of the propositions reproduced above.

(1) How would the use of optional rather than required essay items likely affect the interpretation of the scores obtained?
   *a. It generally distorts norm-referenced interpretations.
   b. It generally affects treatment-referenced interpretations more than norm-referenced ones.
   c. It generally makes criterion-referenced interpretations more accurate.
   d. It generally provides clarification of the domain for domain-referenced interpretations.

(2) How would the use of optional rather than required essay items probably affect test-score variability?
   *a. The standard deviation will be smaller when choices are permitted.
   b. There will be fewer low scores when choices are permitted.
   c. Score variability will be increased when choices are permitted.
   d. Scores are more likely to be spread out through the moderate range when choices are permitted.

(3) What is the probable effect on score reliability of using optional rather than required essays?
   *a. The K–R20 should be noticeably lower.
   b. The K–R20 could be only slightly higher or lower.
   c. The test–retest coefficient should be noticeably lower.
   d. The split-halves coefficient should be unaffected.

In the remainder of this chapter, a number of suggestions will be offered for writing good multiple-choice test items. Most of these reflect conclusions that item writers have reached as a result of their own efforts to produce items that will yield dependable indications of achievement, and many are supported by rational inference. Nonetheless, only a few have been tested in rigorous experiments, and the results have not always clearly supported the suggestions. Rigorous experiments in this area are difficult to manage, and the effect of violating one or a few suggestions is not likely to be great. On the whole, however, item writers are likely to produce better items if they know and follow the suggestions than if they are ignorant of them or disregard them. A comprehensive review of multiple-choice item writing research and lore led Haladyna and Downing (1989a) to develop a taxonomy of item writing rules and to examine the validity of the rules that have been offered by text authors and researchers (Haladyna and Downing, 1989b).

THE MULTIPLE-CHOICE ITEM STEM

The function of the item stem is to acquaint the examinee with the problem that is being posed. Ideally, it should state or imply a specific question. Although one can sometimes save words without loss of clarity by using an incomplete statement as the item stem, a direct question is often better. Not only does a direct question tend to present the examinee with a more specific problem, it also may focus the item writer's purposes more clearly and help him or her to avoid irrelevance or unrelatedness in the distracters.

Focus on Relevance

Irrelevant items fall short in contributing to the purpose for testing for any number of reasons: the stem fails to present a question or specific problem, the wording of the stem is ambiguous, or the question presented is relatively insignificant. A lack of relevance results in frustration for examinees and contributes to unreliable measures. The sample items that follow illustrate poor techniques for beginning the multiple-choice item.

Physiology teaches us that
*a. the development of vital organs is dependent upon muscular activity.
 b. strength is independent of muscle size.
 c. the mind and body are not influenced by each other.
 d. work is not exercise.

Here the subject of a sentence is used as the item stem and its predicate as the correct response. Obviously, the predicate does not *necessarily* follow: Physiology could teach us a variety of things. Even if the stem were rephrased to read, "What does physiology teach us?" the item would be just as bad.

In comparing the period of heterosexual adjustment of our culture with those of other cultures, it must be concluded that
*a. there are tremendous differences that can only be explained on a cultural basis.
 b. there are large differences that must be explained by the interaction of biology and the more influential culture.
 c. although there are some differences, the biological foundation of puberty is fundamental.
 d. in most cultures puberty is the period of heterosexual adjustment.

Here, again, there are any number of conclusions possible on the basis of a study of a particular period of human development. Until the examinee reads all the responses, she or he has no clear idea of what the question is asking. The item as a whole is not focused on any specific problem. This opens the way for confusing multiple interpretations.

Absolute and relative correctness.   Ideally, the intended answer to a multiple-choice question should be a thoroughly correct answer, admitting no difference of opinion among adequately informed experts. This kind of absolute correctness, however, is difficult to achieve except in formal logical systems or in statements that simply reproduce other statements. Few, if any, inductive truths or experimentally based generalizations can be regarded as absolutely true. Test constructors must base many of their items on propositions that are not absolutely true but are strongly probable. They should, however, guard against basing items on statements whose validity would be challenged by competent scholars.

Another guideline to follow is that the stem of a multiple-choice item should ask a question that has a definite answer. Indeterminate questions may provide interesting topics for discussion, but they do not make good items for testing achievement. For example:

Which event in the following list has been of the greatest importance in American history?
*a. Braddock's defeat
 b. Burr's conspiracy
 c. The Hayes–Tilden contest
 d. The Webster–Hayne debate

It is unlikely that scholars can agree on which of these events is of the greatest importance in American history. The importance of an event depends on the point of view of the person making the judgment and the context in which that individual is thinking of it.

While each multiple-choice item should have a definite answer, it may not always be an absolutely correct answer. Many good items ask the examinee to choose the best answer, as in this example.

Which statement best characterizes the man appointed by President Eisenhower to be Chief Justice of the United States Supreme Court?
 a. An associate justice of the Supreme Court who had once been a professor of law at Harvard
*b. A successful governor who had been an unsuccessful candidate for the Republican presidential nomination
 c. A well-known New York attorney who successfully prosecuted the leaders of the Communist party in the United States
 d. A Democratic senator from a southern state who had supported Eisenhower's campaign for the presidency

For many of the most important questions that need to be asked, it is impossible to state an absolutely correct answer within the reasonable limits of a multiple-choice test item. Even if space limitation were not a factor, two experts would probably not agree on the precise wording of the best possible answer. Items whose "correct" answer is simply the best among the alternatives offered often permit the item writer to ask much more significant questions and free him or her from the responsibility of stating a correct answer so precisely that all authorities would agree that the particular wording used was the best possible wording.

Opinions and authoritative sources. What about items that involve expressions of opinion? If it is an opinion on which most experts agree, then a reasonable multiple-choice item can be based on it.

Which of these statements is most consistent with Jefferson's concept of democracy?
  a. Democracy is part of the divine plan for mankind.
  b. Democracy requires a strong national government.
c. The purpose of government is to promote the welfare of the people.
  d. The purpose of government is to protect the people from radical or subversive minorities.

The responses to this question represent generalizations on the basis of Jefferson's speeches and writings. No authoritative sanction for one particular generalization is likely to be available. Yet scholars familiar with Jefferson's work would probably agree on a best answer to this item. In such cases the use of an item based on expert opinion is entirely justifiable. However, if the item asks the examinee for a personal opinion, it is subject to criticism. For example:

What do you consider the most important objective of staff meetings?
a. To establish good working relations with your staff
  b. To handle routine matters
  c. To help teachers improve instruction
  d. To practice and exemplify democracy in administration

There is one sense in which any answer to this item must be considered a correct answer. On the other hand, what the item writer obviously wanted to do was to test the examinee's judgment against that of recognized authorities in the field of interpersonal relations. It would have been better to ask students directly to "choose the most important objective of staff meetings." Their answers will obviously be what *they* consider the most important objective, but all answers will be open to criticism and possible correction should they differ from the judgment of recognized experts.

But even experts disagree, particularly in areas that experience continual change due to new advancements in the field. An instructor may present one viewpoint or recommend a specific technique, but the textbook adopts a different or opposing position. When it is relevant to examine students on these topics, it may be necessary to specify the authoritative source in the stem. Expressions like "According to your instructor" or "According to Ebel and Frisbie," for example, may be needed to establish a frame of reference from which students should respond. However, such situations probably ought to be quite rare. It seems more relevant for examinees to understand the rationale for a particular point of view than, for example, to remember Smith's viewpoint.

Good multiple-choice items deal with important, significant ideas, not with incidental details, as does the first item following, nor with particular, unique organizations of subject matter, as does the second.

This question is based on the advertising campaign of Naumkeag Mills to retain the market leadership of Pequot bed linen. What was the competitive position of Pequot products in 1927?
  a. Ahead of all competitors among all customers
b. Strong with institutional buyers but weak with household consumers
  c. Second only to Wamsutta among all customers
  d. Weak with all groups of consumers

This advertising campaign may indeed provide an excellent illustration of the problems involved and the practices to follow in advertising campaigns. But it seems not entirely appropriate to measure students' ability to handle an advertising campaign by asking them to recall the details of one illustration used in instruction.

The second principle of education is that the individual
 a. gathers knowledge.
 b. makes mistakes.
 c. responds to situations.
 *d. resents domination.

The only person capable of answering this question is one who has studied a particular book or article. Whether a given principle of education is first or second is usually a matter of little importance. Educators have not agreed on any particular list of principles of education or any priority of principles. This item shows an undesirable close tie-up to the organization of subject matter used by a specific instructor or writer.

Instructional insertions. Informational preambles that serve only as window dressing and do not help the examinee understand the question being asked should ordinarily be avoided. Here are two examples.

While ironing her formal, Jane burned her hand accidentally on the hot iron. This was due to a transfer of heat by
 *a. conduction.
 b. radiation.
 c. convection.
 d. absorption.

The introductory sentence suggests that the item involves a practical problem. Actually the question asked calls only for knowledge of technical terminology.

In purifying water for a city water supply, one process is to have the impure water seep through layers of sand and fine and coarse gravel. Here many impurities are left behind. Below are four terms, one of which will describe this process better than the others. Select the correct one.
 a. Sedimentation
 *b. Filtration
 c. Chlorination
 d. Aeration

The primary purpose of a test item is to measure achievement. While much learning may occur during the process of taking a test, deliberate inclusion of instructional materials may reduce its effectiveness as a test more than its instructional value is increased. It might be better to ask the purpose of filtration in purifying city water supplies or the type of filter used.

Introducing novelty.   Novel questions and unique problem situations reward the critical-minded student who has sought to understand what he or she was taught and penalize the superficial learner. Consider this example:

If the radius of the earth were increased by 3 feet, its circumference at the equator would be increased by about how much?
  a.   9 feet
  b.   12 feet
 *c.   19 feet
  d.   28 feet

Requiring students to predict what would happen under certain unusual, even impossible, circumstances is a good way to measure their understanding of the principle involved. This type of task does a good job of discriminating between the student who can estimate an answer based on a thorough understanding of the principles and the student who must rely on formula and tedious computations.

It is usually desirable to avoid using the same questions or problems in a test that were used during instruction. In general, bona fide questions such as would be asked by a person honestly seeking information are likely to be more important than quiz-type questions, which would only be asked by someone who already knew the answer. Here is an example of a bona fide question:

J. B. Matthews, one-time employee of Senator McCarthy's subcommittee, charged that a large number of supporters of communism in the United States would be found in which of these groups?
  a.   Wall Street bankers
  b.   Newspaper editors
  c.   Professional gamblers
 *d.   Protestant clergymen

Unintended clues.   Multiple-choice items sometimes provide unintended hints about the correct answer that offer considerable help to a poorly prepared examinee. In some cases, key words from the stem, or their synonyms, are repeated in the correct answer. In others the correct response is more consistent grammatically or semantically with the stem than is any of the other responses. Finally, sometimes the stem of one item will inadvertently suggest the answer to another item. Here are some examples of items that provide relevant clues in the stem:

When used in conjunction with the T-square, the left vertical edge of a triangle is used to draw
 *a.   vertical lines.
  b.   slant lines.
  c.   horizontal lines.
  d.   inclined lines.

The use of the word *vertical* in both the stem and the correct response of this item provides an obvious clue.

Minor differences among organisms of the same kind are known as
  a. heredity.
*b. variations.
  c. adaptation.
  d. natural selection.

The plural term *differences* in the stem calls for a plural response, which can only be response *b.*

The major weakness of our government under the Articles of Confederation was that
  a. there were no high officials.
*b. it lacked power.
  c. it was very difficult to amend.
  d. there was only one house in Congress.

There is an obvious relation between lack of power and weakness of government. If a person knew nothing about the Articles of Confederation, common sense would nonetheless dictate the correct response.

     Any test item that is either much too easy or much to difficult for a group of examinees cannot provide much useful information about their relative levels of achievement. If on inspection or after tryout an item is found to be inappropriate in difficulty, some corrective action may be needed.

Manipulating difficulty.   To some extent the difficulty of a multiple-choice item is inherent in the idea on which it rests. There are, however, techniques that give the writers of multiple-choice test items some control over the difficulty of the items they produce on a given topic. In general, stem questions can be made easier by making them more general or harder by making them more specific. The following pair of items is illustrative.

A tariff is a tax on
  a. gifts of money.
*b. goods brought into a country.
  c. income of immigrants.
  d. real estate.

Only the most general notions about a tariff are required to respond successfully to this item, which is thus suitable for use at the lowest level of achievement. Much more knowledge of tariffs is required to respond successfully to the following item.

A high protective tariff on Swiss watches in the United States is intended to most directly benefit
  a. Swiss watchmakers.
  b. United States citizens who buy Swiss watches.

c. United States government officials.

d. United States watchmakers.

This pair of items illustrates how the generality or specificity of a question can be used to help control its difficulty.

Focus on Clarity

It is desirable to express the stem of the item so that it requests the essential knowledge being tested as directly, accurately, and simply as possible. The following item stem seems needlessly complex:

Considered from an economic viewpoint, which of these proposals to maintain world peace derives the least support from the military potentialities of atomic energy?

a. An international police force should be established.

b. Permanent programs of universal military training should be adopted.

c. Sizes of standing military forces should be increased.

d. The remaining democratic nations of the world should enter into a military alliance.

Even after repeated careful readings, the meaning of this item stem is not clear. It involves a negative approach and seems to combine two dissimilar bases for judgment, economics, and atomic energy. The wording of this item might seem to reflect lack of clarity in the thinking of the person who wrote it.

Using negatives. It sometimes seems desirable to phrase the stem question to ask not for the correct answer, but for the incorrect answer. For example,

In the definition of a mineral, which of the following is incorrect?

a. It was produced by geologic processes.

b. It has distinctive physical properties.

c. It contains one or more elements.

d. Its chemical composition is variable.

Items that are negatively stated, that is, that require an examinee to pick an answer that is not true or characteristic, tend to be somewhat confusing. They appear unusually attractive to examination writers because so much of the instructional material is organized in terms of parallel subheadings under a main topic. This suggests the easy approach, that of asking for something that is *not* one of those subheadings. However, such questions are rarely encountered outside the classroom and thus lack the practical relevance that is usually desirable. At times, negatively worded stems seem to be the best means of stating a problem to achieve both brevity and clarity. This item is an example:

Under which of these circumstances would a speaker at a political rally NOT be protected by the First Amendment?

a. When asking the audience to join in a protest march

b. When telling the audience to take violent action

c. When denouncing the president of the United States

d. When calling for the creation of a new political party

By capitalizing or underlining the negative word, the item writer draws the examinee's attention to it and ensures that the careless reader who knows the answer will not overlook this key word.

Introducing qualifications.   The purpose of the words and syntax chosen in writing a multiple-choice test item is to communicate explicit meaning as efficiently as possible. Habits of colorful, picturesque, imaginative, creative writing may serve the item writer badly by impairing the precision and definiteness of a communication. Few written words are read with such careful attention to meaning, expressed and implied, as those in objective-test items. Item writing makes rigorous demands on the vocabulary and writing skill of test constructors as well as on their mastery of the subject matter and their familiarity with the caliber of the students to be tested. Simple carelessness in grammar, usage, punctuation, or spelling may interfere with the effectiveness of an item and will certainly reflect no credit on the item writer. Skill in expository writing and careful exercise of that skill are essential to the production of good objective-test items.

It is well to specify all conditions and qualifications necessary to make the intended response definitely the best of the available alternatives. Consider this example:

What change occurs in the composition of the air in a lighted airtight room in which the only living things are growing green plants?

  a. **Carbon dioxide increases and oxygen decreases.**

b.* **Carbon dioxide decreases and oxygen increases.

  c. **Both carbon dioxide and oxygen increase.**

  d. **Both carbon dioxide and oxygen decrease.**

As originally worded, this item simply asked, "What change occurs in the composition of the air in a room in which green plants are growing?" Only if one specifies that the room is lighted, so that photosynthesis can take place; that it is airtight, so that changes in air composition will not be neutralized by ventilation; and that there are no other living things that might consume the oxygen faster than it is produced, is it possible to give a firm answer to this question.

Sometimes when item writers seek to limit a question in order to elicit a definitely correct answer, they reduce its dimensions to the point that the question itself becomes inconsequential. For example, it is important to know why the armed forces of the United States were ordered into combat in Korea in 1950, but it is difficult to give a thoroughly correct answer to such a question. On the other hand, it is quite easy to give an unequivocally truthful answer to the question, "What explanation for U.S. military action in Korea was given in an editorial in the *Chicago Tribune* on Friday, June 30, 1950?" But the knowledge this question tests is of dubious value.

Introductory sentences.   Item writers should never settle for a best answer when a correct answer to the same question is available. They should be sure that, in the eyes of competent experts, the best alternative is clearly superior to all the others.

At the same time, however, they should not avoid important questions simply because there is no absolutely and completely correct answer. If many descriptive or qualifying ideas are required, the clearest expression may be achieved by placing them in separate introductory sentences.

The term *creeping socialism* appeared frequently in political discussions in the early 1950s. Which of these is most often used to illustrate creeping socialism?
*a. Generation and distribution of electric power by the federal government
b. Communist infiltration of labor unions
c. Gradual increase in sales and excise taxes
d. Participation of the United States in international organizations such as the United Nations

The use of two sentences—one to present background information and the other to ask the question—frequently adds to the clarity of the item stem. Combining these two elements into a single-question sentence probably would make it considerably more complex.

In other situations a separate introductory sentence is necessary to establish the setting or context. Such statements differ from the instructional preambles and window dressing mentioned earlier. Here is an example:

"When we look at the world as a whole, it is clear that the problem of economic progress is really the most important." This statement is best classified as
*a. a value judgment.
b. a scientific conclusion.
c. an established fact.
d. an analogy.

Obviously, these statements could be merged to form a single question. But for examinees whose reading skills may not be well developed, greater clarity of task can be achieved by using the format illustrated.

PREPARING THE RESPONSE CHOICES

Once a suitable item stem has been prepared, a correct response should be written and then the set of distracters (incorrect responses) can be developed. Several different techniques can be employed to prepare plausible distracters, responses that will enhance the clarity and efficiency of the item without providing irrelevant clues that lead the uninformed to the correct response.

Obtaining Distracters

The purpose of a distracter in a multiple-choice item is to discriminate between those students who have command of a specific body of knowledge and those who do not. To do this, the distracter must be a plausible alternative. One way of obtaining plausible distracters is to use true statements that do not correctly answer the question presented in the stem. For example:

What is the principal advantage of a battery of lead storage cells over a battery of dry cells for automobile starting and lighting?
  a.   The storage cell furnishes direct current.
  b.   The voltage of the storage cell is higher.
  *c.   The current from the storage cell is stronger.
  d.   The initial cost of the storage cell is less.

Lead storage cells do furnish direct current, and at a higher voltage than dry cells, but this is not the reason why the storage cell is preferred. Judgments concerning the relevance of knowledge may be as important as judgments concerning its truth. Multiple-choice items should make frequent use of this device for testing an achievement that is sometimes thought to be testable only by using essay examinations.

Another source of plausible distracters are familiar expressions, phrases that have been used in common parlance and that may seem attractive to students whose knowledge is merely superficial.

Which of these has effected the greatest change in domestic plants and animals?
  a.   Influence of environment on heredity
  b.   Organic evolution
  *c.   Selective breeding
  d.   Survival of the fittest

Phrases like "organic evolution" or "survival of the fittest," which a student may have heard without understanding, provide excellent distracters at the elementary level of discrimination for which this item is intended.

Here are some specific tactics that item writers can use to generate good distracters for a multiple-choice item.

1. Define the class of things to which all the alternative answers must belong.   For example, if the question asks what cools an electric refrigerator, the class of possible answers is defined as "things that can cause cooling," such as ice, moving air, expansion of gas, and so forth.

2. Think of things that have some association with terms used in the question.   For the electric refrigerator question, these might be such things as "flow of electricity through a compressed gas" or "electromagnetic absorption of heat energy."

3. If the item calls for a quantitative answer, make the responses distinctly different points along the same scale.   For example, in response to the question, "How many questions should the average student answer correctly on a good multiple-choice test?" the alternative answers might be 40 percent, 60 percent, 80 percent, and 90 percent. Such a scale is illustrated in this item.

How did (X) the estimated amount of petroleum discovered in new fields in the late 1970s compare with (Y) the amount extracted from producing fields in the same years?

  a. X was practically zero.
*b. X was about half of Y.
  c. X just about equaled Y.
  d. X was greater than Y.

In many situations the precise value of a quantitative answer is less important than knowledge of a general level or relationship. One systematic approach to testing in quantitative situations is to categorize the responses to represent intervals on a scale of quantities. The use of code letters for the two quantities to be compared shortens the response options and probably adds to their clarity.

Sometimes it is possible to establish a qualitative scale of responses, as in this item.

Some cases of lung cancer may be attributed to cigarette smoking. What was the status of this idea in the late 1980s?

*a. The theory had been clearly established by medical evidence.
  b. It was a controversial matter and some experts considered the evidence to be inconclusive.
  c. The theory had been clearly disproved by surveys of smokers, former smokers, and non-smokers.
  d. The theory was too recent to have been subjected to any tests.

The responses to this item represent a scale of values from complete establishment to complete indefiniteness. The use of a qualitative scale of responses helps to systematize the process of test construction and to suggest desirable responses.

4. Phrase the question so that it calls for a "yes" or "no" answer plus an explanation. Here is an example.

Is the ratio of discretionary income to disposable income usually higher in a senior-citizen household than in a young-married household? Why?

  a. Yes, because seniors have greater savings income to spend.
  b. Yes, because seniors have no major future expenses (house, college costs) to save for.
  c. No, because social security payments seldom cover all fixed expenses of seniors.
*d. No, because disposable income is always higher, by definition.

5. Use various combinations of two elements as the alternatives.   Thus four responses might occasionally assume this form:

  1. Only A
  2. Only B
  3. Both A and B
  4. Neither A nor B

An item illustrating this tactic is:

What was the general policy of the Eisenhower administration during 1953 with respect to government expenditures and taxes?
- *a.* Reduction of both expenditures and taxes
- **b.* Reduction of expenditures, no change in taxes
- *c.* Reduction in taxes, no change in expenditures
- *d.* No change in either expenditures or taxes

If the two elements each have two different values, for example rise–fall, rapidly–slowly, they can be combined in this way to give four alternatives.

1. It rises rapidly.
2. It rises slowly.
3. It falls slowly.
4. It falls rapidly.

6. Finally, if alternatives still remain elusive, consider using a different approach in the item stem. It is also useful sometimes to back off from the writing job and to ask just what the item is supposed to be testing. If the proposition on which it is based is self-evident, or if a plausible false alternative to it does not exist, the idea may just as well be discarded and a new start made with a better idea.

In developing the distracters it is possible to manipulate the overall difficulty of the item, to make the correct response more or less difficult for examinees to identify. The more homogeneous the responses are, the more fine the content discrimination required, and consequently the more difficult the item will be. Compare the responses of the first item that follows with those of the second.

An embargo is
- **a.* a law or regulation.
- *b.* a kind of boat.
- *c.* an embarkment.
- *d.* a foolish adventure.

Because the responses to this item vary widely, only an elementary knowledge of embargoes is required for successful response.

An embargo is
- *a.* a tariff.
- *b.* a customs duty.
- **c.* the stoppage of goods from entry and departure.
- *d.* an admission of goods free of duty.

The homogeneity of responses in this second question makes it considerably more difficult.

Another means of making an item easier is to provide more than one basis for choosing the correct answer, as in this item.

Which of the following are known for their writings in colonial America?
*a. **Thomas Paine and Ben Franklin**
 b. **Mark Twain and Henry Clay**
 c. **William Penn and Paul Revere**
 d. **Robert Frost and Ernest Hemingway**

The use of the names of two individuals fitting the specification in the item stem makes it somewhat easier. The examinee need only know one of the colonial writers—or know that one in each of the distracters was not known for his writing in the colonial period—to respond successfully.

It has occurred to some item writers that they might use as distracters the wrong answers students give to short-answer or completion items (Loree, 1948). Some useful ideas are quite likely to be obtained in this way, but the gain in quality of items or in ease of item writing seldom seems to justify the labor of obtaining the student responses (Owens, Hanna, and Coppedge, 1970; Frisbie, 1973).

Striving for Clarity

Each of the alternative answers offered in a multiple-choice test item should be appropriate to the question asked or implied by the item stem. Careless, hasty item writing can sometimes result in the inclusion of inappropriate answer choices, as in this example:

The chief difference between the surface features of Europe and North America is that
 a. **the area of Europe is larger.**
 b. **Europe extends more to the south.**
 c. **the Volga River is longer than the Missouri–Mississippi.**
*d. **the greater highlands and plains of Europe extend in an east–west direction.**

Only the correct answer really describes a surface feature of Europe. Either the question should not be limited to "surface features" or the responses given should all conform to that category.

Since multiple-choice responses are all intended to be answers to the same question, they should all be parallel (that is, similar) in grammatical structure, in type of content, in length, and in complexity. Unfortunately, this is not always the case.

Slavery was first started
*a. **at Jamestown settlement.**
 b. **at Plymouth settlement.**
 c. **at the settlement of Rhode Island.**
 d. **a decade before the Civil War.**

The first three responses to this item are places; the fourth is a time. In questions of this type, it is not difficult to visualize an instance in which two responses would be correct. Use of a direct question stem might help to prevent this type of ambiguity.

Since alternative responses are intended to represent a set of distinct options to the stem question, it is helpful to the examinee and to the effectiveness of the test item if they do indeed present clear choices.

Meat can be preserved in brine due to the fact that
a. salt is a bacterial poison.
*b. bacteria cannot withstand the osmotic action of the brine.
c. salt alters the chemical composition of the food.
d. brine protects the meat from contact with air.

Both responses *a* and *b* could be judged correct. Response *b* simply explains why response *a* is correct. In a case like this, it is undesirable to count only one of two almost equally correct responses.

Familiar expressions and phrases provide a useful source of plausible distracters, but obscure distracters are undesirable.

A *chaotic* condition is
a. asymptotic.
*b. confused.
c. gauche.
d. permutable.

If the words *chaotic* and *confused* represent an appropriate level of difficulty for this vocabulary test, then the remaining terms used as distracters are obviously too difficult. It is unreasonable to expect the examinee to know for sure that one of them might not be a better synonym for "chaotic" than the intended correct answer.

The search for plausible distracters may sometimes induce an item writer to resort to trickery, as in this item.

Horace Greeley is known for his
a. advice to young men not to go West.
b. discovery of anesthetics.
*c. editorship of the *New York Tribune*.
d. humorous anecdotes.

Insertion of the "not" in the first response spoils what would otherwise be the best answer to the question and thus makes the item more a test of students' alertness than of their knowledge of Horace Greeley. Trickery of this kind reflects badly on the ethics of the item writer and is likely to spoil the discriminating power of the item. Such ploys tend to have detrimental effects on well-prepared examinees who are able to detect them. The message to them is "Read *every* word carefully because someone is out to catch you off guard." As a result, students are likely to require more time to make their responses, and their levels of frustration are likely to rise.

Gaining Efficiency

The need for parallel structure between the stem and the responses sometimes requires that all responses begin with the same word. But if the same group of words is repeated in each response, the possibility of including that phrase in the stem should be considered.

Which is the best definition for a vein?
*a. **A blood vessel carrying blood going to the heart**
 b. **A blood vessel carrying blue blood**
 c. **A blood vessel carrying impure blood**
 d. **A blood vessel carrying blood away from the heart**

This item could probably be improved by using an incomplete statement stem such as, "A vein is a blood vessel carrying. . . ." Occasionally, some repetition provides the most convenient way of making the item clear, but in this case, the repetition seems excessive.

Another problem arises when responses are long and complex so that examinees have difficulty perceiving and keeping in mind the essential differences among the alternatives.

Systematic geography differs from regional geography mainly in that
 a. **systematic geography deals, in the main, with physical geography, whereas regional geography concerns itself essentially with the field of human geography.**
 b. **systematic geography studies a region systematically, while regional geography is concerned only with a descriptive account of a region.**
*c. **systematic geography studies a single phenomenon in its distribution over the earth in order to supply generalizations for regional geography, which studies the arrangement of phenomena in one given area.**
 d. **systematic geography is the modern scientific way of studying differentiation of the earth's surface, while regional geography is the traditional and descriptive way of studying distribution of phenomena in space.**

A better question might ask, "What characteristic of systematic geography distinguishes it essentially from regional geography?"

Brevity in the responses simplifies the task for the examinee by removing an irrelevant source of difficulty. Brief responses also tend to focus attention on the essential differences among the alternatives offered. Other things being equal, the multiple-choice test item having shorter responses will be superior. But a test composed largely of items using one-word responses or very short phrases is likely to place more emphasis on vocabulary than on command of knowledge. The item writer should not sacrifice importance and significance in the questions to gain brevity in the responses. By way of illustration, if the purpose of an item is to test understanding of the word *monogamy*, the first of the following items will probably do the job better than the second.

What is monogamy?
  a. **Refusal to marry**
  b. **Marriage of one woman to more than one husband**
  c. **Marriage of one man to more than one wife**
  *d. **Marriage of one man to only one wife**
A marriage in which one woman marries one man is called
  a. **unicameral.**
  b. **dualism.**
  c. **monotheism.**
  *d. **monogamy.**

It is usually desirable to list the responses to a multiple-choice item rather than to arrange them in tandem, as in this example.

The balance sheet report for the Ajax Canning Company would reveal (*a*) The company's profit for the previous fiscal year *(*b*) The amount of money owed to its creditors (*c*) The amount of income tax paid (*d*) The amount of sales for the previous fiscal period.

Responses in tandem save some space but are much more difficult to compare than those placed in list form. Another good rule is that whenever the alternatives form a quantitative or qualitative scale, they normally should be arranged in order of magnitude from smallest to largest or largest to smallest. This may avoid some confusion on the part of the examinee and eliminate an irrelevant source of error.

The population of Denmark is about
  a. **2 million.**
  *b. **4 million.**
  c. **7 million.**
  d. **15 million.**

Common practice in writing multiple-choice tests calls for three or four distracters for each item. If good distracters are available, the larger the number of alternatives, the more highly discriminating the item is likely to be. However, as one seeks to write more distracters, each additional one is likely to be somewhat weaker. There is some merit in setting one's goal at three good distracters to each multiple-choice item and in struggling temporarily to reach this goal. Not all good distracters are immediately apparent. Some will emerge only after considerable brain racking.

On the other hand, there is no magic in four alternatives and no real reason why all items in a test should have the same number of alternatives. It is quite possible to write a good multiple-choice test item with only two distracters (three responses), and occasionally with only one distracter, as Smith (1958) and Williams and Ebel (1957) have shown. After tryout, one can actually improve some items by dropping those alternatives that don't distract poor students or that do distract good ones.

Eliminating Unwanted Clues

A common device for adapting multiple-choice items to questions that seem to require several correct answers is to add as a final alternative the response, "all of the above." But use of this response as the correct answer is strictly appropriate only if all preceding alternatives are *entirely correct* answers to the stem question. It is not uncommon on some classroom tests to find "all of the above" as the correct answer for each or most of the items in which it appears. Occasionally, just the opposite situation is found. In both cases such a pattern introduces an irrelevant clue to the correct answer or to an incorrect answer. When "all of the above" is used—and it should be used sparingly—it ought to be the correct answer on *some* occasions, but never on *all* occasions in which it appears.

The response "none of the above" is also sometimes used, either as the intended answer or as a distracter. It is particularly useful in multiple-choice arithmetic or spelling items where the distinction between correctness and error is unequivocal. But this response, like "all of the above," should *not* be used unless the best answer is a thoroughly correct answer. Here are examples of correct (first) and incorrect (second) usage of these responses.

Which word is misspelled?	**What does the term *growth* mean?**
a. Contrary	*a. Maturation
*b. Tendancy	b. Learning
c. Extreme	c. Development
d. Variable	d. All of these
e. None of these	e. None of these

The overuse of both of these response alternatives probably derives from the misconception that all multiple-choice items should have at least four (or five) response alternatives. These phrases are used as filler when the item writer encounters difficulty in finding a sufficient number of distracters. In such circumstances, the overuse of each becomes a clue to the testwise, underprepared student who recognizes that "all of the above" or "none of the above" is seldom the correct answer when it does appear. As was pointed out in the previous section, there is no compelling reason for all items in a test to have the same number of alternatives.

The use of distracters that are less difficult than the correct answer is sometimes criticized because it permits a student to respond successfully by eliminating incorrect responses. However, students who can respond successfully on this basis usually possess more knowledge than those who cannot. Hence the discriminating power of an item is not impaired by this characteristic. Of course, a distracter that is absurd or highly implausible will contribute little or nothing to the effectiveness of a test item.

Which of the following has helped most to increase the average length of human life?

a. Fast driving

b. Avoidance of overeating

c. Wider use of vitamins

*d. Wider use of inoculations

Some teachers may feel that the abilities of some of their students cannot possibly be underestimated, but they should not let this feeling of frustration lead them to employ such an unreasonable distracter as response *a.*

A lack of parallelism in the alternative choices often leads poorly prepared examinees to the correct answer. There is a tendency for unskilled item writers to express the correct answer more carefully and at greater length than the other alternatives. Sometimes the correct response is more general and inclusive than any distracter. At other times a familiar verbal stereotype is used as the correct answer, allowing some students to respond successfully simply by recalling vaguely that they had encountered those same words before. Here are some examples of items that provide unwanted cues:

How did styles in women's clothing in 1950 differ most from those in 1900?
a. **They showed more beauty.**
b. **They showed more variety.**
c. **They were easier to clean.**
*d. **They were easier to live in, to work in, to move in, and were generally less restrictive.**

The greater detail used in stating the correct response makes it undesirably obvious.

History tells us that all nations have enjoyed participation in
a. **gymnastics.**
b. **football.**
*c. **physical training of some sort.**
d. **baseball.**

Response *c* obviously provides a more reasonable completion to the stem than any of the other responses. It represents a consistent style of expression. This is one of the dangers inherent in the use of incomplete-statement item stems.

All these irrelevant clues to the correct answer are undesirable, of course, and should be avoided. It is entirely appropriate to plant such clues deliberately in the distracters to mislead the testwise but poorly prepared student. To give all the relevant clues—those useful to well-prepared examinees—while avoiding the irrelevant clues is an important skill in writing multiple-choice test items.

Reducing Complexity

In some medical and health-related content areas it has become popular to group answer choices and have examinees select the correct combination of choices. Such items have been referred to as "multiple multiple choice," "complex multiple choice," and "K-type items." Here is a sample item:

A form of exercise that is intended mainly to help build endurance is

a.	swimming.	**1.*	a and b
b.	jogging.	2.	a and c

c. lifting weights.	3. b and e
d. push-ups.	4. c and d
e. trunk-twisting.	5. d and e

Research comparing complex multiple-choice, multiple true–false, and multiple-choice tests point to these generalizations: (1) complex items are more time-consuming, are less efficient, and yield less reliable scores, (2) complex items are more difficult and examinees perceive them to be more difficult, (3) complex items can provide clues about correct and incorrect options because of the particular combinations of choices offered or because of the frequency with which certain options are included, and (4) examinees express greater preference for multiple true–false or multiple choice as a true measure of what they know. (See Dryden and Frisbie, 1975; Albanese, Kent, and Whitney, 1977; Albanese and Sabers, 1978; Frisbie and Ory, 1980; Kreiter and Frisbie, 1989; and Haladyna and Downing, 1989b, for data supporting these generalizations.)

The multiple true–false format, described in the previous chapter, overcomes all the limitations of the complex multiple-choice format noted above. It is highly efficient, it yields the most reliable scores, it samples the content domain most thoroughly, and examinees have shown a distinct preference for it (Frisbie and Sweeney, 1982). There seems to be no logical or empirical basis for the continued use of complex multiple-choice items.

SUMMARY PROPOSITIONS

1. The most highly regarded and widely used form of objective test is the multiple-choice form.
2. Critics of multiple-choice items tend to exaggerate both the number of faulty items that appear on tests and the seriousness of the consequences of those faults.
3. The important aspects of educational achievement that can be measured by objective tests are largely identical with those that can be measured by essay tests.
4. A student who selects the correct response to a good multiple-choice item by eliminating responses she or he knows are incorrect demonstrates achievement of relevant subject matter.
5. Multiple-choice items should be based on sound, significant ideas that can be expressed as independent and meaningful propositions.
6. The stem of a multiple-choice item should state or clearly imply a specific direct question.
7. A multiple-choice item calling for a best answer can be as effective as one that contains only one absolutely correct answer.
8. Good multiple-choice items can be based on matters of opinion if most experts share that opinion or if the authoritative source is specified.

9. A good multiple-choice item ordinarily should not ask for the examinee's opinion.
10. Items testing recall of incidental details of instruction or special organizations of subject matter ordinarily are undesirable.
11. The item stem should pose the essence of its question as simply and accurately as possible.
12. Item stems including the word *not*, asking in effect for an incorrect answer, tend to be both confusing to the examinee and somewhat superficial in content.
13. The stem of a multiple-choice item should be expressed as concisely as possible without sacrificing clarity or omitting essential qualifications.
14. Brevity is desirable in multiple-choice responses, but it should not be achieved by reducing significant questions to less important or trivial ones.
15. True statements that do not provide good answers to the stem question often make good distracters.
16. Item writers can make some multiple-choice items easier by making the stem more general and the responses more diverse; they can make items harder by making the stem more specific and the responses more similar to each other.

17. All the responses to a multiple-choice item should be parallel in type of content, grammatical structure, and general appearance.
18. The responses to a multiple-choice item should be expressed simply enough to make clear the essential differences among them.
19. The responses to a multiple-choice item should be listed rather than written one after another in a compact paragraph.
20. While most multiple-choice items provide at least four alternative responses, good questions can be written using only two or three alternatives.
21. There is no compelling reason for all multiple-choice items in a test to have exactly the same number of response alternatives.
22. The responses "none of the above" and "all of the above" are appropriate only when the response choices given to the question are absolutely correct or incorrect (as in spelling or arithmetic problems).
23. The distracters in a multiple-choice item should be definitely less correct than the answer, but plausibly attractive to the uninformed.
24. The intended answer to a multiple-choice item should be clear, concise, correct, and free of clues.

QUESTIONS FOR STUDY AND DISCUSSION

1. What is the most serious limitation of the multiple-choice format for measuring achievement (in your opinion) and how could that limitation be overcome?
2. How does the process of elimination, inherent in the multiple-choice format, contribute to less valid scores when objective-referenced rather than norm-referenced interpretations are needed?
3. Why is it preferable for the stem of a multiple-choice item to be written as a question rather than an incomplete sentence?
4. What are some advantages to the item writer of being able to use a "best answer" rather than "absolute correct answer"?
5. How can the difficulty of a multiple-choice item for a given group be altered without changing the basic underlying proposition being measured?
6. What are some potential drawbacks to using compound choices (for example, A and B; A, B, and C; and so on) as multiple-choice alternatives?
7. Under what circumstances might the use of "none of the above" contribute most to obtaining valid scores?
8. How can the use of multiple true–false items in place of multiple choice improve the measurement of achievement?

10 _____

Other Objective-Item Formats

SHORT-ANSWER ITEMS

A short-answer test item aims to test knowledge by asking examinees to supply a word, phrase, or number that answers a question or completes a sentence. Completion and fill-in-the-blank are other common labels for short-answer items. Here are several examples:

(1) Who discovered the insulin treatment of diabetes?   __Banting__

(2) The name of the holy city of Islam is   __Mecca__

(3) In what year was the battle of Hastings fought?   __A.D. 1066__

What is the common name of each of these chemical substances?

(4) $CaCO_3$ __limestone__

(5) $NaCl$ __salt__

(6) $C_{12}H_{22}O_{11}$ __sugar__

(7) $NaOH$ __lye__

(8) NH_3 __ammonia__

Items 4 through 8 constitute a cluster of similar short-answer items based on the same question.

Short-answer items deal mainly with words and numbers. They ask for names of persons, places, things, processes, colors, and so forth. They may also ask for English words, foreign equivalents, or symbols that represent words in shorthand, mathematics, chemistry, music, or logic. Common responses also include numbers representing dates, distances, costs, and populations. If they call for a phrase, it is usually something short, specific, and familiar, such as "spontaneous combustion" or "discovery of America." An item that calls for a collection of somewhat longer responses, for example, "Give three reasons why . . ." or "List the traits of . . ." is classified as a short essay question rather than a short-answer item.

This means that short-answer items test mainly for factual information. As the foundation of all reliable knowledge, facts constitute an important substratum. But there is much, much more to knowledge than the facts that can be reported in single words, short phrases, or numbers. What short-answer items can test is much more limited than what true–false or multiple-choice items can test. Thus, while any short-answer item can be converted to a true–false or multiple choice item, only a few true–false or multiple-choice items can be converted to the short-answer form.

Short-answer items are very much less affected by guessing than are true–false or multiple-choice items. They also are supposed to test recall rather than recognition, which in the eyes of some instructors makes them more demanding and more valid as tests of achievement. However, as we have already seen, not only is blind guessing a rather rare phenomenon, but the harm that it can do to the score on a reasonably good, reasonably long test is actually rather slight. And in response to the contention that recall is a more strenuous mental process than recognition, it may be said that good choice-type items seldom can be answered by simple recognition. In fact, they are more likely than are short-answer items to test understanding and to require reflective thinking.

Despite these limitations, short-answer items have a place in educational measurement. They are reasonably easy to write. They are efficient, providing many separate scorable responses per page or per unit of testing time. And if the group to be tested is reasonably small, the scoring that must be done by the teacher or a competent aide is not unreasonably burdensome.

Short-answer tests are widely and justifiably popular in the primary and intermediate elementary grades, where basic vocabularies are being built in subjects like spelling, geography, and arithmetic, and in those parts of science where names of structures, substances, and symbols must be learned. When used simply, they are the test item of choice when examinees have identifiable reading or writing problems.

Writing Short-answer Items

1. Word the question or incomplete statement carefully enough to require a single, unique answer. A common problem with short-answer items is that a question that the item writer thought would call for answer A elicits from some of the examinees equally defensible answers B, C, or D. For example, the question, "What is coal?", to which the intended answer was "a fuel," might also elicit such answers as "petrified vegetable matter," "a burning ember," or "impure carbon." To prevent this dual ambiguity—indefiniteness in what is tested and consequent difficulty in scoring—the question should be reworded so as to elicit a more specific answer.

For what purpose is most coal used?
From what substance was coal formed?
What name is applied to a glowing coal in a fire?
Coal consists mainly of what chemical element?

2. Think of the intended answer first. Then write a question to which that answer is the only appropriate response. The focus of a short-answer question should be on the intended answer. If item writers keep that answer in mind and word their questions accordingly, they will probably succeed in avoiding indefiniteness and multiple correct answers. An alternative, but inferior, method of obtaining short-answer items is to find a textbook sentence from which a word can be deleted to make a short-answer item. For example:

Thunderstorms form when columns of_____air rise to cooler altitudes.

Possible correct answers to this item include "warmer," "lower," and "moist." This example also serves to illustrate the next three suggestions for writing short-answer items.

3. If the item is an incomplete sentence, try to word it so the blank comes at the end of the sentence. This will often make the intent of the item clearer and avoid some of the indefiniteness and possibility of multiple answers.

4. Use a direct question, unless the incomplete sentence permits a more concise or clearly defined correct answer. When an incomplete sentence is arranged so the blank comes at the end, it will often be apparent that a direct question would be just as easy to write and possibly a shade easier to understand. For example:

The name of the holy city of Islam is_____.

versus

What is the name of the holy city of Islam?

However, answers to the question:

Why did the United States declare war on Japan in 1941?

are likely to be more variable and somewhat longer than completions of the sentence:

The immediate cause for the U.S. declaration of war on Japan in 1941 was the <u>bombing of Pearl Harbor.</u>

5. Avoid unintended clues to the correct answer. The word *cooler* in the item on thunderstorms suggests that the air before it rose must have been warmer. Or consider this item:

Steamboats are moved by engines that run on the pressure of_____.

It takes little knowledge or insight to guess that the correct answer to this item must be "steam." For what purpose is a question like this one being asked at all? Focusing on the answer before writing the question is likely to result in more important questions that have more specifically unique answers. It is also important to remember that questions written with a specific answer in mind are likely to be more relevant and more concise than sentences lifted from text material.

Another common but unwanted cue helps the examinee determine the length of the intended responses. Each blank used in a set of short-answer items should be exactly the same length. The short-answer directions should indicate if only a single word or if either a word or phrase may be used as a valid response. Consider this item:

The names of the two rivers that meet at Cairo, Illinois, are the_____and_____.

The long blank to accommodate "Mississippi" and the short blank intended for "Ohio" make this item easier for all, but particularly for students who are unsure about the names.

6. Word the item as concisely as possible without losing specificity of response. Clear ideas are expressed in concise statements or questions. Excess words waste the examinee's time and may confuse the idea to be expressed.

7. Arrange space for recording answers on the right margin of the question page. This practice not only makes the items easier to score, which is its main justification, but also encourages the use of direct questions or placement of blanks at the end of incomplete sentences.

8. Avoid using the conventional wording of an important idea as the basis for a short-answer item. Use of the usual wording may encourage and reward study to memorize rather than to understand. For example:

Gain or loss divided by the cost equals the gain or loss in_____.
Two lines perpendicular to the same line in the same plane are_____to each other.

Better versions of these items would be:

To determine the percent of gain on a transaction, by what must the actual gain be divided?_____
If two lines are drawn perpendicular to the same line on a sheet of paper, the two lines are_____.

MATCHING ITEMS

Matching-test items occur in clusters composed of a list of premises, a list of responses, and directions for matching the two. In many clusters the distinction between premises and responses is simply in the names given to them. The two lists can be interchanged without difficulty. In other clusters, such as the following example, it is convenient to use descriptive phrases as the premises and shorter names as responses.

Directions: **On the blank before each of the following contributions to educational measurement, place the letter that precedes the name of the person responsible for it.**

	Premises	*Responses*
_e_	16. Developed the Board of Examiners at the University of Chicago	a. Alfred Binet
_c_	17. Developed high-speed electronic test-processing equipment	b. Arthur Otis
_d_	18. Published the first textbook on educational measurement	c. E. F. Lindquist
		d. E. L. Thorndike
		e. L. L. Thurstone

A wide variety of premise–response combinations can be used as the basis for matching-test items: dates and events; terms and definitions; writers and quotations; quantities and formulas; color samples and names of colors; and so on. Names of an animal's organs or structures can be matched to parts shown on a sketch of the animal.

Closely related to the matching-test item is the classification or key-list item. Responses for this item consist of a list of classes such as the parts of speech, periods of history, classes of plants or animals, types of chemical reactions, cause–effect sequences, branches of government, or nations or states. The premises consist of names, descriptions, or examples that are to be classified among the responses provided. Here is an illustration.

Directions: **After each event in the list below, put the number**
  1. **if it happened before the birth of Christ (4 B.C.)**
  2. **if it happened after the birth of Christ but before the Magna Carta was signed (A.D. 1215)**
  3. **if it happened after the Magna Carta was signed but before Columbus arrived in America (1492)**
  4. **if it happened after Columbus arrived in America but before the Declaration of Independence (1775)**
  5. **if it happened after the Declaration of Independence (1775)**

36.	Battle of Hastings	2
37.	Eruption of Mt. Vesuvius	2
38.	Guttenberg Bible printed	3
39.	Pilgrims landed at Plymouth	4
40.	William Shakespeare was born	4

Apart from the use of classes or categories as responses (the key list), classification items differ from typical matching items in that the same response is "matched" to more than one premise, and the number of premises is usually greater than the number of responses. In typical matching items there are more responses than premises.

Matching items have something in common with multiple-choice items in offering explicit alternative answers. They also have something in common with short-answer items. They are usually limited to specific factual information—names, dates, labels, and so on. They are poorly suited for testing understanding. They are also poorly adapted for testing unique ideas, since a cluster of related items is a prerequisite to the writing of such items. Clustering can reduce the breadth of sampling of questions in a test, concentrating attention on particular narrow aspects of achievement.

There are, on the other hand, some attractive features of matching-test items. They are efficient in that they yield many independent scorable responses per test page or per unit of testing time. They may also motivate students to cross-reference and integrate their knowledge and to consider relations among the items in the lists of responses and premises. Yet seldom can a whole test be composed of matching- or classification-test items. Some aspects of achievement may, however, be ideally suited to this item form. Here are some suggestions for using it effectively.

1. Choose homogeneous premises and responses for any matching cluster. The premises and responses in the list that follows are not homogeneous.

_____13. dark, hard wood		*a.* board foot
_____14. tool for smoothing		*b.* drawing
_____15. 12″ × 12″ × 1″		*c.* plane
		d. shellac
		e. walnut

Is it necessary to supply a key for the correct answers to the items in this cluster? As this example illustrates, if the lists are not homogeneous, the items are likely to test only the simplest associations and to provide many commonsensical clues to the correct answer.

2. Make the lists of premises and responses relatively short. It is easier to keep short lists homogeneous. The task involves less irrelevant difficulty if examinees do not have to hunt through long lists for a match. Adding responses beyond four or five reduces the chance of successful guessing only a very little. The difference in the probabilities of a correct answer by chance between a five- and a six-response item is only about 0.03. Common practice among expert item writers is to use a list of three premises to be matched by one of five responses.

3. Do not attempt "perfect" matching, in which each response is matched once and only once to each of the premises. In perfect matching, the final match may be given away by the other matches. Or if an error is made in one match, there is certain to be an error in another. Thus the items are not wholly independent. Using more responses than premises eliminates these potential dangers of perfect matching.

4. Provide directions that clearly explain the intended basis for matching. While the intended basis may be self-evident in simple matching clusters, in most cases it should be made explicit to avoid any misunderstandings. Classification items usually require fairly detailed directions.

5. Arranging responses or premises or both in alphabetical order usually prevents giveaway clues that can occur in item writing. Item writers are likely to think of a premise and its responses together. If they are written down just as they are thought of, their sequence may make the task of matching easier than it should be. Rearranging one or both lists in alphabetical order will eliminate such clues. However, if any logical order exists among the responses (for example, quantities or dates) preserving that order will remove an irrelevant difficulty from the examinees' task.

6. If the responses are numerical quantities, arrange them in order from low to high.

7. Use the longer phrases as premises, the shorter as responses.   Both of these actions will tend to simplify the examinees' task in finding the correct match and may eliminate irrelevant difficulty.

NUMERICAL PROBLEMS

While numerical problems can be presented as multiple-choice test items, they are most often presented in short-answer form. Numerical problems provide the basis for a wide variety of test items in arithmetic and other branches of mathematics, in the sciences, in bookkeeping and accounting, and in any fields of study where exact quantitative relationships have been developed.

Numerical problems provide good measures of achievement in learning. They are performance tests that assess application of knowledge. Many novel problems can easily be produced by changing the given quantities and the ways in which they are presented, and these novel problems are an excellent way to test understanding in contrast to mere recall. The answers are usually concise and hence easy to score, even in short-answer form. All these are virtues of numerical problems as short-answer test items. But sometimes there are minor difficulties in using them.

The problem of avoiding a number of correct responses, which plagues other short-answer items, takes a somewhat different form in numerical problems. How precisely correct must the answer be to receive credit? How much partial credit should be given if the process is correct but the answer incorrect because of computational errors? No blanket answer can be given to these questions, but the following suggestions may help to avoid serious difficulties on these points.

1. Use the simplest numbers possible.   The purpose of the item is to test understanding of a process, not computational accuracy. If accuracy needs to be tested, test it in separate items, using numbers as complex as may be necessary.

1a.   **How many circles of radius 1 5/8" can be obtained from an 8 1/2" by 11" sheet of paper?_____ .**

1b.   **How many circles of radius 1" can be obtained from an 8 " × 12" sheet of paper?_____ .**

Clearly the same problem-solving ability is measured by both items, but the computational load required by the first will make it more time consuming, more difficult, and less relevant as a measure of problem-solving ability.

2. If possible, choose the given quantities so that the answer will be a whole number. To do this will help to avoid uncertainty about how far a decimal fraction should be carried out.

2a. What is the area in square feet of the largest rectangle that can be formed from an isosceles trapezoid having bases of 20" and 35" and altitude of 17"?

2b. What is the area in square feet of the largest rectangle that can be formed from an isosceles trapezoid having bases of 24" and 30" and altitude of 18"?

The numbers in the first problem yield a (rounded) correct response of 2.36, which also could be expressed as 2.4 or 2. The second problem requires the same thought processes but yields a correct response of 3 square feet and requires no rounding.

3. Specify the degree of precision expected in the answer.   If students are uncertain about what they are being asked to do, and if they guess wrongly, the measurement of what they are able to do will be made less accurate.

4. If a fully correct answer must specify the unit of measure in which it is expressed, tell the examinee this as part of the problem.   It is easy for a distracted examinee to forget to write the units in which an answer is expressed. If knowing what the units should be is an important part of the problem, ask for them separately, thus:

4a. What number expresses the intensity of illumination on this surface?_____
4b. In what units is this illumination intensity expressed? <u>foot-candles</u>

5. If possible, divide a single complex multiple-step problem into a number of simpler single-step problems.   It is a mistake to believe that the more complex the problem, the better it will test the examinee's ability. Just the reverse is usually true. Any complex problem involves a number of procedural choices, as well as a number of quantitative calculations. Each of these can be made the basis of a separate test item. Success in solving the whole problem involves nothing more than success in making the separate choices and calculations. Consider these two items. The first is relatively complex, but the second is more efficient and likely will contribute more to high reliability.

5a. Last year Marcy sold 60 cars at an average price of $2,000. Her goal this year is to sell 50% more cars. If Marcy earns a commission of 10% for each sale, how much more will she earn this year than last year if she reaches her goal?

5b. Last year Marcy sold 60 cars at an average price of $2,000. Her goal this year is to sell 50% more cars. Marcy's commission is 10% for each sale.

   1. How many cars does Marcy hope to sell this year?
   2. How many dollars did Marcy earn last year from her sales?
   3. How many dollars does Marcy hope to earn this year?

Breaking down a complex, multiple-step problem in this way will minimize the problem of partial credit. It will result in more independent indications of achievement or lack of it. That will improve the reliability of the test scores.

6. Express the numerical problem clearly and as concisely as possible. Clarity requires full information and simple direct statements. Conciseness, the elimination of unnecessary words or distracting comments, also aids in achieving clarity. A study was made some years ago to test the hypothesis that inclusion of irrelevant data would improve the measuring characteristics of physics test problems (Ebel, 1937). This hypothesis was based on the assumption that giving the examinee only the numerical information needed was not true to life and might help students who lacked understanding to stumble onto the correct answer. But the inclusion of complicating irrelevant data did not improve the items. Evidently they were quite complicated enough without it.

SUMMARY PROPOSITIONS

1. Short-answer items are used mainly to test for factual information.
2. A much wider range of achievements can be tested with true–false or multiple-choice items than with short-answer items.
3. The difficulty examinees have in producing the correct answer to a short-answer item is an advantage of limited value.
4. Short-answer items do not provide a more valid measure of real achievement than do choice-type items.
5. Short-answer items are efficient and relatively easy to prepare.
6. Short-answer items need to be conceived and written carefully to avoid the possibility of multiple-correct answers.
7. In writing short-answer items, it is advantageous to think first of the answer and then write the question that will elicit it.
8. A direct question generally will result in a less ambiguous short-answer item than will an incomplete sentence.
9. Item writers should avoid "lifting" intact sentences from textual materials as the basis for short-answer items.
10. Matching items, like short-answer items, usually are limited to testing for factual information.
11. Matching items are efficient and useful in emphasizing relationships between ideas.
12. Short, homogeneous lists should be used in any matching cluster.
13. Perfect matching of the two lists on a one-to-one basis is undesirable.
14. Directions should be explicit about the basis to be used in matching.
15. The list of responses in a matching cluster should be presented in either scrambled or alphabetical order to avoid clues.

QUESTIONS FOR STUDY AND DISCUSSION

1. How might the responses to a set of short-answer items be used as the basis for developing multiple-choice items?
2. Why is it not possible to convert all true–false or multiple-choice items to useful short-answer items?
3. How can matching items be used to measure achievement beyond the recall level?
4. What can be done to reduce or eliminate the role of computational skill in testing numerical problem-solving ability?
5. What are some drawbacks associated with reducing a multiple-step numerical problem to a set of single-step problems?

11

Essay-Test Items

THE PREVALENCE OF ESSAY TESTING

Essay tests continue to be a very popular form, especially among scholars and at the higher levels of education. Their history of usage dates back earlier than 2300 B.C. in ancient China, and until the turn of the century they were about the only form of written examination in wide use. Thus they have the sanction of tradition (Coffman, 1971).

However, there are other reasons for their popularity. One is convenience. In contrast with objective tests, essay tests are relatively easy to prepare—the difficult part of the job is usually grading students' answers. Another is the security they provide to the examiner. Writers of essay questions are seldom required, as are composers of objective-test items, to defend the "correct" answer or to demonstrate that none of the "wrong" answers is as good as the correct answer. Essay questions require the student to create an explicit answer that the scorer can rate without describing the basis of any rating scale or without showing his or her own version of an ideal answer. Thus the deficiencies of an essay question are seldom so readily available for observation as are those of an objective-test item.

It is also quite easy for the grader of an essay test to control the general level and distribution of scores. Whether the examiner allows no points, five points, or even seven points for a seriously inadequate answer is a matter of personal decision. Thus, no matter how inappropriate the level of difficulty of an essay test, the grader can adjust the standards so some—but not too many—will receive scores below some preset minimum passing score. The fact that test-item difficulty is not a crucial factor contributes in no small measure to the popularity of the essay test.

The distinction between an essay test and an assessment of writing is an important one. While both use writing as the medium of expression, essay scoring focuses on the content expressed in and with the writing. Writing assessment, on the other hand, uses the content of a prompt but focuses on the quality of the writing itself. Thus, writing is a means to an end with essay testing, but it is an end in itself with writing assessment. A similar parallel can be drawn between the reading introduced by a multiple-choice test and the reading required by a test of reading comprehension.

Our purpose in this chapter is to direct attention to the use of essay tests for measuring educational achievement. The distinction between the purposes of essays and writing assessments is important to keep in mind so that the essay exercises, the scoring criteria, and the scoring procedures will yield scores that represent achievement in the relevant content domain, not abilities in written expression.

THE VALUE OF ESSAY TESTING

Those who argue for essay tests and against objective tests usually do so on the ground that essay tests provide a better indication of students' real achievements in learning. Students are not given ready-made answers but must have command of an ample store of knowledge that enables them to relate facts and principles, to organize them into a coherent and logical progression, and then to do justice to these ideas in written expression. Recall is, of course, involved in the composition of an answer to an essay-test question, but it would be a gross oversimplification to characterize an essay test as simply a measure of recall.

Furthermore, the answers given to an essay-test question can often provide clues to the nature and quality of students' thought processes. Some writers of essay-test questions occasionally deliberately choose indeterminate issues as the basis for their questions. What the student concludes, they say, is unimportant. The evidence on which the examinee bases the conclusion and the cogency of his or her arguments in support of it are said to be all-important.

Many of the traits that essay tests have been said to measure, such as critical thinking, originality, and ability to organize and integrate, are not at all clearly defined. Those characteristics of the answers that serve to indicate which students have more and which have less of these traits are seldom set forth explicitly. When the scores awarded to essay-test answers are explained or defended, deductions from a maximum possible score are usually attributed to some combination of these deficiencies:

1. Incorrect statements were included in the answer.
2. Important ideas necessary to an adequate answer were omitted.
3. Correct statements having little or no relation to the question were included.
4. Unsound conclusions were reached, either because of mistakes in reasoning or because of misapplication of principles.

5. Bad writing obscured the development and exposition of the student's ideas.
6. There were flagrant errors in spelling and the mechanics of correct writing.

Mistakes in the first four categories can be attributed either to weaknesses in the student's command of knowledge or to lack of clarity and specificity in the examiner's question. Mistakes in the last two categories either indicate a weakness in written self-expression or reflect the difficulties of the hand in keeping up with a mind racing ahead under the pressure of a time limit. As essay tests are typically used, the unique functions they have that are beyond the scope of objective tests seem somewhat limited and indefinite. Odell's (1927) scales for rating essay-test answers suggest strongly that the length of a student's answer may be closely related to the score it receives. Longer answers tend to receive higher ratings.

Influence of Writing Ability

Essay tests are also valued for the emphasis they place on writing. However, this is both an advantage and a disadvantage. Written expression is an important skill that essay tests do encourage. However, the practice that essay tests give in writing may be practice in *bad* writing—hasty, ill considered, and unpolished. Worse, skill in writing, or lack of it, may influence the scorer's judgment regarding the content of the answer. Uniform, legible handwriting and fluent, graceful sentences can compensate for some deficiencies in content (Chase, 1979; Hughes, Keeling, and Tuck, 1983). On the other hand, flaws in spelling, grammar, or usage can detract from the scorer's evaluation of the content.

Students occasionally use writing skill to compensate for lack of knowledge. Students who are hard put to answer adequately the question asked can transform it subtly into a related question that is easier for them to answer. If they perform well on the substitute task, the reader may not even notice the substitution. Or the student may concentrate on form rather than on content, on elegant presentation of a few rather simple ideas, in the hope that this may divert the reader's attention from the lack of substantial content.

Not all readers of essay examinations are easy to bluff. Then, too, students likely to be most in need of the kind of assistance that bluffing might give them are usually the least able to use such techniques. For this reason, bluffing on essay tests is hardly more serious a problem than guessing one's way to success on an objective test.

Influence on Examinee Preparation

That the nature of the examination expected affects the preparation students make for it is attested by experience, reason, and research (Meyer, 1935; Terry, 1933). Surveys of student opinion conducted about 50 years ago suggest the students then studied more thoroughly in preparation for essay examinations than for objective examinations. The absence of more recent research on this topic may suggest a lack of interest in the topic, a lack of awareness of the potential differences, or an implicit indication that students obviously prepare differently for the two types of tests.

With respect to the influence of examinations on study, the really important question is not how students say they study for examinations of different kinds—or even how they actually do study—but how these differences affect their achievement. In the absence of adequate research, we venture to make the following inferences:

1. The kind of study and achievement that a test stimulates is probably more a function of the kind of questions asked than of the mode of student response.
2. To the degree that tests in different forms measure the same kinds or aspects of achievement, they should stimulate the same kind of study and have the same effect on achievement.

It is not uncommon to see students who have been handed a multiple-choice test begin to write memorized notes or lists on the back pages of their test booklets. These are likely the same kinds of notes these students would make upon beginning an essay test. An inspection of objective-test booklets after the completion of testing often reveals significant note making, most often in a form that may be intelligible only to the maker.

Many potent factors other than examinations affect how and with what success students study. These factors interact in complex ways to facilitate or to inhibit learning. The chances are small, therefore, that research will ever demonstrate clearly which form of examination, essay or objective, has the more beneficial influence on study and learning.

RELIABILITY OF ESSAY-TEST SCORES

The most serious limitation of essay tests as measures of achievement in classroom settings is the low reliability of the scores they typically yield. Low reliability means that there is a good deal of inconsistency between scores obtained from successive administrations of the same test or equivalent tests, or from independent scorings of the same test. On the whole, three conditions are responsible for this low reliability: (1) the limited sampling of the content covered by the test, (2) the indefiniteness of the tasks set by the essay questions, and (3) the subjectivity of the scoring of essay answers.

In general, the larger the number of independent elements in the sample of tasks chosen for an achievement test, the more accurately performance on those tasks will reflect overall achievement in the field. It is true that the answer to a complex essay-test question often involves many separate elements of achievement. Yet they are dealt with as a more or less integrated whole by both the student and the grader, not as independent elements.

Few, if any, experimental studies of the sampling reliability of essay tests relative to that of objective tests have been made. The difficulty of obtaining sufficiently objective scoring of essay-test answers may be part of the reason. But there have been some theoretical analyses of the problem. Ruch (1929) has shown a direct relation between the extensiveness of the sample of tasks in a test and the precision with which different levels of achievement can be differentiated. Posey (1932) demonstrated that examinees' luck, or lack of it, in being asked what they happen to know is a much greater factor in the grade they receive in a 10-item test than in one of 100 items.

On many essay-test questions, the task and the basis for judging an examinee's success in completing it are not clearly specified. Essay questions *can* be explicit; they can guide students to produce those answers that will signify achievements. Often, however, they do not. Similarly, scoring directions *can* be written in a concise, easy-to-follow manner. Again, they often fall short of the mark. The more detailed and explicit the directions to both student and scorer, the more objective and reliable the measurements obtainable from an essay-test question ought to be.

The classic studies of Starch and Elliott (1912, 1913a, 1913b) exposed the appallingly wide variations in the grades that typical teachers assigned to the same student's answers to questions in geometry, literature, and history. Later studies confirmed these findings in other contexts (Finlayson, 1951; Vernon and Mellican, 1954). Thus, although it has been shown elsewhere that essay-test answers can be graded reliably when the job is done under careful supervision, the fact that essay tests typically yield highly subjective and unreliable measures of achievement was established beyond dispute.

The score on any test is a means of communicating and recording a measurement or an evaluation. It is useful only insofar as it is meaningful. It must mean something to the person who determined it, not only at the moment of determination, but days or weeks later. It must mean as nearly as possible the same thing to the student who receives it as it did to the teacher who assigned it. To the degree that other qualified observers would assign different scores, the measurement lacks objectivity and hence utility. Measurements of school achievement, like other reports, must be trustworthy in order to be useful. To be trustworthy means that they are capable of independent verification. If the same teacher were to assign totally different scores to the same essay-test answer on different occasions—or if different teachers were to disagree in the same way—our confidence in the scores would be shaken and their usefulness seriously diminished.

A particularly difficult distinction for students of educational measurement to comprehend is the difference between (1) the reliability of essay scores for a group of examinees and (2) the reliability of essay ratings from multiple readers. The reliability of essay scores relates to the collection of concerns we might have about the consistency of any test scores—objective, essay, problem, or performance. Would retesting on another occasion yield very similar results? Would retesting with an equivalent set of items yield similar results? Thus, to determine essay-score reliability, the same test must be given again, an equivalent test must be given somewhat concurrently, or multiple essay-item scores on the test must be used with coefficient alpha to estimate internal consistency.

The reliability of essay ratings raises questions about the extent to which different raters assign the same relative scores to the same essay responses. The main question raised is, "Does the score assigned to an essay depend too much on who does the scoring?" When multiple raters of a set of essay responses are consistent in applying the scoring criteria, the rank orderings of students produced by each rater will be about the same. That is, the correlation between scores assigned by any pair of raters on the same essays will be quite high. The most defensible method of estimating the reliability of ratings is a correlational method presented by Ebel (1951).

PREPARING ESSAY ITEMS

Implicit in what has been said in this chapter about the values and limitations of essay tests are a number of suggestions for improving essay-type questions.

1. Ask questions or set tasks that will require the student to demonstrate a command of essential knowledge.   Such questions will not simply call for reproduction of materials presented in the textbook or classroom. Instead of looking exclusively backward to the past course of instruction, they will also look forward to future applications of the things learned. The questions will be based on novel situations or problems, not on the same ones used for instructional purposes.

2. Ask questions that are determinate, in the sense that experts could agree that one answer is better than another.   Indeterminate questions are likely to function only as exercises in exposition, whose relation to effective behavior may be quite remote. Such questions will probably not be especially relevant to the measurement of a student's useful command of essential knowledge. Furthermore, and most importantly, the absence of a good best answer may make it much more difficult for a reader to judge a given student's level of achievement. On controversial questions, which many indeterminate questions are, the reader's opinions and biases may considerably influence any evaluation of the student's answer.

3. Define the examinee's task as completely and specifically as possible without interfering with measurement of the achievement intended.   The question should be carefully phrased so that examinees fully understand what they are expected to do. If the task is not clearly evident in the question itself, add an explanation of the basis on which answers will be evaluated. Do not allow students more freedom than is necessary to measure the desired achievement. If the question permits variation in the extent and detail of the answer given, but this is not a relevant variable, specify about how long the answer is expected to be.

4. In general, give preference to more specific questions that can be answered more briefly.   The larger the number of independently scorable questions, the more thoroughly the content domain can be sampled and, therefore, the more reliable the scores are likely to be. Narrower questions are likely to be less ambiguous to the examinee and easier for scorers to grade reliably. Occasionally, an instructor may find it necessary to base an essay test on only a few very broad questions. These occasions are not frequent, however, and the instructor should be sure that the need for extended answers is sufficient to warrant the probable loss in score reliability.

5. Avoid giving the examinee a choice among optional questions unless special circumstances make such options necessary.   If different examinees answer different questions, the basis for comparing their scores is weakened. Clearly, when students choose the questions they can answer best, the range of test scores is likely to be narrower—hence the reliability of the scores would be expected to be somewhat less. Research indicates that this expectation is justified.

When college students in psychology were given the choice of omitting one of five essay questions, Meyer (1939) found surprisingly that only 58 percent of them omitted the question on which they would do least well. He "suggested that unless the various questions are weighted in some suitable fashion the choice form of essay examination be discontinued." Stalnaker (1951) concluded a survey of the problems involved in the use of optional questions with these words:

> No experimental evidence has been published to show that skills and abilities can be adequately sampled by the use of optional questions; on the other hand, several studies have shown that optional questions complicate measurement and introduce factors of judgment which are extraneous to the ability being measured. For sound sampling, it is recommended that optional questions be avoided and that all examinees be asked to run the same race. (p. 170)

Optional questions are sometimes justified on the ground that giving students a choice among the questions they are to answer makes the test "fairer." But if all the questions involve essential aspects of achievement in a course (as they ordinarily might), it is not unfair to any student to require answers to all of them. Furthermore, an opportunity to choose among optional questions may help the poorer student considerably, but may actually distract the well-prepared student.

Optional questions may be justifiable when a test of educational achievement must cover a broad area and when the students who take it have received unequal training in different areas. Even in such a situation, however, the advantages of using optional questions are highly dubious. Optional tests, separately scored, might be preferable to a common test, yielding a single score, based on different sets of questions.

6. Test the question by writing an ideal answer to it.   Writing the ideal answer at the time a question is drafted serves an immediate purpose. It gives the test constructor a check on the reasonableness of the question and on the adequacy of his or her own understanding. Perhaps some change in the question could make it easier, if that seems desirable, or more discriminating, which is always desirable. Also useful, if it can be arranged, is to have a colleague in the same field try to answer it. Comparison of such ideal answers might shed additional light on the question's suitability and might suggest additional ways of improving it.

The deferred purpose served by drafting an ideal answer to each essay-test question is to provide guidance and a point of reference for the later scoring of students' answers. If someone other than the instructor is to grade the questions or to help with the grading, the ideal answer is almost indispensable to uniformity in grading.

SCORING ESSAY ITEMS

The decisions to be made when selecting a method for scoring essays involve the type of score interpretation desired—norm-referenced or criterion-referenced—and the amount of diagnostic information needed about individuals' responses.

Holistic and Analytical Methods

The most common procedures used for scoring essay responses are the holistic (sometimes called global-impression) and the analytical methods. The primary-trait method is applicable to scoring writing assessments based on a specific mode of discourse, but like other methods used in large-scale writing assessments, it is not applicable to assigning scores to essays that are intended to measure achievement of content.

The *holistic method*, as the name implies, involves assigning a score to each response depending on the overall quality of the answer. The assigned score represents quality in relation to some relative standard—as when it is compared with the response of all other students—or in relation to some absolute standard—as when it is compared with a set of sample papers that represent predetermined gradations of quality. Figure 11–1 shows how the holistic method can be used to obtain scores based on relative standards. The scorer reads each response quickly and places it on one of three piles depending on how that response compares with others that have been read. After the first reading is completed, papers in the "high" stack are shuffled, reread, and sorted into grade (or numeric) piles. The percentages in parentheses indicate the scorer's expectations for the number of papers that should be assigned each grade, presumably based on the grading procedures established for the course.

When criterion-referenced interpretations are needed and holistic scoring is to be used, the scorer must describe, in advance, the characteristics that differentiate responses at each score-scale point. For example, in evaluating responses to an essay about the impact of the transcontinental railroad on westward expansion, the grading guide may indicate that social, political, and economic impact all should be addressed and that examples of each should be given. The scoring standards might be represented on a scale like this:

5 = All 3 aspects are included, all with relevant examples
4 = At least 2 of 3 aspects are included, both with relevant examples

Figure 11-1. Sample Sorting Procedure for Holistic Norm-Referenced Scoring

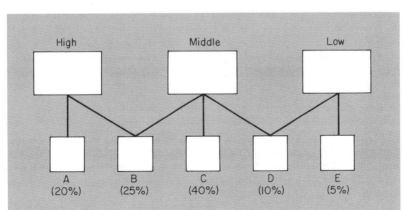

3 = At least 2 of 3 aspects are included, at least one with relevant examples

2 = At least 1 of 3 aspects is included with relevant examples

1 = At least 1 of 3 aspects is included, no pertinent examples

0 = No response, irrelevant response

Note that the scorer is not looking for particular examples and that, when one aspect of the response is missing, it makes no difference which one it is.

With the *analytical method,* crucial elements of the ideal response need to be identified and scored separately. The scorer accumulates points for each element appearing in the response or points are deducted for each missing element. The higher the proportion of crucial elements appearing in the student's response, and the less they are contaminated by inaccuracies or irrelevancies, the higher the student's score will be. Analytical scoring allows the scorer to pay attention to the organization and integration of the responses, as well as to the relations between crucial elements that appear. But when these relationships are complex or subtle, analytical scoring may prove to be too cumbersome and tedious to be effective.

The grading guide used with analytical scoring defines absolute standards and, thus, provides scores that are ready for criterion-referenced interpretation. Of course, once those scores are available, interindividual comparisons also can be made. The quality of the norm-referenced interpretations made with scores from the analytical method depends on the skill of the individual who created the grading guide definitions and on the skill and care of the scorer.

In general, holistic scoring is simpler and faster than analytical scoring. In some situations it may yield more reliable scores. But holistic scoring does not provide any clear justification of the score (grade) assigned, nor does it give students any indication how their answers fell short of the standard. Analytical scoring can provide such indications. In addition, it is well suited to questions that are likely to elicit detailed, uniformly structured answers.

Techniques to Promote Objectivity

As has been mentioned, the efficacy of essay tests as measures of educational achievement depends primarily on the quality of the scoring process. The competence of the scorer is crucial to the quality of this process, yet even competent scorers may inadvertently do things that make the results less reliable than they could be. Here are some suggestions for scorers of essay-test answers to consider if they are committed to making their results as accurate as possible.

1. Score the answers question by question rather than student by student. This means that the scorer will read the answers to question 1 on all students' papers before going on to their responses to the next question. Such a procedure is obviously required with the holistic method. It is also advantageous in analytical scoring, since concentration of attention on one question at a time helps to develop specialized skill and to foster independent judgment in scoring (Hales and Tokar, 1975).

2. If possible, conceal from the scorer the identity of the student whose answer he or she is scoring.   The purpose of this procedure is to reduce the possibility that biases or halo effects will influence the scores assigned. Ideally, the answers to different questions would be written on separate sheets of paper, identified only by a code number. These sheets would be arranged into groups by question number for the scoring process and then recombined by student name for totaling and recording. This process can reduce the halo effect associated with the student's name and reputation or with the high or low scores on that student's preceding answers.

3. If possible, arrange for independent scoring of the answers, or at least a sample of them.   Independent scoring is the only real check on the objectivity, and hence the reliability, of the scoring. Since it is troublesome to arrange and time consuming to carry out, it is seldom utilized by classroom teachers. But if a school or college were to undertake a serious program for the improvement of essay examinations, such a study of the reliability of essay-test scoring would be an excellent way to begin.

To get independent scores, at least two competent readers would have to score each question, without consulting each other and without knowing what scores the other had assigned. At least 100, preferably 300, answers should be given this double, independent reading. (The answers need not all be to the same question. Reading the answers of 30 students to each of 10 questions would be quite satisfactory.) The correlation between pairs of scores on individual questions would indicate the reliability of the ratings.

SUMMARY PROPOSITIONS

1. The popularity of essay tests is due partly to their convenience in preparation, the freedom from dispute they provide the examiner, and the control of the score distribution they afford.
2. Essay questions are less vulnerable to examinee criticism than are objective questions.
3. An essay test may permit the examiner to assess the examinee's thought processes.
4. Essay tests usually do not provide valid measures of complex mental processes such as critical thinking, originality, or ability to organize and integrate.
5. The emphasis essay tests place on the ability to write is both advantageous and disadvantageous.
6. Essay scores tend to be low in reliability because of limited content sampling, indefinite test tasks, and subjective scoring.
7. Essay scores must possess significant amounts of objective meaning to be useful.
8. Good essay questions require the examinee to demonstrate a command of essential knowledge.
9. Essay-score reliability can be enhanced by making the questions specific enough so that all good answers will be nearly identical.
10. Reliability can be enhanced more by using more questions that call for short answers than by using fewer questions that require long answers.
11. Optional questions should be avoided in essay testing.
12. Advance preparation of an ideal answer to each essay item facilitates reliable scoring and permits a check of the quality of the question prior to its use.
13. The holistic method of essay scoring involves the assessment of overall quality based on either relative or absolute standards.
14. The analytical method of scoring involves assigning scores to components of a response based on absolute standards.

QUESTIONS FOR STUDY AND DISCUSSION

1. How can the grader of an essay test control the distribution of test scores?

2. How can a social studies teacher obtain a measure of students' analytical abilities with an essay test while controlling the influence of both social studies knowledge and writing skills?

3. Why is essay testing considered "bad practice in writing" by some educators? Is it?

4. What are some of the causes of low essay-score reliability? What are some of the causes of low essay-rater reliability?

5. Why is the use of optional essay items more problematic for norm-referenced than criterion-referenced situations?

6. How can the analytical scoring process result in norm-referenced score interpretations?

7. Why is the "primary trait" method not useful for scoring essays?

8. What purposes are served by scoring an essay test item by item rather than student by student?

12

Test Administration and Scoring

Unless the class is very large, unless the classroom is poorly suited for test administration, or unless other special problems are encountered, test administration usually is the simplest phase of the whole testing process. In the administration of standardized tests, the golden rule for the test administrator is: *Follow the directions in the manual precisely.* In classroom testing there is usually no such manual, and the need for rigidly standardized conditions of test administration is much less. Nevertheless, here, as in most other areas, advanced planning usually pays dividends. Also, there are some persistent problems associated with test administration, such as the questions of preparing test takers, of cheating, and of guessing on objective tests. These, together with a consideration of computer-assisted testing, will provide the subject matter of this chapter.

PREPARING THE STUDENTS

Preparing the students for the test goes hand in hand with preparing the test for the students. Though each can be accomplished separately, the neglect of either certainly will result in lost effort and less valid measures of achievement. As a start, students should know that a test is coming. Any important test should be announced well in advance. If a test is to have the desirable effects in motivating and directing efforts to learn, students need to know not only when the test is coming but what kinds of achievement the test will require them to demonstrate. This means the teacher should plan tests *before* the course begins, using the instructional objectives and learning materials prepared during the planning stages of instruction.

Some instructors favor surprise tests in the belief that such tests keep the students studying regularly and discourage cramming. In some situations these tactics may be necessary and effective. However, most instructors see some elements of unfairness in surprise tests. Furthermore, cramming is unlikely to be effective with, or to be encouraged by, a test of students' command of knowledge. This type of learning cannot be achieved in a few short sessions of intensive cramming. Cramming is most essential and effective if the test requires no more than superficial memory of prominent details and if only short-term remembering is required. Advance announcement and description of test content are likely to do more to encourage productive study than the surprise administration of a test whose nature has been kept secret from the students.

Students tend to seek more information about an upcoming test than most instructors believe they need to know in advance. How many questions will there be? Will there be true–false or only multiple choice? How many points will there be? By answering such questions, the instructor might reduce unnecessarily high levels of anxiety in some students and simultaneously make all students aware that the teacher is striving for the best measure of their performance that is obtainable.

Test-Taking Skills

In addition to knowing that a test is coming and to having a good general idea of what to expect in it, the students need to know how to give a good account of themselves on the test. The measurement of achievement requires active cooperation from the students. If they lack skill in test taking, their scores may fall short of their true achievements. Test taking is not a highly specialized skill nor is it difficult to master. But almost anyone who has taken more than a few tests can testify from personal experience how easy it is to go astray on an examination, how failure to heed all directions, carelessness, unwarranted assumptions, or ignorance of some crucial rule of the game has marred an otherwise creditable test performance.

What are some of the legitimate and essential test-taking skills that examinees ought to possess?

1. They ought to be aware of the danger of failing to read or listen attentively when directions for taking the test are presented and of the danger of failing to follow those directions exactly.
2. They should find out the basis on which responses will be scored. Will points be subtracted for wrong responses or for errors in spelling, grammar, or punctuation? Will any questions carry more weight than others?
3. They should be aware of the premium that most human scorers, and most scoring machines, place on legibility and neatness. Accordingly, they should take pains in writing the answers or marking the answer sheet. For students beyond the elementary school level, a general explanation of how a scoring machine reads stray or multiple marks might instill a greater awareness of the need to make clean erasures and to check responses before the answer sheet is turned in.
4. They should put themselves in the best possible physical and mental shape for taking the test. Fatigue induced by an all-night cram session, even when partially

offset by stimulants, is a heavy handicap. Examinees should realize that last-minute cramming is a poor substitute for consistent effort throughout the course, particularly if the test they are facing is likely to be a well-constructed measure of their command of knowledge. Some anxiety is useful in motivating examinees to do their best, but jitters are even less helpful than fatigue.

5. Students should pace themselves so as to have time to consider and respond to all the test questions. This means that they must not puzzle too long over a difficult question or problem, or write too extensively on an essay test question, even when a long answer seems easy to write.

6. They should know that ordinary guessing corrections really do not penalize even blind guessing, but simply seek not to reward it. Hence, students should act in their own best interest by attempting to answer all questions, even those that they have only a slight basis for answering.

7. In answering an essay question, students should take time to reflect, to plan, and to organize their answer before starting to write. They should decide how much they can afford to write in the time available. And in all cases they should write something, however flimsy it may seem to be, as an answer.

8. If they are making responses on a separate answer sheet, students should check frequently to be sure their mark actually indicates the response they intended and that it is marked in the spaces provided for that question.

9. If possible, examinees should take time to reread their answers, to detect and correct any careless mistakes. It is a common misconception among teachers and students that the first answer given is more likely to be correct than a changed answer. However, research evidence has shown that answer changing tends to improve test scores when the changes are based on new insights rather than random guessing (Mueller and Wasser, 1977). In addition, Crocker and Benson (1980) found that test quality is not eroded by encouraging students to reconsider their original answers.

Since examinations do count, students and their teachers are well advised to spend some time considering how to cope with them most skillfully. Some good books on the subject, giving more detailed help than we have suggested here, are available (Millman and Pauk, 1969; Divine and Kylen, 1979; Annis, 1983).

Skill in test taking is sometimes called *testwiseness*. Students who are richly endowed with this attribute are supposed to be able to score well on any test, whether they know anything about the subject or not. Furthermore, it is supposed by some that objective tests inevitably are better measures of students' testwiseness than of their real achievements.

There is some basis for this concern. Certain tests, especially some kinds of intelligence tests, include novel, unique, and highly specialized tasks—for example, figure analogies or number series. For test items of this nature, the main problem of the examinee is to "get the hang of" solving them. They do not reflect previous learning, nor is the skill developed in solving these test problems likely to be practically useful in other settings. Their use in intelligence testing is justified on the grounds that brighter students will get the hang of solving novel problems sooner, and more fully, than duller students.

Items of this type are seldom used in classroom tests. But there are common faults in item writing that may allow an examinee to substitute testwiseness for knowledge. Some of these, involving unintended clues to the correct answer, were discussed in the chapters on true–false and multiple-choice test items. They are outlined and discussed in greater detail in an article by Millman, Bishop, and Ebel (1965). In a good test, however, the item writer will avoid dropping very many clues of this or any other kind. Given a test that measures command of knowledge and is free of technical flaws, error in measurement is likely to be due to too little, rather than too much, testwiseness.

Test Anxiety

The problem of test anxiety was mentioned in the preceding section. Anxiety is a frequent side effect of testing, whether that testing occurs in the classroom, on the athletic field, in the art exhibit hall, in the courtroom, in the conference room where a crucial business decision is being discussed, or in the legislative chamber where a bill is being debated. Test anxiety in the classroom is not something unique. It is a part, though hopefully not too large a part, of life itself.

Those who study test anxiety conceptualize the trait as having two main aspects—worry (about one's performance) and emotionality (intrinsic, neural reactions to testing) (Hembree, 1988). The worry, fear, and turbulence seem to stem from a fear of negative evaluation or negative consequences as a result of test performance (or whatever other form of performance evokes the reactions). That is, test-anxious examinees may fear that their "low" score may trigger peer rejection or ridicule, loss of respect, or expressions of disappointment from the teacher, parents, or friends. From this standpoint, test anxiety is a misnomer because it is not the test that produces such feelings; it is the anticipated and unwanted response that *might* result from a "low" score that is the source. Those who take tests anonymously or tests having no personal consequences are unlikely to demonstrate any of the cognitive or behavioral disabilities that test-anxious examinees report.

Because human beings are complex and the situations in which they are tested are diverse, it is unlikely that any simple, universal answers will be found to questions concerning the cause and cure of test anxiety. Some research has been done on test anxiety, particularly among young children. However, the measurement of anxiety is no simple problem. It is not surprising that few generalizations of wide applicability can be defended solidly on the basis of research findings. Yet, combining what controlled experimentation has reported with common observations of human behavior, we can offer a few generalizations that seem reasonably safe.

1. There is a negative correlation between level of ability and level of test anxiety. Those who are most capable tend to be least anxious when facing a test (Hembree, 1988; Tryon, 1980).
2. There is a positive correlation between level of anxiety and level of aspiration. Those who are most anxious when facing a test tend to be those who have the greatest need or desire to do well on it.
3. Mild degrees of anxiety facilitate and enhance test performance. More extreme degrees are likely to interfere with and depress test performance.
4. The more frequent a student's contact with tests of a specific type given for a specific purpose, the less likely he or she is to be the victim of extreme anxiety.

5. Test anxiety can be educationally useful if it is distributed, at a relatively low level, throughout the course of instruction, instead of being concentrated at a relatively high level just prior to and during an examination. Skillful teaching involves the controlled release of the energy stimulated by test anxiety.

McKeachie (1988) has concluded, after more than 30 years of research related to anxiety and study strategies, that the poor performance of anxious students may be due to inferior study techniques:

> I have been concerned about students whose performance is impaired by excessive anxiety, particularly anxiety about achievement tests. Our research has revealed some techniques to help these students perform better on tests. Other researchers have also developed methods of reducing anxiety, but even when such students have learned to relax and control their feelings of anxiety, their performance has not improved. Our more recent research indicates that such students perform poorly on tests not simply because they are anxious but because they are poorly prepared. Highly anxious students study, but they study ineffectively, memorizing details and reading and rereading. (p. 7)

Evidence to support the belief that some students of good or superior achievement characteristically go to pieces and do poorly on every examination is hard to find. Since individuals differ in many respects, it is reasonable to suppose that they may differ also in their tolerance of the kind of stress that tests generate. On the other hand, it is conceivable that apparent instances of underachievement on tests may actually be instances of overrated ability in nontest situations. In other words, a student whose achievement is really quite modest may have cultivated the poise, the ready response, and the pleasing manners that would ordinarily mark the person as an accomplished and promising scholar.

TEST-PREPARATION CONSIDERATIONS

Objective tests generally are presented to students in printed or duplicated booklets. Sometimes the questions for essay or problem tests are written on the chalkboard as the test period begins. This saves duplication costs and helps to maintain test security, but it gives the teacher the double responsibility of copying the questions and of getting the students started to work on them, all at a time when minutes are precious and when everyone is likely to be somewhat anxious to begin working. Then, too, when the chalkboard has been erased, no one has a valid record of exactly how the questions were stated.

Oral dictation of test questions, especially short-answer or true–false items, can be accomplished with success, but most students prefer to look at each item while they are trying to decide on a response. This permits the student, rather than teacher, to set the pace. Some instructors put test items on slides or transparencies and project them in a semidarkened room. This enables the examiner to pace the students and ensures that each examinee will give at least brief consideration to each item. Studies have indicated that examinees answer about as many items correctly when they are forced to hurry as when they choose their own pace (Curtis and Kropp, 1962; Heckman, Tiffin, and Snow, 1967). With a reasonably rapid rate of item presentation, more items can be used and more reliable scores can be obtained in a given testing period. But there are drawbacks to dictation as well. Students generally are unhappy with this type of time pressure. Their attention is not so firmly fixed on their own answer sheet, making test proctoring somewhat more tedious. And make-up tests present a serious and nagging problem.

Probably the best method of test presentation is to duplicate enough copies of the test for all students. With printed test copy, legibility of print and of format are prime considerations. Computer-printed master copies should be letter-quality documents; distortions due to poor resolution, worn ribbons, and formatting limitations of the software can reduce test efficiency and introduce measurement errors. Some classroom tests are duplicated unskillfully on inadequate equipment. Then, too, some items are crowded too closely together. Instead of being listed in a column, the response options to multiple-choice items might be written in tandem to form a continuous, hard-to-read paragraph. Faults like these can be avoided by the test maker if reasonable care is exercised in layout and duplication.

The use of a separate cover page on which directions are printed helps to emphasize those directions, provides a reminder of points covered during previous test-preparation discussion, and keeps the students from seeing the items prematurely. Here are some ideas to be addressed by a set of comprehensive directions on a cover sheet:

1. How to use the separate answer sheet and how to grid in names and ID numbers
2. How many items there are and how many pages there are in the test booklet
3. Whether notes, textbooks, translation dictionaries, or other aids are permitted
4. Whether questions may be asked of the instructor during the test
5. How much time is available
6. What special directions should be followed for each of the separate types of items
7. How many points will be awarded for correct responses for each type of item
8. Whether students should guess (or bluff) when they do not know the answer
9. What to do when finished with the test and whether the test booklet needs to be turned in

For multiple-choice tests, a check of the frequency with which each answer choice is the keyed answer should be made. With four-choice items, for example, response A should be the correct answer for about one-fourth of the items. There is a tendency for some item writers to use certain positions (first and last, for example) for the keyed answer. The unintentional use of a pattern in keying items provides an advantage to the testwise, uninformed examinee and serves to lower the quality of the test generally (Haladyna and Downing, 1989b). If the position of the correct answer is determined by a random procedure, each position will be used nearly an equal number of times.

Open-book examinations, in which the examinees are permitted to bring and use textbooks, references, and class notes, have attracted some interest and attention from instructors and educational research workers. Instructors have seen in them a strong incentive for students to study for ability to use knowledge rather than for ability simply to remember it. Such examinations also encourage instructors to eschew recall-type test questions in favor of interpretation and ap-plication types. In this light there is much to be said in favor of the open-book examination. On the other hand, students soon learn that the books and notes they bring with them to class are likely to provide more moral than informational support. Looking up facts or formulas may take away from valuable problem-solving time.

An experimental comparison of scores on the same multiple-choice examination, administered as an open-book test in one section and as a closed-book test in another section of the same course in child psychology, was reported by Kalish (1958). He concluded that, although "the group average scores are not affected by the examination approach, the two types of examinations measure significantly different abilities." Kalish also suggested some possible disadvan-tages of the open-book examination:

1. Study efforts may be reduced.
2. Efforts to overlearn sufficiently to achieve full understanding may be discour-aged.
3. Note-passing and copying from other students are less obvious.
4. More superficial knowledge is encouraged.

The take-home test has some of the same characteristics as the open-book test, with two important differences. On the pro side is removal of the pressure of time, which often defeats the very purpose of a classroom open-book test. The disadvantage is the loss of assurance that the answers students submit represent their own achievements. For this reason the take-home test often functions better as a learning exercise than as an achievement test. Students may be permitted, even encouraged, to collaborate in seeking answers in which they have confi-dence. The efforts they sometimes put forth and the learning they sometimes achieve under these conditions can be a pleasant surprise to the instructor. But the take-home test must be scored and the scores must count in order to achieve this result. And, as with any effective testing procedure, the correct answers should be reported to the students, with opportunity for them to question and discuss. One precaution: it is especially hazardous to use a take-home test of low or unknown quality. Student cross-examination can be devastating.

If time limits for the test are generous, as they usually should be for achievement tests, the order of presentation of the items has little effect on stu-dent scores, as shown by Sax and Cromack (1966). If time is restricted, the items probably should be arranged in order of increasing difficulty. It is reasonable to suppose that to begin a test with one or two easy questions would help to lessen excessive test anxiety. It also seems reasonable to group together items that deal with the same area of subject matter. However, empirical evidence that these practices improve the validity of the test scores is difficult to obtain.

TEST-ADMINISTRATION CONSIDERATIONS

As we have stated earlier, the actual administration of most tests involves rela-tively few and simple problems. Since the time available for the test is usually limited, and seldom as long as some of the students wish, every available minute should be used to good advantage. By giving preliminary instructions the day before the test, by organizing test materials for efficient distribution, and by keeping last-minute oral directions and answers to questions as brief as possible, the teacher can ensure that students have the maximum amount of time to work on it. Corresponding provisions for efficient collection of materials and advance notice to the students that all work must stop when time is called help to conclude the test on time and in an orderly fashion.

During almost any test administration, some students are likely to feel the need of asking an occasional question. Questions such as those growing out of errors in the test copy or ambiguities in the directions or test questions require answers if the students are to respond properly. Teachers should help students understand the tasks but should stop short of giving clues to the answer. Sometimes the dividing line is hard to determine.

Such questions as those stimulated by obvious but noncritical typographical errors should not even be asked. Since the process of asking and answering a question during the course of an examination is always disturbing to others, even if it is done as quietly and discreetly as possible, and since the answer to one student's question might possibly give that individual an advantage over the others, students should be urged to avoid all but the most necessary questions. Discussion of this point can well be undertaken prior to the day of the examination.

Special consideration may need to be given in settings where some examinees use English as a second or foreign language. In classroom testing situations, these students should be encouraged to ask questions related to general vocabulary or cultural situations presented in test items, information with which they may not be familiar. In some cases, special test administrations may be appropriate to permit additional testing time for slower readers. The general goal of good test administration is to present and maintain the conditions that will permit all examinees to demonstrate their true level of achievement without giving advantage to any examinee.

Reduce Opportunities for Cheating

In addition to giving directions, answering questions, and helping students keep track of time, the instructor has at least one other major responsibility during the course of administering a test. That is to prevent cheating. This problem, which students, teachers, and educational administrators tend to agree is serious, seems to receive more attention in the popular press than in technical books and articles on testing. Cheating on examinations is commonly viewed as a sign of declining ethical standards or as an inevitable consequence of increased emphasis on test scores and grades.

Any activity of a student or group of students whose purpose is to give any of them higher grades than they would be likely to receive on the basis of their own achievements is cheating. Thus the term covers a wide variety of activities, such as:

1. The sidelong glance at another student's answers
2. The preparation and use of a crib sheet

3. Collusion between two or more students to exchange information on answers during the test

4. Unauthorized copying of questions or stealing of test booklets in anticipation that they may be used again later

5. Arranging for a substitute to take an examination

6. Stealing or buying copies of an examination before the test is given or sharing such illicit advance copies with others

Although these various forms of cheating differ in seriousness, none should be viewed with indifference. The typical student has many opportunities to cheat, and the willingness to do so has been observed as early as kindergarten (Frisbie and Andrews, 1990). Some circumstances may even encourage examinees to cheat, but none justifies their doing so. Students may conclude, not without some justification, that the ethical standards of many of their peers are not very high, at least where cheating on examinations is concerned. They may go on to infer that this fact requires them to lower their own standards or justifies them in doing so. Whatever other conditions may contribute to it, cheating would not occur if all students were to recognize that it is always dishonest and usually unfair.

Some acts of cheating are no doubt motivated by desperation. The more extreme the desperation, the more ambitious and serious the attempt to cheat is likely to be. A major factor contributing to cheating is carelessness on the instructor's part in safeguarding the examination copy before it is administered and in supervising the students during the examination.

Emphasis on grades is sometimes blamed as a primary cause of cheating. But since grades are, or should be, symbols of educational achievement, we cannot indict grading as a cause of cheating without also indicting the goal of achievement in learning. Does anyone really want to do that? No doubt most students would find it easier to resist the temptation to cheat if no advantage of any consequence were likely to result from the cheating. But refusal to recognize and reward achievement may be as effective in reducing achievement as in reducing cheating. Such a price seems too heavy to pay.

Increased use of objective tests has also been cited as a cause of cheating. The mode of response to objective tests makes some kinds of cheating easier, but the multiplicity of questions makes other kinds of cheating more difficult. No form of test is immune to all forms of cheating. The quality of a test, however, may have a direct bearing on the temptation it offers to students to cheat. Demand for detailed, superficial knowledge encourages the preparation of crib sheets. If the examination seems to the students unlikely to yield valid measures of their real achievements, if it seems unfair to them in terms of the instruction they have received, if their scores seem likely to be determined by irrelevant factors anyway, the "crime" of cheating may seem less serious.

What cures are there for cheating? The basic cure is related to the basic cause. Students and their teachers must recognize that cheating is dishonest and unfair and that it deserves consistent application of appropriate penalties—failure in the course, loss of credit, suspension, or dismissal. Reports on the prevalence of cheating, no doubt sometimes exaggerated, should not be allowed to establish cheating as an acceptable norm for student behavior or to persuade instructors that cheating is inevitable and must be accommodated as gracefully as possible.

It is the responsibility of the instructor to avoid any conditions that make cheating easy—before, during, or after an examination. The security of the examination must be safeguarded while it is being written and duplicated and when it is stored. If the class is large and if students must sit in close proximity, alternate forms of the examination should be distributed to those sitting in adjacent seats. Alternate forms can easily be prepared by arranging the same questions in different order. Finally, instructors should take seriously the task of proctoring their examinations as part of their responsibility to the majority of students who will not cheat and who should not be penalized for their honesty.

Teachers have considerable authority in their own classroom. They should not overuse it under stress or underuse it when the situation demands it. If a teacher is satisfied beyond any reasonable doubt that a student is cheating, she or he needs no other justification for:

1. Collecting the examination materials and quietly dismissing the student from the room
2. Voiding the results of the examination, requiring an alternative make-up examination, or giving the student a failing grade on the examination
3. Bringing the incident to the attention of the school authorities if further action seems necessary

One frequently mentioned proposal for dealing with the cheating problem is the establishment of an honor system. Such systems seem to work best in educational institutions of moderate size with rich traditions that encourage strong group identification and loyalties. The spirit of honor on which the system depends seldom arises or maintains itself spontaneously. It must be cultivated carefully and continuously. The things that must be done, or avoided, to maintain personal honor and the honor of the group usually are defined clearly in a code or by well-rehearsed tradition. The degree to which student experience with an honor system in such an environment cultivates a general and lasting spirit of personal honor in a world where no such system is in effect is open to question. That such systems have worked to limit, or eliminate, cheating in certain institutions seems beyond doubt. That they sometimes break down, disastrously, is also beyond doubt. The adoption of the honor system as a feasible answer to the problem of cheating on examinations is a highly questionable practice in any school.

Issues of Test Security

Instructors and administrators, especially at the college level, are occasionally beset by rumors that copies of this or that examination are "out" in advance of the scheduled administration of the examination. Sometimes the rumors are founded on fact. More often they result from misinformation that anxious students are only too eager to pass along. Finally, the rumor (not so identified, of course) reaches the ears of the instructor, often via one or a number of anonymous telephone calls. What is the instructor to do?

Clearly, the instructor must determine whether or not the rumor is founded on fact, a task that must be pursued with the most vigorous effort. If the instructor is ready to enlist the aid of the informants and if they are willing to help, even anonymously, the task may be possible. If the informants are unable or unwilling to supply any leads, then they should be told courteously but plainly that their information is worthless and their transmission of it harmful.

If verifiable evidence is obtained that some students have, or have seen, advance copies of the examination, the only reasonable course of action is to prepare a new examination, even if it means changing the form of the examination and possibly losing a night of sleep. But if such evidence cannot be obtained even by a thorough search, the rumor had probably best be allowed to die as quietly as it will.

Problems of this kind are most likely to arise and to cause most serious difficulties on college campuses, which is not to say that they are totally absent from high schools. Newspaper stories have documented the "leaks" in test security that have occurred in state testing programs as well. Care in safeguarding examinations before they are given is the best preventative. But it is also helpful to be ready to respond wisely, and vigorously if the situation warrants, when the rumors that a test is out *do* begin to circulate, as they almost surely will sooner or later.

SCORING PROCEDURES AND ISSUES

Student answers to objective-test items may be recorded either on the test copy itself or on a separate answer sheet. Tests given in the elementary grades are almost always arranged so that the answers can be recorded in the test booklet. This avoids complicating the task of responding for the beginner. Cashen and Ramseyer (1969) found that the test scores of first-grade students were lowered substantially when they were required to record their answers on a separate answer sheet. On the average, scores of second-grade students were lowered somewhat, but those of third-grade students were unaffected. These findings followed and confirmed the pioneering work of Hieronymus (1961) on this topic and have been substantiated by more recent work (Ramseyer and Cashen, 1985). Recording answers in the test booklet lessens the danger of purely clerical errors and makes the corrected test copy easier to use for instructional purposes. The use of a separate answer sheet, on the other hand, makes the scorer's task much easier. It also makes possible the reuse of the test booklet. If a scoring machine is to be used, the answers must be recorded on an answer sheet that the machine is designed to handle.

If the answers are to be recorded on the test booklet, space for the answers should be provided near one margin of the test pages. To speed scoring and minimize the possibility of errors, the scorer may record correct answers on the columns of a separate answer key card, using one column for each page of answers and positioning the answers in the column so that they will match the answer spaces on the test copy.

In scoring the answers recorded in test booklets, the scorer may find it helpful to mark the answers, using a colored pencil. A short horizontal line through the student's response can be used to indicate a correct response. Sometimes it is advantageous to mark all responses using, in addition to the horizontal line for correct responses, an × to indicate an incorrect response and a circle around the answer space to indicate an omitted response.

Responses are indicated on most separate answer sheets by marking one of the several response positions provided opposite the number of each item. Such answer sheets may be scored by hand, using a stencil key with holes punched to correspond to the correct responses. Transparent keys, which can be prepared on the film used to make transparencies for an overhead projector, have some advantages, as Gerlach (1966) has noted. When a separate answer sheet and a punched key are used, it is possible to indicate incorrect or omitted items by using a colored pencil to encircle the answer spaces that the student marked wrongly or did not mark at all. This kind of marking is useful when the answer sheets are returned with copies of the test for class discussion.

Most classroom tests of educational achievement are scored by the instructor. If the test is in essay form, the skill and judgment of the instructor or of someone equally competent are essential. The task of scoring an objective test is essentially clerical and can often be handled by someone whose time is less expensive than an instructor's time and whose skill and energy are less in demand for other educational tasks.

Some school systems and colleges maintain central scoring services. Usually, these services make use of small scoring machines, several of which are now available. But even if all the scoring is done by hand, a central service has the value of fostering the development of special skills that make for rapid, accurate scoring. Institutional test-scoring services often provide statistical and test-analysis services as well, and sometimes they even offer test-duplication services that provide expert assistance in the special problems of test production and in the maintenance of test security.

Instructors sometimes use the class meeting following the test for test scoring. Asking each student to check the answers of a classmate may on occasion be a reasonable and rewarding use of class time, but often the process tends to be slow and inaccurate. A difficulty encountered by one student on one test paper may interrupt and delay the whole operation. Most important, if the student scorers are concentrating on mechanical accuracy of scoring, as they probably should be, the circumstances will not favor much learning as a by-product of the scoring process.

Optical Scanning Equipment

Recent advances in computing technology have contributed to the development of an array of electronic scoring machines that are practically useful and economically accessible to school districts and colleges of all sizes. These optical scanners can be operated independently by relatively unskilled workers or they can be integrated into a variety of complex computer equipment configurations. They may be attached to a large computer directly or they may send information to such a computer over transmission lines. They can be attached to a microcomputer or minicomputer. As a self-contained system, some scanners can read the answer sheets, compute the score for each, and print the score on the answer sheet. Smaller machines do so at the rate of 300 sheets per hour, but larger ones process as many as 6000 or more per hour. Most machines require that specially printed answer sheets be used, forms produced with a type of paper and ink that are compatible with the optical sensing system of the machine. These special forms are available in a variety of sizes and can accommodate more than 200 five-choice multiple-choice items per form.

Optical scanners were first developed to provide efficient and accurate scoring of educational tests, but their value to the teacher now extends well beyond test scoring. The evaluation applications that can be scanned are many and varied, limited only by the ingenuity of the document designer and the budget of the user. Scannable forms can be developed to serve as evaluation questionnaires, performance rating forms, observational records, and descriptive surveys. The variety of uses to be made of a "scoring machine" has increased as the price of equipment has decreased and as the computer software has become more friendly. Few schools need be without optical scanning equipment anymore.

Correction for Guessing

Scores on objective tests are sometimes corrected for guessing. The purpose of such a correction is to reduce to zero the gain in score expected to result from blind guessing. In other words, a guessing correction is intended to give the student who guesses blindly on certain questions no reasonable expectation of advantage in the long run over the student who omits the same questions.

Suppose a student were to guess blindly on 100 true–false test items. Since there are only two possible answers, one of which is certain to be correct, the student has reason to expect a score somewhere around 50. Another student, knowing no less than the first but reluctant to guess blindly, might attempt no answers and thus receive a zero. Without correction for guessing, the score of the first student would be higher than that of the second when, in fact, the two scores should be the same.

To correct the first student's score for guessing, it is necessary to subtract from that score an amount equal to the expected gain from blind guessing. Since on a true–false test the student can expect to answer one question wrongly for every question he or she answers correctly, the number of wrong answers is simply subtracted from the number of right answers. If the questions provided three equally likely answers instead of two, the student would expect to give two wrong answers to every right answer. In this case, one would subtract one-half of the number of wrong responses from the number of right responses to correct for guessing. If multiple-choice items list five alternative possible answers to each question, only one of which is correct, the expected ratio of wrong to right answers is 4 to 1, and the guessing correction would call for subtracting one-fourth of the number of wrong answers from the number of right answers.

Logic of this kind leads to a general formula for correction for guessing:

$$S = R - \frac{W}{N - 1} \tag{12.1}$$

where

S = score corrected for guessing
R = number of questions answered rightly
W = number of questions answered wrongly
N = number of possible alternative answers equally likely to be chosen in blind guessing

It is easy to see that this formula becomes

$$S = R - W \tag{12.2}$$

in the case of two-alternative (true–false) items, or

$$S = R - \frac{W}{4} \tag{12.3}$$

in the case of five-alternative multiple-choice test items.

Instead of "penalizing" the student who guesses, one could correct for guessing by "rewarding" the student who refrains from guessing. That is, instead of subtracting 50 units from the score of the guesser, we could add 50 units to the score of the nonguesser. This too would eliminate the expected advantage from blind guessing. The assumption in this case is that, if the nonguesser had guessed, she or he would have given the right answer to one-half of the true–false items. On three-alternative items, the nonguesser would have given correct answers to one-third of the items.

Logic of this kind leads to a second general formula for guessing correction:

$$S' = R + \frac{O}{N} \tag{12.4}$$

where

S' = score corrected for guessing on the basis of items omitted
R = number of items answered correctly
O = number of items omitted
N = number of alternative answers whose choice is equally likely on the basis of blind guessing

Again, it is easy to see that this general formula becomes

$$S' = R + \frac{O}{2} \tag{12.5}$$

in the case of true–false items, or

$$S' = R + \frac{O}{5} \qquad\qquad (12.6)$$

in the case of five-alternative multiple-choice test items.

If the same set of test scores is corrected for guessing in two different ways, by subtracting a fraction of the wrong answers and by adding a fraction of the omitted answers, two different sets of corrected scores will be obtained. But, although the two sets of scores will differ in their average value (with the omit-corrected scores being higher in all cases) and in their variability (with the omit-corrected scores being more variable almost always), the two sets of scores will be perfectly correlated. If student A makes a higher score than student B when the appropriate fractions of their wrong responses are subtracted from the total of their right responses, A will also make a higher score than B when the appropriate fraction of their items omitted is added to the total of their correct responses.

Correction for guessing by subtracting a fraction of the wrong responses is sometimes criticized on the ground that it is based on a false assumption—the assumption that every wrong response is the result of blind guessing. But the falseness of that assumption (and usually it is completely false) does not invalidate the correction formula that rests on it: No such assumption is made in the formula for guessing correction on the basis of items omitted, and yet the two formulas yield scores that agree perfectly in their relative ranking of students. Scores corrected by subtraction may be regarded logically as too low in absolute value, just as those corrected by addition may be regarded logically as too high in absolute value. But they are equally sound in relative value. With scores on tests of educational achievement, the absolute value is usually far less significant than the relative value.

It is also worth noting here that if no items are omitted, scores corrected for guessing by subtracting a fraction of the wrong responses correlate perfectly with the uncorrected scores, that is, with the numbers of right responses. This indicates that the magnitude of the effect of a guessing correction depends on the proportion of items omitted. Only if considerable numbers of items are omitted by at least some of the students will the application of either formula for correction for guessing have an appreciable effect.

Here are some considerations that should influence the test maker's decision regarding the use of a correction for guessing on objective achievement tests:

1. Scores corrected for guessing will usually rank students in about the same relative positions as do uncorrected scores.
2. The probability of obtaining a respectable score on a good objective test by blind guessing alone is extremely small.
3. Well-motivated examinees who have time to attempt all items guess blindly on few, if any, of them.
4. Seldom is any moral or educational evil involved in the encouragement of students to make the best rational guesses they can.
5. Students' rational guesses can provide useful information about their general level of achievement.

6. If a test is timed, a guessing correction removes the incentive for slower students to guess blindly.

7. Scores corrected for guessing may include irrelevant measures of the examinee's testwiseness or willingness to gamble.

Contrary to what students sometimes seem to believe, the typical correction for guessing applies no special penalty to the one who guesses. It simply tends to eliminate the advantage to the student who guesses blindly in preference to omitting items. Testwise students know they have nothing to lose, and perhaps something to gain, by making use of every hunch and scrap of information in attempting to answer every item. The test-naive student, or the one who tends to avoid taking chances, may be influenced by a guessing correction to omit many items on which his or her likelihood of correct response is well above the chance level (Rowley and Traub, 1977; Wood, 1976). To the degree that scores corrected for guessing give a special advantage to the bold or testwise student, their validity as measures of achievement suffers.

Differential Item Weighting

All objective-test scores are obtained by adding weighted response scores. The simplest system of scoring weights, and the one most often used, is $+1$ for the correct response to each test item and 0 for any response not correct. Correction for guessing involves a slightly more complex set of scoring weights, such as $+1$ for each correct response, -1 or $-\frac{1}{2}$ or $-\frac{1}{3}$, and so on, for each wrong response, and 0 for each omitted response.

Some test constructors believe that certain items in their test should carry more weight than others because they are more important items—items of better technical quality, items of greater complexity or difficulty, or items that are more time consuming. For example, in a test composed of 50 true–false and 25 multiple-choice items, the test constructor may decide that each multiple-choice item should be worth 2 points and each true–false item should be worth only 1 point.

Reasonable as such differential weights seem to be on the surface, they rarely cause the test to which they are applied to yield more reliable or valid scores. Nor do they ordinarily make the test a much worse measure. Like guessing corrections, to which they are closely related, they tend to have relatively small effects. The data shown in Table 12–1 support this generalization (Evaluation and Examination Service, 1982). All four instructors requested a slightly different weighting scheme when presenting their examination for test scoring. The value in the last column shows the correlation between uncorrected scores (weights of $+1$ and 0) and corrected scores using the requested weights. The rank order of students was essentially the same in both test-score distributions, and the Kuder–Richardson reliabilities were nearly identical. There is no obvious advantage to using the differential weights in any of these cases. Sabers and White (1969) reached the same conclusion:

from the point of view of test construction, weighted scoring is probably not worth the effort. The same advantages can be gained by adding more items or by selecting only the best items from a larger pool. From the administrative point of view, unweighted scoring saves time and offers fewer possibilities for errors in calculating the scores; in addition, the resulting raw scores are probably easier to interpret.

If an achievement test covers two areas, one of which is judged to be twice as important as the other, then twice as many items should be written over the more important area. This generally will result in more reliable and valid measures than if an equal number of items is written for each area and those for the more important area are double-weighted.

Complex or time-consuming items should be made to yield more than one response, each of which can be independently scored as right or wrong. The advantages of multiple true–false items for such situations were described in Chapter 8. Very difficult items are likely to contribute less than moderately difficult items to score reliability. Giving the more difficult items extra weight lowers the average effectiveness of the items and thus lowers the effectiveness of the test as a whole.

It has occurred to some test constructors that differential weighting of responses to test items might be useful in improving score reliability or validity. For example, in a question like the following:

A child complains of severe pain and tenderness in the lower abdomen, with nausea. What should the child's mother do?

a. **Give the child a laxative.**

b. **Put the child to bed.**

c. **Call the doctor.**

choice of the first response might result in a score of -1, of the second in a score of 0, and of the third in a score of $+1$. In this case the scoring weights were determined a priori. It has also been suggested that they might be determined experimentally, so as to maximize score reliability or validity.

Table 12-1. Effect of Differential Item Weighting Applied to Four Tests

Test Number	No. of Students	No. of Items	Type of Weighting	Correlation
1	83	41	Rights = +4 Wrongs = −1	0.945
2	50	160	Rights = +1 (1–140) Rights = +3 (141–160)	0.923
3	34	105	Rights = +1 (1–70) Rights = +2 (71–105)	0.983
4	21	90	Rights = +1 (1–45) Rights = +3 (46–90)	0.976

But in this case also the experimental results have been disappointing (Downey, 1979). Seldom have any appreciable, consistent gains in reliability or validity been found. It seems clear that to gain any real advantage by this means one would need to write items with this purpose specifically in mind. Most item writers, even skilled professionals, have enough difficulty writing items good enough for simple right or wrong scoring. To make them good enough for more finely graded differential weighting seems a formidable task. Test improvement through additional, good, simply scored items looks more promising to most item writers.

Exceptions will be found, of course, to the generalization that differential weighting of items, or of item responses, is not worthwhile in the scoring of classroom tests of educational achievement. But it is a good general guide to the constructor of an educational achievement test to settle for simple right or wrong scoring of individual items, with each item carrying the same weight as every other item, regardless of its importance, complexity, difficulty, or quality. Increasing the number of scorable units and making each unit as good as possible seem generally more effective than differential weighting of items or responses as a means of test improvement.

COMPUTER-ASSISTED TEST ADMINISTRATION

Computerized testing has long been a part of the computer-assisted instruction programs that have developed to greater levels of complexity as computer technology has improved and become more accessible. Today computers are used for test-administration purposes primarily in programs of individualized instruction, for both formative and summative evaluation. A key advantage of this procedure, in conjunction with item banking, is that tests need never be printed. The computer can be directed to select items from the bank in a prescribed fashion so that, if the bank is large enough, no two examinees would be administered the same set of items. The corresponding disadvantage is that the scores of these examinees may not be comparable if their tests were too different.

The computer offers speed, accuracy in computing, and storage capacity that make it a logical candidate for taking on test-administration chores. It can be programmed to select items for each examinee according to rigorous content and item-difficulty specifications. It can use the examinee's score on a given item to decide which item should be presented next. It can score an item immediately and store the result in each of several locations in its memory. It can use its internal clock to monitor the amount of time each examinee takes to respond to each item. It can store information about test-item performance as well as examinee performance. It can provide examinees with their test score as soon as they respond to the last test item. The potential of the computer for streamlining test administrations seems bounded only by our imaginations in telling the computer what it can do for us.

A new and promising test-administration approach, *adaptive testing*, uses the advantages of the microcomputer and requires a relatively new theory of testing called *item-response theory*. Adaptive testing is based on the assumptions that the trait being measured can be described by a single psychological continuum and that the responses of examinees to test items can be used to place the individuals on that continuum. The computer selects from the test-item bank an item that an average examinee would be expected to answer correctly. If the test taker answers correctly, a more difficult item is chosen for the next try. If the first answer was incorrect, an easier item is chosen for the second try. Since each item in the pool has been calibrated in advance to a particular location on the continuum, the examinee's position on the continuum can be located through successive selections of easier and harder items. A chief advantage of adaptive testing over conventional testing is that only about half the number of items are needed to obtain "equivalent" results (Green, 1983). There are problems yet unresolved with adaptive testing, but its anticipated advantages—shorter testing time, adaptability to more valid item types, and greater test security—make it one of the most promising developments for educational and psychological testing in the last decade of the century.

There are problems to be overcome before mass testing by computer becomes commonplace. For example, there must be a large pool of test items in the computer's bank so that, for test security purposes, every examinee does not receive exactly the same items that those previously tested received. The items different examinees receive must be relatively equivalent in content and difficulty; otherwise their test scores will not be comparable. In addition, there is no assurance that a bank of test items can be maintained without permitting unauthorized access to those items. One computer whiz seems able to "outfox" the other to break security codes designed to limit access and preserve confidentiality. The old-fashioned lock and key still appear to be the safest way to store test items or booklets in preparation for test administration. Finally, research on computer-assisted test administration has drawn attention to additional concerns. Moe and Johnson (1988) found that the terminal screen presented a variety of problems to examinees: 63 percent reported noticeable eye fatigue, 39 percent objected to the brightness, and 25 percent were bothered by glare. One-fourth of the examinees also complained about the lack of opportunity to review items to which they had already responded. Sarvela and Noonan (1988) pointed out the same limitation: inability to reconsider responses, change answers, and recover from key entry errors adds an element of unfairness that reduces the reliability and validity of the scores.

On the plus side, 91 percent of the 315 subjects in the Moe and Johnson (1988) study expressed a preference for taking an aptitude test by computer terminal rather than by conventional paper and pencil procedures. In addition, computer-test administrations show promise for providing more valid test scores with handicapped examinees than can be obtained from paper and pencil tests. No writing is required and, with the availability of voice synthesizers, no reading may be needed. For those who lack the fine motor coordination required to use the keyboard of a standard computer terminal, a touch-sensitive screen on the monitor provides an alternative. There is no way to predict the magnitude of the impact of these devices in providing opportunities in education and employment for those who heretofore have seen mostly barriers. But there is every reason to be optimistic!

SUMMARY PROPOSITIONS

1. Students should be told in advance when an important test is to be given and what the nature of the content is to be.
2. Students at all educational levels should be taught essential test-taking skills.
3. The test developer should avoid clues in the test items that enable an examinee to substitute test-wiseness for command of knowledge.
4. Test anxiety is seldom a major factor in determining a student's score on a test.
5. Research has suggested that the poor test performance of anxious students may be due to incomplete learning and poor study technique.
6. Objective classroom tests usually should be presented in duplicated test booklets.
7. Many aspects of classroom management related to test administrations can be addressed effectively with thorough written instructions on the test booklet coversheet.
8. The position of the correct answer in multiple-choice items should be distributed somewhat evenly so that overuse or underuse of a position does not provide a clue to examinees.
9. Both open-book and take-home tests offer advantages that are outweighed by their disadvantages relative to in-class, closed-book tests.
10. There is no conclusive research evidence that supports the ordering of items in a test according to difficulty level or on the basis of subject-matter areas.
11. The test administrator should help students to adjust their rate of work on a test according to the amount of time remaining.
12. Special test-administration procedures for classroom tests may be needed to accommodate students with language handicaps.
13. The instructor should be responsible for both the prevention and the punishment of cheating on classroom examinations.
14. The development of an honors system is not a promising solution to the problem of cheating during examinations.
15. The instructor should be responsible for preserving the security of a test prior to its administration.
16. The use of separate answer sheets facilitates rapid clerical or machine scoring of objective tests.
17. Recent advances in computer technology have made test-scoring machines more readily available for use by schools in scoring classroom tests.
18. The purpose of using a guessing correction is to reduce to zero the expected score gain from blind guessing.
19. Scores may be corrected for guessing by subtracting a fraction of the wrong responses from, or by adding a fraction of the omitted responses to, the number-right score.
20. Scores corrected for guessing usually will rank the examinees in about the same order as the corresponding uncorrected scores.
21. The probability of getting a respectable score on a good objective test by blind guessing alone is small.
22. Students should be encouraged to make rational guesses about the answers to objective-test items.
23. Giving different weights to different items in a test, or to different correct or incorrect responses within an item, seldom improves score reliability or valid score use appreciably.
24. Adaptive testing is a relatively new and promising method of computer test-administration that has the potential for improving the efficiency, realism, and security aspects of the more traditional testing methods.

QUESTIONS FOR STUDY AND DISCUSSION

1. What are the pros and cons of using "surprise tests" that are intended for summative evaluation purposes?
2. How might a student's deficiency in test-taking skills lead to achievement scores of questionable validity? How do such students cause the reliability of the scores from their class to be lower than it should be?
3. How could a student's self-reports of test anxiety be verified through other means?

4. A teacher allows 40 minutes of testing time for students whose native language is not English, but allows only 30 minutes to all other students. Does this seem like an equitable policy? Why?

5. Why do students cheat on tests instead of preparing themselves thoroughly for scoring well?

6. One instructor allows students to keep their test copies when they leave the exam and she develops a new test for the next time that exam is needed. What are the pros and cons of this procedure for present students, future students, and the instructor?

7. How can it be shown that the use of a correction for guessing formula does not penalize examinees?

8. What kinds of controls would a teacher need to introduce to prevent cheating by students on a computer-administered test? (Answer for individualized testing and group testing separately.)

13

Evaluating Test
and Item Characteristics

What makes an achievement test a good test? This question concerns both students and teachers whenever a test is given, and the answer has direct implications for instruction and for future test development work. With respect to instruction, the feedback loop that leaves and then reenters the performance assessment component of the Basic Teaching Model (described in Chapter 2) is significant. It indicates that the teacher should assess the quality of the tools of assessment. If students' test performances are below expectation, perhaps the explanation is with the methods of evaluation rather than with inadequate learning on the students' part. Tests should be evaluated, then, to determine if the scores they yield have value for the purpose for which they were originally intended.

There is another practical reason for teachers to analyze the test scores and the test from which they were derived. When tests have been scored and returned to students for discussion, considerable learning can occur. However, unless the test-review session has been planned well by the teacher in advance, the opportunities for learning can be preempted by lengthy debates about correct answers and item semantics. A teacher who is prepared with information about poorly performing test items and possible explanations for them stands a better chance of maintaining control of the class session and clearing up misconceptions or misunderstandings revealed by the test-item data.

A third reason for analyzing and evaluating a test after the administration relates to the teacher's professional development. Test and item data can reveal technical flaws and errors of judgment made by the item writer. By making use of these data, teachers can improve their item-writing skills and, at the same time, revise their test items for future use. Eventually, a large pool of high-quality test items should accumulate, and the ability to develop high-quality items will be enhanced in the process.

TEST CHARACTERISTICS TO EVALUATE

The characteristics to consider in evaluating the quality of an achievement test are the same as those to which the test developer attends in trying to build a good test. Some of these important factors are relevance, balance, efficiency, specificity, difficulty, discrimination, variability, and reliability. Though some of these characteristics are evaluated with different criteria for criterion-referenced or norm-referenced measures, each characteristic is important to consider, regardless of the type of score interpretation the test is intended to furnish.

Relevance and Balance

Relevance indicates the extent to which the test items reflect the test specifications and contribute to achieving the stated purpose for testing. Assessing the relevance of test items requires qualitative judgments rather than quantitative criteria. Are the test specifications and purpose sufficiently explicit to allow the test reviewer to decide which items are relevant and which items are not? In view of the test purpose, does an item like this belong in this test? Items that are judged to be relevant are not necessarily of high quality, but they are items that appear to measure the abilities that the test constructor set out to measure.

Relevance is judged by an item by item review of test content with attention directed at these criteria:

1. *Content appropriateness.* Does the item content fit as an element of the domain definition, or does the item content match a specific instructional objective? Can the task presented by the item be found in its general form in the instructional materials used by examinees?

2. *Taxonomic level.* In terms of Ebel's Relevance Guide or Bloom's Taxonomy, are the items written at the appropriate intellectual level? Are the lower levels minimized in favor of the use of knowledge, application, and problem solving? Are the abilities required by each item either too far beyond or well short of the cognitive demands on which instruction was focused?

3. *Extraneous abilities.* To what extent does each item require knowledge, skill, or abilities outside the content domain of interest. Does vocabulary level, reading ability, or creativity play too much of a role? How much specialized background knowledge, outside the domain of instruction, must the examinee call upon to answer the item? To what extent do the norms, customs, or practices of the majority culture influence item interpretation or the selection of the most correct answer?

Most test constructors seek *balance* in their tests. They hope that the items they select for their test will sample representatively all the important tasks—

knowledge, skills, and understandings—outlined in the test plan. The table of specifications developed in the planning stage is intended to be a guide to choosing items for the test. An assessment of test balance is simply a judgment about the extent to which the ideal specifications were achieved in terms of both content representativeness and cognitive abilities. There are two aspects to the assessment of the balance of a test. First, do the weights assigned to content subdomains in the test specifications seem appropriate? For example, *should* there be twice as many items dealing with "rest and sleep" as with "exercise programs?" *Should* there be twice as many items measuring knowledge of terms compared to recommended action? Second, how well were the intentions of the table of specifications carried out? Would an independent judgment of the requirements of each item result in content and abilities distributions like those in the table of specifications?

Efficiency and Specificity

A test that yields a large number of independently scorable responses per unit of testing time is an *efficient* test. Efficiency is a relative characteristic that must be judged by comparing a test with other hypothetical tests that could have been used to serve the same purpose. In general, a multiple-choice test will be more efficient than an essay test, and a true–false test is likely to be more efficient than a multiple-choice test. A multiple true–false test may be the most efficient of the four types. But items of any given type may be more or less efficient as well. For example, multiple-choice items that contain implausible distracters are less efficient than those that do not. Unnecessarily wordy true–false items are less efficient than shorter but relevant statements. Relevance need not and should not be sacrificed to achieve greater efficiency. Though multiple-choice items generally are more efficient than essays, if a testing situation calls for the use of essay items, the efficiency of multiple choice should not even be an issue.

As a test characteristic, efficiency relates to maximizing the amount of information about achievement that can be obtained in a specified time period. A test can also be more or less efficient to develop or to score. Essay tests usually are more efficient to build than objective tests because they require fewer items, but they are less efficient to score. Because test preparation and scoring impinge on teacher "prep" time, efficiency is somewhat important in these terms, also. But in view of the limited amount of instructional time ordinarily devoted to summative evaluation, the most critical aspect of efficiency relates to obtaining the largest number of independently scorable responses per hour of testing.

A test shows high *specificity* if a testwise novice in the subject matter achieves a score near the chance level on the test. Under such circumstances there is good assurance that the test measures content specific to the objectives of instruction rather than general information. To the degree that any achievement test is a test of reading or writing ability, or general intelligence, it suffers in specificity. The most useful evidence for assessing specificity is obtained from the responses of proficient test takers who do not have competence in the field covered by the test.

Difficulty and Discrimination

How difficult a test *should* be relates to the purpose for testing and the kind of score interpretation desired. A good norm-referenced test should be harder, intentionally, than a good criterion-referenced test. But how hard a test turns out to be also depends on how well students learned the content required by the test tasks. If *difficulty* were strictly a characteristic of the test, a given test would be equally hard or easy for every group to whom it was administered.

For norm-referenced purposes, tests that are too easy or too difficult for the group tested will produce score distributions that make it hard to identify reliable interindividual differences. Under these circumstances the goal of the test developer is to use items that will produce moderate difficulty—a mean score that is about halfway between a perfect score and the mean chance score. Thus, the *ideal difficulty* of a 40-item test composed of 5-option multiple-choice items is 24, halfway between 40 and 8 (one-fifth of 40). The difficulty of a test is obviously determined by the difficulty of the items that comprise it. The difficulty of an item, its *p-value*, is the proportion of the group that responds correctly. The ideal difficulty of a 5-choice item is 0.60, halfway between 1.00 and 0.20. Considerable skill is required by item writers to develop and manipulate item content to achieve the appropriate level of difficulty.

How difficult should tests intended for criterion-referenced interpretations be? Because the elements of the domain to be measured are made explicit by the domain definition, the notion of difficulty is built into the test specifications. In this case the item writer is not free to manipulate item content to influence difficulty directly. To the extent that difficulty *is* manipulated, relevance may suffer.

When a rating scale is developed to describe the absolute standards against which performance will be judged, difficulty is accounted for in describing the various scale points. The stimulus presented to the students, whether a theme prompt, a speech topic, or a laboratory skill, must be prepared by the evaluator to be consistent in difficulty with the demands inherent in the objectives of instruction. For example, an impromptu speech about the detriments of smoking would be easier for a high school student than one about how water softeners work. In this case inappropriate difficulty—too hard or too easy—would contribute to a lack of relevance.

Generally, we expect tests geared to criterion-referenced interpretations to be easier, in terms of mean score, than those used for norm referencing. But it is possible for a good criterion-referenced test to yield low scores. In the criterion-referenced situation the goal is not to make tests that are hard, moderate, or easy in difficulty. Instead, the purpose is to translate the test specifications—the domain definition—into relevant test tasks. High degrees of success at translation will automatically take care of difficulty.

The ability of a norm-referenced *test* to discriminate between high- and low-achieving students is a function of the ability of each *item* to do just that. If a large proportion of the "good" students get an item right, and a small proportion of the "poor" students get it right, that item has discriminated properly and has contributed to the test purpose. *Discrimination* is closely related to difficulty:

items that are too hard or too easy are not as capable of discriminating between high and low achievers as items of moderate difficulty.

The items in a criterion-referenced test should also discriminate among students as long as some students have not learned the content measured by those items. But since the purpose of such a test is not to differentiate examinees, items that fail to discriminate are not regarded as poor items, at least on that basis. Of course, if more low achievers than high achievers answer a certain item correctly, that item is a negative discriminator and it interferes with *all* measurement purposes.

Variability and Reliability

As long as differences in student learning exist, and as long as the purpose for testing is to identify such differences, the distribution of test scores should exhibit high *variability*. The larger the standard deviation of the scores, the more successful the test constructor has been in identifying the individual differences in achievement. The role of difficulty and discrimination in obtaining variability should be apparent. Extremely easy or hard tests yield skewed distributions with relatively small standard deviations. Tests composed of items of moderate difficulty stand the best chance of discriminating between levels of achievement and producing high score variability.

Good criterion-referenced tests may produce score variability, but they need not do so. A high-quality graduation test that everyone passes, a spelling test on which everyone obtains a perfect score, or a musical selection that all piano students play without error—all are examples of criterion-referenced situations where variability is quite small or even nonexistent.

When norm-referenced score interpretations are needed, the *reliability* of the scores obtained is the most important *statistical* indicator of their quality. Of course, reliability means very little if relevance has not been established: the user may have succeeded in measuring some irrelevant abilities quite accurately. The goals of high score variability, high item discrimination, and moderate item difficulty all contribute to the major aim of obtaining high score reliability.

Methods used to estimate the reliability of norm-referenced scores may not be very useful for many criterion-referenced situations. These methods are mostly based on correlation coefficients, and the use of correlation depends on variability in scores. When dichotomous decisions such as pass–fail are to be made with scores, decision consistency is of greater concern than score reliability. But in criterion-referenced contexts in which variability naturally occurs, as with grading on the A–F scale, score reliability should be of concern. In such situations the traditional reliability estimate may be appropriate to use, but the standards of goodness used in norm-referenced contexts may be too stringent. For example, a K–R20 of 0.35 would not be acceptable for norm-referenced scores, but it may not be too low for certain criterion-referenced circumstances.

The test characteristics we have reviewed in this section are important to examine in evaluating the quality of an achievement test, no matter what our primary testing purpose is. The evaluation of each characteristic can provide clues regarding the ways in which the test items might be revised and improved for future use. Further discussion of these characteristics and the criteria for judging their goodness follows.

ITEM-ANALYSIS PROCEDURES

The analysis of student responses to objective-test items is a powerful tool for test improvement and for accumulating a bank of high-quality items. The procedures described in this section have been used traditionally with items from norm-referenced measures, but they can be used also for items from criterion-referenced tests. (Procedures specifically designed for criterion-referenced testing will be described in a subsequent section.) Item analysis can indicate which items may be too easy or difficult and which may fail, for whatever reasons, to discriminate properly between high and low achievers. Sometimes these procedures suggest why an item has not functioned effectively and how it might be improved. But most often item analysis only identifies problems, and the evaluator must search for the probable causes and possible solutions.

Item analysis begins after the test has been scored. Of the many sets of analysis procedures in use, one has been chosen to illustrate how the process works. And though most microcomputers can do the calculations described below, the process is described in detail to help you develop a complete understanding of the information that results. A classroom teacher who chooses to complete the procedures by hand would follow these six steps:

1. Arrange the scored test papers or answer sheets in score order from highest to lowest.
2. Identify an upper group and a lower group separately. The upper group is the highest scoring 27 percent (one-fourth) of the group and the lower group is an equal number of the lowest scoring of the total group.
3. For each item, count the number of examinees in the upper group that chose each response alternative. Do a separate, similar tally for the lower group.
4. Record these counts on a copy of the test at the end of the corresponding response alternatives. (The use of colored pencils is recommended.)
5. Add the two counts for the keyed response and divide this sum by the total number of students in the upper *and* lower groups. Multiply this decimal value by 100 to form a percentage. The result is an *estimate* of the index of item difficulty.
6. Subtract the lower group count from the upper group count for the keyed response. Divide this difference by the number of examinees in one of the groups (either group since both are the same size). The result, expressed as a decimal, is the index of discrimination.

An Example

An illustration of the data obtained by this process for one item is presented in Figure 13–1. Answer sheets from a social studies test were available for 178 students, so the upper and lower groups consisted of the 48 students having the highest and the 48 having the lowest scores. The keyed response is marked

---

74% What change in life expectancy (number of years a person is likely to live) has been
0.48 occurring?

    *a. It has been increasing. (47–24)
     b. It has been declining due to rising rates of cancer and heart disease. (0–10)
     c. It has increased for young people but decreased for older people. (0–5)
     d. It has remained quite stable. (1–7)
       Omits (0–2)

Figure 13-1. Illustration of Item-Analysis Data

with an asterisk. The figures in parentheses following each response alternative indicate how many of the upper group (first figure) and how many of the lower group (second figure) chose each response. Of the 48 in the upper group, 47 students chose the first response (the keyed answer) and one chose the fourth response. Of the 48 students in the lower group, 24 chose the first response, 10 the second, 5 the third, and 7 the fourth. Two of the lower group students failed to respond to the item at all. (Note that we do not know how the middle 46 percent of scorers responded to this item.)

The moderate degree of difficulty of the item is indicated by the 74 percent of correct response in the two groups combined, calculated as follows:

1. Add the two counts for the keyed response:

    47 + 24 = 71

2. Divide this sum by the total number of students in both groups:

    71 ÷ 96 = 0.74

3. Convert the decimal value to a percentage:

    0.74 × 100 = 74%

This difficulty value is actually an estimate of the difficulty index that would be obtained if we determined the percentage of the entire group, all 178 students, that answered the item correctly. The estimate will be quite satisfactory for large classes, but it may be fairly inaccurate for smaller classes. Of course, for small classes the time required to tally the responses of all students to compute the difficulty index would not be great.

The reasonably good level of discrimination of the item is indicated by the Upper–Lower Difference Index, the difference in proportions of correct response between the upper and lower groups [(47 − 24) ÷ 48 = 0.48]. And each of the distracters functioned reasonably well since each attracted some responses and these were largely from students in the lower group. In sum, the moderate difficulty level permitted reasonable discrimination and a useful contribution to score reliability.

SELECTION OF THE UPPER AND LOWER GROUPS

The type of item analysis we describe in this chapter, like most such procedures, makes use of an internal criterion for the selection of groups of high and low achievement. That is, the total score on the test to be analyzed is used as the criterion rather than some other independent (external) measure of achievement. In order to conclude that an item showing high discrimination is a good item, one must assume that the entire test, of which that item is a part, is a good test.

Such an assumption is ordinarily quite reasonable. Most test constructors come close enough to the mark on their first attempt to make the total score a fairly dependable basis for distinguishing between students of high and low achievement. However, it must be conceded that item analysis using an internal criterion can only make a test a better measure of *whatever it does measure*. To make the test a better measure of what it *ought* to measure, one would need to use some better criterion than the total score on the test itself. Obviously, this would be an external criterion. Yet an external criterion has no real advantage over an internal criterion unless it is truly a better measure of whatever the test is supposed to measure.

The use of total-test score as a basis for selecting upper and lower groups for item analysis has two important advantages. The first is relevance. Within limits set by the wisdom and skill of the test constructor, the score on a teacher-made test does come closer than any other measure is likely to come to measuring what that person wished to measure. The second is convenience. The total score on the test whose items are being analyzed is always readily available.

The selection of highly discriminating items, using total test score as the criterion, results in a test whose items are valid measures of what the whole test measures. In this sense, item analysis is a technique of item validation. But the kind of analysis and selection we have been considering does not demonstrate, and might not even improve, the validity of the test as a whole. What it can do to the test as a whole, and this is no small thing, is to make the scores more reliable, and thus probably more valid, too.

Step 3 in the process of item analysis called for the counting of responses in upper and lower 27 percent groups. Why 27 percent? Why not upper and lower fourths (25 percent), thirds (33 percent), or even halves (50 percent)? The answer is that 27 percent provides the best compromise between two desirable but inconsistent aims: (1) to make the extreme groups as large as possible and (2) to make the extreme groups as different from one another as possible. Kelley (1939) demonstrated that when extreme groups, each consisting of approximately 27 percent of the total group, are used, one can say with the greatest confidence that those in the upper group are superior in the ability measured by the test to those in the lower group.

Although upper and lower groups of 27 percent are best, they are not significantly better than groups of 25 or 33 percent. Test analysts who prefer to work with simple fractions like one-fourth or one-third should feel free to use upper and lower fourths or thirds. However, those who do should guard against the intuitive feeling that 33 percent is better than 27 percent because it involves groups of larger size or that 25 percent is better than 27 percent because the difference between the groups is greater. In each case the supposed advantage is slightly more than offset by the opposing disadvantage. The optimum value is 27 percent.

Counting the Responses

The counting of responses to the items is likely to be the most tedious and time-consuming part of the analysis. However, for many classroom tests the number of papers in each extreme group may be less than ten, which makes the task seem less formidable. A chart can be developed that has items numbered down the left side and response alternatives labeled across the top as column headings. The chart helps to organize the work and, if many copies of it are duplicated at one time, a supply can be kept on hand for future tests or to share with colleagues. Often clerical staff or aides can perform the tallying work and computation with minimal guidance.

Some teachers obtain response counts by a show of hands in class, as suggested by Diedrich (1960), or by using student volunteers. But neither of these approaches is recommended here, because each fails to maintain the confidentiality of the test scores that students and their parents should expect to be respected. Optical scanners and computers are the most efficient tools available for obtaining the item-analysis counts and indices. Many school districts and colleges with data-processing and computing facilities make such analysis available to teachers.

INDEX OF DIFFICULTY

Historically, two measures of item difficulty have been used. One, which is slightly harder to calculate but slightly less confusing to interpret, defines the index of difficulty of a test item as the percentage of a defined group of examinees who did *not* answer it correctly. Under this definition, the larger the numerical value of the index of difficulty is, the more difficult the item. The second measure defines the difficulty index as the percentage of the group who answered the item correctly. The larger the value of the index is, the *easier* the item. Despite the minor confusion associated with it, the second definition is used in this book because it has been so consistently adopted by measurement specialists in the literature related to achievement testing.

The numerical value of the index of difficulty of a test item is not determined solely by the content of the item. It reflects also the ability of the group responding to the item. Hence, it is more appropriate to say, "When this item was administered to that particular group, its index of difficulty was 63 percent," than to say, "The index of difficulty for this item is 63 percent."

The Distribution of Difficulty Indices

It is quite natural to assume, as many test constructors do, that a good norm-referenced test must include some easy items to test the low achievers and some difficult items to test the high achievers. After all, it must discriminate among students over a fairly wide range of achievement levels. But the actual testing circumstances rarely warrant such an assumption. The items in most norm-referenced tests are not like a set of hurdles of different heights, all presenting the same task but varying in their difficulty. Such norm-referenced items do differ in difficulty, but they differ also in the kind of task they present.

Suppose a class of 20 students takes a test and 12 of the students answer item 6 correctly, but only 8 of them answer item 7 correctly. A reasonable assumption is that any student who answered the harder question (7) correctly also answered the easier question (6) correctly. Anyone who missed the easier question also would be expected to have missed the harder one. But such assumptions and expectations are often mistaken when applied to achievement tests.

Table 13–1 presents data on the responses of 11 students to six test items. A plus (+) in the table represents a correct response, a zero (0) an incorrect response. In this exhibit the students have been arranged in order of ability, and the items in order of difficulty. Note that the item missed by good student B was not one of the most difficult items. Poor student J missed all the easier items but managed correct answers to two of the more difficult items.

It is possible to imagine a test that would give highly consistent results across items and across students when administered to a particular group. Results would be called consistent if success by a particular student on a particular item practically guaranteed success on all other items in the test that were easier for the group than that item. Correspondingly, failure on a particular item would almost guarantee failure on all harder items if student responses were highly consistent. But a test showing such a degree of consistency among the responses would also be characterized by much higher reliability than ordinarily obtained with the same number of items. Such tests can be imagined but are seldom met with in practice. This is another reason why specifications requiring that the test include items ranging widely in difficulty are seldom warranted.

Most item writers produce some items that are ineffective (nondiscriminating) because they are too difficult or too easy. Efforts to improve the accuracy with which a test measures, that is, to improve its score reliability, usually have the effect of reducing the range of item difficulty rather than increasing it. The differences in difficulty that remain among items highest in discrimination are usually more than adequate to make the test effective in discriminating different levels of achievement over the whole range of abilities for which the test is expected to be used.

Some data from a simple experimental study of the relation between

Table 13-1. Responses of 11 Students to Six Test Items

Student	A	B	C	D	E	F	G	H	I	J	K
Item 1	+	+	+	+	+	+	+	+	+	0	0
Item 2	+	+	+	+	+	+	0	+	0	0	+
Item 3	+	0	+	0	0	+	+	+	+	0	0
Item 4	+	+	0	+	0	0	+	0	0	+	0
Item 5	+	+	+	+	+	0	0	0	0	0	0
Item 6	+	+	0	0	+	0	0	0	0	+	0

spread of item-difficulty values, on the one hand, and spread of test scores and level of reliability coefficients, on the other, are presented in Figure 13–2.

Three synthetic tests of 16 items each were "constructed" by the selection of items from a 61-item trial form of a social science test. This trial form had been administered to over 300 college freshmen and an item analysis performed to yield indices of difficulty and discrimination for each item. The items constituting the three 16-item tests were selected so as to yield tests differing widely in difficulty distributions.

Figure 13–2. Relation of Distribution of Test Scores to Distribution of Item Difficulty Values

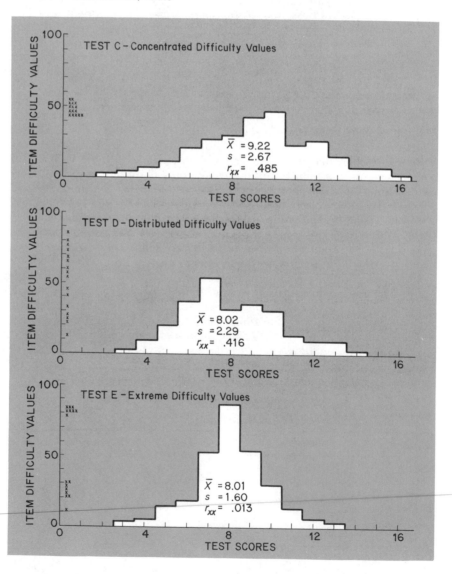

In Test C, the items selected were *concentrated* in difficulty values as near the middle of the entire distribution of difficulty values as possible.

In Test D, the items selected were *distributed* in difficulty values as uniformly as possible over the entire range of available difficulty values.

In Test E, the items were selected for *extreme* difficulty values, including the eight easiest and the eight most difficult items.

When these three 16-item tests were scored on a set of 253 answer sheets for the 61-item tryout form, the distributions of scores displayed in the histograms of Figure 13-2 were obtained. The distributions of item difficulties are indicated by the tally marks along the vertical scales to the left of each histogram.

Note the inverse relation between the spread of item difficulties and the spread of test scores. The wider the dispersion of difficulty values, the more concentrated the distribution of test scores. Note, too, the very low reliability of scores on the test composed only of very easy and very difficult items and the somewhat higher reliability of the scores from those tests composed of items more nearly in the mid-range of difficulty. In short, the findings of this study support the recommendation that items of middle difficulty be favored in the construction of achievement tests.

INDEX OF DISCRIMINATION

Upper–Lower Difference Index

The index of discrimination that results from step 6 was first described by Johnson (1951). Since then it has attracted considerable attention and approval. It is simpler to compute and to explain to others than such other indices of discrimination as the point-biserial correlation, biserial correlation, Flanagan's coefficient (Flanagan, 1939), and Davis's coefficient (Davis, 1946). It has the very useful property, which most of the other correlation indices lack, of being biased in favor of items of middle difficulty. As we have already seen, it is precisely these items that provide the largest amounts of information about differences in levels of achievement and that thus contribute most to score reliability. If the primary goal of item selection is to maximize reliability, as it should be for norm-referenced tests, the items having highest discrimination in terms of this index should be chosen. Item difficulty need not be considered directly in item selection, since no item that is much too difficult or much too easy can possibly show good discrimination when the upper–lower difference index is used.

Item discrimination indices of all types are subject to considerable sampling error (Pyrczak, 1973). The smaller the sample of answer sheets used in the analysis, the larger the sampling errors. An item that appears highly discriminating in one small sample may appear weak or even negative in discrimination in another small sample. The values obtained for achievement-test items are also sensitive to the kind of instruction the students received relative to the item. Hence the use of refined statistics to measure item discrimination seldom seems to be warranted.

But even though one cannot determine the discrimination indices of individual items reliably without using large samples of student responses, item analysis based on small samples is still worthwhile as a means of overall test improvement. How much better a revised test composed of the most discriminating items can be expected to be will depend on how large the samples and how small the sampling errors are.

Biserial and Point-biserial Indices

The biserial and point-biserial correlation coefficients are presented as discrimination indices in some item-analysis reports generated by a computer. Their computation is too complex and time consuming to warrant our attention, but because they are popular indices of discrimination, it is worth comparing each with the upper–lower difference index discussed above.

The *biserial correlation coefficient* describes the relationship between two variables: score on a test item and score on the total test for each examinee. High positive correlations are obtained for items that high-scoring students on the test tend to get right (item score = +1) and low-scoring students on the test tend to get wrong (item score = 0). Such items are interpreted to be high in discrimination. Negatively discriminating items show the opposite relationship: Most students with high test scores have scores of zero on the test item and many with low test scores have scores of +1 on the item. The *point-biserial correlation coefficient* differs from the biserial coefficient computationally and theoretically, but for item-analysis purposes the two can be interpreted in essentially the same manner.

When both are computed with data from the same test item, the biserial coefficient will yield a value that is always at least one-fourth larger than the point-biserial (Guilford, 1965, p. 324). Neither coefficient is as biased in favor of items of moderate difficulty as is the case with the upper–lower index. Thus, it is possible to obtain relatively high point-biserial or biserial discrimination indices for very hard or very easy items. This point is worth remembering when selecting items on the basis of their discrimination indices to build a test or to determine which items may be in need of revision.

ITEM SELECTION

One of the two direct uses that can be made of indices of discrimination is in the selection of the best (that is, most highly discriminating) items for inclusion in an improved version of the test. How high should the index of discrimination be?

Experience with a wide variety of classroom tests suggests that the indices of item discrimination for most of them can be evaluated in these terms:

Index of Discrimination	Item Evaluation
0.40 and up	Very good items
0.30 to 0.39	Reasonably good but possibly subject to improvement
0.20 to 0.29	Marginal items, usually needing and being subject to improvement
Below 0.19	Poor items, to be rejected or improved by revision

It probably goes without saying that no special effort should be made to secure a spread of item-discrimination indices—the higher each item-discrimination index, the better. Of two tests otherwise alike, the one in which the average index of item discrimination is the higher will always be the better, that is, will produce more reliable scores.

A simple relation can be shown to exist between the sum of the indices of discrimination for the items of a test and the variance of the scores on the test (Ebel, 1967). It is expressed in the formula

$$s_x^2 = \frac{(\Sigma\ D)^2}{6}$$

This formula indicates that the score variance, s_x^2, is directly proportional to the square of the sum of the discrimination indices, $(\Sigma\ D)^2$. Since it is true in general that the larger the score variance for a given number of items, the higher the reliability of the scores, the formula also indicates that the greater the average value of the discrimination indices, the higher reliability is likely to be.

Of course, discrimination should be secondary to content as a criterion for selecting the items for a norm-referenced test. One way of ensuring test balance while maximizing reliability is to sort the available items into content piles that correspond to the content areas of the table of specifications. Then, within each pile, items can be arranged in order of their discrimination index (based on a previous administration to a similar group). Finally, the most discriminating items can be selected until the numbers required by the table of specifications are obtained.

ITEM REVISION

The second use that can be made of indices of item discrimination is in the revision of the test items. Five items illustrating the revision process on the basis of item-analysis data are presented and discussed here. These items were written to test the background knowledge of high school students in the natural and social sciences areas. They were administered to a large cross section of students in a preliminary item tryout. Then item-analysis data were used to select the most satisfactory items for the final form of the test. Among the items that were rejected there appeared to be some that could be salvaged by revision. After making revisions, the items were tried out with another representative group of students and reanalyzed. Results of the tryouts before and after revision are indicated in the following paragraphs.

The first item deals with the distinction between the terms *climate* and *weather*.

37% **What, if any, is the distinction between climate and weather?**
0.13

    a. **There is no important distinction. (1–6)**

    b. **Climate is primarily a matter of temperature and rainfall, while weather includes many other natural phenomena. (33–51)** *c.* **Climate pertains to longer periods of time than weather. (43–30)**

   d. **Weather pertains to natural phenomena on a *local* rather than a *national* scale. (23–13)**

This item is somewhat too difficult for the group tested (only 73 correct responses among 200 students) and does not discriminate well (only 13 more good than poor students answered it correctly). Examination of the response counts indicates that response *b* was attractive to a considerable number of good students and that response *d* was more attractive to good students than to poor. Since the stem of the question seemed basically clear and since the intended correct response seemed reasonable, efforts in revision were concentrated on changing distracters *b* and *d*. It appeared that response *b* could be made less attractive by making it simpler and somewhat more specific. Since response *d* seemed much too plausible to the better students in the group being tested, it was "spoiled" by substituting a more obviously incorrect response. The revised item (revisions in uppercase letters) reads:

62%   **What, if any, is the distinction between climate and weather?**
0.58

   a. **There is no important distinction. (2–22)**

   b. **CLIMATE IS PRIMARILY A MATTER OF RAINFALL, WHILE WEATHER IS PRIMAR- ILY A MATTER OF TEMPERATURE. (3–25)**

   c. **Climate pertains to longer periods of time than weather. (91–33)**

   d. **WEATHER IS DETERMINED BY CLOUDS, WHILE CLIMATE IS DETERMINED BY WINDS. (4–20)**

Analysis data of the revised item reveal that the revisions were effective. The changed item is much easier and much more highly discriminating than the original. Only nine of the good students chose distracters. Equally important is the fact that these revisions did not appreciably increase the number of poor students choosing the correct response. It is interesting to note that on the second tryout the number of poor students who chose response *a* increased markedly, even though this response had not been altered.

     The next item deals with the common misconception that meteors are "falling stars."

36%   **Do stars ever fall to the earth?**
0.35

   a. **Yes. They may be seen often, particularly during certain months. (12–28)**

   b. **Yes. There are craters caused by falling stars in certain regions of the earth. (30–43)**

   c. **No. The earth moves too rapidly for its gravitational force to act on the stars. (5–11)**

   d. **No. The falling of a single average star would destroy the earth. (53–18)**

     This item again is somewhat too difficult, though its discriminating power is fairly good. The item might be made somewhat easier by revising the response *b*. This response can be legitimately criticized as "tricky" because there are *meteor* craters. Hence in the revision, this response alone was changed.

42%   **Do stars ever fall to the earth?**
0.56
    a.   **Yes. They may be seen often, particularly during certain months. (20–68)**
    b.   **NO. PLANETS LIKE THE EARTH HAVE NO ATTRACTION FOR STARS. (1–4)**
    c.   **No. The earth moves too rapidly for its gravitational force to act on the stars. (9–14)**
   d.*   **No. The falling of a single average star would destroy the earth. (70–14)

Note that the difficulty of the item improved only slightly, but the change obviously spoiled the attractiveness of the second response. However, the change did not increase the proportion of poor students choosing the correct answer. Apparently, most of their choices shifted to response *a*, which had not been modified in the revision.

      The next item attempted to deal with the relationship between the number of time zones spanning a geographic area and the size of that area.

23%   **There are eleven time zones in the U.S.S.R. This fact indicates that**
0.09
    a.   **much of the area of the U.S.S.R. is above the Arctic Circle. (12–26)**
    b.   **the U.S.S.R. is wider (east–west) than it is long (north–south). (56–40)**
   c.*   **the U.S.S.R. occupies a large geographic area. (27–18)
    d.   **Some areas of the U.S.S.R. are above the equator and some are below the equator. (5–16)**

This item is much too difficult and is very low in discrimination. The major problem appears to be with choice *b*. It was a very attractive choice overall, but more attractive to good students than to poor ones. A new second response was written that was expected to be less closely related to the idea expressed by the keyed response.

49%   **There are eleven time zones in the U.S.S.R. This fact indicates that**
0.58
    a.   **much of the area of the U.S.S.R. is above the Arctic Circle. (4–32)**
    b.   **MOST OF THE AREA OF THE U.S.S.R. IS IN THE EASTERN HEMISPHERE. (11–25)**
   c.*   **the U.S.S.R. occupies a large geographic area. (78–20)
    d.   **some areas of the U.S.S.R. are above the equator and some are below the equator. (7–23)**

This revision improved both the difficulty level and discrimination of the item markedly. Most good students were able to decide on the correct response, but it appears that poor students distributed themselves nearly evenly across all four responses, much as would be expected if the examinees were blindly guessing.

      The next item deals with cause of shortage in the ground water supply.

48% **Water shortages in many localities have been caused by which, if any, of these factors?**
0.17
    a. **Removal of natural plant cover allowing faster run-off into streams (17-13)**
    b. **Increased demands for water in homes, businesses, and industry (15-26)**
    c. **Neither *a* or *b* (12-22)**
   *d. **Both *a* and *b* (56-39)**

This item is of appropriate difficulty but is not highly discriminating. In this case it appeared that the fault might lie with the design of the item itself. The question was framed in such a way that there were two important, correct answers, and hence it was necessary to include each of these as a single, supposedly incorrect response and to make "both" the correct response. This approach is apparently somewhat confusing. Furthermore, no opportunities are provided for the use of bona fide distracters. In the revision one of the correct responses was placed in the stem of the item and three bona fide distracters were provided as follows:

53% **WHAT FACTOR, OTHER THAN INCREASED WATER USE, HAS BEEN RESPONSIBLE**
0.62 **FOR WATER SHORTAGES IN MANY LOCALITIES?**
    a. **RESTRICTION OF STREAM FLOW BY HYDROELECTRIC DAMS (3-22)**
    b. **DISTURBANCE OF NORMAL RAINFALL BY ARTIFICIAL RAINMAKING (3-18)**
    c. **INTENSIVE FARM CULTIVATION, WHICH PERMITS MOST RAINFALL TO SOAK INTO THE GROUND (10-38)**
   *d. **REMOVAL OF NATURAL PLANT COVER ALLOWING FASTER RUN-OFF INTO STREAMS (84-22)**

The item was made somewhat easier and much more discriminating. In this case, the revision process worked in a way that gladdened the heart of the item writer.

      The final item to be illustrated deals with knowledge of the type of information found on a physical map of a region.

12% **A physical map of a state would show**
0.21
    a. **the state's railway network. (20-25)**
    b. **average rainfall by month for the state. (20-34)**
    c. **the location of the largest cities in the state. (38-40)**
   *d. **the state's highest elevation. (22-1)**

The item writer decided that this item called for too fine a discrimination. All responses were attractive to good students because no single response seemed best. Some physical maps do show major transportation systems and some maps show rainfall patterns, though not usually monthly averages. Finally, major cities are occasionally used as points of reference on physical maps. Each distracter was modified to reduce its attractiveness to good students while maintaining a certain level of plausibility for poor students.

43%   **A PHYSICAL MAP OF A STATE WOULD SHOW THE STATE'S**
0.40
      a.   AVERAGE SUMMER RAINFALL. (2-11)

      b.   POPULATION DENSITY. (20-25)

      c.   MOST IMPORTANT CITIES. (15-40)

    **d.*   HIGHEST ELEVATION. (63-23)

The revised item turned out to be reasonably discriminating and easier, but it is still a bit more difficult than most item writers would prefer. Either students are not clear about the unique features of a physical map or the second and third distracters still represent legitimate correct answers relative to keyed response *d.*

These five items do not illustrate all the possible ways in which item-analysis data may be interpreted to aid in item revision. What they do indicate is the general nature of the process and the fact that it *may* be highly successful.

OTHER CRITERION-REFERENCED PROCEDURES

The procedures for item analysis described in this chapter are equally useful for judging the quality of items from norm-referenced and criterion-referenced measures. However, the standards used to differentiate good and poor items in the two types of measures vary and, consequently, an item earmarked for revision for one type of measure may be selected without change for use in the other type.

In the preparation of items for criterion-referenced measures such as mastery tests, minimum competency tests, and some professional certification tests, item writers need not make a conscious decision to write items that will be about moderate in difficulty. As we have said, the rigid content specifications of the test should indicate with some precision what the test items should measure. If the pool of examinees is expected to be well prepared, the item writer should expect difficulty indices in the range of 70 to 100 percent. By these standards, no well-written test item likely will be judged to be too easy, but items can be identified that are too difficult. However, items that, say, 95 percent of a group answers correctly are not automatically good items for a criterion-referenced measure. For example, those that contain several implausible distracters or that give internal clues suggesting the correct response are still bad items. The analysis of "easy" criterion-referenced items for appropriateness in difficulty should include a review of the items for technical adequacy. The reviewer should be convinced that a high proportion of the students actually knew the content measured by items that show high difficulty indices.

The upper–lower difference index can be used to assess the quality of criterion-referenced items as well, but generally it is much less useful in this situation. No test item, regardless of its intended purpose, is useful if it yields a negative discrimination index. But many good items used in criterion-referenced measures may have discrimination indices of zero or only slightly higher. The explanation for this phenomenon relates to the fact that score distributions from criterion-referenced measures tend to be quite negatively skewed and low in variability. The upper and lower criterion groups tend to be very similar in terms of total test score. In fact, the average *true* scores for the two groups may be barely distinguishable in some cases.

Alternative indices to the upper–lower index or point-biserial correlation have been proposed for use with items from criterion-referenced measures. For example, Cox and Vargas (1966) suggested a pre-post difference index to judge the ability of items to discriminate. The proportion of students who answer an item correctly prior to instruction (pre) is subtracted from the proportion of the same group to respond correctly after instruction (post). The larger the value of the index, the more highly discriminating the item is judged to be. (Because of the way it is computed, some have labeled this as an "index of instructional sensitivity.")

Another index, used primarily for items from mastery tests, is based on the phi correlation coefficient. An item index is computed by correlating item score (0 or +1) with the mastery decision (master or nonmaster) using a two-by-two frequency table like that shown below.

Mastery Decision

		Master	Nonmaster
	+1	A	B
Item Score	0	C	D

If "masters" tend to answer correctly (A is large) and "nonmasters" tend to answer incorrectly (D is large also), the item discriminates well between the two levels of achievement. When the values B and C are large, the item shows negative discrimination. The phi coefficient has greater utility than the pre-post difference index because it requires no pretest administration. But unless the number of nonmasters is sufficiently large, the phi coefficient will provide a misleading indication of the discriminability of the items.

The index of discrimination can be used to select the best items for inclusion in a criterion-referenced measure, also. To do so, items first must be grouped according to the content categories outlined in the table of specifications or according to the objectives being measured. Then the number of items required from each category can be selected on the basis of their discrimination indices. This procedure will ensure that the content balance required to make valid score interpretations will be achieved.

The decision consistency procedures described in Chapter 5 provide alternative methods for assessing the quality of scores from a criterion-referenced test, especially when the traditional reliability analysis seems less appropriate.

POSTTEST DISCUSSIONS

Once the classroom test has been scored, the results can be used to promote additional learning or to contribute to the kind of overlearning that resists forgetting. Testing postmortems can be profitable to students as well as to teachers if they are planned well and conducted in a businesslike manner. The feedback from students to teacher about the nature of misinterpretations or ambiguities can lead to item improvements as well as clarification of misunderstandings.

The main preparation by the teacher for these discussions is the completion of an item analysis and a review of the most difficult items. Hypotheses about why certain items were too hard can serve as a springboard to further analysis and reflection by students. If correct answers are marked on student papers, or if an answer key is displayed on a transparency, class time will not be needed to answer key-related questions.

The class discussion should focus on the items that were most difficult for the class; questions about other items can be handled on an individual basis, if necessary, after class or during some other off-class time. Students who missed the item under discussion should be encouraged to explain how they answered and to indicate ambiguities they may have detected. Disagreements occurring between a student and the teacher that seem not to contribute substantively to class discussion should be suspended until a later time.

It is unlikely that postmortems should lead to the revision of the scoring key or to a deletion of any items from scoring. Obviously, clerical errors in scoring or in preparing the scoring key should be rectified, but controversial item keys should not be changed. There is room to take these and other types of measurement error into account in using the scores, that is, in grading and setting cutoff scores. Such methods of accounting for error should be explained to students so that they are aware that "errors" will be addressed in an equitable way.

SUMMARY PROPOSITIONS

1. Item analysis is a useful tool in the progressive improvement of achievement tests.
2. The relevance of a set of items is established by judging their relationship with instructional content, the appropriateness of their taxonomic level, and the potential for influence by extraneous factors.
3. The degree of match between a table of specifications and the test-item content is an indication of the degree of balance achieved in the test.
4. The most efficient test includes as many independently scorable responses per unit of testing time as is possible without sacrificing relevance.
5. Persons who lack special competence in the subject covered by the test will obtain scores near the chance level if the test is appropriate in specificity.
6. A norm-referenced test is appropriate in difficulty if its mean is midway between the perfect score and the expected chance score.
7. All tests should discriminate achievers and non-achievers of the content they attempt to measure, no matter what the testing purpose may be.
8. The more variable the scores from a test, the more likely the test has succeeded in differentiating between examinees who possess different amounts of the abilities measured by the test.
9. The most significant statistical measure of the quality of an achievement test is the reliability of its scores.
10. Item analysis begins with the counting of responses made by high- and low-achieving students to each of the items in the test.
11. While logical objections can be made to the use of the total score on a test as a criterion for analyzing the items in the test, the practical effect of these shortcomings is small and the practical convenience of disregarding them is great.
12. It is convenient and statistically defensible to consider as "good" students those whose scores place them in the upper 27 percent of the total group and to consider as "poor" students those whose scores place them in the lower 27 percent of the total group.
13. The proportion of correct responses to an item by the combined upper and lower 27 percent groups

provides a satisfactory estimate of the difficulty index of the item.

14. For most classroom tests, it is desirable that all the items be of middle difficulty, with none of them extremely easy or extremely difficult.

15. In general, the wider the distribution of item difficulty values in a classroom test, the more restricted the range of scores will be and the lower the reliability of those scores will be.

16. A convenient and highly satisfactory index of discrimination is simply the difference in the proportions of correct response between the upper and lower 27 percent groups.

17. Good norm-referenced achievement-test items should have indices of discrimination of 0.30 or more.

18. The higher the average discrimination index for items in a test, the more variable the scores are likely to be and the more reliable the scores are expected to be.

19. The item-analysis procedures used with norm-referenced measures are appropriate for items from criterion-referenced measures also, but the standards for differentiating between good and poor items are likely to vary for the two situations.

20. The value of posttest discussions in class is highly dependent on advance preparation by the teacher, focused discussion, and active student participation.

QUESTIONS FOR STUDY AND DISCUSSION

1. What minimum qualifications probably should be met by those who are asked to judge the relevance of a given test?

2. In what sense might a very poor test have excellent balance?

3. What factors might cause content-parallel multiple-choice and true–false tests to be equally efficient?

4. Why might it be possible for a test to be judged highly relevant but low in specificity?

5. How could we decide if a 20-item, 4-choice multiple-choice test was about as difficult for the same group as a 40-item true–false test when both are used for norm-referenced purposes?

6. How could the relative size of the standard deviation be estimated for a specific norm-referenced test?

7. What factors influence the size of the difficulty index of a test item?

8. If the same test is given to three sections of the same class, why might it be preferable to conduct item analysis with the combined groups rather than doing three separate analyses? Why might separate analyses be useful?

9. What is meant by the statement, "The upper–lower index is biased in favor of items of middle difficulty"?

14

Nontest and Informal Evaluation Methods

Imagine this scenario from a sixth-grade science classroom:

> Ms. Franke is using the overhead projector to explain how the steps of the scientific method can be thought of as the main outline for preparing a laboratory write-up after an experiment. In glancing around the room she noticed a puzzled look on Dino's face.
>
> "Dino, can you differentiate the findings of an experiment from the conclusions?" she asked.
>
> "I think so," he replied. "The findings are numbers but the conclusions are words."
>
> "That's often true," Ms. Franke allowed, "but how do their purposes differ?"
>
> "Well, the findings tell what happened, what the result of the experiment was. And the conclusions are supposed to be a summary or general statement. Conclusions tell what we think will happen if we do the same thing again."
>
> "That's a convenient way to describe the difference," the teacher noted. And her presentation continued.

This snapshot from Ms. Franke's science class demonstrates that teachers continually gather data and make judgments and decisions during instruction. It also illustrates the variety of techniques teachers use incidentally to obtain formative evaluations of class and student progress:

1. *Observation* of the class was used to detect such nonverbal indicators as lack of attention, positive nods of the head, or (in this case) expressions of incomplete understanding.

2. *Questioning* was used to determine the nature and extent of misunderstanding of a student.

3. A *checklist* of some form was used by Ms. Franke to take a mental excursion down the ordered steps of the scientific method to determine which steps were creating confusion.

4. A *rating scale* was created, again in the mind of the teacher, to help decide if the quality of student response was sufficient for questioning to cease.

Teachers spend considerable amounts of their professional time with assessment-related activities, as much as 30 percent by some estimates (Stiggins, 1988). Though this time includes the development, administration, and use of their own tests and the preparation for and giving of standardized tests, much of the time is no doubt devoted to less formal methods geared primarily to formative evaluation: observation, quizzes and inventories, checklists, rating scales, oral questioning, and the like. In fact, teachers at both the elementary and secondary level regard the information obtained by their own observations as "crucial or important" to a variety of instructional decisions they make (Dorr-Bremme and Herman, 1986).

In view of the frequency of their use and because of the importance teachers attach to the results, the quality of nontest and informal assessments is a significant matter. The accuracy of the results obtained and their validity for instructional decision making are just as important as for the more formal measures we have discussed in previous chapters. Some of the attributes characteristic of informal methods—lack of planning, lack of comparability of results across students, and failure to record outcomes—can contribute to information that is deficient in accuracy and relevance. But these shortcomings are not so inherent in the methods as they are in the historical use of the methods by teachers. That is, planning often *can* be done, characteristics to be judged *can* be defined to enhance comparability, and methods of recording accurately and conveniently *can* be devised and implemented.

Finally, despite the value of well-developed objective and essay achievement tests, there are many areas of the curriculum in which these test methods are inappropriate, or less appropriate, than certain nontest methods might be. For example, instructional objectives that require speaking, writing, and listening—whether in English or second-language learning—most often require a communicative production. In addition, skills in such areas as physical education, home economics, industrial technology, science laboratory, and performing arts often require demonstrations of either processes or products. Many of the nontest methods and informal assessments are particularly useful for monitoring achievement in areas that cannot be measured directly by more formal measurement methods.

The purpose of this chapter is to describe and illustrate procedures that can be used to supplement test information or to provide information when tests seem ill suited to the task. The main goal is to create a greater awareness of the need to think in terms of reliability and validity when creating such procedures or using the results from them.

OBSERVATIONAL TECHNIQUES

Observation is a fundamental medium for obtaining information that, strictly speaking, cannot be acquired in any other way. Observation schedules and checklists are useful devices for directing our attention to certain behaviors we intend to observe; observational schedules, records, checklists, and rating scales all are devices for recording observations so that the events observed can be preserved as a relatively permanent account of the occurrences. All these devices can serve to ensure that the proper behavior is noted and that it is recorded in an accurate, reproducible fashion. That is, proper development of the aids to observation will contribute to highly reliable and valid outcomes. Of course, the very best charts, lists, or tables cannot overcome severe deficiencies in the observation act itself. Observers who see things that are *not* there, miss things that *are* there, or miscategorize the behaviors they see should be considered just as hazardous as a multiple-choice test comprised of items containing too many ambiguous or implausible distracters. Both forms of assessment are likely to provide highly misleading information.

Spontaneous Observation

Most of the observations teachers make in an instructional setting are unplanned, coincidental, and quickly forgotten, at least apparently so. They are spontaneous because the teacher was not intending to watch for a specific action or interchange. It just happened! Such observations can be very useful in formative evaluation and as an impetus and basis for further planned and focused observation. Here is an example.

> While Mr. Voss was giving some individual assistance to Hank, he noticed that Jana used a dictionary to look up the spelling of several words as she was writing an impromptu theme. She always started at the beginning of the book and turned 5 to 6 pages at a time before locating the proper letter section. Then she turned one page at a time, noting the word in the lower right corner of the page, until she found the proper page.

This spontaneous observation can be the beginning step toward making Jana a more efficient user of the dictionary, but it must be remembered or recorded so that individualized help can be provided later at a more convenient time. Obviously, if the teacher can act on the observed information immediately, the need to record it is diminished.

Of course, an overreliance on spontaneous observation can result in many information voids. That is, planned and systematic observation will help ensure that significant activities are observed, that the most important aspects of those activities are noted, and that all pertinent individuals will be observed. Spontaneous observation often results in "tunnel vision": we see those students who are most demanding of our attention, and we may never get to see the reactions or performances of others in situations that are important but rare occurrences.

Spontaneous observations can be unexpected bonuses, and the information they provide may influence immediate judgments or subsequent decisions. Just as first impressions can sometimes unknowingly or unintentionally influence interpersonal relationships, so the outcomes from incidental observations can shape subsequent decisions in unexpected ways. For this reason, the observer needs to realize how easily the failure to analyze observations for possible causes and potential implications can lead to faulty conclusions. For example, Jana may know about dictionary guide words and how to use them but, for some unapparent reason, she does not use them. Here are some guidelines that might help to create and maintain an awareness that observed behavior usually can be explained by multiple factors.

1. A behavior should not be considered typical unless verified in a convincing way. Verification may mean (a) repeated on other similar occasions, (b) corroborated by another observer on *other* occasions, or (c) rejection of all other reasonable competing explanations.

2. A significant action should be observed again for verification. But if conditions are created intentionally and artificially with the hope that the behavior will recur, the loss of the naturalistic setting may inhibit the expected behavior or it may promote a more socially desirable response by the student.

3. If the observation is of a significant event, then the setting, circumstances, and objective description are important documentation needed for proposing alternate explanations. Such records form a common information base that can be shared with several interpreters to collect independent judgments regarding causality. Reliance on memory is more likely to provide less complete, less detailed, or insignificant information.

4. Since spontaneous observations are unplanned, by definition, a recording form that can accommodate such situations will not be available. Consequently, whatever preconceived notions the observer may hold are apt to be confirmed. There is a natural tendency for observers to attend to details that seem most familiar, to notice those aspects of an event that best fit their existing knowledge base. In other words, the expectations formed from our prior experience are more likely to be fulfilled than are events that are "farthest from our wildest dreams."

Planned Observation

A self-proclaimed "people watcher" can easily overwhelm a willing listener with the peculiarities, unpredictable similarities, and newly discovered diversity observed in a park, on a street corner, or in a busy shopping mall. When we set out to watch particular events, actions, or objects, we seem to be more motivated to accomplish our purpose and more satisfied to have done so than if we just happened to have seen something unusual. So it is in the classroom. Though unexpected events can be exciting and interesting, planned observations can provide revealing, unique information about learners that can be used to manipulate the conditions for learning in a positive way. Such intentional observation is an efficient way to gather information about learning styles, methods of problem solving, motor-skill development, frustration level, and cognitive abilities. Spontaneous observation is continual, by definition; it even occurs *during* the process of planned observation. But the planned approach is likely to be more fruitful—higher in instructional value, more efficient, and resulting in more objective results.

The quality of a set of observations is influenced greatly by the quality of the form that was designed to direct the observer's focus and to record the behaviors. In addition, the utility of the observational data will be determined by the care of the observer in avoiding each of these common problems:

1. *Observer subjectivity.* "Looking with blinders" and "watching without seeing" are common expressions that point to the selective looking some observers experience unknowingly. Such selectivity can be unintentional—and therefore not easily controlled—or intentional, and probably even more difficult to control. It is easier to ignore the inappropriate giggles of a "good" student, for example, than the mild but vocal yawn of a chronic troublemaker. Having a list of specific behaviors to be noted and having multiple observers (an uncommon classroom luxury) are ways of heightening observers' awareness about subjectivity problems.

2. *Observer inference.* The reason for a particular behavior is not always apparent, or sometimes apparent reasons are incorrect. For example, when Jon does a multiple-step computational problem with his calculator, he does one step at a time, writing down each result before entering the next computation. Thus, $[(5^2 + 8^2 + 11^2) \div 3]$ takes six separate steps rather than a single continuous one. Obviously, Jon does not know how to use his calculator most efficiently. Alternatively, Jon has a calculator that does not allow cumulative addition. Or Jon lacks the self-confidence to use the more efficient but more complex method. Few single observations of any significance can be explained without resorting to additional data, usually from another source or by a different method of collection.

3. *Observer presence.* Those who believe that teacher absence from a classroom will influence students' behaviors must necessarily accept that teacher presence also influences the activities that occur (or do not occur). Most teachers can become unobtrusive observers among their own students, and most students will display their typical behavior in such settings. However, those same teachers could manipulate the discussion participation of their class by flaunting a clipboard and by making exaggerated pencil strokes at the conclusion of each student's oral contribution. Planned observations of typical behavior must be carried out in such a way that students will not become too cooperative. Usually, a small effort toward concealment, an increased number of observations, and more extended observation periods will help to overcome the negative effects of observer presence.

4. *Trait ambiguity.* When the characteristic to be observed is described in general, implicit terms, considerable inference will be required of the observer to detect instances of it. If the goal of observation, for example, is to determine the number of times Rodney is "off-task" in a 30-minute period, we are in trouble from the start. How will we know when he is off-task? And how will we know when he is on-task again so that the next occurrence of off-task behavior can be noted? More valid information is likely to be obtained if the task behavior is

defined (for example, silent reading in the textbook, writing out homework assignment) and the most likely behaviors to occur during that task are listed and then checked at systematic time intervals. For the reading task, for example, the list might include: looking down at the book, page flipping, or looking away from the book momentarily (10 or less seconds). Traits that are described in observable terms can be noticed more readily, they can be recorded more accurately, and their antecedents can be determined with greater assurance.

5. *Subject consistency.* Upon listening to a student's excellent speech, there is a tendency to generalize about the excellence of future speeches by the same student. On the other hand, we might be tempted to question the generalizability of a poorly delivered speech. We are less likely to posit that the student had too good a day than to wonder if he or she had a bad day. A single observation is no certain indication about the typical quality of performance on the same task. Repeated observations on similar tasks on other occasions provide the best evidence about performance consistency.

6. *Observer consistency.* If you watch the same film on separate occasions, are you likely to notice some things the second time that were not apparent on the first viewing? Does the same idea carry over to planned classroom observation? When you watch a new film with a friend, do your postviewing discussions reveal that, at times, you saw different things or failed to notice the same things, whether character details, event sequence, or subtle comments or behaviors? Might the same sorts of disagreements arise if two teachers were to observe the activities of a classroom concurrently? Lack of attention to the same attributes, differences in interpretation of observed actions, and differences in ability to use the recording instrument can singly or in combination explain such differences. Of course, to the extent that such differences are frequent and/or sizable, the data are inconsistent and of limited value. The use of multiple observers, a near impossibility for typical classrooms, is ideal for detecting the presence of such errors. In addition, care in instrument and procedural development can help to prevent many of the errors stemming from observer inconsistency.

7. *Recording problems.* Most recording problems stem from deficiencies in the form to be used for recording. For example, a form is inconvenient to use if the behaviors listed are densely packed on the page, if the places for checking or tallying are scattered, or if multiple pages or both sides of a single page need to be used. Furthermore, if the observer must look for too many things at one time, the actions of some individuals will be missed. Or if elaborate coding schemes or detailed note taking are required, observation will become incomplete and, perhaps, slanted toward the most easily handled recording. The most effective coding forms contain a limited scope of variables to be observed, provide for separation of observations and subjective interpretations, use simplified coding schemes, and are formatted for convenient use.

Observation Schedules

Planned observation calls for the use of a schedule, chart, or record form to direct the observer's attention and to facilitate the creation of a permanent record of what was seen. The sample schedule in Figure 14–1 was developed by a history teacher to help determine how wisely students would use the last 10 minutes of the class period if he offered the time daily for students to begin their

Date: October 11		Class: World History		Period: 3

Seatwork Observational Record		
Behavior Observed	*8* *Minutes Left*	*5* *Minutes Left*
1. Working on assignment		
– alone	卌 卌	卌 |
– with other student	| |	|
2. Doing assignment for other class	| |	| |
3. Reading library book or magazine	| |	|
4. Talking with another student (non-work)	卌	卌 | |
5. Resting (head down)	|	|
6. Sitting idly	| |	卌 |
7. Other	|	

Figure 14-1. Sample Observation Schedule

assignments. The sample schedule illustrates several of the features of a good observational record form: (1) The number of categories is limited to a manageable number for purposes of deciding how to code a given behavior. (2) The behaviors to be observed are described in relatively unambiguous terms. Note, for example, that it is possible to distinguish working with another student from socializing with them. Some level of inference is still required, but if "talking with another student" were listed alone, there would be no way to show the more positive behavior—sanctioned collaboration on an assignment. (3) The use of tallies is convenient and the marking locations are identified for ease of use. Behaviors are listed in a column that can be scanned quickly and the descriptions are not too densely packed. (4) There is room at the bottom or on the back side for supplementary notes or interpretations of the recorded data.

If the data shown in Figure 14-1 are typical of the students' behaviors over a period of 4 to 5 days, what useful information do they provide? How should they be interpreted? First, only half of the students were working on their history assignment when only 8 minutes were left. Four others were doing productive things. In sum, two-thirds were working and the rest were "satisfying other needs." Second, with 5 minutes left, only seven were working on history; altogether ten were doing productive things. Over half of the class was involved in social talk or idle time. The teacher shared this information with the class and asked for their advice about whether the free-time period should be continued. What would your approach and decisions be?

Checklists

A checklist is a set of phrases or statements that describes either the essential steps in a procedure or the most important elements of a product. Ordinarily, the evaluator using a checklist will simply check the presence or absence of each step or element, but some checklists permit a rating of the quality of the action observed or the characteristic noted. Pilots go through a checklist before certifying the readiness of their plane for flight, catalog shoppers go through a checklist to ensure that they have completed all aspects of their order form, and most of us use a mental checklist prior to closing our suitcase in preparation for a trip—tooth brush? clean underwear? belt? traveler's checks?

Yelon (1984) has shown how checklists can support many aspects of instruction in addition to assessment. Particularly for skill learning, a checklist provides a sequential order of the performance requirements for the learner so that appropriate practice can be conducted. But most importantly, the checklist provides the criteria for acceptable performance that the learner must internalize so that constant self-evaluation can occur during practice. Eventually, skill learners should be able to evaluate their own performance as thoroughly and as accurately as the instructor.

One goal of a physical fitness unit in a sixth-grade health class is to have students develop and implement an exercise program. The evaluation planning guide in Appendix A shows that students' write-ups of their program will be used as a form of summative evaluation. For purposes of communicating the essential elements of the report and for assessing the completeness of it, the checklist in Figure 14–2 was developed. The checklist would be used in two main ways: (1) It would be given to each student at the time the report assignment was made to help describe the essential ingredients of the report, and (2) it would be used by the teacher in evaluating the quality of each report. Here are some guidelines that were followed in the development of this *product checklist:*

Figure 14–2. Sample Health Report Checklist

Directions: On the line in front of each item, place a plus (+) if the step was completed satisfactorily, place a minus (−) if the step was completed unsatisfactorily, and use a zero (0) if the step was missing.

_____ 1. A doctor's advice about exercising was obtained.

_____ 2. Baseline fitness tests were taken.

        _____ a. Pull-ups or arm hangs

        _____ b. Sit-ups

        _____ c. Recovery index test

_____ 3. Improvement goals consistent with the test results were established.

_____ 4. Exercises appropriate for the goals were selected.

_____ 5. A weekly time schedule was established.

_____ 6. A two-week journal of program use was included.

_____ 7. Personal reactions to program effectiveness, enjoyment, and needs for change were included.

General quality of written expression: _____

_____

_____

_____

_____

1. Obtain or envision examples of good and poor versions of the product to be evaluated.

2. Decide if each judgment should be a simple yes–no, presence or absence of an attribute, or if the quality of each attribute must be assessed. For example, the checklist in Figure 14–2 requires a judgment about quality, satisfactory ($+$) or unsatisfactory ($-$), in addition to present–absent (0). (If finer distinctions in quality are needed, a rating scale would be more useful than a checklist.)

3. Identify the product attribute that must be present and describe how good and poor examples would be expected to differ on each attribute. For example, in step 3 of Figure 14–2, all students may list goals for improvement, but the amount of logical consistency between the goals and the test results is likely to differentiate good and poor exercise plans.

4. List the essential and distinguishing attributes and subdivide those that help to define completeness or provide diagnostic feedback. In Figure 14–2, the three fitness tests were listed individually to help assess completeness (and to convey this criterion in advance to students).

5. When possible, try out a checklist draft on a few sample products to check its comprehensiveness and the relevance of each item. (If the checklist is distributed to students as a grading guide, it should not be modified without giving students an opportunity to take the modifications into account in their product development.)

6. When appropriate, ask a novice to use the checklist. By observing and talking with the novice, it is possible to uncover ambiguities, technical jargon, and missing elements.

The foundation upon which a *performance checklist* is built is a task analysis of the performance to be observed. The procedures for developing a performance checklist are similar to those described above, but there are some important differences.

1. Observe an expert perform the task and record the essential steps. Note the materials and conditions that should be provided to the performer as part of the "givens."

2. Use a draft of the checklist to observe another expert so that differences among experts in performing critical steps of the process can be detected. This step will reduce bias due to idiosyncrasies inherent in the performance of the first expert. Of course, if there are several efficient and effective ways to complete the task in question, a performance checklist may be an inappropriate assessment tool. In such cases the *product* is likely to be more worthy of evaluating than the *process*.

3. When appropriate, attach the criterion of acceptable performance to the description of the step. For example, a checklist for taking someone's blood pressure might have this statement: "Wraps cuff snuggly about upper arm, *but loose enough so that only one finger can be inserted between cuff and arm*." The italicized portion of the statement indicates what "snug enough" means.

4. Use the drafted checklist to observe a novice performer. This step will help ensure that the stages of difficulty experienced by new learners will be identified in sufficient detail. It also will point out the need to insert statements about

what should *not* be done or *how* something should be done. (In addition, it provides a check on whether additional prerequisites need to be incorporated in the teaching objectives.)

Good checklists are time consuming to develop, but they can pay instructional and assessment dividends in a wide variety of situations. Yelon (1984) has identified several circumstances for which a checklist is particularly well suited:

1. When a certain skill is particularly important because it is a prerequisite to learning other skills
2. When a performance is complex, because of the number of its elements or because of the intricacies of particular elements
3. When the fine-tuning of a skill requires fairly detailed feedback to the learner
4. When students depend on self-evaluation, rather than the judgments of an instructor, to check their progress

Rating Scales

Another tool of observation is the rating scale, a method of recording how frequently a certain behavior occurs or how high in quality a characteristic seems to be. Such scales are used to evaluate employee performance, to judge the likelihood of success of applicants to educational programs, to describe the developmental progress of students on various social–emotional traits, and to assess the quality of each of several components of a product or performance. And because rating scales can be used to show variability in quality among several subjects, the ratings that result can be interpreted in norm-referenced as well as criterion-referenced terms. Sometimes, as we will illustrate, the referencing is built into the scale directly.

Developing a rating scale. Like multiple-choice items, rating scales have two parts, a statement or phrase and a set of response options. The primary goal of scale development is to develop these two pieces so that the most valid results will be obtained. A common fault of scale developers is to focus on the careful description of the trait to the exclusion of the meaning conveyed by the response scale itself. Factors to consider in promoting the validity of rating-scale items are detailed and illustrated next.

1. *The trait must be described operationally, either in the stem or in the scale point descriptions.* Items 1A and 1B illustrate several points related to trait definition.

1A **Student is prompt.**
  1. **Always**
  2. **Usually**
  3. **Seldom**
  4. **Never**

1B **Student turns math papers in on time each week.**
  1. **Every day**
  2. **4 out of 5 days**
  3. **3 out of 5 days**
  4. **2 or fewer days a week**

Item 1A provides no context for promptness, but item 1B indicates promptness in completing work rather than, for example, punctuality in coming to school or class. Item B further narrows the context by focusing on math work and by limiting the time period to what is typical in a week. Note that the stem from item 1B and the choices from item 1A together form a fairly ambiguous scale item, also.

Item 2A might appear on a scale for rating the quality of an end table made in a woodworking class.

2A   Quality of the table top surface

1	2	3	4	5
Perfect		Satisfactory		Very Poor

1	2	3	4	5
No sander marks				Sander gouges
No glue distortion				Glue bubbles show
Smooth finish				Sandpaper grooves
No joint seams				Open joint

The first set of scale points is ambiguous and imprecise regarding the attributes of the table top that should be assessed. The criteria of perfection are stated in observable terms with the second set of descriptors so that more objective, reliable measurements are likely to be produced with it.

2. *Scale descriptors should represent a single dimension of either quality or frequency, not both.* Item 3A from a speech evaluation scale is formed with a set of fairly observable scale points, but some points relate to frequency of behavior (2), some relate to eye contact directly (1 and 3), and some relate to use of notes (2, 3, and 4).

3A   Maintains eye contact with audience.
1. **Spans the entire audience**
2. **Occasionally refers to notes**
3. **Tends to look at only 1 or 2 people**
4. **Depends heavily on notes**
5. **Tends to read**

An improved set of responses that focus on eye contact frequency is illustrated by item 3B.

3B   Frequency of eye contact with audience
1. **At least once every sentence**
2. **Once every 2 sentences**
3. **Once in every 3 to 4 sentences**
4. **Less than once in every 3 to 4 sentences**

3. *When norm-referenced ratings are sought, specify the reference group being used.* Items like 4 to 6 appear on rating forms for reporting school progress or for recommending individuals for admission or employment.

4. **How well does the student follow directions?**
5. **How would you assess the applicant's chance of completing a graduate program in education?**

6. **How would you describe the candidate's writing skills?**
    1. **Well above average**
    2. **Above average**
    3. **Average**
    4. **Below average**
    5. **Well below average**

Unless the directions to the rater specify the reference group to use (for example, all pupils in the same class, all graduates of a particular program, all others with similar background qualifications), the rater and the user of the ratings are not so likely to share the same interpretation of the rating. In most cases it is more preferable to state the reference group to be used by the raters than to allow the raters to describe the reference group they decided to use.

4. *When norm-referenced interpretations are desired, use many scale points (5 to 7) rather than few (2 to 3).* More variability in scores can be achieved with a fine scale than a coarse one, and greater score reliability is likely to result. When all scale points need not be defined, bipolar adjectives can be used to define only the end points. Then the number of intermediary points can be varied as deemed suitable by the scale maker.

5. *Raters should be given a chance to indicate that they have had insufficient opportunity to observe.* Depending on the circumstances, a failure to rate can be due to insufficient opportunity to observe or to an unwillingness by the rater to make a negative rating. By using a rating position that says "Too little opportunity to observe," more interpretable ratings are likely to be obtained. In addition, such ratings of a student by a teacher may indicate a need to plan more "target" experience for the student or more opportunities to observe for the teacher.

6. *When several traits or behaviors are to be rated using the same scale, the appropriateness of the scale for each item should be checked.* Items 7 to 10 are from a preschool screening form that uses a 3-point rating scale: above average, average, below average.

7. **Energy**
8. **Posture**
9. **Participates in running games**
10. **Throws a ball**

The directions indicate that present classmates should be considered as the reference groups. What is above average posture (8)? What is above average participation (9)? Throwing a ball, without reference to accuracy or distance, requires a yes–no response, not a norm-referenced rating. As exemplified here, clarity should never be sacrificed for efficiency.

Using a rating scale. Rating scales are prone to certain types of errors that can be minimized by creating an awareness of such errors through rater training. In addition, the procedures for rating can be designed to lessen the chance that rating errors will compromise score validity. For example, when a teacher must rate all 26 students in a class on each of five characteristics, trait by trait rating will be preferable to student by student rating. That is, all students should be rated on attentiveness, then on cooperation, then on using time wisely, and so on, instead of rating Sarah on all five traits, then Michael, and then Chad. This procedure will help avert *halo effect* errors, the tendency to give more positive ratings on all traits to subjects who project an overall positive aura. This recommendation is analogous to the one made regarding the scoring of essays: To prevent the score from one response from influencing the scoring of that person's other responses, all papers should be scored item by item rather than student by student.

Several other kinds of rating errors are also more closely associated with the characteristics of individual raters than with the wording or format of the scales. For example, some raters have a tendency to use only a certain portion of the scale when rating a group of individuals. Some use mostly the negative end of the scale (*errors of severity*) because of their high standards, their wish to "motivate" ratees, or some other unknown reason. Others use mostly the positive end of the scale (*generosity errors*) because of an unwillingness to assign nonpositive ratings, an inability to discriminate levels of quality, or an adherence to fairly low standards. Finally, *errors of central tendency* occur when raters avoid either extreme of the scale and use mainly moderate positions. Such raters often have fairly high standards and are uncomfortable giving very low ratings. Another type of error, *bias* is more difficult to detect. Bias errors may be due to stereotypes held by the rater (red-heads are volatile personalities), unrelated anecdotal information (he hangs out with students who smoke), unrelated personal variables (his mother is a prominent community leader), or history factors (his brother was a very poor reader). For all these kinds of rating errors, the most effective means of prevention are rater training and directions that create an awareness of the potential for such errors and that emphasize the relative uselessness of scores that contain them.

INFORMAL INVENTORIES

There are innumerable instructional situations in which additional information about the learner might help the teacher increase student motivation, activate prior knowledge, choose the most effective approach, or just develop better teacher–student rapport. Some of this information is gathered piecemeal, unsystematically through the constant spontaneous observation teachers do, as in "sizing up," for example. Particularly when teachers need entering behavior information such as prior achievement, interests, attitudes, or preferences for learning styles, various informal and systematic devices can be used economically to build a store of descriptive information. This store of information can be tapped later as needed in a variety of teaching–learning situations.

Questionnaires

Classroom teachers who choose not to rely on last year's teacher for an assessment of the personality of their new class can "take stock" of the new group with a brief inventory, a survey questionnaire tailor-made to achieve the teacher's purpose. The inventory shown in Figure 14–3 provides sample items of the type that would allow the teacher to size up a new class efficiently. The use of open-ended items gives flexibility to respondents but requires the same care in development as the completion test items discussed in Chapter 10. When the teacher is interested in specific options, the second type of item will work better.

The results of an informal inventory provide a class analysis that may raise as many questions as the survey sought to answer. Suppose the results for items 8 to 15 are as shown in Figure 14–4. Here are some new questions that may require further probing, additional planned observation, or a more detailed analysis of specific student responses to this inventory:

1. Would the use of dyads be more effective than small group or committee work?
2. Is this group oriented more to oral–aural stimulus material than visual?
3. Are most students shy about oral reading or do they lack confidence in their reading ability?
4. Have the writing experiences of these students been limited, unsuccessful, or both?
5. How much nonrecreational experience have students had with a microcomputer?
6. Why would a third of the group rather be *told* a puzzle solution than to *figure it out*? (Might it depend on the kind of puzzle they have in mind?)

Figure 14-3. Class Sizing-Up Inventory

Student Name _____ Date _____

Directions: Please complete each of these sentences with a word or two that best describes you.

1. My favorite school subject is _____ .
2. One of my hobbies is _____ .
3. The kind of books I like to read most is _____ .
4. The radio station I most listen to is _____ .
5. My favorite summer activity is _____ .
6. I would rather do homework than _____ .
7. One of my heroes is _____ .

Directions: Please complete each of these sentences by circling the words that best describe you.

8. I prefer to	study alone	study with a friend
9. I prefer to learn by	watching a film	hearing a talk
10. I learn better by	reading	discussing
11. I prefer to	read outloud	read to myself
12. I prefer to	write a story	hear a story
13. To solve a puzzle, I would	like to be told	figure it out
14. To write a paper, I prefer	paper and pencil	a computer
15. I prefer	essay tests	multiple-choice tests

Grade 4 Class		September 1991
8. Prefer	study alone	study with a friend
	卌 ‖	卌 卌 卌 ǀ
9. Learning preference	watch film	hear talk
	卌 卌 ‖	卌 卌 ǀ
10. Learn better by	reading	discussing
	卌 ǀ	卌 卌 卌 ‖
11. Prefer	read aloud	read silently
	‖‖	卌 卌 卌 卌
12. Prefer	write story	hear story
	‖‖	卌 卌 卌 卌
13. Solve puzzle	be told	figure out
	卌 ‖	卌 卌 卌
14. Write paper	pencil	computer
	卌 卌 ‖‖	卌 卌
15. Prefer	essay	multiple-choice
	卌	卌 卌 卌 ‖

Figure 14-4. Summary of Class Inventory Responses

Informal inventories like those described here are very easy and quick to develop, once the teacher has thought about the kind of information needed. A class analysis is important for the teacher's understanding of the group; it also may promote some self-assessment if it is reported back to the group in ways that will not draw attention to the responses of particular individuals. For individual responses, an index-card file system can be used for easy retrieval and for ease of updating after the next survey. (The preferences of youngsters can change rapidly, even daily.)

Similar information can be obtained by the teacher through individual interviews or conversations with students. Though less efficient than questionnaires, these methods permit follow-up questioning for clarification, and they can elicit information without requiring reading, writing, or vocabulary abilities that questionnaires depend upon.

Informal Reading Inventories

Informal inventories in areas like reading and math are needed occasionally to form initial placement judgments about individual students or to obtain diagnostic information for developing an instructional plan. Though commercial products are available for such purposes, it is possible for a group of teachers to collaborate in the development of an inventory that would have a useful span of three or more grades. The procedures illustrated here are for reading, but they could be adapted to other content ares in which there is some natural hierarchical arrangement in the curriculum (for example, math or foreign languages).

Most informal reading inventories consist of a graded word list, graded reading selections, and a set of comprehension questions for each selection. The word list is used as a screening device to determine the most appropriate passage level with which to begin. Students read passages aloud and the teacher records decoding errors. They also read silently and, after each type of reading, the teacher asks five to six comprehension questions. Reading continues until the passages become too difficult, both in terms of the number of decoding errors made and the number of questions answered incorrectly. The results are used to compute reading ability at three levels: independent, instructional, and frustration (Johnson and Kress, 1965). Sample percent-correct scoring criteria prescribed by Evans, Evans, and Mercer (1986, p. 176) are these:

Reading Level	Word Recognition (%)	Comprehension (%)
Independent	98 to 100	90 to100
Instructional	95	75
Frustration	90 or less	50 or less

The following suggestions are offered for developing informal reading inventories that will provide the most meaningful and consistent scores from students in grades 1 thru 12.

1. An existing graded word list may be used or one may be developed by randomly selecting words from each text in a graded basal series. A list of 15 to 20 words from each level, printed on card stock, form a set that is easily administered.

2. Using the same basal series, two passages should be selected from near the beginning of the book for each grade level for which the inventory is to be used. The passages selected should be representative of the subject matter, vocabulary, and language complexity of the grade-level text from which it was taken. Evans, Evans, and Mercer (1986) recommended varying passage lengths according to grade level: preprimer, 50 words; primer and grade 1, 100 words; and grades 2 and up, 200 words. Some inventories use introductory phrases, titles, or illustrations to activate prior knowledge, but such preparatory aids preclude the use of "main-idea" comprehension questions later.

3. A set of eight to ten comprehension questions should be written for each passage. Since the questions are administered orally, the use of free-response rather than multiple-choice format would put a lighter load on short-term memory demands. Most importantly, the questions must require more than recall of factual information or literal interpretation. A premium should be placed on items requiring inference and on generalization questions that get at "why," "how," "what if," or "what next?"

4. Review the graded word lists, passages, and items among a set of teachers representing the same grade levels as the materials. Check for passage representativeness, item ambiguity, item keys (the range of acceptable responses for open-ended items), and scoring criteria for basal-level placements.

The materials developed for an informal reading inventory should be valid for use over a number of years. As long as students have not had an opportunity to read the same passages as part of their regular classroom instruction, inventory results should prove valuable for placement in a series, choosing general reading materials, or diagnosing decoding weaknesses. Teachers might also use the results to make decisions about out-of-level testing prior to the administration of an every-pupil achievement-test battery. (See Chapter 17 for further details about out-of-level standardized testing.)

ORAL QUESTIONING TECHNIQUES

The techniques of oral questioning serve the functions of fostering learning and assessing the extent of learning. Of course, the two purposes often are entwined, particularly when the nature of the assessment is formative rather than summative. The purpose of this section is to demonstrate how oral-questioning methods can produce meaningful assessment data and how methods of recording the outcomes of questioning can contribute to the collection of highly reliable information.

Purposes of Questioning

Though empirical evidence is lacking, both logic and experience suggest that oral questioning is the most frequently employed instructional technique. Why is this probably so? What functions does questioning seem to serve that other techniques accomplish less effectively? In terms of the Basic Teaching Model described in Chapter 2, oral questioning can figure prominently in gathering information about entering behavior, in implementing the instructional procedures, and in assessing performance, particularly in the formative stages. In sum, oral questioning might very well be the first technique used by a teacher to begin a unit of instruction and the last technique used to close out instruction.

The many purposes for oral questioning identified by Stiggins, Rubel, and Quellmalz (1986) and Wilen (1986) can be categorized as primarily supporting either direct instruction or assessment. Both types of purposes will be reviewed here to help differentiate them and to illustrate how inseparable the purposes are at times.

1. *Monitor progress.* Teachers frequently ask questions of the class or direct questions to particular students to make judgments about comprehension and the completeness of learning. The goal is to determine if more examples, practice, or discussion are needed before moving on to the next learning objective. Often these questions are triggered by the teacher's reading of nonverbal cues emanating from student faces.

2. *Encourage application of knowledge.* The "So what?" question that students sometimes raise can be initiated by the teacher to focus on the use of new knowledge—to go beyond the statement of a principle or a general method of problem solving. Such questions stimulate higher-level thinking and heighten interest. The goal here is direct instruction rather than assessment.

3. *Stimulate participation.* Students can be drawn into a discussion through questioning, and those whose attention seems to be elsewhere can be brought into the instructional fold by thoughtful questions. Thus, questioning can stimulate receptivity, a necessary condition for learning to happen.

4. *Review past instruction.* Review sessions sometimes are triggered by a forthcoming summative evaluation, but some also are used as ways of summarizing or providing distributed practice. Such sessions, whether in a game format or in a fast-moving prosecutor style, serve to reinforce (instruct) and to assess (learner and teacher feedback) simultaneously.

5. *Begin discussion periods.* These questions serve the learning function because they focus attention, they activate prior knowledge, and they model metacognitive strategies we hope learners will adopt. For example, questioning at the end of an oral reading session can help learners understand how interpretive and evaluative questioning can improve their own encoding and subsequent retrieval of ideas. That is, they may come to see how this kind of reflective thinking (metacognition) will improve their understanding and subsequent recall.

6. *Encourage creative thinking.* If we want students to think critically and creatively, we must give them practice in doing so and provide them feedback about their efforts. Questions that promote these activities have both instructional and assessment functions. Because students have a tendency to ask questions like those they themselves have been asked, probing questions that provoke thought should be more frequent than recall questions that exercise only memory.

7. *Diagnose student problems.* Successive questioning with carefully chosen probes can lead a teacher to the root of a learning problem. The problem may be missing information, a long-held misconception, a misunderstood step in a process, or the lack of a general approach to understanding a problem. Individual oral questioning, adapted to previous student responses, is a common strategy for diagnosing reading and mathematics problems at the elementary level.

8. *Stimulate student interest.* This instructional technique is used with students who are captured by a puzzle that needs solving or who quickly tune into certain topics. In the first case, we might ask: "If you were confined to a wheel chair because of a broken leg, how would your exercise program need to be modified?" In the second case, we might ask a member of a volleyball team, "How might the rules of six-person volleyball be modified so that the new version has more of the same exercise benefits as aerobic dance?" Direct instruction is the main purpose served here.

When the primary purpose of oral questioning is to serve the assessment function, the methods of forming questions, delivering questions, and interpreting responses are fundamentally important. These techniques determine how reliable and valid the information obtained will be and how sound the subsequent actions of the teacher will be.

Guidelines for Questioning

The issue related to oral questioning that has received the most attention from researchers relates to the taxonomic level of the questions teachers use. To date, the results of that research are clear: despite the rhetoric about fostering higher-order thinking skills, the vast majority of teachers' questions require recall, recognition, and literal comprehension. This is indeed an unfortunate statement about the nature of communication in the classrooms of our schools. Since questions play such a significant role in that communication, it appears that the intellectual level of most verbal interchanges is much lower than it ought to be. How can this sorry state be explained?

First, teachers have little, if any, direct instruction in their preservice programs related to questioning. When they do, the focus is less on taxonomic level and more on the mechanics of conducting a discussion. Second, since higher-level questioning was such an insignificant part of the teacher's own experience as a student, the teacher has not benefited from the modeling of higher-level questioning. Many teaching techniques used by teachers, and not learned directly during preservice instruction, were observed during the teachers' own schooling. High-quality oral questioning was not one of those. Third, oral questioning seems like such a narrow topic, with no perceived positive consquences, that it is not often proposed as an in-service education topic. Besides, the thinking goes, everyone knows how to ask questions—hard ones and easy ones.

Here are some suggestions for making oral questions more challenging for students and for obtaining meaningful information to support instructional decision making.

1. *Be cognizant of the verb used in a question.* The verb can require a simple yes–no response or it can require a description, an explanation, a new plan, or a reasoned judgment. The explicit–implicit distinction made about instructional objectives in Chapter 3 pertains here also. In addition, low-level questions often include such words as who, what, and when; high-level questions tend to use how, why, and which. Here are some examples:

Select the most persuasive editorial.
Compare the persuasive quality of the two editorials.
Name the writer of *Common Sense*.
Cite the time period during which *Poor Richard's Almanac* was written.
Explain how Jefferson's ideals were expressed in the words of the Declaration.

Which editorial is most persuasive?
Why is this editorial more persuasive than that one?
Who wrote *Common Sense*?
When was *Poor Richard's Almanac* written?
How did Jefferson's ideals get expressed in the Declaration?

These sets of "questions" illustrate that oral questioning can be carried out with both declarative and interrogative statements. Behind each declarative statement is a question expressing the same content.

2. *Wait for a response.* The elapsed time between the end of a question and the teacher's next utterance averages about 1 second. Rowe (1974) has shown that these kinds of benefits can accrue by increasing "wait time" to 3 to 5 seconds:

1. Students will give longer responses.
2. More unsolicited, appropriate responses will be given.
3. Fewer cases of nonresponse will occur.
4. Students will become more confident in responding.
5. More speculation and wondering aloud will occur.
6. Teaching will become more student centered.
7. Students will more often supply evidence to support their inferences.
8. Students will ask more questions.
9. Low-achieving students will contribute more.
10. Teacher questioning skills will improve over time.

Teachers tend not to wait very long before rephrasing or asking another question. Ordinarily, the new question is simpler, at a lower level, than the original question. The upshot is, longer wait time ("think time" for students) should preserve the taxonomic level of questioning the teacher intended to use from the start.

3. *Stay with a student who answers incompletely or incorrectly.* If a lower-level follow-up question seems called for, use a sequence of questions to return to the original one. Ask for clarification, restatement, explanation, or evidential support. Students who are abandoned after an incorrect response learn two things: (1) the question must not be very important, and (2) a quick, wrong answer next time will end this kind of "interruption" in short order.

4. *Ask a student to paraphrase or restate the response given by another.* This type of questioning not only demands constant attention from students, it also strengthens comprehension and promotes deeper understanding. Of course, it also provides additional opportunity for formative evaluation.

5. *Call on nonvolunteers regularly.* For higher-order thinking to occur, the thinker must be aware of preceding events that good questioning is likely to build on. Calling on only volunteers helps shy students stay shy, helps unattending students maintain their inattention, and narrows the learning audience to the persistent or self-motivated.

6. *Plan good questions and write them down in advance.* Most good oral questions are as difficult to develop and to word as good written-test items. Consequently, most effective teachers cannot generate many good ones "on the fly." Some teachers develop a card file for certain instructional units, and some write their questions in lecture notes or on overhead transparencies. Spontaneous questioning is more likely to promote knowledge-level thinking than application of knowledge.

Recording Questioning Data

If the responses to oral questioning are to be used for summative evaluation purposes, or if the responses are to be analyzed by the teacher to diagnose group strengths and weaknesses, a permanent record needs to be developed. Documentation at the time of response is nearly always preferable to relying only on memory or to charting from memory at a later time. Of course, if the responses are intended for formative purposes, the teacher is likely to "consume" the information immediately, and documentation is probably unnecessary.

The purpose for questioning and for recording the nature of the responses dictates the characteristics of the recording form to be used. Obviously, one dimension of the form must be student names, but the second dimension is defined by the user's purpose. Figure 14–5 shows two examples of charts that were designed for different purposes. Chart A has a tally mark for each type of question asked of each student and a circle for each appropriate (correct) response. The chart allows the teacher to examine (1) the extent of participation throughout the group, (2) the extent of teacher emphasis on any one type of question, (3) the success rate of students on each type of question, and (4) the overall success of students. The teacher also can determine whether any students are being neglected or if anyone is particularly dominant.

Chart B is intended to show both the quantity and quality of student participation in class recitation or discussion. The focus of this chart is more on the general quality of students' responses than on the nature of the questions they were asked or were able to answer.

Note that for both charts in Figure 14–5 considerable judgment must be exercised by the teacher during the question–discussion period. Did that question require an explanation or was it a prediction? Was that response acceptable? Did Doug add any new slants to the issue or did he mainly say "me too!"? How germane was that comment to the topic, or did it open a new, worthwhile issue? Experience with any single recording form should increase objectivity and, consequently, the usefulness of the data. Forms that require too much inference by the teacher will interfere with the questioning process in detrimental ways: less time will be available for formulating high-quality questions and more dead time will transpire while response quality is transformed into a tally mark in the proper cell of the chart.

Figure 14–5. Alternative Examples of Student Oral Questioning Responses

A. TYPE OF QUESTION ASKED AND ANSWERED

Student	Factual	Explanation	Prediction	Evaluation
Jon	Ⓘ	Ⓘ	ⒾⒾ	
Lori	ⒾⒾ I	I		Ⓘ
Jean	Ⓘ			I
Doug	Ⓘ	Ⓘ I		Ⓘ
Mick		I	I	
Laura	III	ⒾⒾ		I

B. NATURE OF CONTRIBUTION

Student	Major, On Topic	Minor, On Topic	Restate, On Topic	Off Topic
Jon	II	II		
Lori	III			
Jean		I	I	
Doug	I		II	
Mick				III
Laura	I	II	I	

SUMMARY PROPOSITIONS

1. The most common deficiencies associated with informal assessments can be overcome by careful instrument development and advance planning.
2. The quality of observational data is a function of the observation act and the observational recording form.
3. Results from spontaneous observation can influence subsequent judgments or decisions of the viewer in unintended or unknowing ways.
4. Verification of observed behavior is essential to establishing its representativeness and its probable causes.
5. The ability to infer or predict from observational data is limited by such factors as observer subjectivity, observer presence, trait ambiguity, subject inconsistency, and observer inconsistency.
6. The need for objectivity in observational data can be demonstrated to the observer by allocating space on the recording form for the observer to note impressionistic and interpretive comments.
7. A checklist is an observational record that permits systematic recording of the presence or absence of the essential steps in a process or the attributes of a product.
8. The response options of a particular rating scale describe either (a) frequency of occurrence or (b) quality of performance (or of a product).
9. The fineness of a rating scale is related to the amount of score variability it can produce and the level of score reliability that can be attained with it.
10. Detailed rater training can be introduced to rating-scale users to reduce significant errors of severity, generosity, or central tendency.
11. The primary purposes of an informal reading inventory are to provide placement information or to furnish individual diagnostic information for instructional planning.
12. The questioning techniques used by teachers rarely have assessment as their only purpose.
13. The validity of responses obtained from an oral-questioning assessment depends on how well questions are formulated and delivered and how well responses are judged.
14. A thoughtful question can be presented equally well in declarative and interrogative form.
15. Higher-level thinking is more likely to result from wait times of 3 to 5 seconds than 1 to 2 seconds.
16. The purpose of documenting responses to oral questioning is to preserve the meaning of the responses for subsequent decision making.
17. Records of oral questioning that focus on the questions are more likely to be used for teacher evaluation; those that focus on responses are more likely to be used for student evaluation.

QUESTIONS FOR STUDY AND DISCUSSION

1. How could the reliability of the results of oral questioning in a classroom be estimated?
2. What is "informal" about the methods characterized in this chapter as informal assessment methods?
3. Why might the use of an observation schedule or record yield more reliable and meaningful information than could be obtained without either?
4. Why is it absurd to urge teachers to curtail all spontaneous observation in favor of planned observation?
5. What are some typical examples of how spontaneous observations inappropriately influence teachers' decisions?
6. Why might intentional observer selectivity be more difficult to control than unintentional selectivity?
7. What plausible explanations can be given for why subjects are likely to modify their behavior when they become aware that someone is observing them?
8. How might subject inconsistency and observer inconsistency combine to provide distorted information about a subject's performance?
9. What are the likely consequences when the number of different types of behaviors to be observed simultaneously becomes "large"?

10. Why might the results from a checklist be more easily used for criterion-referenced than norm-referenced purposes?

11. How can novices and experts be used effectively in constructing a checklist?

12. What are the expected effects on score interpretation (norm-referenced and criterion-referenced separately) of each of these kinds of rating errors: leniency, generosity, and central tendency?

13. What are the major advantages of using oral questioning for gathering summative achievement information from a class of students?

14. What kinds of questioning techniques by the teacher seem to discourage deep thinking on the part of students?

15. Why might increased "wait time" increase participation as well as the frequency of appropriate responses?

15

Grading and Reporting Achievements

THE NEED FOR GRADES

The uses made of grades are numerous and often crucial. They are used as self-evaluative measures and also to report students' educational status to parents, future teachers, and prospective employers. They provide a basis for important decisions about educational plans and career options. Then, too, education is expensive. To make the best possible use of educational facilities and student talent, it is essential that each student's educational progress be watched carefully and reported as accurately as possible. Reports of school grades serve somewhat the same function in education that financial statements serve in business. In either case, if the reports are inaccurate or unavailable, the venture may become inefficient or the quality of the product may deteriorate.

Grades also provide an important means for stimulating, directing, and rewarding the educational efforts of students. This function of grades has been attacked on the ground that they provide extrinsic, artificial, and hence undesirable stimuli and rewards. Indeed, grades are extrinsic, but so are most other cherished rewards for effort and achievement. Most workers, including those in the professions, are grateful for the intrinsic rewards that sometimes accompany their efforts. But most of them are even more grateful that these are not the only rewards. Few organized, efficient human enterprises can be conducted successfully on the basis of intrinsic rewards alone.

To serve effectively the purpose of stimulating, directing, and rewarding student efforts to learn, grades must be valid. The highest grades must go to those students who have demonstrated the highest levels of achievement with respect to course objectives. Grades must be based on sufficient evidence. They must report the degree of achievement as precisely as possible under the circumstances. If grades are assigned carelessly, their long-run effects on the educational efforts of students cannot be good.

Some students and teachers minimize the importance of grades, suggesting that *what* students learn is more important than the *grade* they get. Their conception rests on the assumption that there generally is not a close relationship between the amount of useful learning a student can demonstrate and the grade he or she receives. Others have made the same point by noting that grades should not be regarded as ends in themselves, and by questioning the use of examinations "merely" for the purpose of assigning grades.

It is true that the grade a student receives is not in itself an important educational outcome—by the same token, neither is the degree or diploma toward which the student is working, nor the academic rank or professional reputation of those who teach that individual. But all these symbols can be and should be valid indications of important educational attainments. It is desirable, and not impossibly difficult, to make the goal of maximum educational achievement compatible with the goal of highest possible grades. If these two goals are not closely related, the fault would seem to rest with those who teach the classes and assign the grades. From the point of view of students, parents, teachers, and employers, there is nothing "mere" about the grading process and the grades it yields. Stroud (1946) underscored this point.

> If the marks earned in a course of study are made to represent progress toward getting an education, working for marks is *ipso facto* a furtherance of the purposes of education. If the marks are so bad that the student who works for and attains them misses an education, then working for marks is a practice to be eschewed. When marks are given, we are not likely to dissuade pupils from working for them: and there is no sensible reason why we should. It simply does not make sense to grade pupils, to maintain institutional machinery for assembling and recording the gradings, while at the same time telling pupils marks do not amount to much. As a matter of fact they do amount to something and the pupil knows this. If we are dissatisfied with the results of working for marks we might try to improve the marks. (p. 632)

Grades are necessary. If they are inaccurate, invalid, or meaningless, the remedy lies less in de-emphasizing grades than in assigning them more carefully so that they more truly report the extent of important achievements. Instead of seeking to minimize their importance or seeking to find some less painful substitute, teachers should devote more attention to improving the validity and precision of the grades they assign and to minimizing misinterpretations of grades by the students, teachers, and others who use them.

SOME PROBLEMS OF GRADING

The problems of using grades to describe student achievement have been persistently troublesome at all levels of education. An important and fundamental reason why problems of grading are difficult to solve permanently is because grading systems tend to become issues in educational controversies. Odell (1950) noted that research on grading systems did not become significant until after the turn of the century. At about that same time, the development of objective tests was ushering in the somewhat controversial "scientific movement" in education. The rise of progressive education in the third and fourth decades of this century, with its emphasis on the uniqueness of the individual, the wholeness of mental life, freedom and democracy in the classroom, and the child's need for loving reassurance, led to criticisms of academic narrowness, the competitive pressures, and the common standards of achievement for all students implicit in many grading systems. However, subsequent renewed emphasis on "back to basics" and on pursuit of academic excellence has been accompanied by pleas for more formal evaluations of achievement and more rigorous standards of attainment (National Commission on Excellence in Education, 1983).

Such drifts and shifts in educational philosophy influence some educational leaders to espouse one philosophy, some another. Some teachers find it easy to accept one position, some another, even when they teach in the same educational institution. Since somewhat differing grading systems are implied by each of these different philosophical positions, it is not surprising that differences of opinion, dissatisfaction, and proposals for change tend to characterize teacher reactions to the entire grading enterprise.

Another reason why grading systems present perennial problems is that they require teachers, whose natural instincts incline them to be helpful counselors and advocates, to stand in judgment over the deeds of others. "Forbear to judge, for we are sinners all," said Shakespeare, echoing the sentiments of the Sermon on the Mount: "Judge not, that ye be not judged." It is never difficult to assign a student a good grade, particularly if it is higher than he or she really expected. But since the reach of many students exceeds their grasp, there are likely to be more occasions for disappointment than pleasure for both students and teachers.

The issues that contribute to making grading so problematic are primarily philosophical in nature. There are no research studies that can answer questions like: What should an A grade mean? What percent of the students in a class should receive a C? Should spelling and grammar be judged in assigning a grade to a paper? What should a course grade represent? These "should" questions require value judgments rather than an interpretation of research data; the answer to each may vary from teacher to teacher. But all teachers must ask similar questions and find acceptable answers to them in establishing their grading policies. With careful thought and periodic review, most teachers can develop satisfactory, defensible grading practices that will yield accurate measures of the achievements of their students. And by attending to the principles that enhance the reliability and validity of other achievement measures, policies and procedures can be developed to produce relevant, meaningful grades at all educational levels.

No system of grading is likely to be found that will make the process of grading easy, painless, and generally satisfactory. This is not to say that present grading practices are beyond improvement. It is only to say that no new grading system, no matter how cleverly devised and conscientiously followed, is likely to solve the basic problems of grading. The real need is not for some new system. Good systems already exist. The real need is in using the existing systems to produce the most valid grades possible for the limited set of purposes grades should serve.

Some Shortcomings of Grades

Two major deficiencies of grades, as they are assigned in many educational institutions, are (1) the lack of clear and generally accepted definitions of what the various grades mean and (2) the lack of sufficient, relevant, and objective evidence to use as a basis for assigning grades (Stiggins, Frisbie, and Griswold, 1989). One consequence of the first shortcoming is that grading standards and the meanings of grades tend to vary from teacher to teacher, from course to course, from department to department, and from school to school within districts (Terwillinger, 1971). Another consequence is that teacher biases and idiosyncrasies tend to reduce the validity of grades (Stiggins, Frisbie, and Griswold, 1989). One outcome of this second shortcoming is that the grades tend to be unreliable. Another is that grades can be inflated—their face value is higher than their actual value.

The absence of explicit definitions for each grade permits teachers to be influenced, either consciously or unknowingly, by extraneous factors in assigning grades. Research on this point from three or more decades ago probably is characteristic of present practice (Carter, 1952; Hadley, 1954; Palmer, 1962). Some teachers deliberately use high grades as rewards and low grades as punishments for behavior unrelated to the attainment of instructional objectives.

The studies of Starch and Elliot (1912, 1913a, 1913b) on the unreliability of teacher's grades on examination papers are classic demonstrations of the instability of judgments based on presumably absolute standards. Identical copies of an English test paper were given to 142 English teachers, with instructions to score it on the basis of 100 percent for a perfect paper. Since each teacher looked at only one paper, no *relative* basis for judgment was available. The scores assigned to the same paper ranged all the way from 98 to 50 percent. Similar results were obtained with test papers in geometry and in history.

Typically, grades such as those Starch and Elliot collected for single examination papers are not highly reliable. For semester grades, however, reliabilities in the range of 0.70 to 0.80 should be common. Semester grades are based on much more extensive and comprehensive observations of student attainments, perhaps as many as 80 hours of observation. Even so, one hour of intensive "observation" under the controlled conditions of a well-standardized achievement test can yield measures with reliability estimates in excess of 0.90. If the tools of performance assessment are not well designed, their collective worth over a semester may be exceeded by a reliable and valid commercially prepared instrument that takes no time for the teacher to prepare and a small fraction of class time to administer. Our purpose here is not to argue for replacing teacher-made evaluation tools with standardized measures, but to dramatize the unfortunate state of affairs in which some teachers find themslves at grade assignment time. We are not facing utter chaos, but considerable room for improvement exists.

THE MEANING CONVEYED BY GRADES

A grading system is primarily a method of communicating measurements of achievement. It involves the use of a set of specialized symbols whose meanings ought to be clearly defined and uniformly understood by all concerned. Only to the degree that the grading symbols have the same meaning for all who use them is it possible for grades to serve the purposes of communication meaningfully and precisely.

The meaning of a grade should depend as little as possible on the instructor who issued it or the course to which it pertains. This means that the grading practices of an instructor, of a department, or indeed of an entire educational institution are matters of legitimate concern to other instructors, other departments, and other institutions. It means that a general system of grading ought to be adopted by the faculty and administration of a school or college. It requires that the meaning of each grading symbol be clearly defined. General adherence to this system and to these meanings ought to be expected of all who issue grades. Such a requirement would in no way infringe the right of instructors to set their own standards or to invent their own meanings for each of the grades issued.

A particular grade carries three distinct pieces of information. First, a grade represents the comparison of a student's performance with either some absolute standard or a relative standard defined by the performance of a specified group. Second, a grade represents quality of performance with respect to either amount of effort expended or amount of achievement demonstrated. Finally, a grade represents either the amount of knowledge possessed at the end of instruction or the amount of learning attributable to the instructional program. The remainder of this section is a discussion of the issues associated with choosing between the alternative meanings that each of the three sources can contribute to the overall meaning of a grade.

Absolute and Relative Standards

A grade represents a teacher's summary evaluation of how well a student has performed a set of tasks in one instructional unit or over a series of several units. These judgments of goodness cannot be made in the absence of a standard of comparison. Performance that is described as good, inferior, adequate, excellent, or inferior obtains its qualitative label when the evaluator compares the performance in question with a performance standard. The standard is either absolute or relative.

Each of the two major grading systems used in the United States since the turn of the century is based on either absolute or relative grading standards. In the early years almost all grading was in percents. A student who learned all that anyone could learn in a course, whose achievement could be regarded as flawless, could expect a grade of 100 (percent). A student who essentially knew nothing about the course content would, theoretically, be given a grade of zero. A definite percent of "perfection," usually between 60 and 75 percent, ordinarily was regarded as the minimum passing grade. The absolute standard to which all students' performances were referenced was the domain of content—the knowledge, skills, and understanding—that defined the course. Because a student's grade presumably is assigned independently of the grades of other students in the course, percent grading usually is characterized as *absolute grading*.

The other major type of grading system is based on the use of a small number of letter grades, often five, to express various levels of achievement. In the five-letter A, B, C, D, F system, truly outstanding performance is assigned a grade of A. The B indicates above-average achievement; C is the average grade; D indicates below-average achievement; and F is used to report failure, achievement insufficient to warrant credit for completing a course. The relative standard to which each student's performance is referenced is the distribution of performance of other students in the class. Thus, letter grading is sometimes characterized as *relative grading*.

Of course, each letter in the grading system can be defined in absolute terms instead of relative terms. A grade of D may indicate achievement of the minimally essential knowledge and understandings; C may represent adequate rather than average achievement; B may indicate a level of advanced achievement with respect to course content; and A may be used to represent exceptional or meritorious achievement. Such general definitions would require substantial refinement to communicate the absolute levels of achievement in any particular course or grade-specific subject matter. The point is, it is not the use of letter symbols that distinguishes absolute and relative grading; it is the nature of the standard against which performance is compared that differentiates the two.

The decision to use either an absolute or a relative grading standard is the most fundamental decision a teacher must make with regard to performance assessment. When the absolute standard is chosen, all methods and tools of evaluation must be designed to yield criterion-referenced interpretations. Absolute standards for grading must be established for each component that is to contribute to the course grade—tests, papers, quizzes, presentations, projects, and other assignments. If the decision is to use a relative standard, all grading components must be geared to providing norm-referenced interpretations. Of course, in both cases cutoff score decisions need to be made as long as several grading symbols are available. The basis for determining the cutoff points will be criterion-referenced in one case and norm-referenced in the other.

Though a clear majority of institutions now use letter grading with relative standards, percent grading is by no means obsolete. Some institutions still use percent grades exclusively; others convert to letter grades from percent grades. Many professional examining boards still prefer to define passing scores in terms of percent scores even though, in some cases, the raw scores are transformed to a percent scale using relative grading methodology. Some instructors voice a preference for absolute grading over relative grading for philosophical reasons but find the task of establishing standards overbearing or, in some cases, too arbitrary.

Achievement and Effort

After the decision has been made about the use of absolute or relative standards, the instructor must decide which aspects of performance or which forms of achievement will be included in the grade. Undoubtedly, some teachers base some of the grades they issue on factors other than the degree of achievement of instructional objectives (Stiggins, Frisbie, and Griswold, 1989). They likely will continue to do so because grades can be used as instruments of social control in the class and because some degree of such control is essential to effective teaching. But the use of grades for these purposes ought to be rare, for it leads to distorted meanings of the grades issued. Indirectly, it conveys to students that social behavior rather than school learning is the most significant purpose of their school program.

One of the important requirements of a good grading system is that the grades indicate as accurately as possible the extent to which students have achieved the instructional objectives in their course of study. If developing students' attitudes toward something or developing their willingness to put forth effort is one of the specific objectives of instruction, and if the instructor has planned instructional procedures to help students develop these behaviors, then it is quite appropriate to consider such behaviors in assigning grades. But usually this is not the case. Accordingly, attitude and effort probably should be excluded from direct consideration in determining the grade to be assigned.

We have argued that grades can and should serve to stimulate, direct, and reward student learning. Certainly, students who exert greater effort and demonstrate greater desire to learn than others ought to be rewarded for their labors. But the *major function* of grading should not be reserved for this purpose. A significant challenge facing each teacher is to identify the forms of reward, other than grades, that appear to stimulate students to perform near their optimum levels of cognitive capability. This is no easy task since students respond differently to words of praise, written notes, smiley faces, and special privileges. The point is that effort and attitude need to be enhanced and sustained through some form of recognition and reward, but grades should not carry this extra burden.

Status and Growth

Some instructors believe that grading is fairer if the grades are based on the amount of improvement students have shown rather than on the level of achievement they demonstrate at the end of instruction. Scores on a pretest, and on other preliminary observations, are used to provide a basis for estimating initial status. The differences between these and subsequent test scores (or other indications of achievement) are used to estimate the amount of change or growth. Hence, high grades are assigned to students who show large gains and low grades are issued to those who display small amounts of change or no growth.

Unfortunately, growth measurements are characteristically low in reliability. Since each test score or observation includes its own errors of measurement, subtracting these scores from other measurements results in an accumulation of errors rather than a cancellation. A difference score probably will be more error laden than either of the scores from which it was derived and, thus, may consist mainly of errors of measurement. If their tests are appropriate and provide reliable scores, instructors may safely use the difference between pretest and posttest mean scores as a measure of their own instructional effectiveness. But few classroom achievement tests are good enough to provide reliable measurements of short-term gains in the achievement of individual students.

In addition to the reliability concern, there are other problems with growth measures. One is that, for most educational purposes, knowledge that a student's achievement is good, average, or poor compared with his or her peers is more useful than knowledge that the student changed more or less rapidly than others during a grading period. Another is that students who get low scores on the pretest have a considerably greater likelihood of showing subsequent large gains in achievement than their peers who earned higher scores initially. Students are quick to learn that, under circumstances of grading on the basis of growth, their pretest scores should be as low as possible to permit the greatest possible observable gain.

It is true that status grading seems to condemn some students to low grades in most subjects, semester after semester. Low grades discourage effort, which in turn increases the probability of more low grades. So the vicious cycle continues, bringing dislike of learning and, possibly, early withdrawal from school. If students are taught to dislike school by constant reminders of their low achievement, the remedy probably is not to try to persuade them that their rate of growth toward achievement is more important than status achieved, for that is a transparent falsehood. The remedy is probably to provide varied opportunities to excel in several kinds of worthwhile activities. The planning and implementation of such efforts certainly would require an alert, versatile, and dedicated teacher. When it is accomplished, though, grading on the basis of status achieved will no longer mean that some students must always win while others must always lose. Instead some students will be able to enjoy some of the rewards of excellence in their own specialties. Cohen (1983), for example, has described alternative procedures for grading the achievement of exceptional students who have been "mainstreamed."

ESTABLISHING A GRADING SYSTEM

The Grade Scale

In general, letter grades and percent grades represent two extremes in terms of precision in grading. Those who first advocated letter grades suggested that the bases on which grades usually are determined are not reliable enough to justify the apparent precision of percent grading. They claimed that the best most instructors could do is to distinguish about five different levels of achievement. Many instructors seemed to agree with this view. Nonetheless, from time to time there has been increased or renewed interest in refining the grading scale by adding plus and minus signs to the basic letters or decimal fractions to the basic numbers (for example, 4.0, 3.5, 3.0, 2.5).

The notion that grading problems can be simplified and grading errors reduced by using fewer categories is an attractive one. Its weakness can be exposed by carrying it to the limit. If only one category is used, if everyone is issued the same grade, all grading problems vanish, but so does the value of grading. A major shortcoming of two-category grading, and to a lesser extent of five-category grading, is the same kind of loss of information. To trade more precisely meaningful grades for grades easier to assign is probably a bad bargain for education.

The use of fewer, broader categories in grading does indeed reduce the frequency of errors in grading. That is, with a few broad categories more of the students receive the grade they deserve because fewer wrong grades are available to give them. But each error is more crucial. The apparent difference between satisfactory and unsatisfactory, or between B and C, is greater than the difference between 87 percent and 88 percent, or between B− and C+. If a fallible instructor (and all of them, being human, are fallible) gives a student a grade of 86 percent when omniscient wisdom would have assigned a grade of 89 percent, the error has less consequence than if the instructor assigns a C when a B should have been given or an "unsatisfactory" grade when it should have been "satisfactory." Hence the use of fewer categories is no royal road to more reliable grading. And, as noted previously, reducing the number of categories reduces the information conveyed by the grade.

Letters versus Numbers

The successful revolt against percent grading was aided by the substitution of letter grades for numbers. Letters helped to emphasize the contrast between clearly relative grading and supposedly absolute percent grading. But the use of letters creates at least two problems. One is that the letters must always be transformed to numbers before they can be weighted or averaged. The other is that letters imply *evaluations* of achievement rather than measurements.

For both these reasons the return to numerical symbols in grading would be advantageous. This advantage must be weighed against the confusion likely to result from the introduction of a new set of symbols, with new and unfamiliar meanings. If an educational institution sets out to improve its grading system, a change in the set of symbols used may help to dramatize and reinforce other, more subtle changes.

Single or Multiple Grades

Achievement in most courses of study is a conglomerate of many factors. There is knowledge to be imparted and understanding to be cultivated; there are abilities and skills to be developed, attitudes to be fostered, interests to be encouraged, and ideals to be exemplified. Correspondingly, the bases used for determining grades include many aspects or indications of achievement: homework, class participation, test scores, apparent attitude, interest and motivation, and even regularity of attendance and helpfulness to the teacher. How can a single symbol do justice to these various aspects of achievement?

The answer of many educators is that it cannot. A grade, some say, is a hodgepodge of uncertain and variable composition. They suggest that grades can be improved by making them more analytical and descriptive. For example, multiple grades or written reports and progress charts have been proposed as improvements over the traditional single letter or number, especially in the elementary school. Expanded reporting forms, for example, are essentially lists of instructional objectives for a subject area that show when formal instruction was presented for each objective and when the student presented evidence of attainment of each (Frisbie, 1976). Such reports are more explicit in communicating what students can do than are letter grades alone. Some school districts use a dual grading system to separate academic progress and the extent of effort exerted. The intent of the dual system is twofold: (1) to provide more information than can be conveyed by a single symbol and (2) to make the academic grade a purer indicator of the level of subject matter competence attained by students.

The dual system is no panacea for the ills of grading; however, under some conditions it can improve grading considerably. Multiple grades require that clear distinctions be made between the aspects of achievement each represents and that sufficient evidence unique to each aspect be obtained as a basis for determining the separate grades. Finally, the larger the number of separate grades reported at one time, the more likely the multiple grades will be influenced by considerable halo effect. That is, the teacher's overall impression of the student may influence each of the grades more than any unique evidence related to the separate aspects of achievement. Certainly, any advantages multiple grading may have to offer an educational institution cannot be realized until the shortcomings of the single-symbol system have been addressed adequately.

There is an eclectic grading system that may appear to be complex, but that has promise for satisfying the needs of proponents of either criterion-referencing or norm-referencing. This system depends on criterion-referenced, minimum competency measures to make passing decisions and uses norm-referenced measures to make relative distinctions between those who have passed. (One version of this method is described by Terwilliger, 1989, in detail.) Only a single grade is assigned to each student, but a failing grade and a passing grade (A, B, C, or D) are referenced to knowledge, skills, and understandings that have been identified as minimally essential. Passing grades in this system reflect the relative standings of students in a class in learning things that the teacher regards as "beyond basics," or important to success in studying more advanced aspects of the subject matter. The eclectic system offers these advantages:

1. Teachers are less likely to assign a barely passing grade (D) to students who have not mastered basic skills than they might be under a conventional relative grading system.

2. Students who fail at first can be retested to improve their grade after they improve their skills. They are not relegated to lasting failure simply because on one occasion they demonstrated less learning than others.

3. Students who excel are rewarded according to their level of achievement. There are incentives to go beyond the minimum essentials defined for passing.

4. The system represents a reasonable compromise for faculties that are split by advocates of an either–or system, absolute versus relative standards.

THREATS TO THE VALIDITY OF GRADES

A distinction should be made between the aspects of performance that a teacher *evaluates* and the subset of those that are appropriate to use for assigning course grades. Components that contribute to determining course grades should reflect students' competence with respect to the instructional objectives. The components of a grade should be academically oriented: grades should not be tools of discipline or rewards for pleasant personalities or good attitudes. A student who is assigned an A grade should have a firm grasp of the skills and knowledge taught. If the student is merely marginal academically but very industrious and congenial, an A grade would be misleading and would render a blow to the motivation of the excellent students in class. Instructors can and should give feedback to students with respect to a variety of traits and characteristics, but only performance based on academic achievement should be used to determine grades. In their recommendations regarding standards and expectations, the National Commission on Excellence in Education (1983) stated that "grades should be indicators of academic achievement so they can be relied on as evidence of a student's readiness for further study." Grades contaminated by other factors give students a false sense of readiness and provide misinformation to those who seek to guide students in their future educational endeavors.

Several aspects of student performance have been labeled as potentially invalid grading components because they represent behaviors that do not reflect directly the attainment of the important objectives of instruction (Frisbie, 1977). Though some exceptions could be noted, these variables generally should not be used in determining course grades.

Neatness in written work, correctness in spelling and grammatical usage, and organizational ability are all worthy traits and are assets in most vocational endeavors. To this extent, it seems appropriate that teachers evaluate these aspects of performance and provide students with constructive comments about them. However, unless the course objectives include instruction in these skills, students should not be graded on them in the course. For example, students' essay examination scores should not be influenced directly by their spelling ability and neither should their course grades. Students whose skills in written expression are weak can and do learn the important knowledge of science, social studies, literature, and other academic subjects. Their writing skills can and should be evaluated in such courses, but their course grades should not suffer directly because of their writing deficiencies. To the extent that they do, these grades are misleading to both students and parents and serve to moderate rather than stimulate interest in the subject area.

Most instructors are attracted to students who are agreeable, friendly, industrious, and kind. They try to ignore or may even reject those who display opposite characteristics. When it appears that certain personalities may interfere with class work or have limited chances for employment in their field of interest, constructive feedback from the instructor may be necessary. But an argumentative or misbehaving student who receives a C grade should have only a moderate amount of knowledge about the course content. The C should not reflect the student's disposition or disruptive behavior directly (Bartlett, 1987).

Most small classes and college seminars depend on student participation to some degree for their success. When participation is an important ingredient in learning, participation grades may be appropriate. In such cases the instructor should ensure that all students have sufficient opportunity to participate and should maintain systematic notes regarding frequency and quality of participation. (See Chapter 14 for sample recording forms.) Waiting until the end of the grading period and relying strictly on memory causes a relatively subjective task to be even more subjective and unreliable. Participation probably should not be graded in most classes, however. Dominating and extroverted students tend to win, and introverted or shy students tend to lose. Instructors may want to provide evaluative information to students about various aspects of the students' personalities, including willingness to participate, but grading should not be the means of doing so.

Students at all levels should be encouraged to attend classes because the lectures, demonstrations, and discussions presumably have been designed to facilitate their learning. If students miss several classes, then their performance on examinations, papers, and projects likely will suffer. If the instructor reduces their grade because of absence, such students are submitted to a form of double jeopardy. For example, a college instructor may say that class attendance counts 10 percent of the course grade, but for students who miss several classes this may effectively amount to 20 percent. Teachers who experience high rates of "cutting" in their classes probably need to examine their classroom environment and instructional procedures to determine if changes are needed. There ought to be more productive means of encouraging students to attend classes than to threaten to lower their grade.

Some instructors are more generous in their grading than they ought to be because they fear that lower grades might bruise their students' self-images. However, as Sadler (1983) has argued, the implementation of this philosophy is not defensible:

> The desire to label everything as good rests on two false assumptions, namely (1) that any negative reaction is bound to stifle personal development and creativity, and (2) that evaluating a performance as a performance is equivalent to judging a person as a person. Not everything produced by human beings, even honest and diligent ones, is good, and students are not so naive. (p. 75)

Judgments about writing and speaking skills, personality traits, effort, and motivation are made by teachers constantly as they interact with their students. To exclude most of these factors from the judgments made about academic progress and promise is no easy task. But accurate and meaningful grades depend on it.

GRADING COURSE ASSIGNMENTS

The assignments discussed in this section are the activities prescribed by the teacher primarily to allow students to demonstrate their level of competence. In this sense, each is a form of summative evaluation and a planned part of performance assessment. Assignments used for formative evaluation purposes, usually labeled homework, are used to provide practice for the learner.

Homework assignments that are intended to provide instruction or formative feedback probably should not be graded and included among the components that enter into course grading. Consider Freddy, for example, who is learning to identify prepositions as they occur in a sentence. On each of the first five daily assignments Freddy missed four to eight sentences out of ten. On the sixth and seventh days he missed none. He missed only one out of twenty on the test given the eighth day. Which grade best describes Freddy's level of achievement? Though he may not have caught on as rapidly as some of his peers, Freddy appears to be able to identify prepositions. Some form of grading might be used to motivate and direct Freddy and his classmates, but all such grades need not enter into determining the final course or term grade.

Perhaps the most frequent shortcoming associated with grading assignments such as papers, reports, presentations, and projects is the failure of the teacher to specify and describe *in advance* what the important aspects of the final product should be like. The lack of "feed forward," as Sadler (1983) has labeled it, produces two undesirable outcomes: (1) some students present incomplete assignments because they misunderstood the teacher's intent, and (2) grading becomes a chore for the teacher because the criteria that distinguish better assignments from poorer ones have not been explicated. The grading guide that seems so logical to prepare for scoring essay items is equally beneficial to the teacher for grading assignments. It can help to accomplish these things:

1. When presented to the students at the time the assignment is made, potential misunderstandings about what to do can be overcome. The nature of the final product can be described completely, and the relative importance of various aspects of it can be presented. Often an example of an A assignment from a previous class is a helpful model.

2. Opportunities for extraneous factors to influence grading are reduced because the relevant elements have been defined. Grading variables and evaluation variables can be separated so that a conscious effort can be made by the teacher to make comments about the nongraded aspects of the work.

3. Grading can be done efficiently because little time is needed to decide which parts of the assignment to weight most heavily. Less time is needed to judge completeness as well.

4. Feedback to students can be somewhat diagnostic because missing segments and student misconceptions are more readily identified.

We discussed in Chapter 12 the importance of preparing students for examinations so that they know what to expect and can prepare themselves further. A grading guide, like the checklist shown in Figure 14–2, can serve this same useful function for assignments, and it also can contribute to more valid and reliable measures of achievement if used wisely by the grader.

COMBINING GRADE COMPONENTS

When teachers determine a course grade by combining grades or scores from tests, papers, demonstrations, and projects, each component may carry more or less weight than the others in determining the final grade. To obtain grades of maximum validity, teachers must give each component the proper weight, not too much and not too little. How can they determine what those weights *ought* to be and what they actually turn out to be? And if these two sets of figures are disparate, what can instructors do? It is not easy to give a firm, precise answer to the question of how much influence each component *ought* to have in determining the composite grade. But several guiding principles can be offered.

In general, the use of several different kinds of indicators of achievement is better than use of only one, provided that each indicator is relevant to the instructional objectives and provided also that it can be observed or measured with reasonable accuracy. Other considerations being equal, the components with the most reliable scores should be assigned the greatest weight.

If component measures of achievement are highly correlated, as they often will be, the problem of weighting them is far less critical than if they are fairly unrelated. For most courses, the various measurable aspects of achievement are related closely enough that proper weighting is not a critical problem. Ideally, the component measures used to determine the final grade will collectively measure all the important objectives in the course. However, two components that cover unique objectives should have greater combined weight than two components that measure many of the same instructional objectives. Note that the emphasis here is on the uniqueness of the objectives and not on the importance of each. More important objectives should have been measured with more components (more test items, more writing samples, more demonstrations) to ensure greater influence in the course grade.

For norm-referenced grading, the actual weight that a component of a final grade *does* carry depends on the variability of its scores and the correlations of those scores with scores from each of the other components. This makes the precise influence of any given component quite difficult to assess. As a first approximation to the weight of a component, the standard deviation of its scores serves quite well. If one set of scores is twice as variable as another, the first set is likely to carry about twice the weight of the second in their total.

Table 15–1 shows that the influence (weight) of one component (for example, scores on one test) on a composite (the sum of scores on three tests, in this example) depends on the variability of the test scores. The top section of the table displays the scores of three students, Tom, Dick, and Harry, on three tests, X, Y, and Z, along with their total scores on the three tests. Dick has the highest total and Tom the lowest. The next section shows how the students ranked on the three tests. Each of them made the highest score on one test, middle score on a second, and lowest score on the third. But note, for future reference, that the ranks of their total scores on the three tests are the same as their ranks on test Z.

The third section of the table gives the maximum possible scores (total points), the mean scores, and the standard deviations of the scores on the three tests. Test X has the highest number of total points. Test Y has the highest mean score. Test Z has scores with the greatest variability.

On which test was it most important to do well? On which was the payoff for ranking first the highest, and the penalty for ranking last the heaviest? Clearly, on test Z, the test with the greatest variability of scores. Which test ranked the students in the same order as their final ranking, based on total scores? Again the answer is test Z. Thus the influence of one component on a composite depends not on total points or mean score but on score variability.

If the three tests should have carried equal weight, they can be made to do so by weighting their scores to make the standard deviations equal. This is

Table 15-1. Weighted Test Scores

Tests	X	Y	Z	Total
Student scores:				
Tom	53	65	18	136
Dick	50	59	42	151
Harry	47	71	30	148
Student ranks:				
Tom	1	2	3	3
Dick	2	3	1	1
Harry	3	1	2	2
Test characteristics:				
Total points	100.0	75	50	225.0
Mean score	50.0	65	30	145.0
Standard deviation	2.5	5	10	6.5
Weighted scores:	×4	×2	×1	
Tom	212	130	18	360
Dick	200	118	42	360
Harry	188	142	30	360

illustrated in the last section of the table. Scores on test X are multiplied by 4, to change their standard deviation from 2.5 to 10, the same as on test Z. Scores on test Y are multiplied by 2, to change their standard deviation to 10 also. With equal standard deviations, the tests carry equal weight and give students having the same average rank on the tests the same total scores.

When the whole possible range of scores is used, score variability is closely related to the extent of the available score scale. This means that scores on a 40-item objective test are likely to carry about four times the weight of scores on a 10-point essay-test question, provided that scores extend across the whole range in both cases. But if only a small part of the possible scale of scores is actually used, the length of that scale can be a very misleading guide to the variability of the scores.

The most efficient means of ensuring proper weight involves the computation of standard scores, perhaps T-scores, for each grading component. Then each component will be represented on a score scale that yields the same standard deviation (10 for T-scores) for each measure. If a teacher has promised a class, for example, that the final grade will be based on five components, weighted as follows,

Unit I test	20%
Unit II test	20%
Term paper	10%
Final exam	30%
Term project	20%

the T-scores of each component can be multiplied by 2, 2, 1, 3, and 2, respectively, to achieve the desired weighting. (Oosterhof (1987) has described the weighting procedures for both criterion-referenced and norm-referenced grading situations.)

One final admonition regarding relative grading and combining scores: It is a mistake to convert test scores to letter grades, record these in a grade book, and then reconvert the letter grades to numbers (A = 4, B = 3) for purposes of computing final averages. A better procedure is to record the test scores and other numerical measures directly. These can be added, with whatever weighting has been adopted, to obtain a composite score that can be converted to a final grade.

Recording of scores rather than letters saves time in the long run, but, more importantly, it contributes to higher grading accuracy. Whenever a range of scores, some higher and some lower, is converted to the same letter grade, information is lost. Each B, whether a high B or low B in terms of the score on which it was based, is given the same value in the reconversion process (for example, B = 4.0). Some of the reliability the teacher struggled to achieve in developing each measure is lost in the process. For this reason it is desirable to record raw scores or standard scores rather than letters or their numerical equivalents.

METHODS OF ASSIGNING GRADES

The procedures a teacher follows for assigning term grades are dictated largely by the meaning the teacher has chosen to attribute to the symbols. The multitude of methods used in practice generally can be categorized in terms of their dependence on either absolute or relative standards (Frisbie, 1978). The popular variations of these two types and their corresponding strengths and weaknesses are described in this section.

Relative Grading Methods

One popular variety of relative grading is called *grading on the curve.* The "curve" referred to usually is the normal distribution curve or some symmetric variant of it. The norm-referenced basis for this type of grading is complicated by the need to establish arbitrary quotas for each grading category. What proportion of the grades should be As? Bs? Ds? Once these quotas are fixed, grades are assigned without regard to actual level of achievement. That is, the highest 10 percent may receive an A, even though the top 20 percent may have achieved at about the same level. Those who "set the curve" or "blow the top off the curve" are merely among the top group, including those who may have scored 20 points lower. The bottom 5 percent may each be assigned an F, even though the bottom 15 percent may be indistinguishable in achievement. Regardless of the quota-setting strategy used, this relative grading method seldom carries a defensible rationale.

The *distribution gap* method, another relative grading variation, is based on the relative ranking of students in the form of a frequency distribution of the composite scores. The frequency distribution is examined carefully for gaps—several consecutive scores that no students obtained. A horizontal line is drawn at the top of the first gap ("Here are the As!") and a second gap is sought. The process continues until all possible grade ranges (A to F) have been identified. The major fallacy with this technique is the dependence on chance to form the gaps. The size and location of gaps may depend as much on random measurement error as on actual achievement differences between students. If the scores from an equivalent set of measures could be obtained from the group, the smaller gaps might appear in different locations or the larger gaps may turn out to be somewhat smaller. Errors of measurement from *different* measures do not necessarily cancel each other out as they are expected to do on repeated measurement with the *same* instrument. The major attraction of the distribution gap method is that, when grades are assigned, few students appear to be right on the borderline of receiving a higher grade. Consequently, teachers receive fewer student complaints and fewer requests to reexamine test papers to search for "that extra point" that would, for example, change a C grade to a B. In situations where the distribution of scores is highly variable, this grading method is likely to yield grades that are similar to those assigned by some other relative grading methods. However, when scores are relatively homogeneous, the gap distribution method actually may be as inequitable to some students as it appears to be.

One other widely used and generally sound relative grading procedure might be labeled the *standard deviation method,* due to the dependence on the standard deviation for determining the grade cutoff points that form equal intervals on the score scale. The first step in this method is to build a frequency distribution for the composite scores. Then the median and standard deviation of the composite scores are computed. Cutoff points for the range of C grades (average performance) are determined by adding one-half of the standard deviation to the median and subtracting one-half of the standard deviation from the median. Then, add one standard deviation to the upper cutoff of the Cs to find the A–B cutoff score. Subtract the same amount from the lower cutoff of the Cs to find the D–F cutoff. Review borderline cases by using the number of assignments completed, quality of assignments, or some other relevant achievement data to decide if any borderline grades should be raised or lowered. Measurement error exists in composite scores, also. A variation of this method that describes the use of relative grading on an institutional basis has been illustrated in considerable detail by Ebel (1972).

Absolute Grading Methods

Various methods that depend on percent scores as their basis have a long-standing history, but their popularity has diminished greatly since the early 1900s. Percent scores from tests, papers, and other projects are interpreted as the percent of content, skills, or knowledge over which students have command—a domain-referenced interpretation. For example, a test score of 83 percent means that the student knows 83 percent of the content represented by the instructional objectives from which test items were prepared and sampled. Percent scores usually are converted to grades by comparing the scores with performance standards established by the teacher for each grading category.

Many teachers assign grades to percent scores using arbitrary standards similar to those set for grading on the curve. That is, students with scores in the 93 to 100 range are assigned an A, 85 to 92 is a B, 78 to 84 is a C, and so on. The restriction here is on the score ranges rather than on the number of students eligible to receive each of the possible grades. But what rationale should be used to determine each grade category cutoff score? Why should the cutoff for an A be 93 rather than 94 or 90? A major limitation of percent grading as used by some teachers is the use of fixed cutoff points that are applied to *every* grading component in the course. It seems indefensible to set grade cutoffs that remain constant throughout the course and over several consecutive offerings of the course. What *does* seem defensible is for the instructor to establish cutoffs for each grading component, independent of the others, depending on the content of each component. For example, the range for an A might be 93 to 100 for the first test, 88 to 100 for a term paper, 87 to 100 for the second test, and 90 to 100 for the final exam.

Those who use percent grading find themselves in a bind when the high-est score obtained on a test was only 68 percent, for example. Was the test much too difficult or did students prepare too little? Was instruction relatively ineffec-tive? Some instructors proceed to adjust the scores by replacing the perfect score, 100 percent, with the highest score, 68 percent in this case. For example, if the highest score was 34 out of 50 points, each student's percent score would be recomputed using 34 as the maximum rather than 50. Though such an adjust-ment may cause all concerned to breathe easier, the new score can no longer be interpreted as originally intended—the proportion of the content domain the student knows, as sampled by the test. A new domain has been established. What useful interpretation can be made of the new scores? How can the new domain be defined?

A final shortcoming of percent grading should be noted. The range of percent scores usually is limited to 70 to 100 because the passing score generally is 70 percent. The test constructor must exhibit great skill to prepare items that will yield scores distributed in this narrow range and that, at the same time, will measure relevant learning as reflected by the instructional objectives. Methods that allow for a lower passing score would permit a greater potential range of scores, likely would yield more reliable scores, and likely would result in more reliable grade assignments, assuming the full range of grades (A to F) is to be used.

A second method of absolute grading, called here the *content-based method,* depends heavily on the judgments of the teacher in deciding the type and amount of knowledge students must display to earn each grade on the A to F scale. It is the method most compatible with mastery or quasi-mastery teaching and learning strategies, but it need not be limited to pass–fail or satisfactory–unsatisfactory grading scales. The procedural steps for establishing performance standards and cutoff scores are outlined below for a 50-item test built to measure achievement in two units of instruction.

1. First, the grade to be assigned to those who demonstrate minimum passing achievement must be established. We will use D for illustration purposes, but it could be C, as is common in graduate-level courses. The teacher must de-velop a description, preferably in writing, of the type of knowledge and under-standing a student who barely passes should possess. Similar descriptions must be developed to describe C, B, and A performances.

2. With the descriptions in hand, the instructor reads the first test item and decides if a student with only minimum achievement should be able to answer it correctly. If so, a D is recorded next to the item number and the same procedure is applied to item 2. If not, the question is posed in terms of C-level achievement. This process continues until the first item has been classified. If the instructor decides that even A students should not necessarily be able to answer the item correctly, another symbol (maybe N) is used to classify the item. (Few such items should exist on a test built by the instructor.) For items that are worth more than a single point, like some essay or problem items, the instructor must decide the minimum number of points to be earned by students in each grade category.

3. This process continues, item by item, until each item has been classified. The estimated cutoff score for a D is determined by adding the number of D symbols preceding the items. Assume that number is 17 for this example. Then the number of C symbols is tallied and added to 17 to obtain the cutoff score for C performance. This process continues until a tentative cutoff score for each grade has been determined. The result might look like this:

A = 48–50
B = 40–47
C = 29–39
D = 17–28
F = 0–16

4. The final cutoff scores can be obtained by adjusting the estimated cutoff score down by 2 to 4 points, depending on test length. The adjustment accounts for negative measurement error, the fact that our measures are less than perfectly reliable. Obviously, positive measurement error will affect some students' scores, but most instructors prefer to give the benefit of doubt to students when it comes to matters of chance. With a 2-point adjustment, the cutoff scores for earning the grades D through A in our example are 15, 27, 38, and 46, respectively.

The content-based method is not without limitations. The instructor must exercise subjectivity in describing the performance that A students, for example, must display. Instructors in the same field, even those teaching the same course, may not completely agree on the knowledge students should be able to demonstrate at each point on the grading scale. They are likely to disagree to some extent about the classification of test items as well. Yet this method is unlikely to be labeled as arbitrary if instructors are willing and able to define performance standards in writing and are able to supply a defensible rationale for their classification judgments. (A similar approach has been described by Terwilliger (1989) in considerable detail.)

Contract Grading

A final method relates to the use of grading contracts, agreements between teacher and student specifying the achievements toward which the student will strive and the grade the teacher will assign as a result. Taylor (1980) reviewed over 100 reports describing contract grading and concluded that "contract grading appears to have a permanent place among the most appropriate current methods of assigning grades to students." However, studies of the effects of contracting generally showed that students like it, teachers assigned more high grades than when conventional methods were used, and student achievement was no higher than with conventional grading. Contract grading appears to be best suited to very small classes or independent studies, courses in which students are given the flexibility to pursue individual interests. In such cases a written agreement should be mandatory so that no misunderstanding will exist regarding what must be accomplished, by whom, and by what deadline.

GRADING SOFTWARE

The time-consuming tasks associated with recording test scores in gradebooks and combining scores for final grades can be handled readily by a microcomputer and any of the numerous software packages available for grading. Some teachers use a spreadsheet program and design their own grading application program; others find the unique features of many of the commercial packages worth their relatively low cost.

Because software and hardware both change more rapidly than most other textbook content, we have chosen not to describe or evaluate specific grading software. However, current information can be located using such references as *Data Sources, Datapro Directory of Microcomputer Software, MENU* (Macintosh), *Education Index,* and *Current Index to Journals in Education* (CIJE). In addition, software reviews and lists of new releases are printed frequently in such journals as *Electronic Learning, inCider, Classroom Computer Learning,* and *The Computer Teacher.* Here are some questions to raise when assessing the utility of a gradebook program:

1. How many students and grading components per student can be accommodated on a single data diskette?
2. For the elementary school level, can the system handle multiple classes for a single group of students?
3. How convenient is it to change grades or to replace scores?
4. Can test scores be imported as a data file so they do not need to be key entered one by one?
5. Does the variety of reporting–printing options satisfy basic needs?
6. Can the data be stored on a data diskette, separate from the program disk, so that copies can be made of the data files?
7. Are there any unusual hardware requirements regarding memory, drives, or printers?
8. Can the program be returned for full refund after a reasonable trial period?

Of course, the main question to ask about any grading software is, "Will the program allow me to use the grading procedures and philosophy I have a-dopted?" For example, software that will not accommodate a teacher's criterion-referenced grading practices should not be considered for adoption, no matter how friendly the package seems to be.

SUMMARY PROPOSITIONS

1. Measurements and reports of student achievement are essential in education, and no better means than grades seem likely to appear.
2. Grades must be reliable and valid to serve their purposes of stimulating, directing, and rewarding student efforts to learn.
3. There is nothing wrong with encouraging students to work for high grades if the grades are valid measures of achievement.
4. Grading is frequently the subject of educational controversy because the grading process is difficult, different philosophies call for different grading systems, and the task of grading is sometimes unpleasant.
5. The major shortcomings of grades relate to a lack of clearly defined meanings for the grades and also to the lack of sufficient good evidence to use as a basis for assigning them.
6. Grades will tend to lose their meaning if the institution lacks a clearly defined grading system or does not require instructors to grade in conformity with the system.
7. The selection of either absolute or relative standards as a basis for grading will be influenced more by philosophical considerations than by empirical ones.
8. Grades should be based primarily on achievement, as reflected by instructional objectives, rather than on attitude or effort.
9. Grades that indicate achievement status tend to be more reliable, meaningful, and constructive than grades that indicate growth.
10. The more grading symbols available in the system, the more reliable the grades will be, but the less convenient the system may be to use.
11. A return to numerical grades would emphasize their use as measurements and would simplify the calculation of grade-point averages.
12. The use of multiple grades on various aspects of achievement can improve grading but requires extra effort relative to using a single grade.
13. Aspects of student behavior that do not indicate achievement directly and that are usually inappropriate as components of a course grade include attendance, class participation, neatness and skill in written expression, and student deportment.
14. Measures used primarily as tools of formative evaluation generally should not be components of a grade intended to represent summative achievement or status.
15. A grading guide for an assignment can be used effectively to communicate the nature of the work to students and to attain a valid evaluation of the assignment.
16. The weight carried by each component measure in a composite score is determined mainly by the variability of the scores from each component.
17. Highly precise weighting of the components on a numerical basis is *not* crucial to the quality of the grades assigned, especially when the number of components is *not* small.
18. Relative grading methods that divide the score scale into equal intervals are preferable alternatives to strict grading on the curve or to the use of score "gaps."
19. It is illogical and impractical to expect that a fixed set of cutoff scores, such as 90 to 100 = A, can be used for all graded work in a course.
20. A defensible absolute grading method requires that the instructor prepare written definitions of the performance standards to be used for assigning grades.
21. The use of contract grading may be advantageous for individual instructional situations but not for grading classes of students.
22. Current microcomputer software can help reduce the clerical effort and the potential for computational errors associated with grading.

QUESTIONS FOR STUDY AND DISCUSSION

1. For what uses are high school course grades most valid?
2. Under what circumstances could it be appropriate to use the grades issued by teachers in a school to evaluate the curriculum of that school?
3. What is grade inflation and what kind of evidence is needed to show that it has or has not occurred?

4. When letter grades are used on report cards at the middle school level, what information should be furnished to communicate the meaning of each grade symbol?

5. What are some effective means of rewarding students for their superb effort to learn, particularly in the face of relatively low achievement?

6. Why is the use of plus and minus letter grading likely to yield more valid grades than simple letter grading?

7. What advantages does letter grading have over numerical grading?

8. What shorcomings, if any, are inherent in the eclectic grading system described in this chapter?

9. What incentives, other than grades, can teachers use to motivate students to participate in class activities and to complete homework or practice exercises?

10. What are the disadvantages of the "feed forward" concept that is recommended for use in grading assignments? How could each disadvantage you identified be overcome?

11. If the scores from three 90-point tests are added together to form a composite for grading, why would each test not necessarily have equal influence (weight) in determining the rank order of individuals in the composite?

12. Under what circumstances might grading on the curve be particularly appropriate?

13. What drawbacks does the standard-deviation method of grading have for relatively small classes?

14. Why might 50 be a more appropriate passing score than 75 in a percent grading system?

15. What are the ideal characteristics of a computer gradebook system for use at each of these grade levels: elementary, middle school, high school, college?

16

The Nature
of Standardized Tests

CHARACTERISTICS OF STANDARDIZED TESTS

The term *standardized test* refers to a test that has been expertly constructed, usually with tryout, analysis, and revision; includes explicit instructions for uniform (standard) administration and scoring; and provides tables of norms for score interpretation purposes, derived from administering the test in uniform fashion to a defined sample of persons. Used loosely, the term can refer to almost any published test or inventory, whether prepared in the manner just described or not. Most precisely, tests or measures that have been standardized provide the means for making score comparisons among examinees who attempt *the same tasks under the same testing conditions and time constraints, and whose responses are scored with the same procedures.* Of course, not all standardized tests, as the term is commonly used, are intended to yield norm-referenced comparisons. Criterion-referenced and domain-referenced achievement tests and some personality measures, all of which may be commercially prepared and uniformly administered, usually provide no tables of norms.

Standardized tests serve the same function in education and psychology as standard weights and measures do in commerce and science. If every meat market had its own type of scale and concept of how much a pound is, we could not be sure that a pound of ground beef purchased at one market would be more or less than a pound obtained at another. The same problem would face the consumer at the gas station, the fabric shop, and the candy counter. Without standardized tests, the achievements and abilities of students from different classrooms and schools could not be assessed readily with a common yardstick. For example, if each fifth-grade teacher in a district were to develop a geography test to measure student achievement, we would likely find tests that varied markedly in the breadth and depth of tasks required, the number of items, the amount of testing time allowed, the quality of test items, and the reliability of the scores obtained. Certainly, it would be illogical and inappropriate to make score comparisons among students from different classrooms and schools under such circumstances.

The distinction made in Chapter 2 between tests and measures will be followed here in detailing the characteristics of test batteries and single-subject tests. In addition, because standardized personality measures and inventories are used so rarely by most teachers and administrators, we have chosen to limit our treatment of standardized instruments to tests in the areas of achievement, cognitive ability, and aptitude.

Test Batteries

Some standardized tests are developed, published, and administered in coordinated sets known as *test batteries*. The number of tests in the set may vary from 3 or 4 to 10 or more, the number of items per test may vary from as few as 20 to 100 or more, and the administration time per test may range from about 10 minutes to more than an hour. The administration of batteries like the *Iowa Tests of Educational Development* or the *Differential Aptitude Tests* may take as many as five separate test sessions.

A primary advantage of using a battery over a collection of separate tests, whether for achievement or aptitude measurement, is that the battery provides comparable scores from the same norm group for all its tests. This is important, for example, if Mindy's achievement in mathematics is to be compared with her achievement in reading, language, and science. Her relative strengths and weaknesses cannot be assessed unless norm-referenced scores using a *single* reference group are available. If separate tests were used, Mindy might seem to do better on the reading test than on the math test simply because students of lower achievement were more prominent in the norm group of the reading test. This illustration explains why aptitude batteries are used so frequently in employment and vocational counseling to help the client understand his or her areas of strength and weakness. The use of separate tests would not permit useful intraindividual comparisons.

An achievement battery is a survey of the subject matter covered by each test; coverage is broad and, therefore, relatively shallow. A battery can provide comprehensive coverage of *most* of the important aspects of achievement at the elementary school level, *many* at the secondary level, and *some* at the college level. The more uniform the educational programs of all students are, the more suitable a test battery will be for all of them.

A very practical advantage of a battery is that the scores from a battery are reported together on a single report. When separate tests are used, a score report is generated for each separate test, creating a most cumbersome accumulation of paper for the user.

The use of a battery of tests that was developed as an integrated whole thus offers substantial advantages. The main disadvantage is the lack of flexibility it affords. A battery may include some subtests that are of little interest to particular users and may omit others they would have preferred. But this is part of the price that must be paid sometimes for the advantages of convenience in use, comprehensiveness of coverage, and comparability of scores. Most achievement-test publishers have overcome this "disadvantage" through creative packaging; a school district can select the tests they wish to use from the original battery, and the publisher will print test booklets containing only the chosen subset of tests.

Single-subject Tests

Tests that measure achievement in one content area, or that measure a single type of aptitude, differ in several respects from their counterparts of similar name that might be found in a battery. The content coverage tends to be slightly broader and more thorough in a single-subject test. And because such tests usually require more testing time than the corresponding test found in a battery, they will contain more total items and more items per skill.

Single-subject tests tend to be used for particular purposes, to make a specific kind of instructional decision, rather than simply to describe students' relative achievement or aptitude levels. For example, readiness tests used at the primary level might help the teacher group students of similar reading or arithmetic achievement levels for instructional purposes. A mathematics test might be used to decide which seventh graders are most likely candidates for eighth-grade algebra. Reading tests are used to help select reading materials that would be most appropriate for developing the reading skills of each student. End-of-course proficiency tests and graduation competency tests are usually single-subject tests that are used to make promotion–retention decisions at key transitional points. Special aptitude tests for musical, artistic, or mechanical ability are used to help students make vocational and educational decisions about future actions in the area tested.

Some single-subject tests resemble a battery in that they contain subtests or they provide skill scores. Some English language tests, for example, provide separate scores on vocabulary, spelling, punctuation, grammar, word usage, and capitalization. A reading test may yield a vocabulary score, a paragraph comprehension score, and a total score. Often such subscores are so highly correlated with one another that their separate diagnostic value is quite limited. However, the total score is probably a comprehensive indicator of achievement in the broad content domain defined by the test specifications.

Most of the standardized tests of cognitive abilities (intelligence) to be described more fully in Chapter 18 are most appropriately classified as single-subject tests. That is, the trait these tests attempt to measure generally is a single, unitary characteristic. Despite the differences among "intelligence" tests in what they purport to measure and in the theory on which they are based, and despite the fact that some yield subtest scores, most intelligence tests are less like batteries and more like single-subject tests.

TYPES OF STANDARDIZED TEST SCORES

Seldom are the raw scores (number correct) obtained by students on standardized tests interpreted directly. Instead, raw scores are converted to some other score scale to facilitate interpretation. These new score scales are designed to permit direct norm-referenced interpretations by referring to a single reference group (status scores) or to several reference groups that have been linked to the same score scale (developmental scores).

Status Scores

Status scores indicate how a student's test performance compares with those of others in a single reference group—a class, school, school district, or national group. Relative position in the group is the focus. Status or standing in the group generally is expressed as a percentile rank, but standard scores like those described in Chapter 4 frequently are used as well. In most cases stanines, *T*-scores, or normal curve equivalents (NCEs) are normalized standard scores derived from percentile ranks. The standard age scores or deviation IQ scores that come from cognitive abilities tests are status scores also.

The primary purpose of status scores is to help in identifying intraindividual differences in achievement (or ability) across tests in a battery. For example, Vic's percentile rank of 14 in vocabulary indicates a relative weakness compared with a reading percentile rank of 42. Science might be considered a strength for Vic and math a weakness if his science stanine score is 7 and his math stanine is 4. Of course, such comparisons are legitimate only when the same reference group has been used.

Note that the use of status scores to monitor year to year progress can mask growth. For example, a student whose reading percentile rank is 87 this year will obtain a similar score next year if normal growth occurs. The sameness conveyed by status scores in this situation could be misinterpreted to mean that no change occurred. In fact, a score of about 87 next year would indicate the student's achievement changed as much as the achievements of others in the norm group. (See the guideline's shown in Chapter 17 for interpreting percentile rank changes.)

Developmental Scores

Developmental scores indicate how a student's test performance compares with those of others in a series of related reference groups (Hoover, 1983). These groups differ systematically and developmentally in average achievement and are defined in terms of school grade or chronological age. Score scales most frequently used to express developmental level include grade-equivalents, age-equivalents, and developmental standard scores (sometimes called expanded standard scores).

Grade-equivalent scores are most appropriately used in grades K to 9 with school subjects that are studied continuously over several years at increasing levels of skill and complexity. To obtain a table of grade equivalents, the test must be given to a large number of students in each of the several grades for which it is intended. Then the median raw score of students in each grade is determined. The raw score is assigned a grade-equivalent score that expresses the grade level and month in that grade in which the raw score was obtained. For example, if the median raw score of third graders tested at the end of October was 22.0, then a grade equivalent of 3.2 would be assigned to that raw score. If the median raw score obtained by fourth graders on the same test at the same time was 30.3, then a grade equivalent of 4.2 would be assigned to that raw score. (Does it make sense that a raw score of 26.0 would be assigned a grade equivalent of 3.7?) Grade equivalents usually are expressed to the nearest tenth, each tenth corresponding roughly to one month of schooling in a school year of approximately 10 months. A grade equivalent of 7.4, for example, represents the median performance of seventh graders at the end of the fourth month.[1] Table 16–1 shows the grade-equivalent score assigned to the typical student in each grade for each of three testing times. Note the average growth rate from year to year is 1.0 and that the same uniform growth is assumed throughout each year.

Grade-equivalent scores can be used to describe a student's developmental level, in terms of school grades, and to measure growth from year to year. But they are less useful for examining relative strengths and weaknesses because, as Table 16–2 illustrates, variability in each test area is different for a given grade group. For example, all sixth graders whose raw scores are at the median in the fall have GE = 6.2, no matter which test area we consider. But performance at the 95th percentile corresponds to a GE of 9.2 for spelling and a GE of 8.0 for math computation. If we looked only at grade equivalents to make judgments about strengths and weaknesses, in this example we would erroneously consider spelling a strength, relative to math computation. Because sixth graders are more homogeneous in math computation achievement than in spelling, the range of grade equivalents needed to describe the bulk of this grade group is 4.2 to 8.0 and 3.2 to 9.2, respectively.

Developmental standard scores are similar to grade equivalents in function and have the same advantages and disadvantages of most other types of derived scores. The developmental standard scores shown in Table 16–3 have average growth rates that decrease as students progress through the grades. These

Table 16–1. Grade-equivalent Scores for Median Performance at Each of Three Times of Year in Each Grade

Time of Year	GRADE								
	K	1	2	3	4	5	6	7	8
Fall	K.2	1.2	2.2	3.2	4.2	5.2	6.2	7.2	8.2
Midyear	K.5	1.5	2.5	3.5	4.5	5.5	6.5	7.5	8.5
Spring	K.8	1.8	2.8	3.8	4.8	5.8	6.8	7.8	8.8

[1] As will be seen in the examples used later, some publishers drop the decimal point when reporting a student's grade equivalent. For example 7.4 and 74 would be interpreted in exactly the same way.

Table 16-2. Differences in Grade-equivalent
Distributions by Test Areas

	GRADE-EQUIVALENT SCORE		
Percentile Rank	Vocabulary	Spelling	Math Computation
95	8.7	9.2	8.0
60	6.6	6.7	6.5
50	6.2	6.2	6.2
40	5.7	5.7	5.9
5	3.5	3.2	4.2

Note: These scores are based on performance in fall of grade 6 on the *Iowa Tests of Basic Skills.*

particular scores, used with the *Iowa Tests of Basic Skills,* illustrate a significant limitation of all developmental standard score scales. There is no meaning or interpretation built into a score. What does a score of 120 mean for a fourth grader tested in April? Without access to a chart, like Table 16–3, we would need to know these things: (1) median performance in fall of grade 3 is defined as 100, (2) median performance in fall of grade 8 is defined as 160, and (3) average annual growth for grades 3 to 8 is 12. Developmental standard scores are not widely used because of the extra baggage required to interpret them and because they are so unfamiliar to teachers and parents.

Grade-equivalent scores are fairly easy to interpret because they are tied to a score scale that is understood by individuals who have little sophistication with tests or statistics. They are subject to misinterpretation just as are status scores, but there is no convincing evidence that developmental scores are more grossly misused or misinterpreted than are status scores (Hoover, 1983). The use of common sense and some basic knowledge about developmental scales are the key ingredients to responsible interpretation of grade-equivalent scores. An example will illustrate.

If Jonnette, a bright fifth-grade girl, gets a grade-equivalent score of 8.4 on an arithmetic test designed for grades 5 and 6, how should her score be interpreted? Chances are this test was not administered to eighth graders, so the value 8.4 is the estimated grade equivalent (by the process of extrapolation). The typical

Table 16-3. Developmental Standard Scores for Median Performance at Each
of Three Times of Year in Each Grade

Time of Year	GRADE								
	K	1	2	3	4	5	6	7	8
Fall	56	73	87	100	112	124	136	148	160
Midyear	60	77	91	104	116	128	140	152	164
Spring	64	81	95	108	120	132	144	156	168
Average growth		17	14	13	12	12	12	12	12

student in the eighth grade, fourth month would score about the same as Jonnette did on this test. However, this does not mean Jonnette can do the same arithmetic as the typical eighth grader. She would need to take a test designed for eighth graders for us to know how she would perform on arithmetic content studied by eighth graders. Students who obtain grade-equivalent scores significantly above or below their own grade level should be retested with a higher or lower test form if the user wishes to obtain more precise indications of their developmental levels. Often the percentile rank, a status indicator, is helpful in making judgments about the value of out-of-level testing for a particular student.

Score Profiles

Only if scores on the several tests used are comparable is a profile of student scores meaningful. Scores will be comparable if they are expressed on the same status score scale (all percentile ranks or all the same type of standard score) and if the same reference (norm) group is used for each one. An example of one student's score profile is shown in Figure 16–1. The horizontal lines on the chart represent various percentile ranks, spaced as they would be if the trait being measured by the scores was normally distributed. There is a vertical line on the chart for each test in the battery. The percentile rank values shown across the top of the chart for each test are marked as dots on the corresponding vertical scales and connected by lines to form the profile. Larry Hill's performance is about average, overall. (His percentile rank for the total test is 52.) His highest achievement levels (relative strengths) are in reading, vocabulary, and work-study skills. His lowest (relative weaknesses) are in language and mathematics.

Profiles are most useful for identifying individual needs of students and for vocational and educational planning. A profile also might be used to identify students who should be tested more extensively or to determine if impressions formed from classroom testing and observation are confirmed. Profiles represent a very compact form of visual communication that makes them convenient for reporting and explaining test results to both students and parents. (Additional examples of profiles can be found in Chapter 17.)

Percentile Bands

In an attempt to stress the fact that test scores are subject to error, some test publishers choose not to report an exact percentile rank for each test score. Instead, they provide a range of values within which the "true" percentile rank probably lies. This range is called a *percentile band.* For example, the test manual may show that the percentile rank for a test score of 63 is between the values 28 and 57; it may go on to stress that the exact percentile rank equivalent is unknown, since it depends on the unknown size and sign (positive or negative) of the error of measurement in the individual's score.

The principle employed in computing percentile bands is the same one involved in using the standard error of measurement (Chapter 5) to find the raw-score range in which the true score probably lies. The width of the percentile band depends on two factors, the reliability of the scores and the degree of certainty that the band includes the true value. Low score reliability or high degrees

Iowa Tests of Basic Skills Form G, H, or J

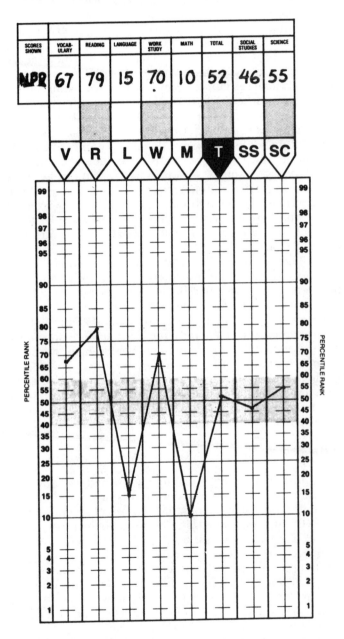

SCORES SHOWN	VOCAB-ULARY	READING	LANGUAGE	WORK STUDY	MATH	TOTAL	SOCIAL STUDIES	SCIENCE
NPR	67	79	15	70	10	52	46	55

NOTE: Each school decides for itself which norms (percentile ranks) are most meaningful. If a label showing ranks appears above, the type of norms used is printed on it (NPR = percentile rank among pupils in the nation; LPR = percentile rank in the local school system; etc.).

Figure 16-1. Sample Student Profile Chart

BCDEFGHIJ-PR-89

of certainty lead to wide percentile bands. Unfortunately, the broader these percentile bands are, the less useful is the information the test provides.

One use of percentile bands in a battery of tests is in deciding whether or not a difference between any two scores of an examinee is large enough to be meaningful. Most manuals suggest that if two percentile bands overlap there is probably insufficient reason to conclude that achievements in the two areas differ. If they do not overlap it is safe to regard the scores as truly different. The purpose of these recommendations is to guard against attaching too much importance to score differences that might be due solely to errors of measurement.

The score report in Figure 16–2 demonstrates the use of percentile bands on scores for Alison Babka from the *Iowa Tests of Basic Skills*. In the upper-right portion of the table, Alison's national percentile rank (NPR) is shown in the second column and the percentile band is plotted in the graph to the right. For vocabulary, for example, Alison's rank appears to be in the range of 59 to 79, which means there is a 50 percent probability that her "true" NPR in vocabulary is in the range.[2] In the bottom of the report are percentile rank bands for skill scores from each test area. Why are some bands wider than others? Why doesn't a percent correct score of 100 always have a percentile rank band at the top of the "HIGH" area?

There is a possibility of underinterpreting test scores using percentile bands, just as one might overinterpret scores without the use of bands. In cases where a test yields highly reliable scores, relatively wide bands may result from selecting high levels of confidence for interpretation. In such cases the user might be better off relying on the percentile rank if additional information is available for decision making. Generally, the larger a score difference, the more confident the user can be that a corresponding achievement difference actually exists. But such interpretations usually are made in a decision-making context using other corroborative test data or auxiliary information pertinent to the decision. When only a test score is available as the basis for making an important decision about an examinee, and this should be an extremely rare occasion, percentile bands are more likely to help than to hinder the process.

Subtest Scores

Just as tests that constitute a test battery provide separate measures of different aspects of achievement, so it is possible to subdivide a single test into separately scored parts to obtain measures of several unique skills. The report in Figure 16–2 demonstrates this. The desire to obtain as much information as possible from a test sometimes leads the test developer to offer a large number of skill scores, each of which may be based on only a few test items. There are two cautions to note with regard to interpreting such skill or subtest scores. First, as the number of separate scores increases, the reliability of each probably diminishes. On many tests, a subtest score based on as few as 10 or 15 items may measure sampling error more than it does true achievement. The percentile bands in Figure 16–2 help alert the user to this possibility.

[2]This report uses a probable error of measurement, a 50 percent confidence band, rather than a standard error of measurement, a 68 percent band. A probable error is approximately two-thirds the size of a standard error.

The Riverside Publishing Company

Iowa Tests of Basic Skills

SERVICE 12:
INDIVIDUAL PERFORMANCE PROFILE

Pupil: BABKA, ALISON
I.D. No:
Class/Group:
Building: MRS NEWTON
DEERFIELD
CRYSTAL FALLS
System: 11 Form G
Norms: FALL
Order No: 000-010192-001

Grade 5
Test Date 10/86
Level: II Form G
Page 2

Figure 16-2. Sample Individual Performance Profile Illustrating Percentile Bands

295

The second caution relates to the validity of subtest scores. When subtest scores are provided, as is true with many single-subject reading tests, the developer should provide subtest intercorrelations in the test manual to show how similar or different the subtests actually are. If the correlations are too high, for example, the subtests are all likely to be measuring the same unitary trait or skill. The responsible test user should focus interpretations on total-test scores in such cases and ignore the availability of the subtest scores.

NORMS

Norms, which report how students actually do perform, should not be confused with *standards,* which represent estimates of how well they should perform. For example, the standard of correctness in arithmetic calculation in most classes is 100 percent, but the norm (average) of student achievement on a given computation test may be only 85 percent. Often the average performance takes on the function of a standard. That is, the average becomes the criterion against which the scores of individuals are judged to determine the score meaning and value. Consequently, few students are regarded as failures in an area of study if their performance is above the norm (or average), and few are regarded as successes if their performance is below it.

Norms are sometimes confused with the various types of scores that are used to report them. Percentile ranks, stanines, grade equivalents, and standard scores are all types of scores, derived from raw scores, to report normative performance; they are not norms themselves. Norms are differentiated by certain characteristics of the reference group that comprise them. There are age norms and grade norms, local norms and national norms, group norms and individual norms, to name only a few. It is possible to combine the characteristics of a norm group in a variety of ways in an attempt to build highly differentiated norm groups. For example, the National Assessment of Educational Progress (NAEP) reports normative performance based on age, geographic region, race, gender, and community type. We could find out how white nine-year-old boys from the rural West score on test exercises, but seldom is it worthwhile to use so many variables in combination to describe test performance. (And, fortunately, NAEP does not use that many classification variables in a single comparison.)

To be accurate, test norms must be based on the scores of large and representative samples of examinees who have been tested under standard conditions, and who take the test as seriously as will other students for whom the norms are needed. The three R's most often used to judge the appropriateness of a set of norms for a given testing situation are *representativeness, relevance,* and *recency.*

Norms obviously must be obtained from students in schools that are willing to take time out from their other responsibilities to help with the norming administration. That very willingness may make them somewhat atypical of the national population of schools and students. To get enough participation from schools to provide a reasonably large norm group is a difficult undertaking. To make it a representative sample is even harder. First, the developer must decide which population the norm sample is supposed to represent. Then the ideal sample that will represent that population must be identified, usually using the most recent census data. Finally, the cooperation of school administrators must be secured and the students in the sample must actually be tested. It is no wonder that Baglin (1981) questioned whether "nationally normed" really means *nationally*. In his review of three norming studies conducted by publishers, the percentage of invited school districts that actually took part was as low as 13 percent in one study and only as high as 32 percent in another.

Even if a set of norms adequately represents the population of students intended by the publisher, the user of that test may not be interested in making comparisons with that particular population. For example, teachers in selective private high schools probably have little interest in representative national norms because nearly all their students would score at or near the 99th percentile. They would rather use norms that help differentiate their better and poorer students. That is, a more relevant set of norms would be students from a representative sample of private high schools in each of four regions of the country— East, South, Midwest, and West.

Finally the steady annual increases in achievement seen nationwide over the past decade have made recency of norms a highly controversial topic. The problem is this. When dated norms are used to make comparisons during a period of increasing achievement, norm-referenced scores will overestimate performance. Figure 16–3 depicts the situation.

The Oxford Schools gave an achievement battery in 1991 that had been standardized (normed) in 1987. The mean grade equivalent of the Oxford fifth graders was 58.9, or a percentile rank for school norms of about 81. That is, 81 percent of the school buildings nationally (fifth-grade classes) had lower average scores than Oxford. But this ranking is based on 1987 performances, the distribution of school building averages nationally in 1987. The frequency polygons in Figure 16–3 for each of the years 1988–1991 show how the national distributions of achievement *would have changed* if the test had been given to the norm group in each of those years. (But it wasn't.) The solid line connects the hypothetical average scores of the norm group in successive years. Note that Oxford's 1991 mean of 58.9 is just slightly above the norm group's 1991 average. (The percentile rank is probably about 55.) In 1991 grade-equivalents terms, Oxford's average is probably more like 53.1, just above the national mean. In fact, had current norms been available, Oxford's percentile rank would have been most accurately described as 55, not 81. What would happen during a period of decreasing achievement if outdated norms were used? If achievement is steady over a long period, are dated norms problematic?

The administration of tests to obtain normative data can take significant amounts of time away from the schools' other important activities. The reluctance of schools to cooperate is somewhat understandable, but it would be quite wrong for administrators and teachers to believe that test administration has no direct educational value for the participating students. A school that "doesn't have time" to cooperate in the tryout or norming of a standardized test suitable to its students' abilities must have a phenomenal program and must be making amazingly good use of teacher and student time. Unfortunately, some of these

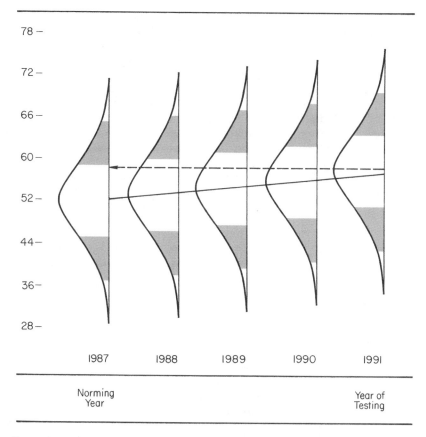

Figure 16-3. The Effect of Outdated Norms for School Averages in a Period of Increasing Achievement

same schools complain of the irrelevant or dated norms provided by the publishers from whom they must select their standardized tests.

Individual versus Group Norms

A somewhat serious error that some test users make is to use norms composed of individual student scores to interpret average scores from school buildings, school districts, or some other aggregate. Although the mean of the school averages for a norm group should be about the same as the mean for the individual student scores, the school averages are likely to be far less variable than the student scores. The standard deviation of the school means will be smaller than that for the student scores. For example, the *average* score in a truly excellent school may be lower than the scores obtained by one-fifth of the students in all schools in the norm group, and the average score in a very poor school may be better than the scores of one-fifth of all students. In other words, when such inappropriate interpretations are made, the percentile ranks of the school averages are not likely ever to be lower than 20 or higher than 80. The most extreme degrees of excellence or deficiency are likely to be underestimated drastically. The most ideal basis for evaluation of school averages, a type of treatment-referenced interpretation, is a separate table of norms for school averages. And the quality of school norms should be judged by the same criteria of relevance, representativeness, and recency as were recommended for individual student norms. Figure 16–3 exemplifies the predicament that can develop when dated norms for school averages are used.

SELECTION OF STANDARDIZED TESTS

Sources of Information

For those who wish to identify published and unpublished tests that measure a particular trait, or those who seek descriptive information or critical reviews of existing measures, a wide variety of sources is available. Most information will be found in print but much of it is accessible through computer retrieval systems as well.

The *Mental Measurements Yearbook* (MMY) generally is regarded as the most comprehensive source of information about published tests. The tenth edition (Conoley and Kramer, 1990), the most current printed edition at the time of this writing, includes such descriptive information about each test as author, publication date, number of forms and levels, number of scores reported, administration time required, and prices for tests and scoring services. In addition, critical reviews by testing specialists and a bibliography identifying research studies in which the measure was used are provided. *Tests in Print III* (Mitchell, 1983) is a summary reference to information detailed in all the *MMY*s published previously. (The fourth edition is scheduled to be published in 1991.)

The Buros Institute of Mental Measurements has made several changes to reduce the severe publication lag that plagued earlier volumes of the *MMY*. First, a biennial publication schedule has begun, and paperback supplements are provided in the alternate years. This means information about current tests is updated in print every year. Second, all *MMY* information is accessible on-line using Biliographic Retrieval Services (BRS). The system (MMYD) is updated continually so that a computer search will uncover the most recent descriptive and evaluative information about available tests.

Another source of descriptive information about published tests, *Tests: A Comprehensive Reference for Assessment in Psychology, Education, and Business,* is a cumulative listing that contains over 3100 entries (Keyser and Sweetland, 1990). A companion publication, *Test Critiques,* provides comprehensive reviews that include recommended applications, technical information, and an overall critique. At the date of this writing, seven volumes had been published (Keyser and Sweetland, 1985–1990).

The most current information about standardized tests is in publisher catalogs and the tests themselves. Those who are charged with selecting tests for a school testing program should review a specimen set for each test under consideration. For a nominal fee, the publisher will provide a copy of one form of the test and the accompanying test manuals to individuals who are authorized to use standardized tests. Publisher representatives can answer questions about their tests and processing services through either telephone inquiries or school visits requested by the test-selection committee.

Some tests have been reviewed by measurement specialists in professional publications like the *Journal of Educational Measurement* or *Measurement and Evaluation in Guidance*. These reviews, as well as validity studies published in *Educational and Psychological Measurement*, can be identified readily through a computerized literature search of *Current Index to Journals in Education* (CIJE) for a very modest price.

Finally, college and university faculty members in education and psychology departments often are available to consult with school personnel regarding test selection and use. Some universities are willing to provide consultation and test-scoring services to school districts through their campus measurement and test-scoring centers. The same services are supplied by some state education departments through area or regional centers established throughout the state to serve school districts.

Selection Criteria

Sources of information available to committees or individuals responsible for selecting standardized tests were described in the previous section. But what information should be sought from these sources and how should the information be weighed in arriving at a selection decision?

Validity. Without question, test content—what the items or test tasks require the examinee to know—is the most important factor to assess. How well the tests or subtests match the curriculum in terms of content coverage and emphasis must be determined in selecting achievement tests. For tests of aptitude and intelligence, a review of the item content is still a significant source of validity evidence. The item types used should be familiar to students, the format of the tests should make them easy for students to use, and the diagrams and figures employed should be legible in terms of size and clarity.

Technical adequacy. A test that has been judged to be sufficiently valid to allow the district to accomplish its purposes for testing should be scrutinized further for technical adequacy. The reliability of test and subtest scores should be assessed from data supplied in the technical manual and comments made by reviewers of the test. Data should be provided in the manual about the equivalency of alternate test forms that may be available. When developmental scores are provided, the user should search for evidence that sufficient data were gathered in the norming process so that reliance on interpolation and extrapolation in scaling the scores was not too great. Sufficient information should be supplied in the manual to permit users to decide that the three R's for evaluating norms are satisfactory.

Practical considerations. Tests that survive a validity and technical screening should be evaluated in terms of certain other important considerations. Schools do not have unlimited funds, but cost should not carry more weight in the decision than validity or technical adequacy. If necessary, trade-offs in scoring and reporting services should be made so that the district can use the most valid measures available. In addition, test administration time required should be weighed in relation to direct instructional time lost. The adequacy of the manuals and other publisher aids for users should be assessed. Finally, tests under consideration should be viewed in terms of the entire district testing program. Is there an appropriate achievement battery available that also was normed on the same group that was used to norm the cognitive abilities test that is under consideration? Is the elementary school battery that is under review linked to a battery that could be used at the middle school or secondary school level? Of course, this question is relevant only to the extent that the upper-level batteries themselves have been judged to be appropriate in validity and technical quality.

The test selection committee must work systematically to gather, organize, and summarize the data about each test under consideration. The topics listed in Appendix D are appropriate for developing in-service programs to help a test-selection committee accomplish the wide range of tasks it faces.

SUMMARY PROPOSITIONS

1. A standardized test is one that has been expertly and carefully constructed, is administered and scored under standard (uniform) conditions, and provides tables of norms for score interpretation.
2. Achievement-test batteries provide for comprehensive coverage of achievements and for comparable scores in different areas of achievement.
3. Single-subject tests provide greater breadth and depth of coverage than their counterparts included in a battery.
4. Status scores permit norm-referenced interpretations and are needed to make intraindividual comparisons from the results of a test battery.
5. Developmental scores depend on the use of multiple reference groups and are most useful for elementary school subjects that are studied continuously over several school years.
6. A grade-equivalent score in arithmetic of 7.4 for a fifth-grade girl on a fifth-grade test does not mean that she is ready for seventh-grade mathematics.
7. Grade-equivalent scores are useful for representing students' year to year growth but not so useful for identifying their relative strengths and weaknesses.
8. A profile of test scores indicates the student's general level of achievement, as well as his or her specific strengths and weaknesses.
9. Percentile bands call attention to the presence of

error in educational measurements but may complicate or distort the interpretation of the results somewhat.
10. Subtest intercorrelations provide evidence about the extent to which the subtests are measures of unique achievements.
11. Part scores from a single test must be sufficiently reliable to be useful.
12. Norms report what is, and standards report what ought to be, but national norms sometimes function as a kind of local standard.
13. To be accurate, test norms must be based on large and representative samples of examinees, tested under standard conditions.
14. The adequacy of test norms depends on their recency, especially in periods of achievement rise or fall within the norm population.
15. Individual-student norms are less appropriate than school norms to use for the interpretation of school or district-average scores.
16. Both descriptive and evaluative information about particular standardized tests can be found in print or can be accessed using a computer retrieval system.
17. Systematic procedures for selecting a standardized measure should give high priority to validity evidence, technical adequacy, and such practical considerations as time requirements and cost.

QUESTIONS FOR STUDY AND DISCUSSION

1. Which characteristics of standardized tests are most significant for tests that will be used to make criterion-referenced interpretations?

2. Why might the national norm groups of two different publishers yield different scores (means and standard deviations) if the groups were given a common test?

3. Why are achievement batteries generally less useful at the high school than elementary school level?

4. If a math test providing three separate scores has intercorrelations of 0.79, 0.85, and 0.83 between subtests, what are the implications for score interpretation?

5. Why should T-scores be regarded as status scores rather than developmental scores?

6. Why might grade-equivalent scores be less useful for interpreting scores of high school seniors than those of third graders?

7. If a sixth grader is working at the level of the typical fourth grader, is it more appropriate to test the student with a test battery designed for grade 4 or grade 6? Explain your response.

8. What is the meaning of a score profile, using percentile ranks, that forms a straight horizontal line?

9. Why are percentile-rank bands particularly useful in interpreting skill or subtest scores?

10. What are the differences between national stanine norms and local percentile rank norms?

11. During a period of national achievement score decline, what impact will the use of dated norms have on the interpretations of students' scores?

12. What does it mean when a school's average score of 33.5 for grade 2 science has a national percentile rank of 97?

13. In what sources are you likely to find the most current critical review of a standardized achievement test?

17

Using Standardized Achievement Tests

There are good reasons why this chapter focuses on *use,* rather than on selecting tests, describing sample test content, or administering and scoring tests. These are all important aspects of standardized achievement testing, but none is so critical as the use of tests and the scores derived from them. The climate of the 1990s threatens valid test use because there is too much testing for purposes for which tests were not designed, and there is too little appreciation for the limited precision with which we are able to measure educational attainments. Consequently, attention in this chapter will be directed toward (1) an analysis of the legitimate uses of standardized achievement tests, (2) illustrations and explanations of score interpretation, (3) planning topics for in-service work in test selection, administration, and interpretation, and (4) an exploration of some issues that affect the quality of a school testing program.

THE STATUS OF STANDARDIZED ACHIEVEMENT TESTING

The great irony of standardized achievement testing today is that, while these tests are being overused to fulfill state and local legislative mandates, their results are being underutilized in serving the instructional needs of teachers and students. To be sure, many school districts have carefully developed testing programs with systematic procedures for interpreting and reporting their test results. But in too many cases the schools are required to give certain tests so that results can be made available for such purposes as interstate and interdistrict comparisons, teacher and administrator personnel decisions, and pupil retention judgments. The many information seekers—legislators, school board members, parent groups, business leaders, and school administrators and teachers—do not share the same agenda and do not, therefore, have need for the same types of information.

Teachers and administrators generally make less use of standardized achievement-test results then they could for two reasons. First, educators tend to understand far less about tests and test scores than would be desirable. Their educational preparation programs and in-service education seldom address the essentials of testing and evaluation. Consequently, teachers often can devote less time than is needed to understand the meaning of test results and to incorporate the information in their instructional planning. Second, teachers who face harsh consequences because of low scores on mandated tests must invest the bulk of their energy and instructional time to preparing their students to do well in the areas (usually reading and math) covered by the accountability assessment. As a result, even if other test scores point to areas of weakness, these teachers cannot afford to split their efforts away from the "high-stakes" mandated assessment.

Part of the explanation for the overdependence on tests by the public has been the "institutionalization" of the standardized achievement test. In fact, Levine (1976) argued that the achievement test has become so uncritically accepted among many educators and the general public that its validity "as a measure of educational accomplishment is virtually unquestioned." To some extent, unfortunately, he may be correct. We do seem ready to question many of the measures we encounter in other aspects of our lives, particularly when they yield results inconsistent with our hopes or expectations. For example, when the bathroom scale gives a higher reading than we expect, how many of us first wonder if the scale is functioning properly? When stopped for a speeding violation, how many drivers first question the accuracy of the radar equipment? But when achievement-test results are lower than we expect, the critical finger is rarely pointed first (if ever) at the instruments themselves. Levine's point is that we may too frequently try to explain substandard test results in terms of teacher quality, funding, or physical resources, and simply assume the appropriateness of the measures that provided those results.

Another explanation for the increased use of standardized achievement tests, particularly mandated assessment, is that the celebrated National Commission on Excellence in Education recommended more. In its report, *A Nation at Risk* (1983), a specific framework with explicit purposes was given.

> Standardized tests of achievement (not to be confused with aptitude tests) should be administered at major transition points from one level of schooling to another and particularly from high school to college or work. The purposes of these tests would be to: (a) certify the student's credentials; (b) identify the need for remedial intervention; and (c) identify the opportunity for advanced or accelerated work. The tests should be administered as part of a nationwide (but not Federal) system of state and local standardized tests. (p. 28)

In outlining the evidence for concluding that we are a nation at risk, the commission reported 14 "indicators of risk," 11 of which depend on the use of standardized test scores as criteria.

Whether or not the achievement test has become an institution is debatable. What seems certain, however, is that good standardized achievement tests will continue to be needed to help educators monitor the effectiveness of their efforts and report the outcomes of their efforts to local boards and parents. Careful test selection and wise test-score interpretation and use can make positive contributions to fulfilling these needs.

USES OF ACHIEVEMENT-TEST RESULTS

Standardized achievement-test scores provide a special kind of information on the extent of student learning. It is special because it is based on a consensus of expert teachers with respect to what ought to be learned in the study of a specific subject, a consensus external to and independent of the local teachers. It thus provides a basis for comparing local achievements with external norms of achievement in similar classes. It is useful information because it helps to inform students, teachers, administrators, and the public at large of the effectiveness of the educational efforts in their schools.

Schools sometimes have been criticized for setting up testing programs, giving and scoring the tests, and then doing nothing with the test scores except to file them in the principal's office. If the school faculty and the individual teachers do not study the test results to identify levels and ranges of achievement in the school as a whole and within specific classes; if they do not single out students of high and low achievement; and if the scores are not reported and interpreted to students, parents, and the public, these criticisms are justifiable. But if the critics mean that no coherent program of action triggered specifically by the test results and designed to "do something" about them emerged from the testing program, then the criticisms probably are not justified.

What a good school faculty "does" about standardized test scores is something like what good citizens do with information they glean from a newspaper. Having finished the evening paper, they do not lay it aside and ask themselves, "Now what am I going to do about all this, about the weather, the accidents, the crimes, the legislative decisions, the clothing sales, the stock market reports, the baseball games won and lost, and all the rest?" They may, of course, plan specific actions in response to one or two items. But most of what is memorable they simply add to their store of latent knowledge. In hundreds of unplanned ways it will affect the opinions they express later, the votes they cast, and the other decisions they make. Information can be very useful ultimately, even when it triggers no immediate response.

Educators who properly deplore judging teacher competence solely on the basis of students' test scores sometimes fail to see that it is equally unwise to take action on school or student problems solely on the basis of those same test scores. Seldom do standardized test scores by themselve provide sufficient guidance for wise and effective educational actions. It follows that these test scores should be regarded primarily as sources of useful information, not as major stimuli and guides to immediate action.

A school faculty or teacher who sees the need and has the opportunity should not hesitate to develop a program for action based partly on the scores provided by standardized tests of achievement. But neither should feel that the testing was a waste of time unless such a program is developed. The immediate purpose to be served by standardized test scores is the provision of instructional information, information that can contribute to the wisdom of a host of specific actions stimulated by other educational needs and developments.

Purposes for Testing

All achievement tests—whether standardized or teacher made—are mainly tools of instruction. That is, they are designed on the basis of the goals of instruction, and their results are intended to show the extent of progress toward those goals. Standardized achievement-test batteries provide surveys of the extent of learning in each of several curricular areas; their scores are expected to improve the decisions teachers make about students. The assumption is that teachers will make better instructional decisions about students *with* such test scores than they would *without* them (Hieronymus and Hoover, 1986). Scores are not intended to supplant teachers' judgments. Instead, they may help to confirm suspicions and expectations, they may provide conflicting information that should trigger reassessment, or they may point out the need for further, more detailed information.

The purposes outlined by the authors of the *Iowa Tests of Basic Skills* indicate the importance of serving instructional needs and, by their absence, the inappropriateness of using such tests for a variety of accountability functions (Hieronymus and Hoover, 1990, p. 1):

1. Describe the developmental level of students so that instructional materials and procedures can be adapted to individuals
2. Diagnose individual strengths and weaknesses in educational development across subject areas and skills within subject areas
3. Determine the extent of readiness to begin instruction, to proceed in an instructional sequence, or to move to an accelerated level of instruction
4. Inform administrative decisions in grouping individuals to accommodate individualized instruction
5. Diagnose group strengths and weaknesses for adjusting curricular content, emphasis, or approach
6. Determine the relative effectiveness of alternate methods or programs of instruction
7. Determine the effectiveness of innovative programs or experimental approaches
8. Provide a means for developing reasonable expectations for student achievement and for describing progress toward such goals
9. Describe student achievement in terms that are meaningful to parents, students, and the general public

Examples of some of these specific purposes will describe how achievement-test scores can be used to select students for remedial attention or for enrichment opportunities, for readiness for planned instruction, or for diagnosing difficulties.

Chapter 1 Selection and Evaluation

Chapter 1 (Title 1) federal dollars are available to schools to operate re-mediation programs in reading and math for students who qualify. The legislation authorizing the expenditures provides that only certain standardized reading (mathematics) tests—from a battery or single-subject test—can be used to identify students eligible for participation. Many schools use the reading (math) score from the administration of a norm-referenced battery to conduct their needs assessment (for example, decide which students qualify for the program as "low achievers").

Program-evaluation procedures, also legislated, require pre–post testing with a standardized test as well. But the pretest and qualifying scores must be from different administrations if they are from the same test. Though all this requires three administrations of the test (not the whole battery) each year, at least one of those can be from the traditional annual battery administration, as long as it occurs during the prescribed dates.

Note that an informal reading inventory, like those described in Chapter 14, could not be used to select eligible program participants. Selection is based on scoring below the 40th percentile, using national norms, and inventories do not provide such normative information. In addition, if local norms were permitted, the lowest 40 percent in *every* school would qualify, regardless of their absolute levels of achievement.

Talented and Gifted Selection

Many school districts provide enrichment activities or before- and after-school programs for talented and gifted (TAG) students. The procedures used to identify eligible students vary among districts, and the selection variables and cutoff scores are often controversial local issues. Standardized achievement-test scores often do, and probably should, be one of several pieces of information considered in the selection process. For example, a typical selection rule might require that one of these conditions be met:

1. Earn a composite score national percentile rank of at least 95 on the *Stanford Achievement Test*
2. Earn a verbal standard age score of at least 125 on the *Cognitive Abilities Test*
3. Be recommended by your teacher *and* be recommended by your parent(s)

A serious drawback of using a high composite score cutoff, as illustrated above, is that it may exclude students who excel in one particular area (for example, science, math, or one of the performing arts). When programs having a narrow focus are provided, as a writing program, then selection involving a test score should depend on a subject-matter score rather than a composite.

It is important that TAG selection criteria permit the use of information other than test scores. Scores from standardized achievement tests are subject to error and those from a single subject, like science, may be based on performance during a 35-minute period on one particular day. In addition, success in TAG programs depends on such nonacademic variables as interest, motivation, persistence, and independence. The nature of the program, the demand for participation, and the extent of local resources may vary enough over time to warrant setting separate criteria for the various TAG program strands available.

Kindergarten Readiness

Standardized achievement-test scores are *not* useful for deciding who should be selected for kindergarten attendance and who should either wait a year or go to prekindergarten. Such placement decisions should be made using information that a readiness test cannot provide. Children who are not ready for kindergarten are those who have some kind of developmental deficit—physical, emotional, social—that needs special attention (or time, in the judgment of some) that the regular kindergarten program does not (and cannot) offer.

Standardized readiness tests are achievement batteries; they do not measure the traits on which the placement decision *should* hinge. Readiness tests tend to measure academic skills in listening, letters and sounds, listening vocabulary, language, and math concepts. Children who show deficiencies in such skills often have not had a preschool or home environment that nourished such skills. But these are cognitive abilities that can be learned relatively quickly, given some concentrated effort by student and teacher. The main value of readiness scores is to provide a picture of student strengths and weaknesses, at the skill level, and to describe the readiness in each subject area of the class of students. Thus, readiness tests are most useful when given in the mid-fall, a time that allows plenty of opportunity for using the results to plan instructional activities in concert with the strengths and weaknesses identified through testing.

Finally, for reasons similar to those cited immediately above, readiness scores obtained in the spring of kindergarten are not useful for making first-grade placement decisions. Decisions to retain, to place in a transitional program, or to promote are not likely to be aided by readiness-test scores. Shepard and Smith (1986) have argued that retention at this decision point has only negative consequences for most students, no matter what criterion is used. Students who show severe weaknesses in prereading skills—listening, letter recognition, letter–sound association, and language relational concepts—may need temporary individual-program plans to remediate their deficiencies. But certainly other considerations should inform the retention decisions, not solely the academic deficiencies of kindergarten.

Diagnosis of Learning Difficulties

Standardized achievement batteries are *not* designed to be diagnostic aids that provide detailed information for work with *individual* students. However, most do provide considerable group diagnostic information, particularly those that display results in special reports that show average test-item scores or average skill scores within tests. Instructional planning for a class can be enhanced by taking such data into account, instructional materials can be selected or developed to improve learning in deficient areas, and time can be reallocated from topics on which students have demonstrated higher levels of accomplishment.

Any achievement test can provide "diagnostic" information of value to individual students if they are told which items they missed. With the teacher's help, these students can then correct the mistakes or misconceptions that led them astray. Highly specific "diagnosis" and "remediation" of this sort can be effective and is often accomplished with classroom achievement tests. But such feedback and discussion are impractical, if not impossible, with standardized tests.

One reason for the lack of success in educational diagnosis in most fields other than elementary reading and arithmetic is that most learning difficulties are not attributable to specific or easily correctable disorders. Instead, they usually result from accumulations of incomplete learning and of distaste for learning. Neither of these causes is hard to recognize; neither is easy to cure. Diagnosis is not the real problem, and diagnostic testing can do little to solve that problem.

Another reason for this lack of success in educational diagnosis is that effective diagnosis and remediation take a great deal more time than most teachers have or most students would be willing to devote. The diagnosing of reading difficulties is a well-developed skill, and remedial treatments can be very effective. Because reading is so basic to other learning, the time required for diagnosis and remediation is often spent ungrudgingly. But where the subject of study is more advanced and more specialized, the best solution to learning difficulties in an area, say algebra, physics, or German, may be to put off study in that area and cultivate learning in other areas that present fewer problems.

Standardized diagnostic tests in both reading and math are achievement tests used by reading or math specialists to gain information about the learning problems of individual students. These tests are built to allow test takers to demonstrate certain kinds of errors or misconceptions held by students who are having difficulties in reading (or arithmetic computation). Often the results of the subject matter test in a battery indicate a general problem, and the diagnostic test is administered to ascertain the specific deficits in terms of skills and subskills. Unfortunately, diagnostic tests, like other achievement tests, help to identify problem areas, but they seldom provide reasons for the difficulties and cannot prescribe solutions to overcome them. A major challenge to the teacher is to synthesize the entering behavior information about a student so that the instructional strategies and materials can be selected that will optimize that student's conditions for learning.

INTERPRETING SCORES OF INDIVIDUALS

Most test publishers offer such a wide variety of score reports and scoring services that schools sometimes have difficulty deciding which ones they should order. The process of deciding can be simplified if a school first reviews its purposes for testing. Such a review will help to identify who needs information—teachers, counselors, administrators, parents—and what kind of information is needed—pupil test and skill scores, building average scores, system-wide averages, classroom percent scores, and so on. The list of needs may seem almost endless, but the review process will help to rule out many reports that are either similar to one another or simply not needed. There is good reason to believe that the underutilization of scores by teachers is due in part to the inconvenient format in which the scores are reported to them. Of course, part of the reason for the inadequate reporting is that teachers are seldom consulted about report formats that would be most helpful to them.

When test results come back to a district, nearly every teacher will receive a list report, an alphabetical listing of students and their corresponding scores. At the middle school and high school levels, reports might be arranged by class period for each English, math, science, and social studies teacher. Figure 17–1 is a sample list report showing scores for Mrs. Newton's fifth-grade class on the *Iowa Tests of Basic Skills*. A review of the scores of Alison Babka will illustrate how scores of individual pupils might be interpreted. Here are some statements that might be made about Alison's performance in the fall of fifth grade:

1. Her Complete Composite grade-equivalent score (the average of the five main scores) is 55, the same as the typical student at the end of the fifth month of fifth grade.
2. Her Complete Composite percentile rank of 60 means that 60 percent of fifth graders nationally have composite scores lower than hers.
3. In sum, Alison's overall achievement seems about average compared with other fifth graders nationally.
4. Alison's relative strengths are in areas in which her percentile rank is noticeably above her Complete Composite percentile rank—punctuation and math computation.
5. Alison's relative weaknesses are in areas in which her percentile rank is noticeably lower than her Complete Composite percentile rank—language usage, math problem solving, social studies, and science.

At this point we should be interested in the particular skills that may have contributed most to the strengths and weaknesses identified by the test scores. A report that makes such analysis possible and that provides percent-correct scores for criterion-referenced interpretation is the Student Skills Analysis report in Figure 17–2. (Note that the Individual Performance Profile report, Figure 16–2, also could be used nicely for this purpose.)

Across the top of Alison's skills report, the test scores—grade equivalents and percentile ranks—from the list report are reproduced for easy reference. The fourth column of numbers in the bottom section of the report is the percent-correct score for Alison, and the next two columns, averages for the class and the nation, permit norm-referenced comparisons. Here are some statements that might be made about Alison's performance based on skill scores:

1. Punctuation is a relative strength of Alison's, partly because of her performance with terminal punctuation and use of commas. Her other skill scores are much like those of the average student in her class.
2. Alison's math computation performance was bolstered by perfect scores on addition/subtraction of whole numbers and decimals. But whole number multiplication/division seems to be a weak skill within this generally strong area.
3. The language usage and expression weakness seems to be explained mainly by usage skills, all of which need improvement.

The Riverside Publishing Company

SERVICE 9B:
LIST REPORT OF PUPIL SCORES

Iowa Tests of Basic Skills

Class/Group MRS NEWTON
Building DEERFIELD
Bldg Code
System CRYSTAL FALLS
Norms FALL
Order No 000-010192-001

Form G
Grade 5
Test Date 10/86
Page 1

Pupil Name / ID. No.	Other Info.	Birth Date / Age	Level / Sex		VOCABULARY V	READING R	LANGUAGE SKILLS: SPELLING L-1	CAPITALIZATION L-2	PUNCTUATION L-3	USAGE L-4	TOTAL L	WORK-STUDY SKILLS: VISUAL MATERIAL W-1	REFERENCES W-2	TOTAL W	MATHEMATICS SKILLS: CONCEPTS M-1	PROBLEMS M-2	COMPUTATION M-3	TOTAL M	COMPOSITES: BASIC	COMPLETE	SOCIAL STUDIES SS	SCIENCE SC
ADEN, MATTHEW		7/76	10	GE	43	42	37	60	60	44	50	41	34	38	57	51	65	58	45	46	49	39
4099091097		10-03	(M)	NPR	28	26	17	68	68	36	46	25	11	18	66	48	92	73	31	35	44	30
BABKA, ALISON		7/76	11	GE	59	61	58	51	69	43	55	51	51	51	54	36	58	49	57	55	42	45
6101090083		10-03	(F)	NPR	69	71	64	48	83	34	58	48	48	49	57	14	75	42	65	60	31	39
BIRCH, TRENT		5/76	11	GE	65	58	54	86	79	61	70	74	55	64	67	69	58	65	60	64	78	67
8112107117		10-05	(M)	NPR	83	64	55	98	93	67	87	93	58	80	87	91	75	89	74	82	86	72
CARSTEN, DEBBIE		6/76	11	GE	100	81	77	90	92	74	83	67	80	74	76	67	56	66	81	81	100	99
9126139124		10-04	(F)	NPR	99	96	93	99	99	87	98	85	98	94	96	89	67	91	99	99	99	99
CRAY, CYNDI		9/74	11	GE	37	38	28	34	39	43	36	49	42	46	58	50	35	48	38	41	34	64
1093090094		12-01	(F)	NPR	16	18	6	12	21	34	14	43	26	36	69	45	5	39	14	21	20	68
DEGALA, SCOTT		4/76	11	GE	61	56	62	86	76			72	59	66	71	72	69	71	62		90	89
7119114127		10-06	(M)	NPR	74	60	72	98	90			91	68	84	93	94	96	96	78		95	94
DIAZ, PATRICK		5/76	11	GE	35	41	43	46	54	39	46	51	33	42	54	36	62	51	42	43	17	45
3114095106		10-05	(M)	NPR	13	24	29	36	55	27	36	48	10	26	57	14	87	49	23	26	2	39
FLAPAN, ALISA		11/75	11	GE	68	61	90	69	82	66	77	64	64	64	73	72	72	72	73	68	64	75
8113104115		10-11	(F)	NPR	88	71	99	84	95	76	95	80	78	80	94	94	97	96	95	90	70	81
GERAMI, MARTY		4/75	11	GE	19	27	37	34	44	25	35	44	22	33	44	36	37	39	30	31	54	51
1072086074		11-06	(M)	NPR	1	4	17	12	32	6	13	30	1	10	26	14	7	11	2	3	54	48
HURKA, MOLLY		12/75	11	GE	57	54	62	54	59	57	58	64	58	61	69	56	57	61	58	58	48	71
6113106110		10-10	(F)	NPR	64	55	72	55	66	60	65	80	65	74	90	62	71	81	68	68	42	77
KARR, ALLEN		11/74	10	GE	28	32	40	52	69	40	50	50	40	45	44	42	49	45	36	40	26	31
2085095090		11-11	(M)	NPR	5	8	22	50	83	28	46	45	22	33	26	24	37	28	10	19	9	18
KMOCH, MIKE		6/77	11	GE	44	38	44	49	49	41	46	62	35	48	40	50	44	45	43	44	59	36
3097094095		9-04	(M)	NPR	30	18	31	43	43	30	36	76	13	41	15	45	19	28	25	29	63	25
LIU, TAMMY		6/75	11	GE	65	72	85	79	88	66	80	49	68	58	62	61	69	64	72	68	82	75
9115112120		11-04	(F)	NPR	83	90	98	94	98	76	97	43	86	67	78	76	96	88	94	90	89	81
MELROY, JACK		5/75	11	GE	46	44	39	54	59	64	54	46	45	46	65	59	56	60	47	50	57	64
5092105101		11-05	(M)	NPR	35	30	20	55	66	72	56	35	33	36	83	70	67	78	37	46	59	68
ORTIZ, ROBERT		8/75	11	GE	40	27	33	49	39	23	36	44	30	37	44	42	45	44	36	37	30	36
1089091089		11-02	(M)	NPR	22	4	11	43	21	4	14	30	7	16	26	24	22	25	10	13	14	25
PAPKE, CARRIE		7/76	11	GE	55	46	60	82	66	57	66	59	45	52	60	58	49	56	54	55	59	60
6094111118		10-03	(F)	NPR	58	35	68	96	79	60	81	68	33	51	74	67	37	67	57	60	63	63
ROVNER, ANDREA		9/75	11	GE	46	51	47	72	69	57	61	65	49	57	58	50	53	54	50	54	51	57
6094091109		11-01	(F)	NPR	35	48	38	88	83	60	71	82	43	64	69	45	55	60	45	57	48	58
RYAN, LAURA		12/74	11	GE	47	47	47	46	54	61	52	52	42	47	44	42	48	45	46	48	34	42
3088085082		11-10	(F)	NPR	37	38	38	36	55	67	51	50	26	38	26	24	33	28	34	40	20	34
SINK, DENNIS		8/76	11	GE	54	56	71	72	82	80	76	61	58	60	65	59	57	60	60	61	45	57
8108123120		10-02	(M)	NPR	56	60	86	88	95	93	94	74	65	71	83	70	71	78	74	75	36	58
SPIRO, KATHI		6/76	11	GE	54	46	51	49	69	66	59	56	48	52	52	54	41	49	50	52	57	48
5111107112		10-04	(F)	NPR	56	35	48	43	83	76	67	61	41	51	51	56	12	42	45	51	59	44
TAO, DANIEL		4/75	11	GE	42	52	49	60	64	49	56	56	49	52	54	56	57	56	50	52	30	29
4082076083		11-06	(M)	NPR	26	50	43	68	76	45	60	61	43	51	57	62	71	67	45	51	14	15
WARING, GINNY		8/74	11	GE	40	36	58	54	54	33	50	41	33	37	52	54	50	52	46	43	22	51
2095119105		12-02	(F)	NPR	22	14	64	55	55	17	46	25	10	16	51	56	42	53	34	26	5	48
AVERAGES			ITBS:	N	22	22	22	22	22	21	21	22	22	22	22	22	22	22	22	21	22	22
				GE	50.2	48.5	53.3	60.4	64.4	51.9	57.0	55.4	47.3	51.4	57.4	53.3	54.0	55.0	51.6	52.0	51.3	56.0
PR OF AVG GE:	NATIONAL	PUPIL NORMS			46	41	53	69	76	50	63	59	39	50	67	54	59	63	50	51	49	56
	N TESTED =	22																				

GE=Grade Equivalent, NPR-S=Nat'l %ile Rank/

Figure 17-1. Sample List Report of Scores

Figure 17-2. Sample Student Skills Analysis Report

4. The weakness in math problem solving is generalized, as might have been expected from the percentile rank of 14. In view of her strength in addition/subtraction skills in math computation, the best starting point for improving problem solving may be to work on single-step problems requiring only addition or subtraction. There may be some value in looking at Alison's responses to the problem-solving test items to determine if a pattern of misunderstanding exists.

5. The social studies skills and scores provide little help in diagnosing problems. (This may be as much a function of the subject matter organization of social studies as anything.)

6. Performance in science is weak overall but particularly with respect to topics in physics and chemistry. (There is a possibility that a general problem-solving weakness exists, in view of the math problem-solving, social studies, and science results just reviewed.)

7. Alison also had some trouble with the reading of graphs and tables in the Visual Materials test. This weakness may relate to social studies and science, classes in which these skills ordinarily get reinforced.

8. Though reference materials was not identified as a weakness, one of the skills, alphabetizing, presented a problem. The fact that Alison did not even guess one of the eight items correctly suggests that she may have a misconception or mistaken rule about the alphabetizing process. An analysis of her responses might reveal the specific problem.

Another aspect of interpreting the scores of an individual student involves checking on growth over the past year. This can be done by referring to the student's cumulative record folder to compare the scores from the previous year with those from the current year. If typical progress was made in each area, the percentile ranks should be about the same on the two occasions. This table, obtained from the teacher's guide for the *Iowa Tests of Educational Development*, helps the user decide how large a difference should be considered "atypical" (Feldt, Forsyth, and Alnot, 1989, p. 11):

Original Percentile Rank	Size of Change in Percentile Rank
85–99	±8
65–84	±11
35–64	±15
15–34	±11
1–14	±8

For example, if Alison's fourth-grade vocabulary percentile rank was 50, her gain to 69 (+19) this year would be considered an unexpected level of growth.

Finally, growth can be estimated using a developmental score, in this case the grade equivalent. Students in the average range should be expected to gain one year or 10 months (or 1.0 when the decimal point is used) in a year. Those below average might gain only 6 to 8 months and those above average could be expected to gain 12 to 14 months. A profile chart containing scores for each of several successive years can provide a useful visual display for assessing the adequacy of growth—overall and in the areas previously noted as strengths or weaknesses.

INTERPRETING SCORES OF CLASSES

A list report of students' scores, like the one in Figure 17–1, is a logical starting point for conducting an analysis of the scores from a single classroom. The bottom row of the list report shows the average grade-equivalent score and the corresponding pupil percentile rank for each test area. When these averages are regarded as the scores of the "average student" in the class, interpretive statements like these can be made:

1. The Complete Composite grade-equivalent score of 52.0 means the average student in the class scored just like the typical fifth grader in the nation who has finished the second month. The percentile rank of 51 verifies this interpretation.
2. The relative strengths of the class are in areas in which the percentile rank is noticeably higher than the percentile rank of the average Complete Composite score (51)—capitalization, punctuation, and math concepts.
3. The relative weaknesses are in the reference materials and reading areas.
4. The students who contribute most to the group's low reading performance are Matthew, Cyndi, Patrick, Marty, Allen, Tammy, Robert, and Ginny. (By identifying these individuals, the teacher can determine whether the results might be due to unexpected test performance by certain students.)

Thus far, in addition to identifying areas of group strength and weakness, we have tried to verify that the student scores most responsible for these extreme group performances are not due to incomplete testing, random responding, or some other erroneous factor. Students who were not motivated to take the tests seriously could have responded in unpredictable ways that would cause their scores to be incongruent with their typical classroom attainments. Such scores should be ignored temporarily so that subsequent group analysis and instructional planning will not be distorted.

The next step is to determine the skills that might explain the relative strengths and weaknesses noted above. The Group Item Analysis report in Figure 17–3 shows the Visual Materials and Reference Materials skill scores and corresponding item scores for Mrs. Newton's class. Since reference materials was a weakness previously identified, we should look at the scores in the right column to gauge performance in that area. The first column of numbers shows the test item number, and each of the next four columns shows the average percent-correct score for (1) all fifth graders in the *nation,* (2) Mrs. Newton's *class,* (3) all fifth graders in the *building,* and (4) all fifth graders in the school *system.* The last column, Diff, is the class average minus the national average. It is this column that can help isolate skill deficiencies and the particular item content that contributed to them.

Mrs. Newton's class seems to have had some trouble with alphabetizing

SERVICE 6: GROUP ITEM ANALYSIS (GIA)

Class Report: Diff = Class minus Nation

Only Differences larger than 5% of National Percent Correct are Printed

Class Group	MRS NEWTON
Building	DEERFIELD
Bldg Code	
System	CRYSTAL FALLS
Norms	FALL
Order No	889-017325-111

Level	11
Form	G
Grade	5
Test Date	10/86
Sheet	4 of 5

Iowa Tests of Basic Skills

VISUAL MATERIALS N Tested = 27 items

	Item	Nat	Cls 20	Bld 20	Sys 38	Diff
MAP READING		55	66	66	68	+11
LOCATING/DESCRIBING PLACES						
1A Using map symbols	21	62	75	68		+13
1A Using map symbols	24	74	90	89		+16
1A Using map symbols	27	49	65	66		+16
1A Using map symbols	31	74	90	89		+16
1A Using map symbols	49	52	70	63		+18
1A Using map symbols	54	54	65	71		+11
1B Using map symbols	25	69	90	89		+21
1B Using map key	52	40	15	29		-25
1C Using distance/direction	29	69	80	87		+11
1C Using distance/direction	55	27	25	45		+10
Avg: 10 items		57	67	67	70	+10
DIRECTION/DISTANCE						
2A Direction: orientation	23	75	90	89		+15
2A Direction: orientation	28	54	70	74		+16
3A Distance: street map	30	29	25	25		
3A Distance: road map	50	51	55	66		
3B Using scale of distance	43	49	50	50		
3C Comparing distances	51	56	60	68		+ 6
Avg: 6 items		52	58	58	63	+ 6
INTERPRETING DATA						
4 Industrial production	44	32	55	45		+23
4 Transportation	45	51	70	61		+22
4 Crop production	46	48	70	59		+14
Avg: 3 items		44	58	58		
LIVING CONDITIONS						
5A Routes of travel	22	70	80	79		+10
5A Routes of travel	42	71	90	84		+19
5A Routes of travel	53	45	55	66		+10
5C Landscape visualization	26	45	60	53		+15
5C Landscape visualization	47	50	60	68		+20
5D Living conditions	32	70	90	97		+11
5D Living conditions	33	84	95	97		+11
5D Living conditions	48	44	55	61		+11
Avg: 8 items		60	73	73	75	+13

VISUAL MATERIALS (continued) N Tested =

	Item	Nat	Cls 20	Bld 42	Sys 50	38	Diff
READ'G GRAPHS/TABLES 16 items		44	42	42	38	45	
READING/COMPARING							
6A Reading: bar graph	36	34	35	35	39		
6C Reading: cell in table	38	68	80	80	76	+12
6C Reading: cell in table	41	74	65	65	76	- 9
7A Comparing: rank	60	44	50	50	50	+ 6
7B Comparing: sums/diff's	34	67	85	85	76	+18
7B Comparing: sums/diff's	56	34	25	25	32	- 9
7B Comparing: sums/diff's	37	41	25	25	32	- 6
7C Determining ratios	61	31	25	25	34	-16
7C Determining ratios	62	31	30	30	18	
Avg: 9 items		47	47	47	48	
INTERPRETING RELATIONSHIPS							
8A Titles and subtitles	35	32	30	30	37	- 7
8B Rates and trends	57	37	30	34	16	-17
8B Rates and trends	39	52	50	50	16	
8C Underlying relationships	63	26	5	5	13	-21
8C Underlying relationships	40	75	90	90	89	+15
8D Drawing conclusions	58	34	30	30	42	
8D Drawing conclusions		33	35	35	41	
Avg: 7 items		40	35	35	41	

REFERENCE MATERIALS N Tested =

	Item	Nat	Cls 20	Bld 20	Sys 38	Diff
ALPHABETIZING						
A Three-step	52	59	30	30	39	-29
A Four-step	53	42	20	20	39	-22
A Two-step	55	61	40	40	45	-14
A Three-step	56	55	35	35	42	-21
A Two-step	57	56	30	30	39	-26
A Three-step	58	58	50	50	55	- 8
A Three-step	59	51	30	30	30	-21
Avg: 8 items		55	34	34	42	-21
USING A TABLE OF CONTENTS						
C Identifying page	20	87	90	90	95	
C Identifying chapter	21	52	50	50	47	
C Identifying chapter	22	52	40	40	53	-12
C Identifying chapter	23	46	50	50	40	
C Identifying chapter	24	64	70	70	79	+ 6
C Identifying chapter	25	53	60	60	68	+ 7
C Identifying information	26	46	50	50	42	
Avg: 7 items		57	59	59	62	
USING AN INDEX						
I Single-step	27	80	80	80	84	
I Single-step	28	66	55	55	63	-11
I Single-step	29	75	75	75	79	
I Multi-step	30	83	90	90	87	+ 7
I Single-step	31	73	85	85	82	+12
I Single-step	32	78	75	75	71	
I Cross-reference	33	72	75	75	76	
Avg: 7 items		76	76	76	77	
USING A DICTIONARY						
D1 Spelling	35	66	80	80	68	+14
D2 Pronunciation	34	60	60	60	74	- 6
D2 Pronunciation	37	47	45	45	45	
D3 Syllabication	41	55	55	55	58	
D6 Meaning	36	49	65	65	66	+16
D6 Meaning	38	56	45	45	47	-11
D6 Meaning	39	51	40	40	53	-11
D6 Meaning	40	57	55	55	53	
Avg: 8 items		56	56	56	54	
ENCYCLOPEDIAS						
E Common class	42	58	50	50	55	- 8
E Major topic	43	45	50	50	47	
E Common class	44	64	60	60	53	
E Common class	45	59	50	50	58	- 9
Avg: 4 items		57	53	53	54	
GENERAL REFERENCES						
R1 Glossary	46	54	45	45	61	- 9
R3 Dictionary	47	54	40	40	54	-14
R6 Atlas	48	39	25	25	37	-14
R7 Magazines	52	45	45	45	42	- 7
R8 Special references		44	16	16	16	-25
R9 Book selection	49	50	50	50	41	+16
Avg: 6 items		46	36	36	41	-10

Figure 17-3. Sample Group Item Analysis Report

and with the use of general references. With respect to alphabetizing, all types seem to be problematic because the differences are all negative and, with the exception of item 58, they are sizable. Mrs. Newton will need to decide if she should plan some instruction in this skill; if she should incidentally introduce alphabetizing tasks in the course of presenting science, social studies, or other such lessons; or if she thinks her upcoming plans will deal with this skill sufficiently. The weakness in general references might have been expected if these fifth graders had not been instructed in the use of atlases, almanacs, and certain book parts. The district curriculum guide would be a useful reference for deciding about reasonable expectations and possible needs for remediation in situations like this.

When schools are departmentalized, as they usually are for middle school and high school grades, score reports can be prepared separately for each of a teacher's classes. Through simple answer sheet coding at the time of testing, Mr. White's period 2 physics students can be grouped together on a list report, and group skills analysis reports, like the one in Figure 17–4, can be provided. This latter report shows the average skill scores of 14 grade 12 students on the *Iowa Tests of Educational Development*. It can be used much like the group item analysis report (Figure 17–3) to find skills that help explain areas of strength and weakness. For example, the Sources of Information class average percent-correct score of 58 was only 3 points less than the national average score. One skill, use of encyclopedias and almanacs, was a weak area and another, use of the *Reader's Guide*, was a strong area. In science, Mr. White's major area of interest, these students performed slightly below the national average, but no skill seemed to be particularly weak or strong. In Quantitative Thinking, another area of interest to a physics teacher, these students performed slightly better than the national average, particularly in the skills of probability/statistics and exponents.

If teachers in departmentalized schools are expected to review the standardized achievement scores of their students, as they should be, reports by class period should be provided for them. It is unreasonable, for example, for middle school teachers to pour over a list report of 240 eighth graders to find the ones in their own classes. Not only would this be a tedious exercise, it would not permit the teacher to obtain a snapshot of a single instructional group. *If score reports are not user friendly, test scores will be underutilized.*

REPORTING TO STUDENTS AND PARENTS

The most basic use of test scores is to report them to all who need to know, along with a simple interpretation of what they mean. They should be reported to students as well as to their parents because both are key ingredients in school learning. Parents that are informed are likely to be more involved—at home and at school—with their children's learning and are more likely to work cooperatively with the teacher.

Students, too, must be informed about their own test results because they make countless decisions about their own instructional involvement—whether to participate, how much to participate, how much effort to devote, and what kind of personal standards to adopt. And unless students are made aware of their

IOWA TESTS OF EDUCATIONAL DEVELOPMENT

CLASS GROUP SKILL PROFILES

ITED™

SYSTEM	BUILDING		TEACHER CODE 10 PERIOD 2	ORDER CODE: 010069-217
LAKE CITY	HILLSDALE			

SERVICE 9 — NORMS: FALL — FORM X8 — GRADE 12 — DATE TESTED 09/29/87 — NORM GROUP NAT'L

Skill Areas	Number of Items	Class Average % Correct	Norm Average % Correct	Diff
Correctness & Appropriateness of Expression	69	62	58	04
Capitalization/Punctuation	09	60	56	04
Grammar	07	57	54	03
Sentence Structure	12	71	65	06
Organization	09	68	63	05
Diction/Clarity/Word Choice	17	59	59	00
Spelling	15	58	53	05
Literary Materials	46	61	56	05
Literal Comprehension	05	73	64	09
Interpretation of Nonliteral Forms	07	66	60	06
Inferences and Relationships	10	53	53	00
Generalizations	08	57	55	02
Literary Techniques/Tone	16	63	53	10
Vocabulary	40	63	53	10

Skill Areas	Number of Items	Class Average % Correct	Norm Average % Correct	Diff
Sources of Information	46	58	61	-03
Books	06	54	57	-03
Dictionaries	06	58	60	-02
Organization of Library Materials	05	66	63	03
Encyclopedias/Almanacs	05	34	69	-35
Common References	08	57	62	-05
Readers' Guide	06	74	60	14
Maps/Atlases	06	54	53	01
Govt. & Private Agencies	04	68	69	-01
Quantitative Thinking	40	49	44	05
Whole Numbers/Fractions/Decimals	07	64	61	03
Percent	06	32	31	01
Geometry/Measurement	06	42	40	02
Estimation/Rounding	04	45	41	04
Probability/Statistics	06	54	44	10
Exponents	04	48	38	10
Graphs/Tables/Formulas	07	55	48	07

Skill Areas	Number of Items	Class Average % Correct	Norm Average % Correct	Diff
Science	60	49	52	-03
Principles of Inquiry/Measurement	05	57	56	01
Interpretation of Information	07	58	60	-02
Inferences and Predictions	11	51	54	-03
Classification of Ideas	04	55	60	-05
Analysis of Experimental Procedures	21	45	48	-03
Evaluation of Evidence	06	46	53	-07
Generalization and Extension of Ideas	06	40	44	-04
Social Studies	60	57	56	01
Literal Comprehension	04	57	61	-04
Interpretation of Information	15	60	55	05
Inferences and Relationships	12	52	53	-01
Classification of Ideas	05	63	62	01
Evaluation of Sources, Evidence, and Conclusions	16	57	54	03
Author's Position and Techniques	08	54	60	-06

THIS REPORT IS BASED ON 14 STUDENTS IN GRADE 12

Figure 17–4. Sample Class Group Skills Profile Report

scores, they are likely to be less motivated to take the next standardized test seriously. When students develop the impression that test scores do not get used or that the scores are not important to others, efforts diminish and test scores lose their usefulness. Such is the unfortunate situation in some high schools where test scores tend to be used administratively by the district, but potential instructional uses are ignored.

Score reports that are marked by simplicity in visual presentation and explanation are most ideal for reporting to others. For example, the Individual Performance Profile report (Figure 16–2) discussed in Chapter 16 is ideal for reporting to parents during a parent–teacher conference. This report has several strengths that permit a comprehensive and comprehensible interpretation of results:

1. Percentile ranks, the easiest type of derived score to understand, are used.
2. Percentile bands allow the idea of error to be incorporated in the interpretation.
3. The arrangement of test and skill profiles permits an easy identification of relative strengths and weaknesses.
4. The presentation of test and skill scores on the same report provides opportunities for diagnosing within areas of weakness within each.
5. Percent-correct scores allow for criterion-referenced interpretations of skill scores.

(Turn to Figure 16–2 and try to visualize how you would use this report in discussing Alison's scores with Mr. Babka.)

When face to face parent–teacher meetings are not possible, reporting test results to parents through the mail can be accomplished with a narrative report like the one in Figure 17–5. The prose summary on the right side is intended to de-emphasize jargon and numbers and to provide a permanent record for parents (and the teacher). The four paragraphs of the narrative describe (1) facts about the test situation, (2) the meaning of the composite score, (3) areas of strength and weakness, and (4) reading achievement. The profile on the left uses a bar graph of percentile ranks to support the analysis of strengths and weaknesses noted in the narrative. The combination of prose explanation and visual representation helps to replace the interpretation a teacher might verbalize in a conference. Narrative reports that provide interpretation in addition to description are the most useful.

School officials are sometimes reluctant, for many reasons, about reporting the results of their testing programs. But a school should seldom, if ever, require all students to take a test whose results are not to be reported to students or their parents. Students and parents are partners with teachers and administrators in the educational process. The process works best if all parties are admitted to full partnership. Finally, the Family Educational Rights and Privacy Act of 1974, also commonly known as the Buckley Amendment, gives students and parents specific rights related to access to records, the accuracy of the recorded information, and the release of personal records. The reporting practices and test record keeping of schools must be developed with these rights and responsibilities in mind.

Iowa Tests of Basic Skills

Published by THE RIVERSIDE PUBLISHING COMPANY

Pupil: TRENT BIRCH
I.D. No:
Grade: 5
Sex: M
Birth Date: 5/76
Age: 10 YRS 5 MOS
Order No.: 000-010192-001

Class/Group: MRS NEWTON
Building: DEERFIELD
System: CRYSTAL FALLS
Norms: FALL
Test date: 10/86
Level/Form: 11/G

Tests	Scores		National Percentile Rank
	GE	NPR	Low 1 10 25 Average 50 75 90 High 99
VOCABULARY	65	83	
READING	58	64	
SPELLING	54	55	
CAPITALIZATION	86	98	
PUNCTUATION	79	93	
USAGE/EXPRESSION	61	67	
LANGUAGE TOTAL	70	87	
VISUAL MATERIALS	74	93	
REFERENCE MATERIALS	55	58	
WORK-STUDY TOTAL	64	80	
MATH CONCEPTS	67	87	
MATH PROBLEMS	69	91	
MATH COMPUTATION	58	75	
MATH TOTAL	65	89	
COMPOSITE	64	82	
SOCIAL STUDIES	78	86	
SCIENCE	67	72	

GE: Grade Equivalent. NPR: National Percentile Rank

COPY FOR THE TEACHER OF TRENT BIRCH

TRENT WAS GIVEN THE IOWA TESTS OF BASIC SKILLS (FORM G, LEVEL 11), IN OCTOBER, 1986. TRENT IS IN THE FIFTH GRADE AT DEERFIELD IN CRYSTAL FALLS. THIS REPORT WILL HELP EXPLAIN THE DETAILS OF THE TEST RESULTS.

TRENT'S COMPOSITE SCORE IS THE BEST INDICATOR OF HIS OVERALL ACHIEVEMENT ON THE TESTS. TRENT EARNED A COMPOSITE GRADE EQUIVALENT OF 64, WHICH MEANS THAT HIS TEST PERFORMANCE WAS APPROXIMATELY THE SAME AS THAT MADE BY A TYPICAL PUPIL IN THE SIXTH GRADE AT THE END OF THE FOURTH MONTH. TRENT'S PERFORMANCE WAS MEASURED WITH THE LEVEL 11 TEST. TRENT'S STANDING IN OVERALL ACHIEVEMENT AMONG FIFTH GRADE PUPILS NATIONALLY IS SHOWN BY HIS COMPOSITE PERCENTILE RANK OF 82. THIS MEANS THAT TRENT SCORED BETTER THAN 82 PERCENT OF FIFTH GRADE PUPILS NATIONALLY AND THAT 18 PERCENT SCORED AS WELL OR BETTER. TRENT'S OVERALL ACHIEVEMENT APPEARS TO BE ABOVE AVERAGE FOR HIS GRADE.

THE SCORES OF ONE PUPIL ARE OFTEN COMPARED WITH OTHER PUPIL'S SCORES. GENERALLY, TRENT'S SCORES ARE ABOVE AVERAGE WHEN DESCRIBED IN THIS WAY. HOWEVER, SKILLS CAN ALSO BE COMPARED WITH EACH OTHER TO DETERMINE AN INDIVIDUAL'S STRENGTHS AND WEAKNESSES. IN TRENT'S CASE, THE HIGHEST SCORES ARE IN CAPITALIZATION AND VISUAL MATERIALS. THESE ARE STRONG POINTS WHICH CAN BE USED TO IMPROVE OTHER SKILLS. TRENT'S LOWEST SCORES ARE IN SPELLING AND REFERENCE MATERIALS. THESE ARE AREAS IN WHICH TRENT APPEARS TO NEED THE MOST WORK.

A PUPIL'S COMMAND OF READING SKILLS IS RELATED TO SUCCESS IN MANY AREAS OF SCHOOL WORK, SINCE MOST SUBJECTS REQUIRE SOME READING. TRENT'S READING SCORE IS SOMEWHAT ABOVE AVERAGE WHEN COMPARED WITH THOSE OF OTHER FIFTH GRADE PUPILS NATIONALLY. TRENT'S READING SCORE IS ABOUT AVERAGE WHEN COMPARED WITH HIS OWN TEST PERFORMANCE IN OTHER AREAS.

Figure 17-5. Sample Profile Narrative Report

SOME INTERPRETATION PROBLEMS

Because the test results of a student, class, building, or district are influenced by a variety of factors, it is impossible to attribute high or low performance to any one factor. That is not to say that attribution should be ignored. But, as we shall point out, inept attempts to explain the test results of a group can lead to feelings of futility among teachers or to the destruction of test scores as a viable information source.

Judging Teacher Competence

Should the results of standardized achievement tests be used to evaluate the competence of teachers, either individually or as a group? Even when we recognize that test results never tell the whole achievement story, that standardized tests have limitations, and that factors other than teacher competence enter the picture, there is still a good case for arguing that poor achievement (or good) *may* be the result of poor teaching (or good). If we agree that the quality of teaching influences the quality of achievement, then we must agree also that good measures of achievement have something to contribute to the complex process of evaluating teacher competence. If we do not agree that good learning requires good teaching, why do we try to hire good teachers or try to train them in the first place?

The concern about whether to use test scores as a partial basis for teacher evaluation has intensified because of the many misuses of students' test scores in personnel decisions. The primary purpose of testing, to improve instruction, has been replaced in some cases by the use of scores to make salary decisions, decide promotions, or assign teachers to buildings. In some instances, teacher retention decisions are made by giving heavy weight to the most recent standardized test results. Giving inordinate emphasis to test results for such purposes has destroyed the instructional value of the scores in the affected schools and has narrowed the "instructed curriculum" to closely match test content, if not to include specific test items.

Too much emphasis on test scores in judging teacher competence also has slowed the search for acceptable alternative measures of effective teaching. The existence of objective, quantified indicators like test scores has contributed to complacency about developmental efforts. Research on teacher evaluation continues, but the prospects for more effective methods are no greater for the evaluation of teacher competence than for the assessment of student achievement.

The gross misuses of standardized achievement-test scores for judging teacher competence we have witnessed over the past decade have caused us to qualify our response to the initial question raised. In the absence of other pertinent information, test results should not be used to make personnel decisions. Test scores that are compromised by attempts to influence personnel decisions are useless for *any* purpose. Any secondary use of standardized achievement-test scores that erodes the basic instructional purpose for testing should be discontinued promptly.

Judging School Quality

As long as the principal task of the school is to facilitate cognitive learning, any information that describes the extent of such learning seems admissible for judging school effectiveness. From this standpoint, the most effective schools are those whose students exhibit the greatest amount of year to year growth in achievement on all dimensions of the curriculum. Scores from standardized achievement tests can contribute to examining annual growth in the curriculum areas tapped by the tests' items.

The surge of interest in state or district report cards has helped to diversify the thinking of educators about a variety of school quality indicators—attendance, retention, graduation rate, college-going rate, ACT or SAT average scores, participation in extracurricular activities, and so on. Unfortunately, there are many aspects of the curriculum that never get assessed and factored into curriculum evaluation because acceptable assessment procedures are not available. Thus, judgments of school quality seldom are based on performance in such academic areas as writing, speech, health, performing arts, foreign languages, and physical education. Scores from standardized achievement tests have much to contribute to the assessment of school quality, but their focus is limited, as the emphasis on them also should be.

School achievement, and consequently test scores, are influenced by a number of factors related to the students, the staff, the school, and the community. Reasonable expectations for school-level achievement, most importantly in terms of year to year growth, should be developed through a consideration of these factors. For example, achievement seems to be related to student ability, motivation, attitudes, and home environment; school-facility quality, learning climate, instructional equipment and materials quality, and curriculum breadth; and community financial resources, support for the schools, and population mobility. Sometimes it is difficult to recognize that achievement is as high in a school as should be expected, given the resources—human and monetary—that have been expended. It is equally difficult to recognize that the high achievement observed in some schools is lower than it ought to be, given the nature of resources committed to it. Obviously, schooling is a joint venture that depends on many constituent groups for its success. A failure on the part of *any* one of them— school board, administrators, teachers, parents, or students—can interfere with achievement, despite the efforts of the others. Consequently, achievement goals and expectations should be developed jointly, and responsibility for achievement outcomes must be held jointly as well.

SCHOOL TESTING PROGRAM ISSUES

A number of decisions face teachers and administrators in the various phases of test selection, preparation, administration, and score interpretation. Some of the guides and manuals that accompany standardized tests speak to these issues, but many do not. The remainder of this chapter is devoted to an analysis of each of several matters that impact test use but are not thoroughly dealt with in most measurement texts.

Teacher In-service Planning

A test-battery selection committee is faced with four major tasks: (1) review or assess the test-related information needs of the school system and its structural units, (2) develop a list of criteria to be used in evaluating the competing achievement batteries from which a selection will be made, (3) determine the procedures to be used to obtain evidence relevant to each selection criterion and to weight the evidence from the various selection criteria, and (4) implement the procedures and make a recommendation. In view of the lack of preparation or experience of many educators with these tasks, an in-service program for most selection committees is essential. The topics listed in Appendix D form a comprehensive agenda from which local plans for in-service might be developed.

When a standardized achievement battery is administered properly, we can be relatively confident that (1) students have responded to the tasks to the best of their abilities, (2) resources provided by the school have been expended judiciously, (3) score interpretations using the publisher's norms are appropriate (meaningful), and (4) year to year growth estimates can be represented accurately. To ensure proper preparation and administration, teacher in-service planned around the topics listed in Appendix E should be provided. The specific in-service needs of a district will depend on the extent of annual staff turnover and the extent of previous experience with the battery in current use, among other factors. In addition, when the staff is formed predominantly by experienced teachers, greater emphasis should be placed on the "why" of various procedures rather than on a rehash of the "what."

Finally, test scores need to be placed in the hands of teachers so that instructional decisions can be made about students, classes, or segments of the curriculum. Teachers must be able to recognize discrepant performance, interpret various kinds of scores, locate scores on particular reports, and relate the score information to expectations and previous achievement levels. In-service topics that address these skills, delineated in Appendix F, are the basis for program planning. Posttest in-service is necessary to ensure that the conscientious efforts of test selection and administration are brought to worthy conclusions.

Curriculum-Test Content Match

It is both unfair and illogical to administer a test to students when that test covers topics students have not had an opportunity to learn about. But the other extreme has its limitations, also, as Linn (1983) has pointed out: "Allowing the match between instructional materials and test items to be too close risks losing the capability to measure understanding." The greatest loss, however, is the ability to generalize about what students may be able to do:

> Literal match of instruction and testing in the sense of practice on the items that appear on the test destroys the measurement value of the test. Inferences about skills and knowledge that are made on the basis of test results become suspect

when the match becomes too close. To test whether a student can apply skills and knowledge to solve a new problem, the problem must be new. Practice on the problem as part of instruction insures match and may improve scores, but eliminates any conclusions regarding problem solving. (p. 187).

The mismatch dilemma illustrates the need for both nationally prepared tests, available from publishers, and local tests developed specifically for the school curriculum. Most importantly, the dilemma further highlights the loss of information that is likely to result from customized testing, especially when items (rather than objectives) are selected by the school. How can higher-order thinking skills be measured, for example, when the match is very close?

Practice and Teaching to the Test

The preparation of students for testing is an issue of curriculum-test match because preparation can be so extensive that, in fact, it becomes the "instructional curriculum." Teaching to the test has become a major concern, particularly in high-stakes testing contexts. How much preparation is legitimate before *teaching to the test* becomes *teaching the test*? Mehrens and Kaminski (1989) have conceptualized the various gradations of practice (and malpractice) using this scale:

1. General instruction without regard for specific objectives measured by the test in question
2. Teaching of test-taking skills
3. Instruction on objectives that may include some specifically chosen because they are known to be measured on *some* standardized tests
4. Instruction on objectives that match those measured by the test in question
5. Instruction on objectives that match those measured by the test, where the test format is also used in instruction
6. Practice using a published parallel form (current or dated) of the test in question
7. Practice using the exact items from the test in question

Most test specialists would agree that the first two approaches are reasonable and that the last two never are. We agree with Mehrens and Kaminski that the most questionable position is item 4. Certainly, if these are the only objectives of instruction, this form of practice would compromise the meaning of the norms (except perhaps in a structured curricular area like mathematics computation). From our perspective, the most reasonable position for a school to take includes the teaching of test-taking skills (2) and instruction that combines positions 3 and 4.

Early School Testing

The use of standardized tests in the early primary grades, beginning in kindergarten, can accomplish the same purposes as testing at other levels. There is just as much need to monitor growth, identify strengths and weaknesses, and estimate developmental levels among the younger students. However, due to the nature of the curriculum and limited skills of primary students, testing conditions must be adjusted. For example, tests are untimed, they are administered orally, and responses are marked directly on the test booklet. The ability of five-year-olds to handle such testing in the fall of kindergarten has been documented in several studies (Frisbie and Andrews, 1990; Wodtke and others, 1989).

Many primary teachers have been convinced that testing in the early grades is a mistake, that the results are very unreliable, and that some students are placed in a traumatic situation by testing. No doubt some of these teachers have observed student behavior that supports their position. Others probably have been influenced by the misuse of achievement scores in making grade retention–promotion decisions or kindergarten admission judgments. With respect to reliability, teachers often do not have ready access to the supporting technical data for a given test or they are uncertain about how to interpret the data.

It appears, however, that many primary teachers object to norm-referenced testing because it puts some students in a position of having to answer questions they are unprepared to answer. Consequently, they might say, the love of learning the teacher has tried so hard to instill is undone in a matter of minutes by a test. Obviously, a test with too many difficult questions should not be given to a child because it may produce unnecessary frustration and probably would provide little useful information. But a test with *some* hard questions is necessary to distinguish students of different achievement levels and to help identify relative strengths and weaknesses. Besides, students have all had experience in their past that created frustration and some degree of failure—tying shoes, buttoning and zipping, riding a bicycle, or printing their name. When students are told by the test directions that some questions might be asked that they cannot answer, most of them understand and accept the conditions without negative consequences.

Perhaps too much early school testing is done because administrators have required it, rather than because teachers have found the results helpful. As long as legitimate purposes for testing exist, it is paramount that appropriate tests be selected, that the administration directions be followed exactly, and that students be encouraged to do their best. Otherwise the results may not be very valid for any purposes, even those of which the teacher may not be fully aware.

Frequency and Time of Year

The reasons for giving standardized achievement tests hold the answers to the questions: When should tests be given? and How often should tests be given? Since different testing purposes do not point to the same answer and because a number of practical factors enter in, answering these two questions means weighing trade-offs.

The costs in dollars and instructional time probably should preclude giving a full battery more than once in a school year. Some pre-post testing may be necessary at times for program evaluation, but ordinarily this should involve the readministration of only one or two tests from a battery.

Some districts have begun to look for ways to respond to the intrusion of the multiple national, state, and district testing programs that erode direct instructional time. One response has been to limit the administration of an achievement battery to alternate years, or to give the battery only in alternate grades (perhaps 3, 5, 7, 9, and 11). The main drawback to such a schedule is that the analysis of growth—for individuals and district-wide grade groups—must be based on a two-year period. Such a plan precludes early detection of learning problems and a corresponding quick response to their resolution. Consequently, minor problems could become major and efforts to remediate could involve months rather than days. Furthermore, when some grades are never tested, curriculum problems are more difficult to isolate and more time consuming to address.

With respect to time of year, instructional purposes are best served by a fall testing program. Results can be returned in time for use in instructional planning for the rest of the year, students still are grouped in classes in the same way the score reports list them, and there is little threat of test scores being used to evaluate teachers. Midyear testing offers the same advantages but allows less time for remediating weaknesses.

End-of-year testing has an implicit accountability purpose associated with it, whether intended or not by school officials. As long as teachers *perceive* that judgments about them may be influenced by the scores of their class, such reactions as "teaching the test" can result. On the positive side, spring testing permits an assessment of the effects of year-long program innovations or of the introduction of new materials. At the primary level, it supplies administrators with current achievement information they often use to reconstitute classes for the upcoming year.

Two other points merit brief attention. First, for purposes of monitoring growth, it makes no difference which time of year testing is done. What does matter, however, is that testing be done at about the same time in consecutive years. Second, and related, testing should be done as near as possible to the dates on which norms were gathered by the publisher. These are often October 31 for fall and April 30 for spring, but the publisher's technical manual should be consulted for specific tests. Fall norms generally would apply to testing done in September through November. Consequently, schools that test in late September, for example, are treated like those that test in late November, at least with respect to normative comparisons. The two-month difference likely will affect status interpretations but not the analysis of strengths and weaknesses or the estimation of growth.

Out-of-Level Testing

Out-of-level testing is a method of adapting testing to the curriculum level that is most appropriate for the group or individual to be tested. For example, it might be decided that a third-grade class to be tested in the fall should be given a test level that is ordinarily more appropriate for spring testing in second grade. If the teacher believes the third-grade test is too advanced in content coverage in most test areas, the decision to "drop back" is likely to yield more useful information.

There are usually dramatic achievement differences among students in the same classroom, and teachers ordinarily work hard to accommodate those differences by individualizing materials, activities, and expectations. In view of such accommodations, it makes sense that testing also be individualized so that those working at markedly lower or higher curricular levels than their classmates will be tested on the objectives to which their instruction has been directed. An average sixth-grade class should not be given a test designed for average seventh graders; neither should a very low achiever in sixth grade be given a test intended for typical sixth graders.

Out-of-level testing can result in major gains for teacher and student with no loss in interpretability of scores. Such scores are likely to be more accurate because students will experience less frustration with foreign content and will be more motivated to complete the test. The test and skill scores are more likely to demonstrate a pattern of strengths and weaknesses rather than a picture of all weaknesses—undifferentiated performance levels. The grade-equivalent scores that result from out-of-level testing have the same meaning as scores derived from in-level testing. That is, these scores are interpreted without regard to the test level taken. Also, the percentile ranks assigned to a pupil show how that pupil's grade-equivalent scores compare with those of others in the same grade. That is, a third grader is always compared with other third graders, no matter which test level was administered.

Testing Special Students

Individualizing testing is one method of accommodating students with special needs, but there are other students who, no matter which test level is selected for them, will require special testing conditions. Students with some form of learning disability, those with visual or auditory deficits, or those with physical handicaps may need extra time, a reader, an answer recorder, or some other form of assistance that requires departure from standard administration conditions. When the goal of testing is to obtain relevant information for individual program planning, all such accommodations should be made. Of course, score interpretations must take into account the special conditions and their effect on the applicability of norms. In such cases, norm-referenced scores are likely to be of little interest or value, except perhaps when local norms are available.

When adaptations are made for individual students, often separate and different report forms may be of value. Reports that focus on skills and subskills and that provide item response information will be most useful for building individual programs of instruction. When such information is coupled with teacher observations from the test-administration sessions, the needs of special students can be addressed within the mainstream of the school testing program.

High School Testing

Much discussion about standardized achievement testing tends to focus on grades K to 8, where these tests are most prominently used, but these tests are administered in virtually every high school, at least in some grades. There are a number of practical reasons why high school standardized testing with achievement batteries presents some unique problems, concerns, or issues.

First, the nature of the high school curriculum precludes the use of a battery that presumes some kind of continuous instruction (and subsequent continuous growth) in each subject-matter area in grades 9 to 12. For example, not all juniors take a math course, sophomore science (chemistry) is not a logical extension or continuation of freshman science (biology), and in eleventh-grade social studies, some students are in world history, many are in American history, some are in sociology, and some may be taking a course like "Family Living." Such curriculum diversity and inconsistent patterns of course enrollment among students make the *traditional* achievement battery somewhat inappropriate for nearly every high school student.

A logical response to this curriculum match problem is to focus assessment on more generalized skills that all students are expected to develop throughout the high school program. For example, writing, reading, quantitative thinking, interpretation of data, and literary analysis are skills that all of us continue to develop in high school, college, and throughout our lives. (We never reach our reading comprehension potential, for example.) Batteries like the *Iowa Tests of Educational Development* were prepared to assess the extent of general development within the broad curricular areas, rather than to measure the achievement of basic skills or the possession of specific knowledge.

A second issue in high school testing relates to the competition of external testing programs. High school students planning for postsecondary school admissions take ACT and SAT tests (as well as the preliminary versions, PACT and PSAT), and scores are returned to the high school as well as to the students. Thus, additional achievement data from an external standardized testing program supplement the information available from the school's norm-referenced testing program. Some teachers perceive less need for the standardized testing program, especially in the upper grades, because of the availability of the admission testing program scores. Partly for this reason, many schools do not administer an achievement battery to high school seniors.

Third, high school teachers use standardized test scores far less than their elementary or middle school colleagues, in part because of the curricular diversity problem. Furthermore, since they tend not to use the scores, high school teachers regard the tests as relatively unimportant and they resist giving them. This "chain reaction" continues. Teachers form a negative attitude about the tests, that attitude carries over to the high school students, and, finally, many of the students fail to take the tests seriously. This lack of motivation in students causes the scores to be of questionable validity for any purpose.

The outcomes from standardized achievement batteries at the high school level seem to be of less concern to students, parents, and teachers than they were at the lower grade levels. Other information is at hand that is perceived as more important for making future career and educational plans. Nonetheless, the results from the batteries are useful for making judgments about the school curriculum—content coverage and emphasis, sequence, and breadth of opportunity presented by course offerings. And when the tests focus on educational development, the scores also are useful for monitoring growth and for identifying strengths and weaknesses. In short, standardized achievement scores can be just as useful at the high school level as at the elementary level, but considerably greater effort must be expended to convince teachers of the value of the information and to help them develop convenient methods of using the information.

SUMMARY PROPOSITIONS

1. The current testing climate is dominated by excessive testing for various accountability purposes to the detriment of instructional improvement efforts.
2. The primary and essential use of scores from standardized achievement tests is to provide information to all who are concerned with the educational process.
3. If scores obtained from a school-testing program are reported and interpreted to teachers, students, and parents, no other formal or elaborate program for using them is necessary.
4. Standardized achievement-test scores are useful primarily in facilitating instruction and in evaluating its results.
5. The use of an achievement composite score for selecting students for gifted educational programs may exclude many who excel in only one particular subject area.
6. Readiness-test scores provide information for instructional planning, but they have much less value for making program placement decisions.
7. Except in the fields of elementary reading and arithmetic, diagnostic testing has proved to be of little educational value.
8. The selection of report formats for standardized-test results should be done on the basis of *who* needs *what kind* of information.
9. An individual's pattern of strengths and weaknesses can be determined by comparing each separate test score with the battery composite-score percentile rank.
10. Skill and subskill scores provide diagnostic information that may account for weaknesses identified at the test level.
11. The strengths and weaknesses of a class can be identified by treating the class averages as the scores of the "average pupil" and then using the interpretive procedures outlined for use with individual's scores.
12. It is a mistake to assume that students are unable to understand the meaning of their own test scores or that they care little about their own scores.
13. Achievement-test scores provide information that can contribute to evaluations of teacher competence, but such scores never should be used as the sole or primary basis for evaluating teachers.
14. Expectations for achievement levels in a particular school should be developed through an analysis of the characteristics of the students, the school plant and program, and the socioeconomics of the community.
15. Schools must provide teachers with in-service education on the topics of test selection, test administration, and test-score interpretation because preservice educational opportunities on these topics are too rare.
16. When the content match between the test and curriculum is too close or when students are taught the test content too directly, the ability to generalize about what students are able to do is diminished greatly or lost altogether.
17. The use of standardized achievement tests in the early primary grades can accomplish the same purposes that testing at higher levels does.
18. Annual fall testing with an achievement battery is optimal for addressing the several instructional purposes that can be served by standardized achievement tests.
19. It is unreasonable to expect that a single test level can be used to measure achievement in a classroom populated by students whose academic developmental levels may span two to three grades.
20. The diverse nature of the high school curriculum and the varied enrollment patterns of the students make the testing of educational development more useful than the testing of achievement of basic skills at that level.

QUESTIONS FOR STUDY AND DISCUSSION

1. What knowledge about standardized testing is needed by the general public to make individuals "informed consumers?"
2. What should a school district do, as a minimum, with its annual standardized achievement-test results?
3. Why should test scores supplement a teacher's judgment about student status and progress rather than teacher judgment supplementing the test scores?

4. What would be a reasonable selection rule for identifying sixth graders for a creative writing program?

5. Why might a child who cannot count or who does not know any letters of the alphabet be able to profit from beginning a traditional kindergarten program?

6. Why are there probably no diagnostic achievement tests in science or social studies?

7. What are the relative strengths and weaknesses of Marty Gerami, shown in Figure 17-1? (Note the Complete Composite score is the average of scores V, R, L, W, and M.)

8. How can percentile ranks be used to describe and interpret year to year growth?

9. What procedures might a teacher follow to explain why the average score of the class is much lower than last year's class?

10. What are some plausible explanations for a student's scores that show negative growth (for example, GE = 5.8 this year but GE = 6.0 last year in reading)?

11. What can be said about relative strengths to a student whose composite-score percentile rank is 99?

12. How does a high mobility rate within a community interfere with some aspects of test-score interpretation?

13. What should be the essential components (goals and methods) in a school district's year-long in-service plan to improve the evaluation-related skills of all teachers?

14. In what way might the teaching of test-taking skills be construed as "teaching the test"?

15. Why is it generally not possible to identify individual or group strengths and weaknesses with scores from a criterion-referenced test?

16. Why might October 28 be considered the most ideal day to begin administering an achievement battery in a school?

17. If a student is expected to obtain nearly the same grade-equivalent and percentile rank scores when tested out of level, what is the point of doing out-of-level testing?

18. What incentives can be used to encourage high school students to perform at their best on standardized achievement tests?

19. What can be done to make the results of standardized achievement tests more useful to high school teachers in virtually all subject areas?

18

Standardized Intelligence and Aptitude Measures

THE CONCEPT OF INTELLIGENCE

Despite widespread acceptance of the idea that intelligence exists, there seems to be no consensus as to just what it is. It presumably has a biological basis in neuroanatomy or brain physiology. Various levels of mental deficiency have been associated with metabolic defects and certain types of prenatal environmental stress (for example, oxygen deficiency, viral infection, and injurious drugs). But thus far no biological basis for differences in intelligence among normal humans has been determined.

In its common and informal usage, intelligence is often characterized as "brightness" or "sharpness." These words suggest responsiveness, perceptiveness, cleverness, and ability to cut through appearances and confusions to reach understanding. Lack of intelligence is associated with dullness, which suggests a lack of attentiveness, awareness, or understanding. Despite their imprecise and informal characterizations, these verbal representations of intelligence are used constantly as we "size up" the abilities of others around us. The outcomes of such informal assessment no doubt have significant impacts on relationships formed, viewpoints entertained, and judgments followed.

Psychologists who study cognitive processes and mental development and functioning differ among themselves in their conceptions of intelligence (Weinberg, 1989). But they are in general agreement with the nonacademicians who perceive intelligence as a composite of mainly three elements: (1) ability to solve practical problems, (2) ability to verbalize, and (3) ability to adapt to various demands of the social environment. Some researchers call it the ability to learn or to do work in school, the same ability that Alfred Binet (1911) was interested in detecting with his early tests. Others characterize it as ability to reason, to solve problems, and to use the "higher mental processes." Still others emphasize original thinking and the ability to adapt to novel situations. In some discussions "creativity" is posited as a component of intelligence, as some see it, or as a separate, but related psychological construct, as others see it.

Definitions: Operational and Analytical

One possible solution to the problem of defining intelligence is to use an operational definition, as is done with a variety of other personality measures. The test used to measure the trait defines what is being measured. That is, intelligence *is* whatever the test measures. But different tests measure different kinds of intelligence depending on the nature of the tasks in them. Obviously, this approach, whatever its virtues in helping us to think more concretely about what we mean by intelligence, is not going to yield a single, generally acceptable definition.

Another possible solution is to use the methods of factor analysis on the responses of a wide variety of persons to a wide variety of tasks (test items) designed to measure intelligence. Factor analysis is a statistical technique that involves examining the correlations between a large number of item responses to determine if certain homogeneous subsets of items, called *factors,* can be identified. This approach has shed much light on the extent to which proficiency on certain tasks tends to be related to, or independent of, proficiency on other tasks. But it has provided no compelling definition of intelligence. Different researchers have not used the same kinds of test tasks and, even when they have, they have interpreted their findings somewhat differently. Spearman (1927), for example, found a common, general intellectual factor, but Thurstone (1938) found seven primary mental abilities. The multidimensional "structure of intellect" model proposed by Guilford (1966) is quite elaborate but of mostly theoretical interest. The tasks he used to conceptualize the measurement of intelligence were subdivided finely into 120 aspects of intellectual functioning based on the process, product, and content characteristic of each aspect. Finally, Vernon (1971) is one of several factor analysts to propose a hierarchical theory of intelligence that helps to explain much of the correlational data that has accumulated on the structure of intelligence.

More recently, cognitive psychologists have proposed information-processing models to describe what happens during intellectual functioning rather than studying what results from the process. For example, the triarchic theory offered by Sternberg (1985) is based on these three premises:

1. Intelligence explains the ability of persons to adapt to their environment, socially or culturally. More intelligent individuals are able to adapt in a wider range of social contexts.

2. Intelligent behavior is goal directed; there is a reason for it. Often the

reason relates to wanting to be able to perform cognitive tasks spontaneously or automatically (like an expert) or wanting to be able to handle a novel problem.

3. Intelligent behavior is bounded by the extent to which information-processing skills and metacognitive strategies have been developed.

The current work of cognitive psychologists seems promising for education because it suggests that the intellectual components of individuals may be isolated. This means the functions can be studied separately and the components can be developed to promote quicker learning, improved memory, or more extensive recall capability. Thus far, however, these theories have had little impact on the instruments that dominate the sales market for cognitive abilities tests.

Because the multitude of definitions proposed by psychologists provides no convergence or consensus, the measures of intelligence available for use in our schools do not have a common basis. The implication for those who must select intelligence tests for their school testing program is clear. The operational definition and theoretical bases of each test under consideration must be reviewed and the test tasks must be examined in terms of the school's purpose for testing. In most cases the nature of the test items will provide a clearer indication of what is to be measured than will whatever criterion-related or construct-related evidence that is supplied by the publisher to support the intended use of the test.

THE NATURE OF INTELLIGENCE TESTS

The different conceptions of the nature of intelligence have contributed to the development of a wide diversity of tasks for testing it. Examples of some of the types most widely used on group-administered tests are presented below. (The wide variety of open-ended questions and performance tasks used on some individually administered tests differ considerably from the tasks shown here.) As you read each of these items, try to describe the characteristics of individuals who likely would answer the items correctly and those who likely would not. When you have read all the items, try to synthesize your descriptions to arrive at a verbal description of intelligence.

I. Verbal

1. *Synonyms (or antonyms)*
   Identify the pair of words in each set that are either synonyms or antonyms.
   a. accident　　　b. bad　　　　c. evil　　　d. worry

2. *Verbal analogies*
   snow: flake: :　　a. cloud: fleecy　c. hail: storm
   　　　　　　　　　b. icicle: eaves　d. rain: drop

3. *Verbal classification*
   pear　apple　peach
   a. beet　　　　　b. grape　　　c. wheat　　　d. green

4. *Similarities*
   Which of these is most like a calf?
   a. colt　　　　　b. cat　　　　c. pony

5. *Sentence completion*
   While most teachers agree that educational tests are useful, one occasionally hears the suggestion that education could go on perfectly well, perhaps much better than in the past, if tests and testing were _____.
   a. abolished   b. criticized   c. praised   d. investigated

6. *Sentence interpretation*
   Given sentence: The date must be advanced one day when one crosses the International Date Line in a westerly direction.
   Interpretive question: If a ship approaches the International Date Line from the east on Tuesday, what day is it on board the ship after the line has been crossed?

II. Quantitative

7. *Number series*
   1   3   5   7   9 _____
   a. 10   b. 12   c. 11   d. 13

8. *Quantitative relations*
   X. 2,000 feet   Y. one mile
   a. X is more   b. Y is more   c. X and Y are the same

9. *Arithmetic reasoning*
   How many 25¢ candy canes can be bought with $1.00?

10. *Relative magnitudes*
    A dollar is how many times larger than a dime?
    a. 2   b. 5   c. 10   d. 100

11. *Number sentence construction*
    3   6   ÷
    a. 1/4   b. 1/3   c. 2   d. 9

III. Abstract Processes

12. *Figure classification*

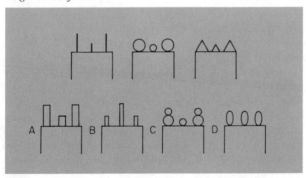

13. *Figure analogies*

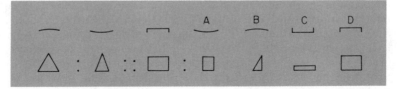

14. *Matrix progression*
Which figure belongs in the blank space?

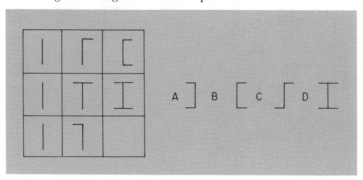

A B C D

School-related Tasks

Some of the exercises used to test intelligence—giving synonyms, interpreting sentences, computing, and solving problems—are the objects of specific instruction in school. Hence, almost identical tasks are likely to be found in general achievement-test batteries. Abilities to handle other tasks such as analogy problems, number sentence construction, and problems of classification usually are learned incidentally (if at all) in school, at play, at home, or elsewhere.

It is sometimes assumed that what a student succeeds in learning incidentally is a better indication of intelligence than is the person's success in intentional learning in school. The assumption may be justified, but the evidence and logic needed to justify it are not obvious. Teaching does indeed assist learning, but it does not make learning automatic nor does it eliminate the need for effort and ability on the part of students. Intelligence contributes to learning in school as well as out of it.

Obviously, if we wish to compare the intelligence of children who have been to school with those who have not, we should not use tasks that the school tries to teach. As a general principle, if we seek to infer basic ability to learn using measurements of success in learning, we must first try to equalize opportunities to learn and then select as test items only problems to which all children probably have been exposed. Yet, as Coleman and Cureton (1954) have pointed out, even if opportunities for in-school learning could be equalized, there would still remain great differences in the availability of incidental learning. These differences in environments and life-styles among different families, different neighborhoods, and different regions of the country cannot, and probably should not, be eliminated. Therefore, the prospects for equalizing opportunities to learn are essentially nonexistent. School-related tasks probably represent the greatest experiential common denominator for children and, thus, the most appropriate source of items for predicting potential for learning in school.

Nonverbal and Culture-fair Tests

Some developers of intelligence tests have attempted to minimize, or to eliminate entirely, the influence of verbal ability on test scores. The tasks they use are based on objects, drawings, or figures that require assembly, classification, arrangement, selection, or some other form of manipulation. Sometimes even the instructions involve no words, but are given in pantomime.

These tests are useful if students who do not all speak the same language must be tested with the same test, or if a student with a severe language handicap must be tested. They may be appealing to those who seek measures of intelligence that are less influenced directly by school learning, particularly language learning. But there is no good reason to believe that these nonverbal tests are more valid measures of intelligence than the verbal tests. Ability to do well on them is learned also. And since verbal facility is so important an element in school learning, and in most other areas of human achievement, the major application for nonverbal tests seems to be with individuals who have significant language problems or with those whose native language is not English.

Most intelligence tests not only require some degree of adeptness with a particular language, but also assume familiarity with a particular culture. This quality limits their usefulness in other cultures. However, attempts to build *culture-free* tests have failed because testing requires communication, and communication is impossible in the absence of culture and the symbols, concepts, and meanings it embodies.

Attempts to build *culture-fair* tests by eliminating items that discriminate between different cultures have been no more successful. If carried far enough, they result in eliminating all the items. There is no difference between individuals in their response to any test item that cannot be attributed to differences in culture, if culture is defined inclusively enough. Each of us lives in a somewhat different culture. Not only Eskimos and Africans, but also Vermonters and Virginians, farmers and city dwellers, boys and girls, even first-born and next born in the same family live in somewhat different cultures. The differences are not equally great in all of these instances, but they exist as differences in all cases, and they can be used to support the contention (as absurd as it may be) that any item that discriminates is unfair. It is logically impossible for a culture-free test or culture-fair test to discriminate among individuals, and there is no reason to use a test that does not discriminate between those who have more or less of an ability of interest to the user.

SCORES REPORTED FROM ABILITY TESTS

Originally the scores reported from intelligence tests were formed by dividing each examinee's mental age score by his or her chronological age. Even though such quotients are no longer computed, the IQ (intelligence quotient) label lives on, both in the popular press and among academics. Today the results from most intelligence or academic aptitude tests are reported as standard scores (normalized) and percentile ranks.

Standard Scores and Percentile Ranks

The raw scores obtained on intelligence tests require norms for interpretation, and these norms—usually age or grade level—are expressed as stanines some other type of standard score, or percentile ranks. Though the standard scores used by various publishers are known by different names, virtually all are defined by a mean score of 100 and a standard deviation of 16 (or 15 in some cases). For example, when age norms are used, the standard score may be called a standard age score, mental age score, age-equivalent score, cognitive skills quotient, or deviation IQ score.

The score ranges in Table 18–1 show the approximate equivalent values of scores commonly reported for intelligence tests. These are the same relationships discussed in Chapter 4 based on the normal curve. The general descriptors are terms that might be used in a narrative report or during a parent–teacher conference to describe a level of performance for either age or grade norms.

Many score reports list standard scores and percentile ranks for both age and grade norms. For students whose chronological age is typical for their grade level, their percentile ranks using either norm group should be the same. But for those who are older or younger than their grade mates, noticeable differences should be expected.

Subtest and Total Scores

In view of the wide range of definitions of intelligence discussed earlier it should not be surprising to find multiple scores produced from some tests and only a single score furnished by others. Tests built on a unitary theory of intelligence should be expected to report a single score, but those based on a multi-faceted theory should produce several, one for each facet perhaps. In addition, theories that promote the idea that intelligent behavior might vary in different content areas would require testing in each of the several distinct domains (for example, mathematical, verbal, abstract, social). In some cases it might be inconsistent with the theory to average the separate scores to obtain a meaningful total (overall) score. For example, when verbal and nonverbal scores are reported, what meaning should be attached to the average of such scores? The specific

Table 18–1.   Relationship between Standard Score, Percentile Rank, and Stanine Ranges Used in Cognitive Abilities Score Interpretation

Standard Score Range	General Descriptor	Percentile Rank Range	Stanines Ranges
128 and up	Well above average	96–99	9
112–127	Above average	77–95	7–8
88–111	Average	23–76	4–6
72–87	Below average	4–22	2–3
71 and below	Well below average	1–3	1

Note: The stanine values show approximate relationships. For example, by definition, 4 percent of the scores are found in each of stanines 1 and 9.

meaning might be impossible to determine, but most cognitive psychologists would probably accept the average as an indicator of general cognitive ability.

There may be considerable diagnostic information in the pattern of an individual's scores on an intelligence-test battery. Consider three students who all have the same average standard score.

Test Score	Rob	Thad	Zach
Verbal	121	96	76
Quantitative	90	97	80
Nonverbal	80	98	135
Average	97	97	97

The patterns shown by the test scores indicate that important information would be concealed by using only a total (average) score. Rob, for example, showed considerable verbal facility, while Zach showed strength in abstract reasoning and a potential for verbal and quantitative deficits. Note that Thad's even pattern of scores would not be misinterpreted by using only the average score. The pattern of strengths and weaknesses apparent from separate test scores has implications for the individualization of content, materials, and approach to instruction. Of course, all scores that represent an extreme or that seem "out of character" for a student should be verified through further observation or testing, perhaps with the assistance of a school psychologist.

Interpreting Scores of Individuals

The main purposes of using an intelligence battery with all students in a particular grade are (1) to identify those who may have an overall *atypical* level of cognitive development and (2) to gain information for individualizing instruction. As is true with the interpretation of scores from any test, the user should look for discrepancies:

1. How do the separate scores from tests within the battery compare?
2. How do the scores from this testing compare with those from the last testing?
3. How do the scores compare with in-class performance tests, behavior in verbal interactions, and performance on written assignments?
4. How do the scores compare with recent scores from standardized achievement tests?

Nearly all intelligence tests used in the schools are measures of developed abilities, skills obtained through experiences both in and out of school. Many of these skills can be nurtured through direct instruction; they need not wait for some kind of maturational unfolding. Consequently, when deficiencies are noted, teachers can intervene with the intent to improve a child's learning strategies—short-term or long-term memory, ability to retrieve information, ability to discriminate the attributes of concepts, or the ability to classify objects or ideas.

The Riverside Publishing Company

SERVICE 9B:
LIST REPORT OF PUPIL SCORES

Cognitive Abilities Test

Class/Group MRS KESSLER
Building LAKEVIEW ELEMENTARY
Bldg Code
System HEXLER COMMUNITY
Norms FALL
Order No 000-014879-000 ==

Form 4
Grade 2
Test Date 9/86
Page 1

VERBAL BATTERY

Pupil Name / ID Number / Other Info	Birth Date / Age	Level (Sex)	No Marked	Raw Score	Grade Scores PR	S	STD Score	Age Scores National PR	S	Local PR	S
APARICIO, ANNA	9/78 8-00	2 (F)	56	46	91	8	118	87	7		
BRADLEY, KRISTIN	6/78 8-03	2 (F)	56	38	52	5	97	43	5		
CASCIO, RYAN	9/78 8-00	2 (F)	56	32	24	4	88	23	4		
DAVIS, ISIAH	9/78 8-00	2 (M)	56	42	76	6	107	67	6		
GAINEY, BRIAN	2/79 7-07	2 (M)	56	41	71	6	109	71	6		
GOMEZ, LUIS	8/78 8-01	2 (M)	56	36	40	5	94	35	4		
JANIK, MELINDA	6/79 7-03	2 (F)	56	40	66	6	111	75	6		
KATO, JOHN	11/78 7-10	2 (M)	56	41	71	6	107	67	6		
LEAPHORN, NADINE	4/79 7-05	2 (F)	56	43	80	7	114	81	7		
MARRERO, GLORIA	3/79 7-06	2 (F)	56	48	97	9	128	96	9		
OMEARA, DANIEL	1/79 7-08	2 (M)	56	47	94	8	122	92	8		
OMORI, JENNIFER	4/79 7-05	2 (F)	56	40	66	6	108	69	6		
REYES, ELENA	1/79 7-08	2 (F)	56	42	76	6	109	71	6		
SAED, FARHAD	1/79 7-08	2 (M)	56	37	44	5	98	45	5		
SAKODA, FUHIKO	7/78 8-02	2 (F)	56	40	40	5	92	31	4		
SALAS, CESAR	10/78 7-11	2 (M)	56	49	98	9	126	95	8		
HABAUNSEE, JOHN	11/78 7-10	2 (M)	56	44	84	7	114	81	7		
WALKER, SHARON	7/78 8-02	2 (F)	56	36	40	5	92	31	4		
CLASS AVERAGES NO. TESTED = 18 N FOR AVERAGES =			18	41.0	6.3		107.4	68	6.0		

QUANTITATIVE BATTERY

No Marked	Raw Score	Grade Scores PR	S	STD Score	Age Scores National PR	S	Local PR	S
56	54	99	9	140	99	9		
56	36	44	5	92	31	4		
56	40	65	6	102	55	5		
56	43	75	6	108	69	6		
56	49	93	8	126	95	8		
56	37	52	5	98	45	5		
56	41	70	6	113	79	7		
56	38	56	5	102	55	5		
56	39	61	6	105	62	6		
56	34	36	4	95	38	4		
56	43	75	6	113	79	7		
56	49	93	8	124	93	8		
56	42	72	6	108	69	6		
56	37	52	5	95	38	4		
56	44	79	7	110	73	6		
56	44	79	7	113	79	7		
56	40	65	6	99	48	5		
18	41.6	6.1		108.3	70	6.0		

NONVERBAL BATTERY

No Marked	Raw Score	Grade Scores PR	S	STD Score	Age Scores National PR	S	Local PR	S
53	49	96	9	129	97	9		
53	33	41	5	93	33	4		
53	24	16	3	81	12	3		
53	44	84	7	112	77	7		
53	45	87	7	119	88	7		
53	30	30	4	91	29	4		
53	24	16	3	88	23	4		
53	34	45	5	99	48	5		
53	45	87	7	119	88	7		
53	45	87	7	119	88	7		
53	47	93	8	123	92	8		
53	35	49	5	102	55	5		
53	40	70	6	107	67	6		
53	35	49	5	100	50	5		
53	29	27	4	87	21	3		
53	47	93	8	121	91	8		
53	47	93	8	123	92	8		
53	32	36	4	91	29	4		
18	38.1	5.8		105.8	64	5.8		

PR = Percentile Rank   S = Stanine

Figure 18–1. Sample List Report of *Cognitive Abilities Test* Scores

Exceptional students who demonstrate highly developed cognitive skills require special attention, also. They might be able to learn faster, handle more complex ideas, and probe greater depths than most of their classmates. Supplemental materials and projects can be used to provide the enrichment they probably need. Extra, high-interest activities need to be kept on hand because, since they may require fewer repetitions to learn, these students are likely to develop more idle time than their peers. The so-called troublemakers in a classroom are as likely to come from the top of the ability scale as the bottom, especially if individualization of instruction is inadequate.

The sample report shown in Figure 18–1 contains the scores from Mrs. Kessler's second-grade class on the *Cognitive Abilities Test* (CogAT) (Thorndike and Hagen, 1986). The procedures described in Chapter 17 for interpreting individual scores can be used with this list report, too. Here are some reasonable statements to make about the performance of Anna Aparicio, the first student listed.

1. In terms of the descriptors in Table 18–1, Anna's performance is above average compared to other eight-year-olds nationally.
2. Since the age of most beginning second graders (nationally) is closer to six years than seven, we should expect Anna's age PR and S scores to be higher than the corresponding grade scores (as they are).
3. Anna's verbal performance could be termed a relative weakness because the other two scores are so high. (In an absolute sense, no weaknesses are apparent.)
4. Quantitative reasoning is both a relative and an absolute strength for Anna. She may progress faster than her classmates in math, more so in math concepts and computational skills than in verbal problem solving.

The class averages in the last row of the report in Figure 18–1 indicate that Mrs. Kessler's class has a fairly even pattern of scores: 107.4, 108.3, and 105.8. This means there are no identifiable *group* strengths and weaknesses to which she might need to adjust. The typical student has scores in the sixth stanine with percentile ranks around 68. Fortunately, there are no students who, on the basis of their battery scores, seem to require further testing to explore the possibility of developmental disabilities.

APTITUDE TESTING

Aptitude tests, like intelligence tests, are not always easy to distinguish from achievement tests because, on the surface, the content seems interchangeable. For example, a collection of math items could be found on any one of the three types. There are differences—sometimes subtle and sometimes gross—that help developers of aptitude tests accomplish purposes that achievement tests ordinarily are not intended to serve.

Aptitude tests are measures of potential—abilities that foreshadow success on related tasks at some future time. Their purpose is predictive and their focus often is narrowed to a single ability or small collection of related abilities. Someone who has the aptitude to do clerical work, for example, has the prerequisite skills in manual dexterity, attention to detail, and speed with repetitive tasks to complete many types of clerical work effectively and efficiently. Of course, if the person has performed clerical work previously, we would not need an aptitude test to predict his or her potential as a clerk. In most walks of life, past performance (achievement) is the best predictor of future performance in the same realm of activity.

The most common forms of aptitude are those used to judge scholastic promise and those used in employment and educational counseling. The American College Test (ACT) and Scholastic Aptitude Test (SAT) are widely used to make predictions about who is likely to succeed in a college undergraduate program. Other similar tests are used for particular admission decisions: graduate school (GRE, Miller Analogies, GMAT), medical school (MCAT), and law school (LSAT). These tests tend to be highly verbal, but several of them also yield separate quantitative, verbal, and total scores. In addition to these, aptitude-test scores are used in counseling situations to assess promise in musical, mechanical, and artistic endeavors, among others.

It is common to include an aptitude battery in a middle school testing program to aid students, parents, and counselors in planning the most appropriate high school curriculum for students to pursue. However, in most cases the scores from standardized achievement tests and the grades from a variety of subject areas may provide an equally useful planning base. Thus, aptitude tests might be administered to an individual for whom past information is incomplete, conflicting, or dated due to unusual intervening events in the student's life.

In sum, aptitude tests are designed to predict future performance and are based on content that may have been learned in or out of school. By contrast, achievement tests are intended to describe the current status of an examinee's learning. The content of an achievement test should represent a knowledge domain that we care to know about. The content of an aptitude test, however, need not be bound to a particular domain because the user will not want to make inferences about *that* domain. Instead, the user of aptitude scores wishes to make inferences about future behavior—what the examinee probably will be able to do, not what he or she can do now.

Intelligence is thought of by many as a general aptitude. In view of the competing theories of intelligence and the nature of the corresponding sets of tasks used to measure it, such aptitudes as verbal, visual–spatial, and quantitative reasoning seem to be fitting descriptors. In addition, the purposes for using intelligence tests are nearly always predictive rather than descriptive. More on the nature of aptitude tests and their relationship to intelligence tests can be found in Cronbach (1984) and Anastasi (1988).

SUMMARY PROPOSITIONS

1. Because of the variety of definitions proposed for intelligence and the lack of consensus regarding how to measure it, schools should not use the results from different tests as though they were measures of exactly the same construct.

2. Educators should prefer verbal to nonverbal intelligence tests, particularly for group testing, and tests that emphasize abilities developed in school rather than those that result from incidental learning.

3. Instead of choosing tests that purport to be "culture free" or "culture fair," schools should choose tests whose content is relevant to the learning tasks of the school.

4. The age and grade norms used to interpret scores from intelligence tests are usually expressed as standard scores or percentile ranks.

5. The scores from an intelligence-test battery can convey an overall ability level, as well as a pattern of strengths and weaknesses.

6. The particular scores a student obtains on an intelligence test may have implications for deciding what skills the student needs to learn and which instructional procedures might be most effective with that child.

7. Test users should not be surprised to get somewhat different scores from somewhat different intelligence tests, or to find that the same student's score shifts upward or downward from time to time when given the same test.

8. Teachers should regard intelligence tests as measures of general ability in school learning, an ability that is based on prior learning.

9. Aptitude tests are designed to forecast success in some future endeavor, presumably by measuring skills that are essential to successful performance in that endeavor.

10. The focus of achievement tests is what the examinee can do now, but the focus of aptitude tests is what the examinee will be able to do in the future.

QUESTIONS FOR STUDY AND DISCUSSION

1. What are some of the practical and theoretical consequences of our inability to agree on a definition of intelligence?

2. What are some examples of individuals adapting to their social environment?

3. How can a prospective user of an intelligence test determine just what the test actually measures?

4. Could meaningful criterion-referenced interpretations be made with scores from an intelligence test? Explain your answer.

5. How could a set of tasks be culture fair without being culture free?

6. Why might the tasks on a nonverbal intelligence test not be considered culture fair?

7. What similarities exist between a total score from an intelligence-test battery and a composite score from an achievement-test battery?

8. Why are the intelligence-test scores of students generally more stable over time than are their achievement-test scores?

9. In view of the differences in purpose of achievement tests and aptitude tests, how might the test-construction procedures differ for the two?

Appendix A

Sample Evaluation Planning Guide
Health Unit:
Physical Fitness (Grade 6)

Assess Entering Behavior

1. Class oral questioning to determine group familiarity with these terms: physical fitness, endurance, body flexibility, body strength, stress, and fatigue.
2. Observation and classification of students as overweight, about right, underweight; physically normal or handicapped; and typical response to physical exertion as tolerant, somewhat stressed, or overly stressed.

Formative Evaluation

1. Periodic short quizzes dealing with terms, concepts, and relationships between ideas.
2. Class oral questioning with examples and non-examples to check concept attainment.
3. Review of draft copy of proposed exercise plan and program.
4. Review, after one week, of exercise and sleep journal entries.

Summative Evaluation

1. Objective test section covering concepts, relationships, and application of principles.
2. Short answer test section dealing with explanations, descriptions, and problem solving.

3. Short essay section requiring the evaluation of a hypothetical exercise program for a healthy sixth grader.

4. Development of a two-week journal with daily entries describing personal exercise and sleep activity.

5. Preparation of an exercise program by the student and a write-up of the effectiveness of the program, recommended changes in the program, and personal reactions to a two-week implementation.

Appendix B

Propositions Obtained from Instructional Materials
Health Unit:
Physical Fitness (Grade 6)

1. Exercise is bodily exertion that contributes to developing and maintaining fitness.
2. Exercise can improve blood vessel capacity and increase heart strength and lung capacity.
3. Exercising to increase muscle strength provides protection from back pain and builds abdominal support.
4. Bone thickness and density can be increased by exercising.
5. Fat tissue is replaced by lean muscle tissue as a result of regular exercising.
6. Exercise can alleviate the symptoms of stress—muscle tension and inability to sleep.
7. Aerobic exercise requires a minimum of 10 minutes of continuous, rhythmic physical activity.
8. Aerobic exercise produces these body effects: increased cardiovascular and respiratory capacity, lower blood pressure and heart rate, and improved endurance.
9. A minimum of three 20-minute sessions weekly is required to achieve the benefits of aerobic exercise.
10. Anaerobic exercise is brief, intense physical activity.
11. Anaerobic exercise improves body movement, strength, and speed, usually without conditioning the cardiopulmonary systems.
12. Planning an exercise program includes these components: physical exam, fitness ratings, goal definition, activity selection, progress monitoring.
13. Fitness goals generally center on cardiopulmonary endurance, muscular endurance, muscular strength, flexibility, and alertness and concentration.

14. The schedule for an exercise program accounts for frequency, intensity, and session length.
15. Target heart rate is the rate that should be maintained during exercise to improve cardiopulmonary fitness.
16. Maximum heart rate is 220 minus age; target heart rate is a percentage of the maximum rate that depends on current fitness level and age.
17. The exercise-session length should be moderate for aerobic activity and longer for a program geared to losing body fat.
18. Symmetric stretching of body parts prior to workout prevents muscle tear and strain and promotes free joint movement.
19. Dehydration can be prevented by drinking cold water before and during exercise.
20. Signs of overexertion include: nausea, unusual tiredness, and lasting aches or pains in joints or muscles.
21. A fitness journal helps monitor progress toward goals and provides information for modifying the program.
22. Exercise and food intake operate jointly to affect weight loss, gain, and stability.
23. Sleep is accompanied by muscle relaxation and reduction in heart rate, breathing rate, and body temperature.
24. Deep sleep stages of the sleep cycle are used to repair body tissue and to rid the tissue of wastes.
25. Dreaming occurs during the rapid eye movement (REM) stages of the several nightly sleep cycles.
26. The sleep cycle can be affected negatively by poor body position, too much light, or too much noise.
27. The amount of sleep a person requires depends on age, activity level, and general health condition.

Appendix C

Sample Instructional Objectives
Health Unit:
Physical Fitness (Grade 6)

At the completion of this unit the student should be able to:

1. Identify increased body system efficiencies that result from regular exercise.
2. Explain how regular exercise relates to both bone stress and increased bone strength.
3. Describe the effects of exercise on the specific symptoms of emotional stress.
4. Distinguish the purposes and features of aerobic and anaerobic exercising.
5. List the essential components of a plan for developing an exercise program.
6. Assess the completeness and appropriateness of an exercise program tailored for another person.
7. Describe how to do a physical activity that would help attain each of these goals: cardiopulmonary endurance, muscular strength, flexibility, and mental alertness and concentration.
8. Explain how to determine each of these rates: maximum heart rate, target heart rate, and resting heart rate.
9. Plan an exercise program consistent with his or her own goals and current health status.
10. Keep a complete daily fitness journal for a two-week period of an exercise program.
11. Describe how nutrition and exercise jointly affect body weight.

12. State the changes in these body systems as a person begins sleep: muscular, circulatory, respiratory, nervous, and excretory.
13. Draw a line graph that shows the number and frequency of dream episodes in one night for most individuals.
14. Estimate the relative amounts of sleep required by individuals who vary in age, activity level, and general health condition.

Appendix D

Test Selection Committee In-service Topics

The teachers and others who are responsible for test selection must have knowledge about (1) the system's curriculum and (2) the essentials of testing to fulfill their obligations. Some of the most significant topics to address in preparing a selection committee for its primary task are listed below.

A. Sources of Information about Tests
  1. References (for example, *Mental Measurements Yearbook, Test Critiques*)
  2. Computer search systems [for example, Bibliographic Retrieval Services, ERIC (CIJE)]
  3. Publisher materials (catalogs, specimen sets)
  4. Test reviews (references, journals, textbooks)
  5. Consultants (publisher's test specialist, selected college education faculty)

B. Test Content and Curriculum Match
  1. Identify the scope of the battery (major test scores)
  2. Within test areas, assess breadth of skill and subskill coverage
  3. Within test areas, determine number of items per skill
  4. Within test areas, determine the taxonomic levels covered and emphasized (for example, knowledge level, variety of higher-order skills)
  5. Need to consider discrepancies between the school's *published* curriculum and the *instructional* curriculum
  6. Take the test with an introspective view toward assessing curriculum match
  7. Judge fairness in gender and ethnic representation—names, roles, interpersonal relations depicted

C. Technical Quality
  1. Evaluate reliability evidence in view of user purpose (skill scores, equivalent forms, difference scores within the battery)

  2. Assess the appropriateness of available norms (relevance of norm population, representativeness of norm sample, recency of data)

  3. Review completion rates and time limits to judge efficiency and speededness

  4. Review difficulty of each test in terms of floor and ceiling; difficulty of items for time of year of testing

  5. Determine reading load in nonreading tests in terms of readabilities, vocabulary levels, sentence structure, and accompanying visual displays

D. Practical Matters

  1. Compute costs of materials and services (for example, consumable versus reusable, processing and scoring charges, local preparation and dissemination of reports)

  2. Determine extent and quality of publisher consultative services (teacher in-service, school board or parent meetings)

  3. Judge usefulness of ancillary materials (manuals, guides, interpretive aids)

  4. Evaluate test administration and preparation time in terms of information gained

  5. Appraise the quality of printed materials (for example, format and type size, legibility of art, usability of answer documents)

  6. Determine the need for and the suitability of practice materials

  7. Determine extent to which a companion test of cognitive skills is available that will meet other needs efficiently and economically

Appendix E

Teacher In-service Topics Regarding Preparation for Test Administration

The list of topics below are among the most relevant to be addressed in teacher in-service programs prior to test administration.

A. Selection of Appropriate Test Levels
 1. Review of test content to establish the most appropriate test level for each grade (or class)
 2. Assess the need for individualized testing (out of level) within classrooms by using individuals' current reading and developmental levels

B. Test Scheduling and Advance Preparation
 1. Identify students for whom adaptation in administration must be arranged (visual, hearing, LD, ED, left-handers)
 2. Prepare students through discussion of testing purposes and, if needed, use of practice materials
 3. Outline procedures and develop schedule for make-ups

C. Test Administration
 1. Review local time schedule and the need to adhere to it
 2. Discuss appropriate and inappropriate methods of preparing students, including the need to motivate students
 3. Review importance of following standard directions exactly and consequences of departures in terms of score invalidity
 4. Describe test security measures to be taken before, during, and after testing
 5. Discuss the importance of reading administration directions prior to testing date
 6. Describe procedures for preparing the classroom for testing (arrangement, bulletin-board displays)
 7. Review systematic procedures for materials distribution and collection

8. Discuss the importance of monitoring test takers, types of permissible assistance during testing, handling irregularities, and proctor responsibilities

D. Postadministration Matters
   1. Describe procedures for checking documents for completion and for quality of student marks
   2. When applicable, review steps for hand-scoring procedures (for example, using scoring masks, converting scores, and recording results)
   3. When applicable, discuss need for and procedures for using special coding areas on the answer documents

Appendix F

Teacher In-service Topics on Achievement-test Score Interpretation

A posttesting in-service program can prepare teachers to understand the meanings of scores, the locations of scores on their reports, and methods of using the reports effectively. This list identifies key concepts and principles teachers must understand to interpret standardized achievement-test scores.

A. Selection of Publisher Score Reports and Services
  1. Review the system's purposes for testing and identify report formats that will facilitate achieving each purpose
  2. Match the specific goals of teachers, counselors, and administrators with the types of reports that facilitate attaining the goals of each group
B. Differentiate the Types of Scores Reported
  1. Distinguish composite, test, skill, and item scores
  2. Describe the purposes of raw and percent scores
  3. Explain the meanings and purposes of developmental scores (GE, SS)
  4. Explain the meanings and purposes of status scores (PR, NCE, stanine)
  5. Describe class average scores in terms of "average student"
C. Understanding the Norms Used in Reporting
  1. Describe the nature of each group (local, national, catholic, large city, and so on)
  2. When appropriate, differentiate norms for pupil scores and norms for school averages
  3. Explain the effect of time of year of testing on GEs and PRs
D. Extracting Information from Test Reports
  1. Assess annual growth of individual students using profile charts or cumulative records

    2. Identify individual strengths and weaknesses in terms of both test areas and skills within each test area

    3. Estimate individual developmental levels within major curriculum areas

    4. Monitor annual growth of classes (or grade cohorts), developing growth expectations and accounting for student migration

    5. Identify class (or grade) strengths and weaknesses in terms of tests and skills within tests

    6. Use group data to describe skill and item performance (norm and criterion referenced)

    7. Explain test results to students and parents

E. Basic Interpretive Considerations

    1. Differentiate the purposes of norm- and criterion-referenced interpretation

    2. Demonstrate how to take measurement error into account with developmental and status scores

    3. Describe how to set reasonable performance standards for use with criterion-referenced interpretations

References

AARON, R. I. (1971). *Knowing and the function of reason.* New York: Oxford University Press.

AIRASIAN, P. W. (1989). Classroom assessment and educational improvement. In L. W. Anderson (ed.), *The effective teacher.* New York: Random House.

ALBANESE, M. A., and SABERS, D. L. (1978). Multiple response vs. multiple true–false scoring: A comparison of reliability and validity. Paper presented at the Annual Meeting of the National Council on Measurement in Education, Toronto.

———, KENT, T. H., and WHITNEY, D. R. (1977). A comparison of difficulty, reliability, and validity of complex multiple choice, multiple response, and multiple true–false items (Research Report No. 95). Iowa City: University of Iowa, Learning Resource Unit, College of Medicine.

ALEXANDER, L., and JAMES, H. T. (1987). *The nation's report card: Improving the assessment of student achievement.* Washington, DC: National Academy of Education.

AMERICAN PSYCHOLOGICAL ASSOCIATION. (1985). *Standards for educational and psychological testing.* Washington, DC: The Association.

ANASTASI, A. (1988). *Psychological testing* (6th ed.). New York: Macmillan, Inc.

ANDERSON, J. R. (1983). *The architecture of cognition.* Cambridge, MA: Harvard University Press.

ANNIS, L. F. (1983). *Study techniques.* Dubuque, IA: William C. Brown.

AYRES, L. P. (1912). *A scale for measuring the quality of handwriting of school children.* New York: Russell Sage Foundation, Bulletin 113.

BAGLIN, R. F. (1981). Does "nationally" normed really mean nationally? *Journal of Educational Measurement, 18,* 97–107.

Bakke v. California. 438 U.S. 265. (1978).

BARKER, D., and EBEL, R. L. (1981). A comparison of difficulty and discrimination values of selected true–false item types. *Contemporary Educational Psychology, 7,* 35–40.

BARTLETT, L. (1987). Academic evaluation and student discipline don't mix: A critical review. *Journal of Law and Education, 16*(2), 155–65.

BERK, R. K. (1984). Selecting the index of reliability. In R. K. Berk (ed.), *A guide to criterion-referenced test construction.* Baltimore: Johns Hopkins University Press.

BINET, A. (1911). Nouvelles recherches sur la mesure du niveau intellectuel chez les enfants d'ecole. *Annee Psychologiquie, 17,* 145–201.

BIRENBAUM, M., and TATSUOKA, K. K. (1987). Open-ended versus multiple-choice response formats—It does make a difference for diagnostic purposes. *Applied Psychological Measurement, 11,* 385–95.

BLOOM, B. S. (1968). Learning for mastery. *Evaluation Comment, 1,* UCLA Center for the Study of Evaluation.

———, and others (1956). *Taxonomy of educational objectives. Handbook I: The cognitive domain.* New York: David McKay Co.

BOULDING, K. E. (1967). The uncertain future of knowledge and technology. *Education Digest, 33,* 7–11.

BUNDERSON, C. V., and INOUYE, D. K. (1987). Computer-aided educational delivery systems. In R. Gagné (ed.), *Instructional technology.* Hillsdale, NJ: Lawrence Erlbaum Associates.

CARTER, R. S. (1952). How invalid are marks assigned by teachers? *Journal of Educational Psychology, 43,* 218–28.

CASHEN, V. M., and RAMSEYER, G. C. (1969). The use of separate answer sheets by primary age children. *Journal of Educational Measurement, 6,* 155–8.

CHASE, C. I. (1979). The impact of achievement expectations and handwriting quality on scoring essay tests. *Journal of Educational Measurement, 16,* 39–42.

354

Code of fair testing practices in education (1988). Washington, DC: Joint Committee on Testing Practices (available from the American Psychological Association).

COFFMAN, W. E. (1966). On the validity of essay tests of achievement. *Journal of Educational Measurement, 3*, 151–6.

—— (1971). Essay examinations. In R. L. Thorndike (ed.), *Educational Measurement* (2nd ed.). Washington, DC: American Council on Education.

COHEN, M. R., and NAGLE, E. (1934). *An introduction to logic and the scientific method.* New York: Harcourt Brace Jovanovich.

COHEN, S. B. (1983). Assigning report card grades to the mainstreamed child. *Teaching Exceptional Children, 15*, 86–9.

COLEMAN, W., and CURETON, E. E. (1954). Intelligence and achievement: The "jangle fallacy" again. *Educational and Psychological Measurement, 14*, 347–51.

Comptroller General (1976). *The national assessment of educational progress: Its results need to be made more useful* (Report to Congress, HRD-76-113). Washington, DC: Author.

CONOLEY, J. C., and KRAMER, J. J. (eds.) (1990). *Tenth mental measurements yearbook.* Lincoln, NE: Buros Institute of Mental Measurements.

COOK, D. L. (1955). An investigation of three aspects of free-response and choice-type tests at the college level. *Dissertation Abstracts, 15*, 1351.

COUNTS, G. S. (1932). *Dare the school build a new social order?* New York: John Day Co.

COX, R. C., and VARGAS, J. (1966). A comparison of item selection techniques for norm-referenced and criterion-referenced tests. Paper presented at the Annual Meeting of the National Council on Measurement in Education, Chicago.

CROCKER, L., and ALGINA, J. (1986). *Introduction to classical and modern test theory.* New York: Holt, Rinehart and Winston.

——, and BENSON, I. J. (1980). Does answer-changing affect test quality? *Measurement and Evaluation in Guidance, 12*, 233–9.

CRONBACH, L. J. (1951). Coefficient alpha and the internal structure of tests. *Psychometrika, 16*, 297–334.

—— (1984). *Essentials of psychological testing* (4th ed.). New York: Harper & Row.

——, and MEEHL, P. E. (1955). Construct validity in psychological tests. *Psychological Bulletin, 52*, 281–302.

CURTIS, H. A., and KROPP, R. P. (1962). *Experimental analyses of the effects of various modes of item presentation on the scores and factorial content of tests administered by visual and audiovisual means.* Tallahassee, FL: Florida State University, Department of Educational Research and Testing.

DAVIS, F. B. (1946). *Item analysis data* (Harvard Education Papers No. 2). Cambridge, MA: Harvard University, Graduate School of Education.

Debra P. v. Turlington. 747 F. Supp. 244 (M.D. Fla. 1979).

DeCECCO, J. P., and CRAWFORD, W. R. (1974). *The psychology of learning and instruction* (2nd ed.). Englewood Cliffs, NJ: Prentice-Hall, Inc.

Diana v. State Board of Education. Civil No. C-70, 37 RFP, (N. D. Cal. 1973).

DIEDRICH, P. (1960). *Short-cut statistics for teacher-made tests* (Evaluation and Advisory Service Series No. 5). Princeton, NJ: Educational Testing Service.

DIVINE, J. H., and KYLEN, D. W. (1979). *How to beat test anxiety and score higher on your exams.* Woodbury, NY: Barron's Educational Series.

DORR-BREMME, D. W., and HERMAN, J. L. (1986). *Assessing student achievement: A profile of classroom practices* (CSE Monograph Series in Evaluation, No. 11). Los Angeles: University of California—Los Angeles.

DOWNEY, R. G. (1979). Item-option weighting of achievement

tests: Comparative study of methods. *Applied Psychological Measurement, 3*(4), 453–61.

DRESSEL, P. L. (1978). Advanced placement examinations. Review in O. K. Buros (ed.), *The eighth mental measurements yearbook.* Highland Park, NJ: Gryphon Press, pp. 627–9.

DRYDEN, R., and FRISBIE, D. A. (1975). *Comparative reliabilities and validities of multiple choice and complex multiple choice nursing education tests.* Paper presented at the Annual Meeting of the National Council on Measurement in Education, Washington, DC.

EBEL, R. L. (1937). Some effects of irrelevant data in physics test problems. *School Science and Mathematics, 37*, 327–30.

—— (1951). Estimation of the reliability of ratings. *Psychometrika, 16*, 407–24.

—— (1961). Must all tests be valid? *American Psychologist, 16*, 640–7.

—— (1965). *Measuring educational achievement.* Englewood Cliffs, NJ: Prentice-Hall, Inc.

—— (1967). The relation of item discrimination to test reliability. *Journal of Educational Measurement, 4*, 125–8.

—— (1968). Blind guessing on objective achievement tests. *Journal of Educational Measurement, 5*, 321–5.

—— (1972). *Essentials of educational measurement* (2nd ed.). Englewood Cliffs, NJ: Prentice-Hall, Inc.

—— (1975). Can teachers write good true–false test items? *Journal of Educational Measurement, 12*, 31–6.

—— (1978). The ineffectiveness of multiple true–false items. *Educational and Psychological Measurement, 38*, 37–44.

—— (1979). *Essentials of educational measurement* (3rd ed.). Englewood Cliffs, NJ: Prentice-Hall, Inc.

—— (1980). Are true–false items useful? In R. L. Ebel (ed.), *Practical problems in educational measurement.* Lexington, MA: D. C. Heath.

—— (1983). The practical validation of tests of ability. *Educational Measurement: Issues and Practice, 2*, 7–10.

EURICH, A. C. (1931). Four types of examinations compared and evaluated. *Journal of Educational Psychology, 22*, 268–78.

Evaluation and Examination Service (1982). *Evidence for not weighting objective test items* (EES Memo No. 51). Iowa City, IA: University of Iowa.

EVANS, S. S., EVANS, W. H., and MERCER, C. D. (1986). *Assessment for instruction.* Boston: Allyn and Bacon.

FELDT, L. S., and BRENNAN, R. L. (1989). Reliability. In R. L. Linn (ed.), *Educational measurement* (3rd ed.). Washington, DC: American Council on Education.

——, FORSYTH, R. A., and ALNOT, S. D. (1989). *Teacher, administrator, and counselor manual—Iowa Tests of Educational Development.* Chicago: Riverside Publishing Company.

FINLAYSON, D. S. (1951). The reliability of the marking of essays. *British Journal of Educational Psychology, 21*, 126–34.

FLANAGAN, J. C. (1939). General considerations in the selection of test items and a short method of estimating the product-moment coefficient from the tails of the distributions. *Journal of Educational Psychology, 30*, 674–80.

FRISBIE, D. A. (1973). Multiple-choice vs. true–false: A comparison of reliabilities and concurrent validities. *Journal of Educational Measurement, 10*, 297–304.

—— (1974). The effect of item format on reliability and validity: A study of multiple choice and true–false achievement tests. *Educational and Psychological Measurement, 34*, 885–92.

—— (1976). Expanded reporting forms—points to ponder. *The Clearing House, 49*, 371–2.

—— (1977). Issues in formulating course grading policies. *National Association of Colleges and Teachers of Agriculture Journal, 21*, 15–18.

—— (1978). Methodological considerations in grading. *Na-*

tional Association of Colleges and Teachers of Agriculture Journal, 22, 30–4.

—— (1988). Reliability of scores from teacher-made tests. *Educational Measurement: Issues and Practice, 7*(1), 25–35.

——, and ANDREWS, K. (1990). Kindergarten pupil and teacher behavior during standardized achievement testing. *Elementary School Journal, 90*(4), 435–448.

——, and DRUVA, C. (1986). Estimating the reliability of multiple true–false tests. *Journal of Educational Measurement, 23,* 99–105.

——, and ORY, J. C. (1980). *Alternatives to the complex multiple choice item: An experimental comparison* (Research Report No. 370). Urbana–Champaign, IL: University of Illinois, Office of Instructional Resources.

——, and SWEENEY, D. C. (1982). The relative merits of multiple true–false achievement tests. *Journal of Educational Measurement, 19,* 29–35.

GAGNÉ, R. M., and DRISCOLL, M. P. (1988). *Essentials of learning for instruction* (2nd ed.). Englewood Cliffs, NJ: Prentice-Hall, Inc.

GERLACH, V. S. (1966). Preparing transparent keys for inspecting answer sheets. *Journal of Educational Measurement, 3,* 62.

GLASER, R. L. (1962). Psychology and instructional technology. In R. L. Glaser (ed.), *Training research and education* (559–78). Pittsburgh, PA: University of Pittsburgh Press.

—— (1963). Instructional technology and the measurement of learning outcomes. *American Psychologist, 18,* 519–21.

—— (1968). Adapting the elementary school curriculum to individual performance. *Proceedings of the 1967 Invitational Conference on Testing Problems.* Princeton, NJ: Educational Testing Service.

GREEN, B. F. (1983). Adaptive testing by computer. In R. B. Ekstrom (ed.), *New directions for testing and measurement: Measurement, technology, and individuality in education.* San Francisco: Jossey-Bass.

Griggs v. *Duke Power Co.* 401 U.S. 424, (1971).

GRONLUND, N. E., and LINN, R. L. (1990). *Measurement and evaluation in teaching* (6th ed.). New York: Macmillan Publishing Co.

GUILFORD, J. P. (1936). *Psychometric Methods.* New York: McGraw-Hill Book Co.

—— (1965). *Fundamental statistics in psychology and education.* New York: McGraw-Hill Book Co.

—— (1966). Intelligence: 1965 model. *American Psychologist, 21,* 20–5.

HADLEY, S. T. (1954). A school mark—fact or fancy? *Educational Administration and Supervision, 40,* 305–12.

HALADYNA, T. M., and DOWNING, S. M. (1989a). Validity of a taxonomy of multiple-choice item-writing rules. *Applied Measurement in Education, 2*(1), 51–78.

——, and —— (1989b). A taxonomy of multiple-choice item-writing rules. *Applied Measurement in Education, 2*(1), 37–50.

HALES, L. and TOKAR, E. (1975). The effect of the quality of preceding responses on the grades assigned to subsequent responses to an essay question. *Journal of Educational Measurement, 12,* 115–18.

HARROW, A. J. (1972). *A taxonomy of the psychomotor domain: A guide for developing behavioral objectives.* New York: David McKay Co.

HECKMAN, R. W., TIFFIN, J., and SNOW, R. E. (1967). Effects of controlling item exposure in achievement testing. *Educational and Psychological Measurement, 27,* 113–25.

HEMBREE, R. (1988). Correlates, causes, effects, and treatment of test anxiety. *Review of Educational Research, 58*(1), 47–77.

HIERONYMUS, A. N. (1961). *Research on the use of a separate answer sheet in grade 3.* Unpublished manuscript, Iowa Testing Programs, University of Iowa.

——, and HOOVER, H. D. (1986). *Manual for school administrators—Iowa Tests of Basic Skills.* Chicago: Riverside Publishing Company.

——, and —— (1990). *Multilevel teacher's guide—Iowa Tests of Basic Skills,* Form J. Chicago: Riverside Publishing Company.

HILLS, J. R., and GLADNEY, M. B. (1968). Predicting grades from below chance test scores. *Journal of Educational Measurement, 5,* 45–53.

HIVELY, W. (1974). Introduction to domain-referenced testing. In W. Hively (ed.), *Domain-referenced testing* (5–15). Englewood Cliffs, NJ: Educational Technology Publications.

Hobson v. *Hansen.* 269 F. Supp. 406 (D.D.C. 1967).

HOEL, P. G. (1947). *Introduction to mathematical statistics.* New York: John Wiley & Sons, Inc.

HOGAN, T. P. (1981). *Relationship between free-response and choice-type tests of achievement: A review of the literature.* ERIC Document Reproduction Service No. ED 224-811.

HOOVER, H. D. (1983). *The most appropriate scores for measuring educational development in the elementary schools: GE's.* Invited paper presented at the Annual Meeting of the American Educational Research Association, Montreal.

HSU, L. M. (1979). Ordering power of separate versus grouped true-false tests: Interaction of type of test with knowledge level of examinees. *Applied Psychological Measurement, 3,* 529–36.

HUGHES, D. C., KEELING, B., and TUCK, B. F. (1983). Effects of achievement expectations and handwriting quality on scoring essays. *Journal of Educational Measurement, 20,* 65–70.

IRVIN, L. K., HALPERN, A. S., and LANDMAN, J. T. (1980). Assessment of retarded student achievement with standardized true/false and multiple-choice tests. *Journal of Educational Measurement, 17,* 51–8.

JOHNSON, A. P. (1951). Notes on a suggested index of item validity: The U-L index. *Journal of Educational Psychology, 62,* 499–504.

JOHNSON, M. S., and KRESS, R. A. (1965). *Informal reading inventories.* Newark, DE: International Reading Association.

JOYCE, B. R., and WEIL, M. (1980). *Models of teaching* (2nd ed.). Englewood Cliffs, NJ: Prentice-Hall, Inc.

KALISH, R. A. (1958). An experimental evaluation of the open-book examination. *Journal of Educational Psychology, 49,* 200–4.

KANE, M. T. (1982). A sampling model for validity. *Applied Psychological Measurement, 6,* 125–60.

——, and BRENNAN, R. L. (1980). Agreement coefficients as indices of dependability for domain-referenced tests. *Applied Psychological Measurement, 4,* 105–26.

KELLER, F. (1968). Good-bye teacher. *Journal of Applied Behavioral Analysis, 1,* 79–89.

KELLEY, E. C. (1962). The fully functioning self. In *Perceiving, behaving, becoming.* Washington, DC: Association for Supervision and Curriculum Development, 1962 Yearbook.

KELLEY, T. L. (1939). The selection of upper and lower groups for the validation of test items. *Journal of Educational Psychology, 30,* 17–24.

KEYSER, D. J., and SWEETLAND, R. C. (eds.). (1985–90). *Test critiques,* Volumes I–VIII. Kansas City, MO: Test Corporation of America.

——, and —— (eds.) (1990). *Tests: A comprehensive reference for assessment in psychology, education, and business* (3rd ed.). Kansas City, MO: Test Corporation of America.

KIBLER, R. J., and others (1981). *Objectives for instruction and evaluation* (2nd ed.). Boston: Allyn and Bacon, Inc.

KRATHWOHL, D. R., BLOOM, B. S., and MASIA, B. B. (1964). *Tax-*

onomy of educational objectives. Handbook II: The affective domain. New York: David McKay Co.

KREITER, C. D., and FRISBIE, D. A. (1989). Effectiveness of multiple true–false items. *Applied Measurement in Education, 2*(3), 207–16.

KUDER, G. F., and RICHARDSON, M. W. (1937). The theory of the estimation of test reliability. *Psychometrika, 2,* 151–60.

Larry P. v. Wilson Riles. 495 F. Supp. 926 (N.D. Cal. 1979).

LEVINE, M. (1976). The academic achievement test: Its historical context and social functions. *American Psychologist, 31,* 228–38.

LIGON, E. M. (1961). Education for moral character. In P. H. Phenix (ed.), *Philosophies of education.* New York: John Wiley & Sons, Inc.

LINDQUIST, E. F. (1960). The Iowa testing programs—a retrospective review. *Education, 81,* 7–23.

LINN, R. L. (1983). Testing and instruction: Links and distinctions. *Journal of Educational Measurement, 20,* 179–89.

LOREE, M. R. (1948). *A study of a technique for improving tests.* Unpublished doctoral dissertation, University of Chicago.

MAGER, R. F. (1962). *Preparing instructional objectives.* Palo Alto, CA: Fearon Publishers, Inc.

MCCALL, W. A. (1939). *Measurement.* New York: Macmillan, Inc.

MCKEACHIE, W. J. (1988). The need for study strategy training. In C. E. Weinstein, E. T. Goetz, and P. A. Alexander (eds.), *Learning and study strategies.* New York: Academic Press, Inc.

MEHRENS, W. A., and KAMINSKI, J. (1989). Methods for improving standardized test scores: Fruitful, fruitless, or fraudulent? *Educational Measurement: Issues and Practice, 8,* 14–22.

MESSICK, S. (1989). Validity. In R. L. Linn (ed.), *Educational measurement* (3rd ed.). Washington, DC: American Council on Education.

——, BEATON, A., and LORD, F. M. (1983). *National assessment of educational progress reconsidered: A new design for a new era* (NAEP Report 83-1).

MEYER, G. (1935). An experimental study of the old and new types of examinations: II, methods of the study. *Journal of Educational Psychology, 26,* 30–40.

—— (1939). The choice of questions on essay examination. *Journal of Educational Psychology, 30,* 161–71.

MILLMAN, J. (1974a). Program assessment, criterion-referenced tests, and things like that. *Educational Horizons, 32,* 188–92.

—— (1974b). Criterion-referenced measurement. In W. J. Popham (ed.), *Evaluation in education.* Berkeley, CA: McCutchan.

——, and PAUK, W. (1969). *How to take tests.* New York: McGraw-Hill Book Co.

——, BISHOP, C. H., and EBEL, R. L. (1965). An analysis of testwiseness. *Educational and Psychological Measurement, 25,* 707–26.

MITCHELL, J. V., JR. (ed.) (1983). *Tests in print III.* Lincoln, NE: University of Nebraska Press.

MOE, K. C., and JOHNSON, M. (1988). Participants' reactions to computerized testing. *Journal of Educational Computing Research, 4*(1), 79–86.

MUELLER, D. J., and WASSER, V. (1977). Implications of changing answers on objective test items. *Journal of Educational Measurement, 14,* 9–14.

National Commission on Excellence in Education (1983). *A nation at risk: The imperative for educational reform.* Washington, DC: The Commission.

NITKO, A. J. (1980). Distinguishing the many varieties of criterion-referenced tests. *Review of Educational Research, 50*(3), 461–85.

ODELL, C. W. (1927). *Scales for rating pupils' answers to nine types of thought questions in English literature.* Urbana, IL: University of Illinois, Bureau of Educational Research.

—— (1950). Marks and marking systems. In W. S. Monroe (ed.), *Encyclopedia of educational research.* New York: Macmillan, Inc.

OOSTERHOF, A. C. (1987). Obtaining intended weights when combining students' scores. *Educational Measurement: Issues and Practice, 6,* 29–37.

OWENS, R. E., HANNA, G. S., and COPPEDGE, F. L. (1970). Comparison of multiple-choice tests using different types of distractor selection techniques. *Journal of Educational Measurement, 7,* 87–90.

PALMER, O. (1962). Seven classic ways of grading dishonestly. *English Journal, 51,* 464–7.

PATTERSON, D. G. (1926). Do new and old type examinations measure different mental functions? *School and Society, 24,* 246–8.

POLANYI, M. (1964). *Personal knowledge.* Chicago: University of Chicago Press.

POSEY, C. (1932). Luck and examination grades. *Journal of Engineering Education, 23,* 292–6.

PYRCZAK, F. (1973). Validity of the discrimination index as a measure of item quality. *Journal of Educational Measurement, 10,* 227–31.

QUELLMALZ, E. S., CAPELL, F. J., and CHOU, C. (1980). Effects of discourse and response mode on the measurement of writing competence. *Journal of Educational Measurement, 19,* 241–58.

RAMSEYER, G. C., and CASHEN, V. M. (1985). The relationship of level of eye-hand coordination and answer marking format to the test performance of first- and second-grade pupils: Implications for test validity. *Educational and Psychological Measurement, 45,* 369–75.

ROSS, C. C. (1947). *Measurement in today's schools* (2nd ed.). Englewood Cliffs, NJ: Prentice-Hall, Inc.

ROWE, M. B. (1974). Wait-time and reward as instructional variables, their influence on language, logic, and fate control: Part one—Wait time. *Journal of Research on Science Teaching, 11,* 81–94.

ROWLEY, G. L., and TRAUB, R. E. (1977). Formula scoring, number-right scoring and test-taking strategy. *Journal of Educational Measurement, 14,* 15–22.

RUCH, G. M. (1929). *The objective or new-type examination.* Glenview, IL: Scott, Foresman and Co.

RYLE, G. (1949). *The concept of mind.* London: Hutchinson and Co., Ltd.

SABERS, D. L., and WHITE, G. W. (1969). The effect of differential weighting of individual item responses on the predictive validity and reliability of an aptitude test. *Journal of Educational Measurement, 6,* 93–6.

SADLER, D. R. (1983). Evaluation and the improvement of learning. *Journal of Higher Education, 54,* 60–79.

SARVELA, P. D., and NOONAN, J. V. (1988). Testing and computer-based instruction: Psychometric considerations. *Educational Technology, 28*(5), 17–20.

SAX, G., and COLLET, L. S. (1968). The effects of differing instructions and guessing formulas on reliability and validity. *Educational and Psychological Measurement, 28,* 1127–36.

——, and CROMACK, T. R. (1966). The effects of various forms of item arrangements on test performance. *Journal of Educational Measurement, 3,* 309–11.

SCRIVEN, M. (1967). The methodology of evaluation. In R. Tyler (ed.), *Perspectives of Curriculum Evaluation.* AERA Monograph Series on Curriculum Evaluation (No. 1.) Skokie, IL: Rand McNally.

SHEPARD, L. A., and SMITH, M. L. (1986). Synthesis of research on school readiness and kindergarten retention. *Educational Leadership, 44*(3), 78–86.

SMITH, K. (1958). An investigation of the use of "double

choice" items in testing achievement. *Journal of Educational Research, 51,* 387–9.

SPEARMAN, C. E. (1927). *The abilities of man.* New York: Macmillan, Inc.

STAFF (1989, Winter). Board says recent court decisions on test use for awarding scholarships is not anti-SAT. *College Board News,* p. 1.

STALNAKER, J. M. (1951). The essay type of examination. In E. F. Lindquist (ed.), *Educational measurement.* Washington, DC: American Council on Education.

STANLEY, J. C. (1971). Reliability. In R. L. Thorndike (ed.), *Educational measurement* (2nd ed.). Washington, DC: American Council on Education.

STARCH, D., and ELLIOTT, E. C. (1912). Reliability of grading high school work in English. *School Review, 20,* 442–57.

——, and —— (1913a). Reliability of grading high school work in history. *School Review, 21,* 676–81.

——, and —— (1913b). Reliability of grading high school work in mathematics. *School Review, 21,* 254–9.

Stell v. *Savannah,* 379 U.S. 933 (1964).

STERNBERG, R. J. (1985). *Beyond IQ: A triarchic theory of human intelligence.* New York: Cambridge University Press.

STIGGINS, R. J. (1987). Design and development of performance assessments. *Educational Measurement: Issues and Practice, 6,* 33–42.

—— (1988). Revitalizing classroom assessment: The highest instructional priority. *Phi Delta Kappan, 69,* 363–8.

——, FRISBIE, D. A., and GRISWOLD, P. A. (1989). Inside high school grading practices: Building a research agenda. *Educational Measurement: Issues and Practice, 8*(2), 5–14.

——, RUBEL, E., and QUELLMALZ, E. (1986). *Measuring thinking skills in the classroom.* Washington, DC: National Education Association.

STROUD, J. B. (1946). *Psychology in education.* New York: David McKay Co.

SUBKOVIAK, M. J. (1984). Estimating the reliability of mastery-nonmastery classifications. In R. K. Berk (ed.), *A guide to criterion-referenced test construction.* Baltimore: Johns Hopkins University Press.

—— (1988). A practitioner's guide to computation and interpretation of reliability indices for mastery tests. *Journal of Educational Measurement, 25,* 47–55.

TAYLOR, H. (1980). *Contract grading* (ERIC/TM Report No. 75). Princeton, NJ: ERIC Clearinghouse on Tests, Measurement and Evaluation (ERIC Document Reproduction Service No. ED 198 152).

TERRY, P. W. (1933). How students review for objective and essay tests. *Elementary School Journal, 33,* 592–603.

TERWILLIGER, J. S. (1971). *Assigning grades to students.* Glenview, IL: Scott, Foresman and Co.

—— (1989). Classroom standard setting and grading practices. *Educational Measurement: Issues and Practice, 8*(2), 15–19.

THORNDIKE, E. L. (1918). *The seventeenth yearbook of the National Society for Study of Education (Part II).* Bloomington, IL: Public School Publishing Co.

—— (1951). Reliability. In E. F. Lindquist (ed.), *Educational measurement.* Washington, DC: American Council on Education.

THORNDIKE, R. L., and HAGEN, E. (1986). *Examiner's manual—Cognitive Abilities Test,* Form 4. Chicago: Riverside Publishing Company.

THURSTONE, L. L. (1938). Primary mental abilities. *Psychometric Monographs,* No. 1.

TRYON, G. S. (1980). The measurement and treatment of test anxiety. *Review of Educational Research, 50,* 343–72.

U.S. Office of Education (1951). *Life adjustment education for every youth.* Washington, DC: U.S. Government Printing Office.

U.S. v. *South Carolina,* 445 F. Supp. 1094 (D.S.C. 1977).

VERNON, P. E. (1971). *The structure of human abilities.* London: Methuen.

——, and MELLICAN, G. D. (1954). A further study of the reliability of English essays. *British Journal of Statistical Psychology, 7,* 65–74.

WARD, W. C. (1982). A comparison of free-response and multiple-choice forms of verbal aptitude tests. *Applied Psychological Measurement, 6,* 1–11.

WAY, W. D., FORSYTH, R. A., and ANSLEY, T. N. (1989). IRT ability estimates from customized achievement tests without representative content sampling. *Applied Measurement in Education, 2*(1), 15–35.

WEINBERG, R. A. (1989). Intelligence and IQ. *American Psychologist, 44*(2), 98–104.

WESMAN, A. G. (1971). Writing the test item. In R. L. Thorndike (ed.), *Educational measurement* (2nd ed.). Washington, DC: American Council on Education.

WILEN, W. W. (1986). *Questioning skills, for teachers* (2nd ed.). Washington, DC: National Education Association.

WILEY, D. E. (1981). Improving policy development. In D. Carlson (ed.), *New directions in testing and measurement: Testing in the states: Beyond accountability.* San Francisco: Jossey-Bass.

WILLIAMS, B. G., and EBEL, R. L. (1957). The effect of varying the number of alternatives per item on multiple-choice vocabulary test items. *The 14th yearbook of the National Council on Measurements Used in Education.* East Lansing, MI: Michigan State University.

WILSON, P. A., DOWNING, S. M., and EBEL, R. L. (1977). *An empirical adjustment of the Kuder-Richardson 21 reliability coefficient to better estimate the Kuder-Richardson 20 coefficient.* Unpublished manuscript.

WODTKE, K. H., and others (1989). *How standardized is school testing? An exploratory observational study of standardized group testing in kindergarten.* Unpublished manuscript, University of Wisconsin—Milwaukee.

WOOD, R. (1976). Inhibiting blind guessing: The effect of instructions. *Journal of Educational Measurement, 13,* 297–308.

YELON, S. L. (1984). How to use and create criterion checklists. *Performance and Instruction Journal, 23*(3), 1–4.

Author Index

Subject Index